MUSICAL SIGNAL PROCESSING

STUDIES ON NEW MUSIC RESEARCH

Series Editors:

Marc Leman, Institute for Psychoacoustics and Electronic Music, University of Ghent, Belgium

Paul Berg, Royal Conservatory, The Hague, The Netherlands

MUSICAL SIGNAL PROCESSING

Edited By

CURTIS ROADS, STEPHEN TRAVIS POPE, ALDO PICCIALLI(†), and GIOVANNI DE POLI

SWETS & ZEITLINGER PUBLISHERS

| LISSE | ABINGDON | EXTON (PA) | TOKYO |

Library of Congress Cataloging-in-Publication Data

Musical signal processing / edited by Curtis Roads ... [et al.].
     p.   cm.
   Includes bibliographical references and indexes.
   ISBN 9026514824 (hb). – ISBN 9026514832 (pb)
   1. Computer composition. 2. Electronic music. 3. Computer
music – – Instruction and study. 4. Electronic music – – Instruction and
study. 5. Signal processing. I. Roads, Curtis.
MT56.M87   1997
786.7 – – DC21   97 – 2598
                                                   CIP
                                                   MN

Cover design: Ivar Hamelink
Printed in the Netherlands by Krips b.v., Meppel

ISBN 90 265 1482 4 (hardback)
ISBN 90 265 1483 2 (paperback)

Contents

Contributors

Angelo Bernardi, Dipartimento di Informatica, Università di Padova, Via Gradenigo 6a, I-35121 Padua, Italy

Gianpaolo Borin, Dipartimento di Informatica, Università di Padova, Via Gradenigo 6a, I-35121 Padua, Italy

Gian-Paolo Bugna, Dipartimento di Informatica, Università di Padova, Via Gradenigo 6a, I-35121 Padua, Italy

Antonio Camurri, DIST Computer Music Laboratory, Università di Genova, Via Opera Pia 13, I-16145 Genova, Italy, music@dist.dist.unige.it

Sergio Cavaliere, Dipartimento di Scienze Fisiche, Università di Napoli, Mostra d'Oltremare, Pad. 20, I-80125 Naples, Italy, cavaliere@napoli.infn.it

Roger Dannenberg, School of Computer Science, Carnegie Mellon University, Pittsburgh, Pennsylvania 15213, USA, rbd+@andrew.cmu.edu

Peter Desain, Nijmegen Institute of Cognition and Information, Nijmegen University, P. O. Box 9104, NL-6500 HE Nijmegen, The Netherlands, Desain@nici.kun.nl

Giovanni De Poli, Dipartimento di Informatica, Università di Padova, Via Gradenigo 6a, I-35121 Padua, Italy, DePoli@dei.unipd.it

Gianpaolo Evangelista, Dipartimento di Scienze Fisiche, Università di Napoli, Mostra d'Oltremare, Pad. 20, I-80125 Naples, Italy

Henkjan Honing, Computational Linguistics, Faculty of Arts, University of Amsterdam, Spuistraat 134, NL-1012 VB Amsterdam, The Netherlands, Henkjan@alf.let.uva.nl

Marc Leman, Institute for Psychoacoustics and Electronic Music (IPEM), University of Ghent, Blandijnberg 2, B-9000 Ghent, Belgium, Marc.Leman@rug.ac.be

Aldo Piccialli (†), Dipartimento di Scienze Fisiche, Università di Napoli, Mostra d'Oltremare, Pad. 20, I-80125 Naples, Italy

Stephen Travis Pope, Center for Research in Electronic Art Technology (CREATE), Department of Music, University of California at Santa Barbara, Santa Barbara, California 93106, USA, stp@create.ucsb.edu

Curtis Roads, Les Ateliers UPIC, 16–18 rue Marcelin-Berthelot, F-94140 Alfortville, France, and Département Musique, Université Paris VIII, 2 rue de la Liberté, F-93526 Saint-Denis, Cedex 02, France

Augusto Sarti, Politecnico di Milano, Dipartimento di Elettronica e Informazione, Piazza Leonardo Da Vinci 32, I-20133 Milan, Italy, sarti@elet.polimi.it

Marie-Hélène Serra, Ircam, 1 place Stravinsky, F-75004 Paris, France, serra@ircam.fr

Xavier Serra, Audiovisual Institute—Phonos Foundation, Pompeu Fabra University, Rambla 31, 08002 Barcelona, Spain, xserra@upf.es

Giancarlo Sica, Centro "Aldo Piccialli"—The Audio Lab, Università Popolare di Caserta, Via Chierici 20, I-81100 Caserta, Italy, sica@na.infn.it

Julius O. Smith III, Center for Computer Research in Music and Acoustics, Department of Music, Stanford University, Stanford, California 94305, USA, jos@ccrma.stanford.edu

Alvise Vidolin, Centro di Sonologia Computazionale dell'Università di Padova, Via S. Francesco 11, I-35121 Padua, Italy, and Tempo Reale, Villa Strozzi, Florence, Italy, vidolin@dei.unipd.it

Preface

Once an esoteric science, the synthesis and processing of digital sound takes on ever greater importance in the age of multimedia computing on a global scale. Recordings and films showcase spectacular sound transformations; synthesizers and sound cards bring audio signal processing to millions of users. Less visible to the public, but in no way less interesting, a new generation of composers versed in signal processing techniques are creating a highly refined form of musical art.

The study of audio signal processing splits into two main branches: engineering and musical. The engineering approach adheres to a standardized body of knowledge and techniques. It often starts from acoustical models, such as a generic speaking voice or a lecture hall. Its typical applications are broadcasting and communications, simulations, compression of data, computational efficiency, and encoding/decoding techniques. Problems in the engineering world are solved with respect to well-defined, quantifiable criteria such as cost, fault rates, speed benchmarks, and differential errors.

The musical approach to sound processing has different goals. It is driven by the sharp demand for electronic music instruments and effects processors, by the creative possibilities of multimedia, and by the expressive needs of musicians. New synthesis techniques extend the musical palette. Musical transformations must satisfy not only mathematical criteria, but must also pass the muster of aesthetics. Sound analysis searches for the musical significance in the data-identifying the source instrument, detecting the pitch, tracing the intensity envelope, separating harmonics and noise, recognizing the rhythm, and isolating formant regions, intermodulations, and other patterns in the spectrum.

Musical Signal Processing opens the door to the main topics in musical signal processing today, beginning with basic concepts, and leading to advanced applications. Part I presents a tutorial on signals, analysis/resynthesis, and synthesis techniques. Part II presents innovative topics on the leading edge of current research. Part III looks at ways of representing and manipulating the macrostructure of music signals. Part IV shows how signal processing can be applied in music compositions.

Origins

Musical Signal Processing has its origins in a music and science conference organized by the editors on the Isle of Capri in 1992. Invited lecturers from around the world gathered together for three days in this dramatic Mediterranean setting to present papers, give demonstrations, and debate the issues in this book.

From the outset, the editors planned a cohesive tutorial-oriented book, rather than a scattered scientific anthology. We have rigorously pruned the contributions to follow a systematic pedagogical line. We strongly encouraged consultations and collaborations among authors, and we believe this has resulted in a much clearer and more popular presentation.

Audience

Prepared over a period of four years, *Musical Signal Processing* is designed to be adopted in courses on musical sound synthesis and sound processing, in research centers, conservatories, and university departments of music, acoustics, computer science, and engineering. The audience includes electronic and computer musicians, engineers, acousticians, and instrument designers. The chapters in *Musical Signal Processing* have been written according to a two-part structure: the first half tutorial, the second half advanced. Thus any chapter should be accessible to students of the field.

In memoriam Aldo Piccialli

Our friend and colleague, Aldo Piccialli, Professor of Physics at the University of Naples, computer music researcher, co-founder and board member of the Italian Computer Music Association (AIMI), and member of the Editorial Advisory Board of *Computer Music Journal*, passed away suddenly in March 1995, during the preparation of this book.

After completing his doctoral dissertation on particle physics in 1960 at the University of Cagliari, he was appointed Assistant Professor of Experimental Physics and Electronics. In 1969 he accepted a double appointment as Researcher with the Cybernetics Laboratory of the National Research Center in Naples and also Professor of Electronics at the University of Aquila, where he helped to organize the Laboratory of Electronics. He assumed the post of Professor at the University of Naples in 1980, when he turned his attention to musical signal processing.

Born in Naples, Aldo Piccialli was a quintessential Neapolitan, and his family house on top of Vomero mountain with his wife Giovanna and daughter Ariana was a respite from the frenetic city around him. He disdained formality and hypocrisy, and to some he may have seemed irreverent. But Professor Piccialli was much loved by his students. He enjoyed channeling their curiousity toward the rich territories spanning electronics and music. He constantly encouraged his students and research colleagues to reach their goals without forgetting the enjoyment of life. His scientific lectures were seasoned with irony and wit, in the manner of a Zen teacher. In a classroom he had the ability to scrutinize physical and acoustical signals from many possible aspects. Through his contagious enthusiasm for signal processing, students often found their own interest increased.

Scientific ideas came to him in bursts. To catch merely a grain of his thought and pursue its consequences would often lead to new ideas and a fresh perspective. Moreoever, he was (and forever will be) an adoptive father for his students, to whom he gave his sincere friendship and help in any kind of situation.

We are obliged to mention his important contributions to the advancement of the discipline of computer music in Italy. He strongly supported coordination

Aldo Piccialli, Capri, 1992.

among Italian centers and individuals involved in music research. A founder and active member of the board of directors of AIMI, he always pushed initiatives in the direction of cooperation.

Among his international colleagues, Professor Piccialli was known as an tireless organizer of important conferences, including the international workshops on *Models and Representations of Musical Signals* in Sorrento (1988) and Capri (1992), and the international conference *Music and Technology* at the magnificent Villa Pignatelli in Naples (1985). In these settings he believed strongly in the importance of collective debate, the exchange of ideas, and the cross-fertilization between different disciplines, with the common denominator of artistic motivation. At the time of his untimely death he was working on the establishment of an annual international workshop devoted to signal processing for the arts.

Through his leadership, a veritable school of audio signal processing emerged from the University of Naples. Over a period of sixteen years Professor Piccialli supervised dissertations on topics ranging from wavelet theory, physical modeling, signal processing architecture, chaos theory, fractal synthesis, granular analysis/synthesis, time-frequency analysis, and speech processing. But above all, his classroom was a school of life, and his energy resonates in us. Thus we dedicate *Musical Signal Processing* to Aldo's memory in the hope that others will follow where he led so enthusiastically.

Part I

Foundations of musical signal processing

Part I

Overview

Curtis Roads

All fields of signal processing have enjoyed success in recent years, as new software techniques ride the surging waves of ever faster computer hardware. Musical signal processing has gained particular momentum, with new techniques of synthesis and transformation being introduced at an increasing pace. These developments make it imperative to understand the foundations in order to put new developments in their proper perspective. This part brings together three important tutorials that serve as introductions to the field of musical signal processing in general.

The development of sound synthesis algorithms proceeded slowly for the first two decades of computer music, due to the primitive state of software and hardware technology. Today the inverse holds: a panoply of analysis and synthesis techniques coexist, and the sheer variety of available methods makes it difficult to grasp as a whole. Chapter 1 by Gianpaolo Borin, Giovanni De Poli, and Augusto Sarti serves as a valuable orientation to this changing domain, putting the main methods in context. Beginning with sampling, their survey touches on fundamental techniques such as additive, granular, and subtractive synthesis, with special attention given to physical modeling—one of the most prominent techniques today, having been incorporated in several commercial synthesizers. As the authors observe, effective use of a synthesis technique depends on the control data that drives it. Therefore they have added a unique section to their chapter devoted to the synthesis of control signals.

First proposed as means of audio data reduction (for which it was not ideally suited), the phase vocoder has evolved over a period of three decades into one of the most important tools of sound transformation in all of musical signal processing. In Chapter 2, Marie-Hélène Serra presents a clear and well-organized explanation of the phase vocoder. The first part of her paper is a review of the theory, while the second part presents the phase vocoder's primary musical applications: expanding or shrinking the duration of a sound, frequency-domain filtering, and cross-synthesis.

Chapter 3 presents an innovative phase vocoder that divides the processing into two parallel paths: a deterministic model and a stochastic model. As Xavier Serra points out, the deterministic analyzer tracks the frequency trajectories of the most prominent sinusoidal components in the spectrum, while the stochastic analyzer attempts to account for the noise component that is not well tracked by the deterministic part. In past systems this noise component was often left out, which meant that the transformations realized by the phase vocoder were sometimes stained by an artificial sinusoidal quality. In addition to improving the realism of a transformation, separating the noise component lets one alter the deterministic spectrum independently of the stochastic spectrum. This opens up many musical possibilities, but it is a delicate operation that requires skill to realize convincingly.

1

Musical signal synthesis

Gianpaolo Borin, Giovanni De Poli, and Augusto Sarti

The sound produced by acoustic musical instruments is caused by the physical vibration of a resonating structure. This vibration can be described by signals that correspond to the evolution in time of the acoustic pressure generated by the resonator. The fact that sound can be characterized by signals suggests quite naturally that computing equipment could be successfully employed for generating sounds, either for the imitation of acoustic instruments or the creation of new sounds with novel timbral properties.

A wide variety of sound synthesis algorithms are currently available either commercially or in the literature. Each exhibits characteristics that could make it preferable to others, depending on one's goals and needs. Technological progress has made enormous steps forward in the past few years in terms of delivering low-cost computational power. At the same time, sound synthesis methods have become more and more computationally efficient and the user interface has become "friendlier". As a consequence, musicians can—without an enormous investment—access a large collection of synthesis techniques and concentrate on exploring their timbral properties.

A sound synthesis algorithm can be thought of as a digital model for a sound itself. Though this observation may seem quite obvious, its meaning for synthesis is not so straightforward. Indeed, modeling sounds is much more than just generating them, as a digital model can be used for representing and generating a whole class of sounds, depending on the choice of control parameters. The idea of associating a class of sounds to a digital sound model is in complete accordance with the way we tend to classify natural musical instruments according to their sound generation mechanism. For example, strings and woodwinds are normally seen as timbral classes of acoustic instruments characterized by their sound generation mechanism. It should be quite clear that the degree of compactness of a class of sounds is determined, on one hand, by the sensitivity of the digital model to parameter variations and, on the other hand, on the amount of control that is necessary for obtaining a certain desired sound. As an extreme example, we can think of a situation in which a musician is required to generate sounds sample by sample, while the task of the computing equipment is just that of playing the samples. In this case the control signal is represented by the sound itself, therefore the class of sounds that can be produced is unlimited but the instrument is impossible for a musician to control and play. An opposite extremal situation is that in which the synthesis technique is actually the model of an acoustic musical instrument. In this case the class of sounds that can be produced is much more limited (it is characteristic of the mechanism that is being modeled by the algorithm), but the degree of difficulty involved in generating the control parameters is quite modest, as it corresponds to physical parameters that have an intuitive counterpart in the experience of the musician.

An interested conclusion that could be already drawn in the light of what we have stated is that the compactness of the class of sounds associated with a sound synthesis algorithm is somehow in contrast with the "playability" of the algorithm. One should remember that the playability is of crucial importance for the success of a synthesis algorithm as, in order for an algorithm to be suitable for musical purposes, the musician needs an intuitive and easy access to its control parameters during both the sound design process and the performance. Such requirements often represents the reason why a certain synthesis technique is preferred to others.

Some considerations on control parameters are now in order. Varying the control parameters of a sound synthesis algorithm can serve several purposes. The first one is certainly the exploration of a sound space, that is, producing all the different sounds that belong to the class characterized by the algorithm itself. This very traditional way of using control parameters would nowadays be largely insufficient by itself. With the progress in the computational devices that are currently being employed for musical purposes, musicians' needs have turned more and more toward problems of timbral dynamics. For example, timbral differences between soft (dark) and loud (brilliant) tones are usually obtained through appropriate parameter control. Timbral expression parameters tend to operate at a note-level timescale. As such, they can be suitably treated as signals characterized by a rather slow rate.

Another reason for the importance of time variations in the algorithm parameters is that the musician needs to control musical expression while playing. For example, effects such as staccato, legato, vibrato, etc., are obtained through parameter control. Such parameter variations operate at a phrase-level timescale. For this reason they can be suitably treated as sequences of symbolic events characterized by a very slow rate.

In conclusion, control parameters are signals characterized by their own timescales. Control signals for timbral dynamics are best described as discrete-time signals with a slow sampling rate, while controls for musical expression are best described by streams of asynchronous symbolic events. As a consequence, the generation of control signals can once again be seen as a problem of signal synthesis.

In this chapter, the main synthesis techniques in use today will be briefly presented from the point of view of the user. We will try to point out the intrinsic and structural characteristics that determine their musical properties. We will also devote a section to the problem of the synthesis of control signals for both timbral dynamics (signal level) and musical expression (symbol level).

Synthesis of sound signals

Sound synthesis algorithms can be roughly divided into two broad classes: *classic direct synthesis algorithms*, which include sampling, additive, granular, subtractive, and nonlinear transformation synthesis. The second class includes *physical modeling techniques*, which contains the whole family of methods that model the acoustics of traditional music instruments.

Sampling

Finding a mathematical model that faithfully imitates a real sound is an extremely difficult task. If an existing reference sound is available, however, it is always possible to reproduce it through recording. Such a method, though simple in its principle, is widely adopted by digital sampling instruments or samplers. Samplers store a large quantity of examples of complete sounds, usually produced by other musical instruments. When we wish to synthesize a sound we just need to directly play one sound of the stored repertoire.

The possibility of modification is rather limited, as it would be for the sound recorded by a tape deck. The most common modification is that of varying the sampling rate (speed) when reproducing the sound, which results in a pitch deviation. However, substantial pitch variations are generally not very satisfactory as a temporal waveform compression or expansion results in unnatural timbral modifications, which is exactly what happens with an varispeed tape recorder. It is thus necessary to limit pitch variations within a range of a few semitones. On the other hand, what makes the sampling method most interesting is certainly the variety of sounds available.

From the viewpoint of implementation, the two contrasting needs are computational simplicity and limited memory usage. In order to reduce the data storage requirements, *looping* techniques are inevitably used on the stationary portion of sounds. One method of improving the expressive possibilities of samplers is interpolation between different sounds, using key velocity to switch between "piano" and "forte" playing modes.

In most cases sampling techniques are presented as a method for reproducing natural sounds and are evaluated in comparison with the original instruments. This is the main reason why the most popular commercial digital keyboards, such as electronic pianos and organs adopt this synthesis technique. Of course, sampling cannot hope to capture all the expressive possibilities of the original instrument. Note that sound samples can also be obtained synthetically or through the modification of other sounds, which is a way of widening the range of possibilities of application of samplers. From the composer's viewpoint, the use of samplers represents a practical, real-time approach to a form of the so-called *musique concrète*.

Additive synthesis

A classic method of synthesizing a complex time-varying sound consists of combining a number of elementary waveforms. The waveforms that are superimposed in additive synthesis are often sinusoidal. Under certain conditions, the individual sinusoids fuse together and the result is perceived as a single rich sound.

The idea behind this method is not new. Indeed, additive synthesis has been used for centuries in traditional instruments such as organs. Organ pipes produce relatively simple sounds that, combined together, contribute to the rich spectrum of certain register stops. Particularly colorful effects are created by using many pipes of different pitch at the same time.

When an almost-periodic sound is analyzed, its spectral energy is concentrated at a few discrete frequencies (harmonics). These *frequency lines* correspond to different sinusoidal signals called *partials*. The amplitude of each partial is not constant and its time-variation is critical for timbral characterization. Indeed, in the initial transitory phase (attack) of a note, some partials that would be negligible in a stationary state, become significant. The frequency of each component, however, can be thought of as slowly varying. In other words, additive synthesis consists of the sum of sinusoidal oscillators whose amplitude and frequency are time-varying. If the control parameters are determined through spectral analysis of natural sounds, then this synthesis technique becomes suitable for imitative synthesis. Additive synthesis techniques are also capable of reproducing aperiodic and inharmonic sounds, as long as their spectral energy is concentrated near discrete frequencies (spectral lines).

Additive synthesis is rather general in its principles, but it requires the specification of a large amount of data for each note. Two control functions for each spectral component must be specified, and their evolution is different for various durations, intensities, and frequencies of the considered sound.

In practice, additive synthesis is applied either in synthesis-by-analysis (see Chapters 2 and 3), usually done through parameter transformation, or when a sound with specific characteristics is required, as in psychoacoustic experiments. This latter method, developed for simulating natural sounds, has become the metaphorical foundation of an instrumental compositional methodology based on the expansion of the time scale and the reinterpretation of the spectrum in harmonic structures.

Granular synthesis

Granular synthesis, together with additive synthesis, shares the idea of building complex sounds from simpler ones. Granular synthesis, however, starts from short sound particles called *grains*, whose durations are measured in milliseconds.

Two main approaches to granular synthesis can be identified: the former based on sampled sounds and the latter based on abstract synthesis. In the first case, a sound is divided in overlapping segments and *windowed*. Such a process is called *time-granulation* and is quite similar to what happens in motion pictures, in which a fast sequence of static images produces a sensation of motion. By changing the order and speed of the windowed segments, however, a variety of sonic effects can be achieved.

A variation on the above method consists of analyzing each windowed segment and resynthesizing each of them with a method called *overlap and add* (OLA). In OLA what matters is the temporal alignment of the grains, in order to avoid phase discontinuities, which give rise to unpleasant acoustic artefacts. OLA is then performed in two different ways depending on the grain's waveform, which makes its control rather difficult. One case where OLA-based methods are useful is represented by the synthesis of the random component of a signal, as described by X. Serra (see Chapter 3). In this case only the evolution of the spectral envelope is controlled.

When the grains are aligned to a grid superimposed on the time-frequency plane, granular synthesis becomes the implementation of an inverse transform derived from time-frequency representations such as the *short-time Fourier transform* (STFT) or *wavelet transform*. When, however, the grains are synchronous with the signal period, *pitch synchronous granular synthesis* is obtained. The technique developed by Aldo Piccialli and his colleagues applies granular control to a form of subtractive synthesis (De Poli and Piccialli 1991; see also Chapter 5).

In abstract granular synthesis, the grains consist of arbitrary waveforms whose amplitude envelope is a gaussian bell-shaped function. The most important and classic type of granular synthesis distributes grains irregularly on the time-frequency plane in the form of *clouds* (Roads 1978, 1991). For example randomly scattering grains within a frequency/amplitude/time region results in a sound cloud that varies over time. The density of the grains, as well as the grain duration, can be controlled on a continuous basis. Notice that it is possible to recognize a certain similarity between this type of granular synthesis and the technique of mosaics, where the grains are single monochromatic tesseras and their juxtaposition produces a complex image.

Subtractive synthesis

Some synthesis algorithms exhibit a feed-forward structure consisting of several processing blocks, some of which generate signals (or acquire them as an input) and some of which transform signals. If the transformation is linear, the technique is called *subtractive synthesis*, where the transformation is best interpreted in the frequency domain as a filter. Subtractive synthesis consists of filtering a spectrally rich signal source, which is what happens when the vibrations of violin strings are transmitted to the resonant body of the violin. The resulting spectral signal is given by the product of the input signal spectrum multiplied by frequency response of the filter, so that some frequencies are attenuated while others are enhanced. According to the frequency response of the filter the general trend of the spectrum can be varied or, for example, a small portion of the spectrum of the signal can be extracted.

If the filter is static, the temporal features of the input signal are maintained. If, conversely, the filter coefficients are varied, the frequency response changes. As a consequence, the output is a combination of temporal variations of the input and the filter. The filter parameters are chosen according to the desired frequency response, and are varied according to the desired timbre dynamic.

This technique is most suitable for implementing slowly-varying filters (such as the acoustic response of a specific hall, or for spatialization) as well as filters that are subject to fast variations (muting effects, emulations of speaking or singing voices, sounds characterized by animated timbral dynamics).

Subtractive synthesis does not make specific assumptions about the periodicity of the source signal. Therefore it can be successfully used for generating non-pitched sounds, such as percussion, in which case noise sources characterized by a continuous (non-discrete) spectrum are employed. Notice also that the white noise source–filter model is a valid means for describing random processes that can be used for characterizing the spectral envelope, eventually considered as being time-varying, which is a most significant perceptual parameter.

If we can simplify our hypothesis about the nature of the input signal, it is possible to estimate both the parameters of the source and the filter of a given sound. The most common procedure is *linear predictive coding* (LPC). LPC assumes either an impulse train or white noise as the input that is passed through a recursive filter (Markel and Gray 1976). By analyzing brief sequential segments of the sound, time-varying parameters can be extracted that. can be used in resynthesis. Since the LPC model is parametric, the data obtained by the analysis has an exact interpretation in terms of the model. This fact supplies reference criteria for their modification. For example, when the excitation frequency is increased for the voice, the pitch is raised without varying the position of the formants. One can also apply the filter parameters to another source, to obtain an effect such as a "talking orchestra". This technique is called *cross-synthesis*.

By means of linear transformations, reverberation, and periodic delay effects can also be obtained. In this case, the filter is characterized by constant delays that are best interpreted as time echoes, reverberations (Moorer 1979) or as periodic repetitions of the input signal (Karplus and Strong 1983; Jaffe and Smith 1983).

In general, the division between the generator and the transformation gives rise to the possibility of controlling separately both the source and filter characteristics. There is, therefore, a greater flexibility of control and better interpretation of the parameters, as well as greater fusion in the class of sounds that can be obtained.

Nonlinear transformations

The filter transformations just described, since they are linear, cannot change the frequencies of the components that are present. By contrast, nonlinear transformations can radically alter the frequency content of their input signals. Nonlinear synthesis derives from modulation theory as applied to musical signals. It therefore inherits certain aspects from the analog electronic music tradition while also partaking of the advantages of the digital age.

Two main effects characterize nonlinear transformations: spectrum enrichment and spectrum shift. The first effect is due to nonlinear distortion of the signal, allowing for control over the "brightness" of a sound, for example. The second effect is due to multiplication by a sinusoid, which moves the spectrum to the vicinity of the carrier signal, altering the harmonic relationship between the modulating signal line spectra. From the perspective of harmony, the possibility of shifting the spectrum is very intriguing in musical applications. Starting from simple sinusoidal components, harmonic and inharmonic sounds can be created, and various harmonic relations among the partials can be established.

The two classic methods for spectrum enrichment and spectrum shift, *nonlinear distortion* or *waveshaping* (Le Brun 1979; Arfib 1979; De Poli 1984) and *ring modulation* have perhaps become less important, giving way to *frequency modulation* (FM), which combines both effects. FM, initially developed by Chowning (1973), Chowning and Bristow (1986), has become a widely used synthesis technique. The core module of FM realizes the following algorithm:

$$s(n) = a(n) \sin \left(2\pi f_c n + \phi(n) \right),$$

where $\phi(n)$ is the input signal (modulating signal) and f_c is the carrier frequency. When $f_c = 0$, the nonlinear distortion of modulating signal can be seen and thus the spectrum is enriched. If, on the other hand, $f_c \neq 0$ it can be shown that the written expression equals the ring modulation of a sinusoid by the distorted signal, resulting in a spectrum shift of a value of f_c.

The bandwidth around f_c depends on the amplitude and the bandwidth of the modulating signal. In the most basic case, the modulating signal is sinusoidal with a frequency f_m and there is a line spectrum, with frequencies $f_c \pm k f_m$, characterized, therefore, by the relationship between the frequencies. Thus, it is possible to control the degree of inharmonicity of the signal by means of the f_c/f_m ratio.

On the other hand, controlling the bandwidth of the produced signal gives filter-like effect, similar to subtractive synthesis.

By combining various modules of this type, richer spectra and a wider range of possibility for variation can be obtained. For example, when various carriers, or a complex periodic carriers are used and modulated by the same modulator, sidebands around each sinusoidal component of the carrier are obtained. This effect can be used to separately control different spectral areas of a periodic sound. It is also possible to use complex modulators.

A similar effect is obtained when modulators in cascade are used. In this case, in fact, the carrier is modulated by an FM signal that is already rich in components. The resulting signal still maintains its frequency, as in the case of parallel modulators, but with more energy in most of the sideband components. An oscillator that is self-modulating in phase can also used to generate periodic sawtooth type signals that are rich in harmonics.

Basic FM synthesis is a versatile method for producing many types of sounds. As of yet, however, no precise algorithm has been found for deriving the parameters of an FM model from the analysis of a given sound, and no intuitive interpretation can be given to many of its parameters. Its main qualities: time-varying timbral dynamics with just a few parameters to control, and low computational cost, are progressively losing popularity when compared with other synthesis techniques which, though more expensive, can be controlled in a more intuitive fashion. FM synthesis, however, still offers the attractiveness of its own timbral space, and though it is not ideal for the simulation of natural sounds, it offers a wide range of original synthetic sounds that are of considerable interest to computer musicians.

Physical modeling synthesis

The popularity achieved in recent years by physical modeling synthesis can be attributed to a variety of factors. The most important of these is that modeling sound production mechanisms instead of just modeling sounds seems to offer the musician more direct tools for producing traditional sonorities and their variations. Given the promise of physical modeling synthesis and its recent prominence, we will focus more on this technique than on the classical direct synthesis methods described previously.

Modeling usually means describing mathematically a certain phenomenon. Mathematical models are often used in science and engineering for understanding physical phenomena, and this is especially true in musical acoustics, where it is common practice to study traditional instruments through experiments on their physical models in order to understand how they work.

For sound synthesis, the goal of mathematical modeling is slightly different from that of traditional acoustics. Rather than analyzing the behavior of physical systems purely for the sake of scientific understanding, in sound synthesis there is a practical agenda. What matters is to implement models can be used by musicians in an intuitive fashion during both composition and performance.

The most attractive characteristics of physical modeling synthesis are as follows:

- timbral richness is determined by the model structure rather than by the complexity of its parametric control; in other words, the model is characterized of its own timbral dynamics;
- there exists a precise relationship between the reaction of the reference physical instrument to a certain action, and the reaction of its model.

In other words, good physical models should give rise to a certain timbral richness, like the traditional musical instruments they reference. Their parametric control should be more intuitive, since the control signals have physical meaning to the musician. Ideally, musicians should have the same type of interaction with the physical model that they have with the actual instrument, therefore there should be less need to learn how to play an entirely new synthetic instrument.

Another attractive characteristic of synthesis by physical models is that it often allows us to access the simulation from different points that correspond to spatially distributed locations on the vibrating structure. This provides us with more compositional parameters and more flexibility than we would have with other approaches. Finally, responsive input devices can be used to control the sound generation, which allows the musician to establish a more natural relationship with the system (Cadoz, Luciani, and Florens 1984).

The sound of an acoustic instrument is produced by the elastic vibrations in a resonating structure. The resonator is usually divided into various parts and exhibits several *access points*, which generally correspond to spatially separate positions on the acoustic instrument. Not only are access points necessary for connecting different parts but they also necessary for providing the structure with excitation inputs and for extracting the signal to listen to. In order to maintain the modularity of the implementation structure it is often necessary to make use of special interconnection blocks whose only aim is to make the parts to be connected compatible with each other.

The synthesis of physical models is generally implemented in two steps. The first consists of determining a mathematical model that describes the essential aspects of the sound production mechanism in the reference instrument. At this stage of the synthesis process, the model is subdivided into several building blocks with strong mutual influence, along with a (usually analog) mathematical description of the blocks. The unavoidable discretization and the algorithmic specification is done in a second step.

A crucial aspect of the first synthesis step is in the specification the algorithmic structure and the parametric control of each of the building blocks. The amount of a priori information on the inner structure of the blocks determines the strategy to adopt for these two aspects of the synthesis problems. In general, what can be done is something inbetween two extreme approaches:

> *black-box*: the model is specified by the input–output relationships of the block;
>
> *white-box*: accurate hypotheses are made on the physics of the blocks and such information appears in the model specification.

In order to clarify the difference between these extreme strategies, consider a linear analog circuit (e.g. a filter) and its possible models. A black-box approach would describe such a filter in terms of its impulse response, while a white-box approach would consist in the discretization of the differential equations that describe all circuit elements and their interconnection.

A black-box approach is usually very limiting because of its lack of flexibility. For example, the propagation of perturbations on a string can be generally described in terms of local string displacement, transverse velocity, transverse force etc. All such signals are equally important when interfacing the string model with an external excitation that is yet to be specified. If the only available model for the string were an *input/output* (I/O) relationship, the choice of signals to use would have to be made beforehand. Furthermore, a black-box strategy makes it difficult to properly choose the operating conditions of the model. For example, we would have to change the whole I/O relationship of a reed-like structure every time we need to modify which tone-holes are closed and which ones are open. The same thing would happen if we changed the position from which we extract the signal to listen to. Another problem with black-box strategies is the impossibility to adapt them when the block to be modeled exhibits a nonlinear behavior. The only exception is when the block is memoryless, in which case its description would be given in the form of a simple nonlinear (instantaneous) characteristic. In conclusion, a black-box strategy is too rigid to be useful for flexible and efficient synthesis, but it may become helpful when developing and experimenting with new synthesis models.

A white-box approach describes the entire mechanism of sound generation. The price to pay for this flexibility is the difficulty of constructing a model. For example, the physics of a string can be specified in terms of the partial differential equations that describe its motion. We may thus decide to convert these equations to discrete form in order to obtain a model of the instrument. It is quite evident that the conversion to a discrete form needs to be done not only on the time variables but also on the space variables, and with an accurate space-discretization the number of elements to simulate can become unacceptably large. In conclusion, the advantage of the white-box synthesis strategy is that it makes models that are easily accessible anywhere in their structure. This is balanced on the negative side by the necessity of simulating all parts of the instrument mechanism. Such a requirement is often unnecessary and results in an unmotivated augmentation of the complexity of the model and its software implementation.

There are exceptions to the tradeoffs between flexibility and accuracy in the white-box approach. We will see later that waveguide models are discrete and efficient and avoid the problems of partial differential equations. This approach, however, suffers from the drawback that it is generally difficult to determine a closed-form general solution of the differential equations that describe the system.

The synthesis approach adopted in normal situations consists usually of a mixed (grey-box) strategy not only because the physics of the musical instrument is often only partially known, but more often because there are computational constraints that prevent us from pushing the model resolution too far. An example of the grey-box approach is when we model accurately only part of the system under exam (e.g. the strings of a piano), while we adopt for the rest of the structure (e.g. the soundboard of a piano) a black-box approach.

As we said earlier, the second step in the model's development consists of converting the analog model (in time and in space) to discrete digital form in order to construct a simulation algorithm. If this conversion does not have enough resolution, the accuracy of the simulation is compromised. This can be particularly critical when the aim is to closely imitate the behavior of an acoustic musical instrument. In the case of non-imitative synthesis, when the model resembles its analog counterpart only in the basic sound-production mechanism, it is important to make sure that the digital form retains the characteristic behavior of the reference mechanism.

It is worth mentioning another problem related to imitative physical modeling techniques. As all physical models of musical instruments are necessarily nonlinear, it is usually very difficult to estimate the model parameters through an analysis of the sounds produced by the reference instrument.

Models

In the past few years, a variety of ad hoc simulation algorithms have been developed for studying the acoustics of specific musical instruments. Nevertheless, some of these algorithms are general enough to be suitable for the simulation of more complex structures, especially when combined with other available models. It is thus worth scanning the main methods that are being commonly employed for sound synthesis purposes. In fact, by means of a modular approach it is simpler not only to simulate existing instruments but also to create new sounds based on a physically plausible behavior.

Mechanical models

The most classical way of modeling a physical system consists of dividing it into small pieces and deriving the differential equations that describe the piecesand the interactions between them. As the solution of such differential equations represents the musical signal of interest, the simulation consists of their digital implementation (Hiller and Ruiz 1971).

Rigid mechanical elements are usually described by models with concentrated masses while for flexible elements it is often necessary to use models with distributed mass-spring elements, in order to take into account the propagation time of perturbations. As a general rule, models based on concentrated masses are associated with a set of ordinary differential equations, while distributed structures implement partial differential equations (with partial derivatives in time and in space). In general, it is necessary to solve such equations by successive approximation in the digital domain. Therefore we need discrete space and time variables. In some simple cases, however, it is possible to determine a closed form solution of the differential equations that describe the system. In this case only the time variable needs to be discrete.

The CORDIS system represents a rather different technique for the simulation of mechanical models (Cadoz, Luciani, and Florens 1984). CORDIS is based on the atomization of excitation and resonance into elementary mechanical elements such as springs, masses, and frictions. These elements are connected through appropriate liason modules that describe the interaction between the elements. Such a method has the desirable property of being modular and is quite suitable for simulating several types of vibrating bodies like membranes, strings, bars and plates. On the other hand it is computationally expensive and not convenient for the simulation of acoustic tubes or wind instruments.

In general, mechanical models can describe the physical structure of a resonator in a very accurate fashion but they are characterized by high computational costs, as they describe the motion of all points of the simulated system. Considering the type of signals that we would like to extract from the model, the abundance of information available in mechanical structures is exceedingly redundant. Indeed the output sound of musical instruments can usually be related to the motion of just a few important points of the resonator. For such reasons, mechanical models are particularly useful for modeling concentrated elements such as the mechanical parts of the exciter, even in the presence of nonlinear elements.

It is important, at this point, to mention a problem that is typical of models based on mechanical structures. When we need to connect together two discrete-time models, each of which exhibits an instantaneous connection between input and output, we are faced with a computability problem. The direct interconnection of the two systems would give rise to a delay-free loop in their implementation algorithm. This type of problem can occur every time we connect together two systems that have been partitioned into discrete elements, and several solutions are available. In mechanical models, however, it is common practice to avoid the problem by strategically inserting a delay in the loops (which corresponds to deciding on an artificial order in the involved operations). One has to be careful in inserting such artificial delays, especially when discontinuous nonlinearities are present in the model. The delays tend to modify the system behavior and, sometimes they cause severe instability.

Digital waveguides and wave digital models

Waveguide digital structures have become quite successful in the past few years for their versatility and simplicity. Waveguide modeling represents a different approach in physical modeling, as it is based on the analytical solution of the equation that describes the propagation of perturbations in a medium (Smith 1987, Chapter 7). For example, the general solution of the differential equation that describes the vibration of an infinitely long string (the ideal one-dimensional wave equation), is a pair of waves that propagate undistorted in the system. We can thus model such propagation by using simple delay lines. Starting from this consideration, it is easy to understand that in waveguide models, instead of using the classical Kirchoff pair of variables (intensive/extensive pair of variables such as velocity/force, flow/pressure, current/voltage, etc.), we employ a pair of "wave" variables, which describe the propagation of perturbations in the resonating structure. Such waves travel undistorted as long as the propagation means is homogeneous. To model a discontinuity, we can insert a special junction that models the *wave scattering*. Certain other physical structures can be modeled by filters. Thus there is a close correspondence between waveguide digital systems and our perception of physical reality.

Waveguides can model complex systems such as the bore of a clarinet (with holes and bell), or groups of strings that are coupled through a resistive bridge.

Since they exploit the nature of the propagation of perturbations in an ideal resonating structure, and since such a propagation mechanism is programmed simply by using digital delay lines, their implementation does not suffer from the problems mentioned earlier concerning mechanical models.

Digital waveguides are well-suited for simulating flexible (distributed) structures, as they model the propagation of perturbations in an elastic means through the solution of the wave equation. The concentrated-element version of waveguide schemes is represented by *wave digital* (WD) systems. WD structures represent a nonlinear version of the *wave digital filters* (WDFs) and they are designed after analog circuits. Because of that, they tend to preserve most of the good properties of their analog counterparts. Even though the WDF theory for the synthesis of linear physical systems is now quite mature, a wave digital theory of nonlinear circuits, is still far from being formalized and developed in a homogeneous way.

One of the problems with nonlinear wave digital structures is that instantaneous reflections of wave variables at nonlinear ports are unavoidable (as the impedance of a nonlinear element depends on the applied signal), which makes it difficult to solve non-computability problems when connecting individually discretized elements of the structure. Moreover, when the nonlinearity is not memoryless, which is the case of reactive elements like nonlinear mechanical springs, the classical theory of WDF's is no longer sufficient. Using the classical elements of WDF's we usually end up with computational problems that can be solved only approximately, either using expensive numerical methods or inserting artificial delay elements in the non-computable loops. Very recently, a new method for modeling nonlinear systems with memory in the wave digital domain has been proposed. It consists in a generalization of the WDF theory, and allows for exact low-cost simulation and automatic modeling.

It is important to stress that digital waveguides and wave digital structures are fully compatible with each other, which makes it desirable to explore new physical models based on the wave representation of physical phenomena.

Transfer function models

The resonator can be generally considered a linear system. Because of this, we can always adopt a black-box approach for its implementation, which consists of determining its transfer function (I/O relationship) and implementing it by using any of the available digital signal processing techniques.

Since the resonator can be treated as a linear filter, its physical structure can be completely ignored for implementation purposes. Sometime, however, it could be useful to use some information about the physical structure of the resonator in order to determine how to efficiently implement its transfer function and how to identify its parameters. In some cases, for example, we can experimentally determine the impulse response of the system by measuring some physical parameters such as the section of the acoustic tube and the acoustic impedance of the air. In some other cases we can analytically derive the transfer function from the equations that govern the physical behavior of the resonator.

The main problem that a technique based on the transfer-function suffers from is that each point of the resonator can be attributed a different impulse response. This means that for each point that accesses the resonator structure it will be necessary to define a different filter. Moreover, we must not forget that, in most cases of interest, we are dealing with time-varying transfer functions, therefore an even small variation of the model parameters usually results in a substantial modification of the filter. In general, musical instruments are strongly time-varying as what carries musical information is their parametric variation. For example, the length of the vibrating portion of a violin string depends on the position of the finger of the performer, while the length of the acoustic tube in a trumpet depends on which keys are pressed.

Modal synthesis

In the panorama of methods for physical modeling, modal synthesis represents a rather interesting approach, particularly for implementing resonators. Modal synthesis uses system theory principles (modal decomposition) in order to implement a linear system with the parallel of second order systems, each of which is realized as a damped oscillator. By doing so, a certain modularity and some structural regularity are maintained (Adrien 1991). With an approach based on modal synthesis, all nonlinearities are concentrated at the interconnection between different parts of the vibrating structure.

What stimulates the interest of researchers in this method, besides the modularity of the resulting structures, is the frequency-domain representation. In fact, nonlinear physical models are normally represented in the time-domain, while sometimes frequency-domain representations can be more desirable for musicians.

Another attractive characteristic of modal synthesis is its robustness. In fact, even though data are not obtained from theoretical considerations or experimental results, the system always produces acoustically coherent results, while other methods often behave in an unpredictable and unpleasant way when parameters are inappropriately chosen.

The main drawback of modal synthesis is that modal parameters are difficult to interpret and to handle. Moreover, a modal structure is usually quite complex to describe and to implement, as it requires a large number of modes for periodical sounds. For example, the modal description of a vibrating string needs approximately 100 modes for an implementation of good quality. Finally, interconnecting the various parts often requires the solution of systems of equations, which increases the complexity of the method even further.

Memoryless excitation

We have already anticipated that the resonator can always be modeled as a linear system as its only aim is to cause the system response to be periodical through the insertion of a certain group delay. The excitator, instead, is characterized by a nonlinear behavior, as it is functionally identified as the element that causes the oscillation and limits their amplitude. Modeling excitators is thus quite a different problem from that of modeling resonating structures.

The simplest nonlinear model for an excitator is represented by an instantaneous relationship of the form $y(t) = f(x(t), x_E(t))$, where $y(t)$ is, in general, the excitation signal, and $x(t)$ is the corresponding response of the resonator. In this expression $x_E(t)$ represents an external input signal which normally incorporates the excitation actions of the performer, and $f(\cdot, \cdot)$ is a nonlinear function. As the function is memoryless, this type of model neglects any kind of dynamic behavior of the excitation element (McIntyre $et\ al.$ 1983), therefore the resulting timbral morphology is entirely attributable to the interaction between an instantaneous device and the resonating structure.

Though very simple, a memoryless excitation is capable of simulating the qualitative behavior of a wide variety of musical excitators. It is possible, for example, to describe the behavior of the reed of a clarinet by means of an instantaneous map $f(p, p_M)$, which determines the air flow entering the acoustic tube as a function of the pressure p_M in the musician's mouth and of the pressure p at the entrance of the acoustic tube.

In general, the shape of the function $f(\cdot, \cdot)$ depends on several physical parameters of the excitation. In the case of the clarinet, for example, changing the force exerted on the reed by the lips of the performer, may result in a dramatic modification of the curve $f(\cdot, \cdot)$. Even though this fact may not be a problem from the theoretical standpoint, such a parametric dependence makes it difficult to implement the function $f(\cdot, \cdot)$ in a table-lookup fashion, which results in higher computational costs for the model.

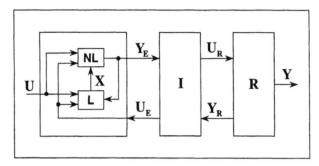

Figure 1. Structure of the excitation given by the interconnection of an instantaneous nonlinearity (NL) and a linear (L) dynamic system. The task of the linear part is to add memory to the nonlinearity.

Nonlinear dynamics scheme

A direct extension of the nonlinear memoryless exciter can be obtained through an appropriate interconnection of an instantaneous nonlinearity and a linear dynamical system (Borin *et al.* 1992). This choice results in a richer and more effective structure of the type shown in Figure 1, whose input/output relationships are:

$$X(n + 1) = F_L[X(n), U(n), U_E(n), Y_E(n)],$$
$$Y(n) = F_{NL}[X(n), U(n), U_E(n)].$$

It is evident from Figure 1 that the memory is concentrated in the linear part of the system while the nonlinearity acts just as an instantaneous map between input and output. Although such a model for the exciter is slightly less general than a nonlinear discrete dynamical system, it is not difficult to realize that it covers many interesting cases. In most physical exciters the nonlinearity is concentrated in the elastic characteristics of one or more of its parts. In general, a good description of these characteristics is either an instantaneous or hysteresis map. The nonlinear element of the model is thus capable of accounting for all instantaneous portions of the elastic characteristics, among which the currently active one is selected through a feedback from the output of the nonlinearity. It is evident that the inertia of the system will be taken into account by the linear part of the excitation.

The synthesis of control signals

In the previous sections we presented the most important models for the synthesis of sound. We also emphasized that the compactness of the class of sounds that can be produced by a sound synthesis model is somehow related to the *playability* of the synthetic instrument. In fact, for a synthesis model to be playable, we need either the class of sounds it can produce to be limited, or to employ an appropriate control signal synthesizer.

The problem of control in synthesis refers to everything that goes from the symbolic description of sounds, as expressed in the score, to the sound, using synthesis models. Traditionally, the score is a series of notes (symbols that describe a sound and its properties on an abstract level) and it is up to the player—with the help of an instrument—to turn this into sound. In general, two levels of abstraction in control can be distinguished, which correspond to different time scales:

- control of the instrument's expressivity;
- control of the spectral dynamics.

The former, which involves the player as an interpreter, refers to the *transformation of symbols into signals* to achieve the desired musical expression. In its most general form, the role of this type of control signal synthesizer is not just that of mapping individual symbols into abrupt variations of parameters but, rather, that of generating a continuous variation of a set of parameters according to their symbolic description, in the *musical phrase* timescale. In other words, such a control signal generator would allow the musician to act in a similar way as the conductor of an orchestra. The second level controls the spectral dynamics of the note and determines the passage from expressive parameters to the underlying algorithm. In this case control signals vary during the evolution of the note.

The notion of "playability" of a synthetic musical instrument, as a consequence, assumes different interpretations depending on which timescale we are considering for the control signals. While always related to the quality of the interaction between musician and musical instrument, in the musical phrase timescale, playability refers to musical expression, while on the note timescale it concerns timbral expression. In both cases, however, the aim of the control synthesizer is that of generating a set of control signals that is as compact as possible and that can be managed by the musician.

Between player and traditional musical instrument, there exists an *interface*, such as a keyboard or a bow, which determines and limits the range of the actions that are compatible with the instrument itself. In a similar way, we can recognize a control interface between musician and synthesis algorithm as well. Such an interface consists of all the musician knows about the instrument and how to interact with it. The control interface maps all possible actions to a set of control parameters that are suitable for the synthesis algorithm in such a way for actions and expectations to be consistent. In the case of commercial musical instruments, the interface is designed by the manufacturer. The use of programmable computers, however, allows the interface to be adapted to the needs of the player, so that different levels of abstraction can be achieved. Programmable interaction makes possible detailed parameteric control à la Music V (Mathews 1969), to completely automatic performance operating directly on musical scores.

Control signals differ from acoustic signals in several respects. For example, their frequency analysis does not seem to have any significant interpretation, therefore control synthesis and manipulation techniques are more suitable to be developed and described in the time domain. In spite of this lack of parallelism, some sound synthesis techniques do have a counterpart in the synthesis of control signals.

Reproduction

When no models are available for the control signals, there is still the possibility of transcribing them from a performance or from an analysis of an acoustic signal. For a few sound synthesis models, sufficiently accurate analysis algorithms are available. For example, for additive synthesis, it is possible to use *short-time Fourier transform* (STFT, see Chapter 2) for estimating model parameters from an acoustic sound in order to reproduce the original sound more-or-less accurately. In this case, the parameters are signals that control the time evolution of frequency and amplitude of each partial of the sound under examination. Through the STFT procedure, several control signals can be obtained from an acoustic sound, provided that they are slowly time-varying. Once a variety of control signal samples are available, their impact on the timbral quality needs to be evaluated and interpreted in order to be able to use them in combination with other time-domain techniques such as *cut and paste*, amplitude or time scaling, etc.

Control synthesis techniques based on recording-and-reproduction are characterized by the timbral richness of natural sounds and the expressivity of acoustic instruments but, similarly to sound synthesis techniques based on sampling, they suffer from a certain rigidity in their usage. In particular, when expressive control signals are derived from the analysis of acoustic samples, all gestural actions are recorded, including those that are characteristic of the performer.

Even though the possibility of modifying control signals appears as being minimal in the case of parameter reproduction, it is always possible to use such signals in a creative way, for instance redirecting some control signals to different control inputs. For example, the pitch envelope could be used for controlling the bandwidth.

Composite controls

A simple synthesis model of control signals consists of combining several elementary signals through superposition or *chaining* or partial overlapping. For example, in the case of sound frequency control, it is possible to add a signal that describes the general trend of the frequency (pitch) to a periodic slow oscillation (tremolo) and to other random or fractal variations.

As far as timbral control is concerned, a control signal can be generated as a chain of different waveforms, each of which describes a different portion of timbral evolution and is selected among a collection of typical trends. For example, the *attack-sustain-decay-release* (ADSR) is a common model for control signals commonly used for modifying the amplitude envelope. This method consists of a chain of four signals that describe characteristic portions (attack, decay, sustain, release) of the timbre.

Interpolation

Interpolation, both linear and nonlinear, is often applied in the synthesis of control signals. Since synthesis can be considered as a process that maps "little" localized information into a continuous variation of a multitude of parameters, the concept of interpolation seems to be quite a natural way of approaching the problem of control parameter synthesis. Starting from the specification of a few significant samples of the control signal (for example, the pitch of the notes that constitute a musical phrase) an interpolation model generates an analog signal that is characterized by properties of smoothness and regularity—characteristic of the interpolator.

Stochastic models

As we said earlier, the reproduction of control signals has the same problems as those typical of sound synthesis based on sampling. In particular, the fact that the whole control function needs to be stored makes this approach not particularly versatile. In order to avoid the intrinsic rigidity of this method, one can think of modeling the control signal with a combination of a deterministic signal that models the average trend of the control signal and a random process that describes its fluctuations. It should be quite clear that, in this case, the statistical properties of the random portion are of crucial importance.

A typical solution for the synthesis of parametric fluctuations through statistical models consists of filtering white noise with an appropriate linear filter (*autoregressive moving average* or ARMA). The parameters of the filter can be estimated by analyzing acoustic samples. This solution can be generally employed whenever it is not possible to make specific hypotheses on the control structure, although it is possible to extract a statistic description of it.

Fractal signal model

In some cases, variations in the control parameters are to be attributed to chaotic behavior of the acoustic mechanism of sound production (such as in an organ pipe driven by a jet of air). When this happens, control signal generators are well-described by fractal models. Typically, the fractal dimension of the signal is first estimated and then used for controlling, for example, a fractional Brownian motion noise generator. There are several types of such generators (each of which is referred to different spectral characteristics of the signal) of the $1/f^*$ type, where * is an appropriate exponent that is related to the fractal dimension and, therefore, to the signal turbulence. These generators are implemented by filtering a white noise or combining several filtered white noises with different bands (Voss 1985). Note that a fractal signal does not reveal its characteristics in the short term. This sometimes leads to the improper use of fractal signal generators.

Iterated maps are often used for producing fractals in a similar way as some popular programs of computer graphics such as Mandelbrot, Julia sets (Peitgen and Richter 1986), etc. Such signals, however, are not effective for the control of musical parameters. Other algorithms, such as that of the *mid-point displacement*, can be used for a fractal interpolation between assigned points, with a local control of the "fractality".

What makes a fractal model interesting is the fact that it captures an important temporal characteristic of natural signals, *self-similarity*, that is, the statistical similarity of some temporal characteristics when viewed from different time scales. In particular, a single generator could be employed for simultaneously generating several signals that evolve on different timescales. For this reason, ARMA filter models are more suitable for modeling self-correlation on a short timescale, while fractal signals are better for modelling self-correlation on a longer timescale.

Physical models

Physical models can also synthesize control signals. In this case, the system is slowly-varying and provides the dynamics for the evolution of the signal. So far, however, this approach has been rarely used for the synthesis of control signals. Most of the available examples are meant for obtaining descriptive physical metaphors for musical processes, rather than for modeling existing mechanisms. For example, Todd suggests a model of a ball accelerating along a surface with several holes in it, for describing the expressive acceleration or slowing down of the musical tempo. Sundberg and Verillo (1980) suggest the analogy between the final slowing down of a musical piece and a person that stops walking. Such models generate parameter variations that can be cognitively perceived as plausible and recognized as natural.

Learning-based synthesis

When the signal to be synthesized belongs to a class of which a variety samples is available, then it is possible to estimate parameter signals through specific "learning" processes applied to the signal samples. One example of this method consists of using signal generators based on *feedforward neural networks* which, when suitably trained, exhibit good generalization properties and, therefore, are capable of producing plausible results even when the final result is quite different from the training samples. For example, spectral dynamics have been obtained through the interpolation of static spectra with properly trained neural networks.

Rule-based synthesis

So far, only synthesis methods based on signal models have been considered. Under specific circumstances, however, it is possible to roughly model the behavior or a human performer by means of a *controller model* operating in a symbol space rather than a signal space. A commonly employed solution for the controller model consists of signal generators based on rules. This choice assumes that it is possible to extract complex "behavioral rules" for the controller, through an heuristic approach. Rules can be deduced from the analysis of the performance from acoustic samples of different performers.

In some situations, the set of rules is characterized by a degree of uncertainty that makes them difficult to implement as binary rules. In these cases, controllers based on *fuzzy logic* seem to be a good choice. Fuzzy controllers are specified a set of rules based on linguistic variables (e.g. "If the note is long ...") and the action to take if the membership conditions are satisfactory (e.g. "... elongate it a little more"). It is then possible to obtain numerical values necessary for control through an operation called "defuzzification".

Assessment of control signal synthesis

The methods presented up to here represent only a selection among many possible techniques that are currently being used for the synthesis of control signals. It is quite common, in practice, to find hybrid methods that combine two or more of the above methods.

It is natural to feel that the methods currently available for the synthesis of control signals are too simple, considering the complexity of the synthesis problem. This is particularly true for expressive control because it has not yet been studied in depth. The reasons behind the lack of results can be attributed to the fact that no suitable methods for analyzing expressive controls are presently available. Furthermore, this type of synthesis, concerns both technical and artistic aspects of computer music, therefore it depends on the personal tastes and opinions of each artist.

As far as control of spectral dynamics, there currently exist adequate analysis instruments but there is apparently not enough motivation for focusing on new synthesis models. This is mainly because the quality of sounds produced by simple models is often considered satisfactory, which definitely confirms the validity of such methods. On the other hand, one should remember that more flexible and accurate models would allow the musician to operate at a higher level of abstraction.

Conclusions

Since the time of the earliest experiments in computer music, many techniques have been developed for both reproducing and transforming natural sounds and for creating novel sonorities. This chapter has described a variety of classical sound synthesis techniques, mostly from the viewpoint of the user, and outlined their principal strengths and weaknesses. Particular emphasis has been placed on the physical model approach to sound synthesis, which is currently one of the most promising avenues of research.

Another important topic discussed in this chapter is the problem of the synthesis of control signals. We believe that once the potential of a synthesis technique is well understood, the researcher's interest should shift to the problem of control, which is the next higher level of abstraction in music production.

Any number of techniques may be used to obtain a specific sound, even though some are more suitable than others. For musical use a versatile and efficient technique is not sufficient, but it is necessary for the musician to be able to specify the control parameters to obtain the desired result in an intuitive manner. It is then advisable for musicians to build their own conceptual models for the interpretation of a technique, on the basis of both theoretical considerations and practical experimentation. This process is necessary because a "raw" synthesis method does not stimulate either the composer or the performer. On the other hand, a solid metaphor for the sound-production mechanism can provide the composers with better stimulae and inspiration, and help performers improve their interpretive skills.

References

Adrien, J.M. 1991. "Physical model synthesis: the missing link." In G. De Poli, A. Piccialli, and C. Roads, eds. *Representations of Musical Signals*. Cambridge, Massachusetts: The MIT Press, pp. 269–297.

Arfib, D. 1979. "Digital synthesis of complex spectra by means of multiplication of nonlinear distorted sine waves." *Journal of the Audio Engineering Society* 27(10): 757–768.

Borin, G., G. De Poli, and A. Sarti. 1992. "Sound synthesis by dynamic systems interaction." In D. Baggi, ed. *Readings in Computer-Generated Music*. New York: IEEE Computer Society Press, pp. 139–160.

Cadoz, C., A. Luciani, and J. Florens. 1984. "Responsive input devices and sound synthesis by simulation of instrumental mechanism: the Cordis system." *Computer Music Journal* 8(3): 60–73.

Chowning, J. and D. Bristow. 1986. *FM Theory and Applications: by Musicians to Musicians*. Tokyo: Yamaha Foundation.

Chowning, J. 1973. "The synthesis of complex audio spectra by means of frequency modulation." *Journal of the Audio Engineering Society* 21(7): 526–534. Reprinted in C. Roads and J. Strawn, eds. 1985. *Foundations of Computer Music*. Cambridge, Massachusetts: The MIT Press, pp. 6–29.

De Poli, G. and A. Piccialli. 1991. "Pitch synchronous granular synthesis." In G. De Poli, A. Piccialli, and C. Roads, eds. *Representations of Musical Signals*. Cambridge, Massachusetts: The MIT Press, pp. 187–219.

De Poli, G. 1984. "Sound synthesis by fractional waveshaping." *Journal of the Audio Engineering Society* 32(11): 849–861.

Florens, J.L. and C. Cadoz. 1991. "The physical model: modelisation and simulation systems of the instrumental universe." In G. De Poli, A. Piccialli, and C. Roads, eds. *Representations of Musical Signals*. Cambridge, Massachusetts: The MIT Press.

Hiller, L. and P. Ruiz. 1971. "Synthesizing musical sounds by solving the wave equation for vibrating objects: Part I and II." *Journal of the Audio Engineering Society* 19(6): 462–470 and 19(7): 542–551.

Jaffe, D.A. and J. Smith. 1983. "Extensions of the Karplus–Strong plucked-string algorithm." *Computer Music Journal* 7(2): 56–69.

Karplus, K. and A. Strong. 1983. "Digital synthesis of plucked-string and drum timbres." *Computer Music Journal* 7(2): 43–55.

Le Brun, M. 1979. "Digital waveshaping synthesis." *Journal of the Audio Engineering Society* 27(4): 250–265.

Markel, J.D. and A.H. Gray, Jr. 1976. *Linear Prediction of Speech*. Berlin: Springer-Verlag.

Mathews, M. 1969. *The Technology of Computer Music*. Cambridge, Massachusetts: The MIT Press.

McIntyre, M.E., R.T. Schumacher, and J. Woodhouse. 1983. "On the oscillations of musical instruments." *Journal of Acoustical Society of America* 74(5): 1325–1345.

Moorer, J. 1979. "About this reverberation business." *Computer Music Journal* 3(2): 13–28.

Peitgen, H.O. and P. Richter. 1986. *The Beauty of Fractals.* Berlin: Springer-Verlag.

Roads, C. 1978. "Automated granular synthesis of sound." *Computer Music Journal* 2(2): 61–62.

Roads, C. 1991. "Asynchronous granular synthesis." In G. De Poli, A. Piccialli, and C. Roads, eds. *Representations of Musical Signals.* Cambridge, Massachusetts: The MIT Press, pp. 143–185.

Smith, J.O. 1987. "Waveguide filter tutorial." In *Proceedings of the 1987 International Computer Music Conference.* San Francisco: International Computer Music Association, pp. 9–16.

Sundberg J. and V. Verrillo. 1980. "On anatomy of the ritard: A study of timing in music." *Journal of Acoustical Society of America* 68(3): 772–779.

Todd, N.P. 1992. "The dynamics of dynamics: a model of musical expression." *Journal of Acoustical Society of America* 91(6): 3540–3550.

Truax, B. 1988. "Real time granular synthesis with a digital signal processing computer." *Computer Music Journal* 12(2): 14–26.

Voss, R.R. 1985. "Random fractal forgeries." In R.A. Earnshaw, ed. *Fundamental Algorithms for Computer Graphics.* Berlin: Springer-Verlag.

2

Introducing the phase vocoder

Marie-Hélène Serra

The *phase vocoder* is a special technique that belongs to a family of sound analysis/synthesis systems. Analysis/synthesis not only allows sound transformations, but also sound synthesis from analysis data, and development of musical structures based on acoustic properties (Roads 1985; Moorer 1985; Risset 1993; Saariaho 1993). Typical analysis/synthesis systems include the phase vocoder (Gordon and Strawn 1985), additive analysis/synthesis (Serra 1989), formant analysis/synthesis (Rodet 1980), and linear prediction (Markhoul 1975). Because they bring a new understanding of the acoustic world, these systems have brought forth a new vision and practice of musical composition.

The application of sound analysis/synthesis in computer music began in the late 1960s (Risset 1966; Beauchamp 1969). Until recently, these techniques were available only to a small group of composers because they required powerful computers with large memories and high-quality digital-to-analog converters. Today, thanks to the technical and economical advance of personal computers, they are accessible to a larger group of potential users. Commercial applications with real-time hardware appeared in 1987, including the Lyre and Technos music systems. Software applications that offer more or less control are also available, including SMS (Serra 1989, 1994), Lemur (Tellman, Haken, and Holloway 1994), SoundHack (Erbe 1994), and SVP (Depalle 1991). Furthermore, recent progess in interactive graphic tools (Puckette 1991; Settle and Lippe 1994) has sparked new interest in analysis/synthesis.

The phase vocoder converts sampled sound into a time-varying spectral representation, modifying time and frequency information and then reconstructing the modified sound. Its use requires some elementary knowledge of digital signal processing. Very good introductory texts on the phase vocoder have been published in recent years (Gordon and Strawn 1985; Dolson 1986; Moore 1990). The phase vocoder can be interpreted and implemented in two different ways that are theoretically equivalent: with a bank of filters or with the short-time Fourier transform. This paper will refer only to the second category.

The short-time Fourier transform is the first step towards the computation of other parameters like spectral peaks, spectral envelope, formants, etc. That explains why today the phase vocoder is only one part of other sound processing methods. This is the case for the program AudioSculpt of Ircam (Depalle 1993) which has been called "Super Vocodeur de Phase" because it includes more than the traditional phase vocoder. Among the possible extensions of the phase vocoder, cross-synthesis between two sounds offers a great musical potential.

The rest of this paper presents the essential sound modification techniques that are made possible with the phase vocoder and other techniques derived from it. The first part reviews the digital signal processing aspects of the phase vocoder (considered here to be a short-time Fourier based analysis/transformation/synthesis system). The second part presents various musical applications.

Generalities

Sound analysis encompasses all the techniques that give quantitative descriptions of sound characteristics. Parameters such as pitch (Figure 1), amplitude envelope, amplitude and phase spectrum, spectral envelope, harmonicity, formants, noise level, etc, are derived from signal processing algorithms. The input of the algorithm is a sequence of samples and the output is a sequence of numbers that describe the analyzed parameters. Because sound evolves with time, sound analysis algorithms generally produce time-varying results. This implies that the algorithms repeat the same procedures on successive short sections of the sound. This kind of processing is called *short-time analysis*.

Spectral analysis is a special class of algorithms which give a description of the frequency contents of the sound. The most famous, the short-time Fourier transform gives a short-time spectrum, that is a series of spectra taken on successive temporal frames. The time evolution of the amplitude part of the short-time

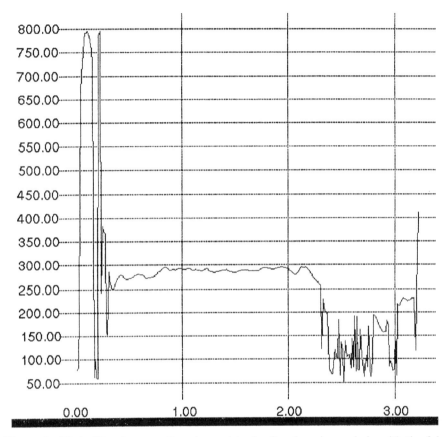

Figure 1. Pitch (Hertz) versus time (seconds) of a female voice melody with the following sounds "Te-ka-ou-la-a-a".

Fourier spectrum (the amplitude spectrum) can be displayed as a sonogram, as shown in Figure 2.

Once descriptive parameters of the sound are obtained, it is very interesting for the musician to be able to modify them and then resynthesize the sound. If the parameters are intuitive and independent, the control of the modification is made easier. The short-time spectrum is very interesting in that aspect. It is an intuitive representation for the musician, because it functions much in the same way as the human auditory system, which detects the frequencies that make up a sound at any given instant. The resulting sound transformations are closely linked to acoustic perception and therefore relatively easily controlable by the musician. Furthermore the short-time spectrum gives a representation of the sound where temporal and frequential information are separated. It is then possible to control independently time-dependent information and frequency-

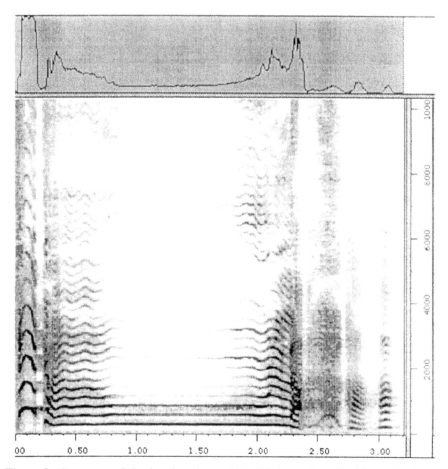

Figure 2. Sonogram of the female voice melody "Te-ka-ou-la-a-a" with amplitude envelope of the sound above.

dependent information. For instance it is possible to stretch the sound without perturbing its timbre.

Sound transformations based on the short-time Fourier transform require a lot of computation due mostly to the transition (at the analysis stage) from the samples to the spectrum and (at the synthesis stage) from the spectrum back to the samples. That is why until very recently real-time execution was a challenge, all the more so because control of the transformations add to the computational load. Recent developments are to be mentioned (Settle and Lippe 1994). More progress is needed in real-time execution speeds and control for sound transformation.

On the other hand, simpler techniques such as delay, chorus, pitch shifting, harmonizing, reverberation, and digital filtering that are applied directly to the sound samples can easily run in real-time, as in the GRM Tools and Hyperprism applications for MacOS. Furthermore the combination of signal processing units, made easier with graphical programming environments such as Max (Puckette 1991) and SynthBuilder, can produce numerous and varied sound effects. Nevertheless a wide range of musical applications are difficult, if not impossible, without the extraction of the short-time spectrum. For instance, filtering one sound with the spectral envelope of another one, called *cross-synthesis*, requires an analysis of both sound spectra.

Basically, the short-time Fourier transform converts the one-dimensional temporal signal (amplitude versus time) into a two-dimensional representation where the amplitude depends both on frequency and time. The later representation gives the evolution of the spectrum with time. The notion of spectrum is reviewed in the next section.

The spectrum

Consider an analog signal $s(t)$ where t is the time expressed in seconds. The spectrum of $s(t)$ is given by the Fourier transform defined as

$$S(f) = \int_{-\infty}^{+\infty} s(t)e^{-j2\pi ft}\, \mathrm{d}t, \tag{1}$$

where the variable f is the frequency in Hz. The result of the transform $S(f)$ is a complex number and can be written in terms of its magnitude and phase:

$$S(f) = |S(f)|e^{j\theta(f)}.$$

$|S(f)|$ is called the *amplitude spectrum* and $\theta(f)$ the *phase spectrum*.

Figure 3 shows a theoretical example of a periodic sound with its spectrum. Several features appear in the spectral representation. The periodicity of the signal is represented in the frequency domain by a line spectrum formed of the fundamental and the harmonics. If the signal is not periodic, the spectrum is continuous because the energy of the signal is distributed continuously among the frequencies. The *spectral bandwidth* is the interval where the energy is not zero. The *spectral envelope* is a smooth curve that surrounds the amplitude spectrum.

Two properties are to be noticed: for all the sounds (that are real signals), the amplitude spectrum is symmetric and the phase spectrum is anti-symmetric. Therefore only half of the spectrum is useful. We usually consider the positive half.

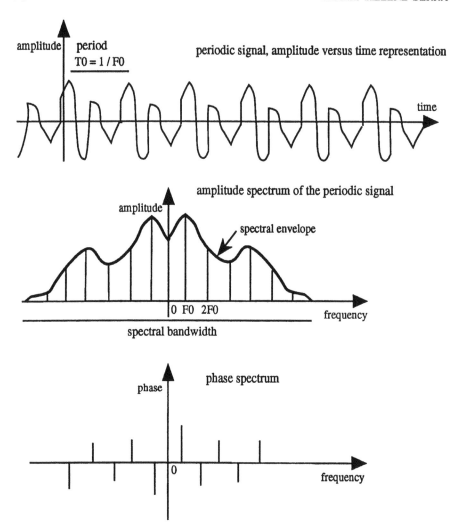

Figure 3. Two representations of a sound. The amplitude versus time representation and the spectrum.

The inverse Fourier transform gives the signal $s(t)$ in terms of its spectrum:

$$s(t) = \int_{-\infty}^{+\infty} S(f)e^{j2\pi ft}\,\mathrm{d}f. \tag{2}$$

In this expression we see more clearly the signification of $S(f)$. The signal $s(t)$ is represented by an integral (continuous sum), over frequency, of the frequency-depending terms $e^{j2\pi f}$ which are weighted by $S(f)$. The term $e^{j2\pi f}$ is called complex exponential and can be written as

$$e^{j2\pi f} = \cos(2\pi f) + j\sin(2\pi f).$$

The Fourier transform expresses the signal as a sum of frequencies (sine and cosine) with different amplitudes $|S(f)|$ and phases $\theta(f)$.

It is important to emphasize that the two different representations of the signal, the temporal representation $s(t)$ and the frequency representation $S(f)$ are equivalent. The transformation of one into the other is accomplished with no loss of information. In other words, $S(f)$ contains all the information that is necessary to recover the temporal signal $s(t)$.

The discrete Fourier transform

The question is how to compute the spectrum of a given sound. The sound, which has a finite duration, must be stored in the computer as a sequence of numbers. This is done via an analog to digital converter. The continous signal $s(t)$ is thus represented by a discrete sequence $s(m)$, where m is the sample number that goes from 0 to $M - 1$, M being the total number of samples. The sample rate F_s of the converter gives the number of samples per second.

The spectrum of the digital sequence is computed with the *discrete Fourier transform* (DFT), which can be viewed as a discrete version of the Fourier transform. The input of the DFT is the sequence of samples $s(m)$ and the output is a sequence of numbers $S(k)$, which express the spectrum at different points k on the frequency axis. The DFT is computed with the following formula (Oppenheim and Shafer 1975; Moore 1985):

$$S(k) = \sum_{m=0}^{M-1} s(m)e^{-j\frac{2\pi}{M}km}, \quad k = 0, \ldots, M - 1, \tag{3}$$

where M is the number of samples in the input sequence.

For M input samples the DFT produces M values corresponding to points of the spectrum. This comes to sampling the spectrum at M points that correspond to the frequencies $f_k = kF_s/M$. These points, called frequency bins, are equally spaced between 0 and the sampling frequency F_s.

The DFT spectrum $S(k)$ is complex and can be converted into a discrete amplitude spectrum $|S(k)|$ and a discrete phase spectrum $\theta(k)$. The amplitude $|S(k)|$ and the phase $\theta(k)$ are the amplitude and phase of the complex exponential

$$e^{j2\pi\frac{k}{M}} = \cos\left(2\pi\frac{k}{M}\right) + j\sin\left(2\pi\frac{k}{M}\right), \text{ where frequency is } k\frac{F_s}{M} \text{ Hz.}$$

An interesting approach consists in viewing the DFT as a projection of the vector $s(m)$ on a basis of M orthogonal vectors, which are the complex sinusoidal of frequencies kF_s/M (Harris 1978; Jaffe 1987). The coefficients $S(k)$ are the results of this projection. If $S(k)$ is null, for a given k, it means that the signal has no energy at the corresponding frequency.

As an example, let us consider a discrete signal made out of the sum of two sine waves with frequencies F_0 and F_1 and amplitudes A_0 and A_1. The sample rate is F_s and the total number of samples is M:

$$s(m) = A_0 \sin\left(2\pi \frac{F_0}{F_s}m\right) + A_1 \sin\left(2\pi \frac{F_1}{F_s}m\right), \quad m = 0, \ldots, M-1. \quad (4)$$

The sequence $s(m)$ is computed with the following parameters:

$F_s = 10000$ samples per second,

$M = 1000$ samples,

$F_0 = 1000$ Hz,

$F_1 = 4000$ Hz,

$A_0 = 1$,

$A_1 = 0.5$.

The sequence is made of two frequencies 1000 Hz and 4000 Hz, which are harmonics. It is periodic, with a period of $F_s/F_0 = 10000/1000 = 10$ samples.

Figure 4 shows only 10 cycles of the signal. The x axis indicates the sample number corresponding to the time in hundredths of a second (with a sample rate of 10000 samples per second, 100 samples equal one hundredth of a second). The y axis indicates the amplitude of the signal. Because the first sine wave is scaled by 1, and the second by 0.5, the sum of the two sine waves goes from -1.5 to 1.5.

The DFT of the sequence $s(m)$ is computed with (3). The amplitude spectrum is shown in Figure 5. The amplitude spectrum $|S(k)|$ is plotted for k between 0 and $M - 1$, which correspond to frequencies between 0 to F_s (10000 Hz). The frequency bins are distant of F_s/M which in our case is $10000/100 = 100$ Hz.

The two sine waves appear as lines at frequencies F_0 and F_1 and at frequencies $F_s - F_0$ and $F_s - F_1$. This is a result of the sampling of the signal $s(t)$ and of the symmetry of amplitude spectrum. Sampling the signal $s(t)$ in time introduces a periodization of the spectrum with a period equal to the sampling frequency F_s (Rabiner 1987). The frequencies $F_s - F_0$ and $F_s - F_1$ are the replica of $-F_0$ and $-F_1$ which form the negative half of the spectrum (see Figure 3).

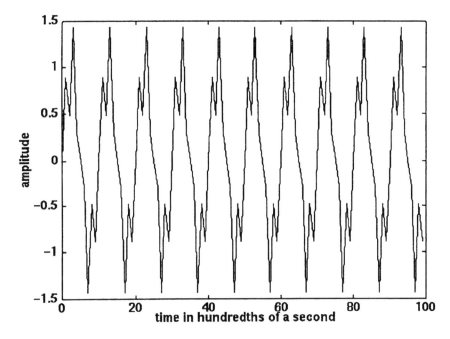

Figure 4. Ten cycles of a periodic sequence. The sampling rate is 10 kHz.

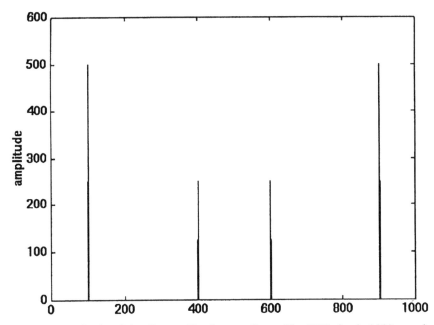

Figure 5. Amplitude of the discrete Fourier transform. The DFT size is 1000 samples. The sample rate is 10 kHz.

Because the DFT is periodic, with period M (Rabiner 1987; Moore 1990) and symmetric in $M/2$, an equivalent representation can be obtained with k between $-M/2$ and $M/2$, which correspond to frequencies between $-F_s/2$ and $F_s/2$.

In Figure 5 the amplitude spectrum has been normalized, so that the amplitudes of the two sine waves are retrieved. The normalization consists in scaling the magnitude spectrum by a factor of $M/2$. (In the literature, the DFT expression (3) can be found with the normalizing factor $1/M$. In this case the scaling factor for retrieving the true amplitude of the sine components is $1/2$. The normalizing factor $1/M$ has to be present either in the DFT expression or in the inverse DFT.) Indeed the DFT amplitude at a given frequency (except for zero frequency) is half the "true" amplitude of the component at this frequency, multiplied by the DFT size M (see Appendix 1). Figure 6 shows the normalized amplitude spectrum (multiplied by the inverse of $M/2$) between $-F_s/2$ and $F_s/2$.

The two frequencies F_0 and F_1 appear in the amplitude spectrum as vertical lines at specific frequency bins ($k = 10$ and $k = 40$). Indeed when the DFT size M is a multiple of the period of the input sequence, the frequency components of the signal (fundamental and harmonics) correspond exactly to DFT bins. In such a case it is straightforward to measure the exact amplitudes of the harmonics. This property is exploited in *pitch-synchronous analysis* (Moorer 1985).

When the DFT size is not an exact multiple of the period, the harmonics in the amplitude spectrum exhibit a different shape. Figure 7 shows the spectrum

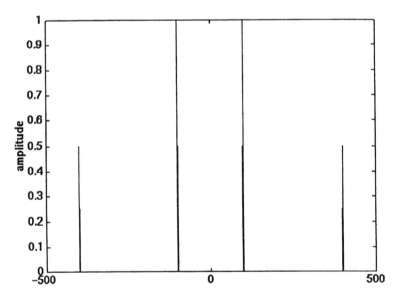

Figure 6. Normalized amplitude of the DFT. Plot between frequency bins $k = -M/2$ and $k = M/2$.

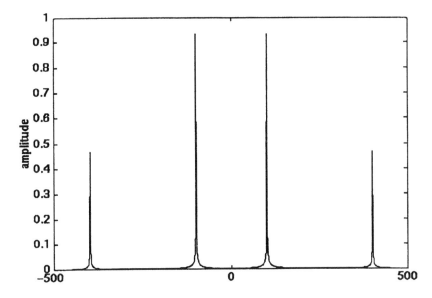

Figure 7. Magnitude spectrum computed with a DFT size of 998 points.

of the same sequence as before but with a DFT size of 998 points. The two input frequencies do not appear as lines but as narrow peaks. The energy of one harmonic is now distributed over several DFT bins. In such cases only an estimation of the harmonic amplitude can be performed (Oppenheim and Shafer 1975; Serra 1989). The same can be said about the DFT of a sound which is not periodic. The partials (sine components) appear in the amplitude spectrum as narrow peaks.

This phenomenon can be explained if one considers that expression (3) is the DFT of a sequence that is multiplied by a rectangular window (of amplitude one). This multiplication involves, in the frequency domain, a convolution between the Fourier transforms. The Fourier transform of the rectangular window is shown in Figure 8. In order to create this figure, the rectangular window has been *zero-padded* up to 4096 samples before taking its DFT (see further on in this section).

The magnitude DFT of the rectangular window is expressed as:

$$|W(f)| = M \left| \frac{\sin(\pi M f)}{\sin(\pi f)} \right| \quad \text{and is zero for } f = \frac{n}{M}, \quad n \text{ integer.}$$

Figure 9 depicts the convolution operation. The convolution of the sound's line spectrum with the Fourier transform of the rectangular window implies that each line is replaced by a copy of the Fourier transform of the window, scaled by its amplitude, and the copies are added together. Thus each spectral line

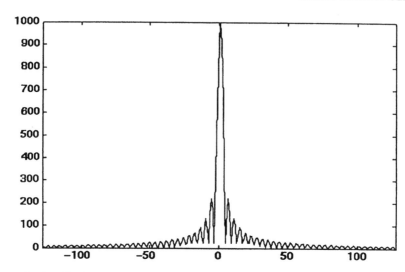

Figure 8. Amplitude of the DFT of a rectangular window of 1000 samples.

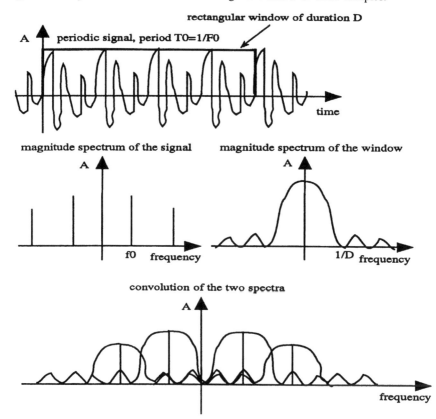

Figure 9. Convolution of a periodic sound with a rectangular window.

is widened due to the primary lobe of the rectangular windows spectrum, and there is interference between overlapping secondary lobes. The widening of the spectral lines due to the size of the primary lobe is inversely proportional to the window size. When the window size (or equivalently the DFT size) is an integer multiple of the period, the only effect of the window is a scaling in amplitude of the harmonic. This is because the amplitude of the function $W(k)$ is zero everywhere except at the point where the DFT is computed. When the window size is not a integer multiple of the period F_s/M, the convolution gives rise to *spectral leakage*.

The mathematical definition of the DFT implies that the input signal is periodic with period F_s/M. (The inverse DFT creates a periodic signal in which the period equals the input sequence of the DFT.) Taking a DFT size which is not equal to a multiple of the period is equivalent to truncating the period, which results in the creation of new frequencies that are not periodic inside the rectangular window. These frequencies are responsible for the spectral leakage. It is possible to reduce the spectral leakage by applying windowing functions different from the rectangular window that attenuate the discontinuities at the window boundaries. As it will be confirmed in the next section, the role of the window is essential in the short-time spectral analysis.

In practice, it is very difficult to adjust precisely the DFT size to the period. This is because, in general, most pitched sounds are not strictly periodic, and many sounds are not at all periodic. Furthermore even if the period is stable, it is not necessarily equivalent to an integer number of samples. A major drawback of taking the DFT of the whole input sequence is that it does not lead to a spectral representation that shows the time evolution. Therefore the idea is to compute a DFT of successive small sections of the sound (the input sequence of the DFT is a section of the sound) while reducing the window's effect so that the spectrum is best estimated.

The ratio F_s/M (sample rate divided by the DFT size) which separates the frequency bins is called the *analysis frequency* or the *spectral definition* of the DFT. It gives the smallest interval for the distinction between two partials. If partials are between two DFT bins they will not be seen. However, one partial can spread over several bins because of the convolution process. (We distinguish between spectral definition and *spectral resolution*. Spectral definition gives the smallest frequency interval that is measurable. Spectral resolution means separation of the partials of the sound. It is related to the window type and size.) For a given sample rate, it is possible to increase the spectral definition by increasing the DFT size M. As it was introduced (3), the DFT size M is the length of the input sequence (the total number of samples of the input sequence). To provide more samples to the DFT, it suffices to add the desired number of samples with zero amplitudes. This process increases the spectral definition (number of bins per frequency interval) but does not interfere with the spectral resolution (separation of partials). This process is called zero-padding.

Before introducing the short-time approach, let us consider the reconstruction of the input sequence from its discrete spectrum $S(k)$. We assume that $S(k)$ has N points, N being equal to or different from M.

The *inverse discrete Fourier transform* (IDFT) allows the computation of a sequence of samples from a discrete spectrum (Rabiner 1987):

$$s(m) = \frac{1}{N} \sum_{k=0}^{N-1} S(k) e^{j \frac{2\pi}{N} km}, \quad m = 0, \ldots, N-1. \tag{5}$$

Given an N point spectrum, the IDFT produces a sequence of N samples. Depending on N, three cases can be distinguished:

> $N = M$, the number of frequency bins equals the length of the input sequence: the reconstructed sequence is equal to the initial one. (More precisely the sequence is reconstructed as a periodic signal whose period equals the initial sequence.)

> $N > M$, the number of frequency bins is greater than the length of the input sequence: the reconstructed sequence is equal to the initial one with samples of zero amplitude added. These samples can be dismissed. (As in the previous case where $N = M$, the reconstructed sequence is periodic and its period equals the input sequence with zeros added.)

> $N < M$, the number of frequency bins that are taken by the IDFT is less than the number of samples in the input sequence: the reconstructed sequence is "time-aliased".

Time aliasing (Figure 10) causes distortion to the reconstructed sequence. It comes from the addition of the "copies" of the inverse DFTs, as it is the case for frequency aliasing, when "copies" of the spectrum are superposed.

The reconstruction of an input sequence from its DFT can be obtained exactly with the IDFT if the DFT size is greater than or equal to the sequence length. The use of an oversampled DFT ($N > M$) is a means for increasing the spectrum definition but it is also necessary when multiplicative modifications (multiplying the spectrum by the response of a filter) are brought to the spectrum. This is because filtering in the spectral domain is equivalent to convolution in the time domain (Smith 1985). After multiplying the DFT spectrum by the filter frequency response, the filtered sound is obtained by performing an IDFT on the

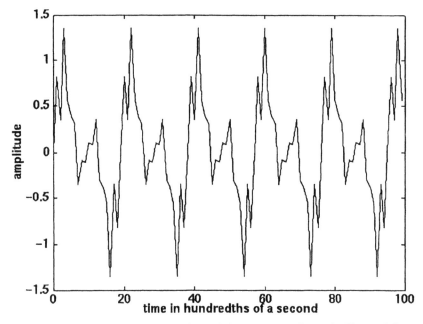

Figure 10. Time aliasing: reconstruction of the sequence shown in Figure 4 from an undersampled DFT.

filtered spectrum. Because of the convolution in the time domain, the length of the IDFT output, the filtered sequence, is equal to the sum of lengths of the input sound and the impulse response of the filter. That is why the filtered spectrum must be defined with more points than the input sequence.

The DFT can be calculated very efficiently using an algorithm called the *fast Fourier transform*, or FFT. This algorithm optimizes the calculation of the values of the discrete spectrum $S(k)$, when the number of frequency bins to be calculated is a power of two. If the number of samples of the sound is not equal to a power of two, zero padding is performed before the FFT is achieved. Zero padding results in better spectral definition.

The short-time discrete Fourier transform

The DFT gives the frequency image of the whole sequence $s(m)$. It is an interesting representation that could serve as a basis for sound transformations (Arfib 1991), but it makes it difficult to apply modifications at specific times. The short-time discrete Fourier transform (STFT) overcomes this by giving a time-dependent version of the discrete Fourier transform.

The computation of the STFT is equivalent to computing a DFT on successive frames of an input sound (Figure 11). For theoretical reasons (see section on the analysis step size), the frames must overlap. A frame is a section of the signal that is obtained by multiplying the signal with a window. The windowed sequence is input to the discrete Fourier transform which transforms it into a discrete spectrum. The window position is moved by an amount called the *step size* or the *hop size*, another frame is computed, and the DFT analysis is repeated. At the end of the computation the sound has been transformed into a set of frames represented by their DFT spectrum.

Several parameters control the computation of the STFT: the window type, the window size, the step size and the DFT size. These parameters are determinant because they control the shape of the short-time spectrum on which modifications are performed. For instance, the quality of a time-stretching can be drastically improved if the window size is correctly set according to the nature of the input sound. Figure 12 shows the amplitude spectrum of a section of a double bass sound obtained with two different window sizes.

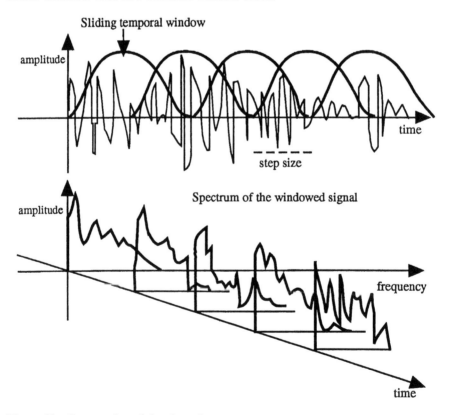

Figure 11. Computation of the short-time spectrum.

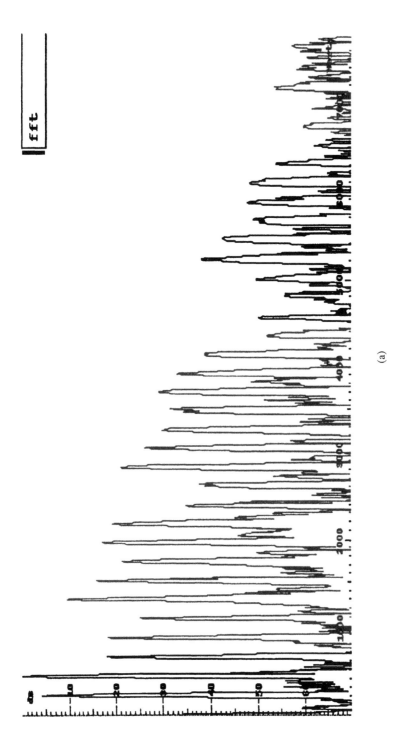

(a)

Figure 12. Amplitude spectrum of a section of a double bass sound. (a) Window size is 0.2 s. (b) Window size is 0.05 s.

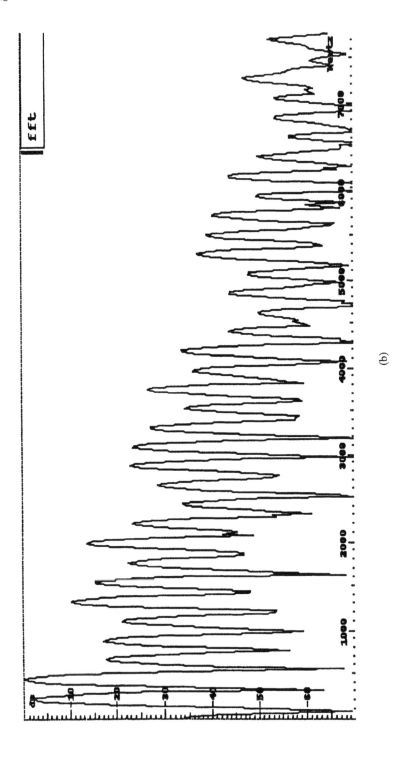

Figure 12.   (Continued.)

The STFT is expressed as:

$$S(rI, k) = \sum_{m=0}^{M-1} s(m)w(rI - m)e^{-j\frac{2\pi}{N}km}. \tag{6}$$

It is a function of two discrete variables, the time rI and the frequency k. The index rI is the position of the window, r being the frame number and I the step size of the analysis window.

By an appropriate rearrangement, equation (6) can be written in the form of a DFT (4) (Dolson 1986; Rabiner and Shafer 1987; Crochiere 1980), and the computation of the STFT can take advantage of the FFT. (From now on the FFT size is used in place of the DFT size.)

$S(rI, k)$ can be seen as the spectrum of the sequence $s(m)w(rI - m)$, which is the input sequence $s(m)$ multiplied by the window shifted at position rI. It is not the exact spectrum of the input sequence, but its convolution with the windows Fourier transform. $S(rI, k)$, which is a smooth version of the input sequence spectrum, is possibly modified. Because the goal is to modify the input sequence, the effect of the window on its spectrum must be reduced as much as possible. This implies that the window's Fourier transform should appear as an impulse with respect to the input spectrum.

After the modification is performed, the output sound is synthesized using an overlap-add method. First, the modified spectrum $\bar{S}(rI, k)$ at frame r is transformed into a sequence of samples $\bar{s}(rI, m)$ with the inverse DFT transform:

$$\bar{s}(rI, m) = \frac{1}{N} \sum_{k=0}^{N-1} \bar{S}(rI, k)e^{j\frac{2\pi}{N}km}, \quad m = 0, \ldots, N-1, \tag{7}$$

which gives a buffer of N output samples, where N is the FFT size. The synthesis formula (7) can also be expressed as:

$$\bar{s}(rI, m) = \frac{1}{N} \sum_{k=0}^{N-1} |\bar{S}(rI, k)|e^{j\left(\frac{2\pi}{N}km+\theta(r\bar{I},k)\right)}, \quad m = 0, \ldots, N-1, \tag{8}$$

where $|\bar{S}(rI, k)|$ and $\bar{\theta}(rI, k)$ are the modulus and the phase of the modified spectrum at frame r. The synthesized buffers from each frame are then combined.

There are several methods for the combination of the synthesized buffers depending on the different formulations of the analysis/synthesis problem (Griffin and Lim 1984). The standard *overlap-add* procedure consists in adding together the buffers and dividing by the sum of the shifted windows (Allen 1977). The output signal $y(m)$ is expressed as:

$$y(m) = \frac{\sum_{r} \bar{s}(rI, m)}{\sum_{r} w(rI - m)}.$$ (9)

With this method the input signal can be exactly reconstructed if there is either no modification of the STFT or a very restricted type of modification. Another synthesis equation has been derived by (Griffin and Lim 1984):

$$y(m) = \frac{\sum_{r} w(rI - m)\bar{s}(rI, m)}{\sum_{r} w^2(rI - m)},$$ (10)

which guarantees that the output signal has a spectrum which best approximates (according to a mean-square error criterium) the modified spectrum. This is the method used in the Ircam phase vocoder (Depalle 1991).

Window type and window size

Several types of windows are commonly used in musical sound analysis: rect-angular, Hamming, Hanning, and Blackman (Harris 1978; Nuttal 1981). The latter three windows share a similar temporal and spectral form.

Different parameters are used to characterize the spectral shape of windows (Harris 1978). For our purpose, we will retain two parameters: the main lobe width, and the difference in the amplitudes of the primary lobe and the first secondary lobe (Figure 13). The main lobe width can be defined as the distance between the two zero crossings of the primary lobe. As such, it is inversely proportional to the window size. If β/M is the main lobe width, the coefficient β

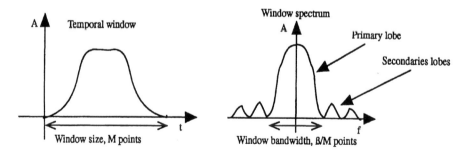

Figure 13. General window type and its spectrum.

depends of the type of window. For a rectangular window, it has the value 2, and for the Hamming window, it is 4.

The relationship between the amplitudes of the primary lobe and the secondary lobes also depends on the type of window. For the rectangular window, the secondary lobe is at -13 dB with respect to the primary lobe. For the Hamming window, the secondary lobe is at -43 dB.

The frequency components (see Figure 9) will be better separated if the window bandwidth is large and if the dynamic ratio between primary and secondary lobes is large. Among windows of equal duration, the rectangular window gives a spectral resolution that is superior to the Hamming window, whose primary lobe is twice as large, but the Hamming windows secondary lobes are much smaller. Therefore a compromise is necessary.

Given a window type, the window size can be adjusted so that the partials are separated. For a quasi-periodic sound, it is possible to adjust the window size according to the period, so as to separate the partials. As illustrated in Figure 9, the enlarged frequency components are discernible if the size of the primary lobe is less than or equal to the distance separating the partials. If the partials are equally spaced (if they are harmonics), the width of the primary lobe must be greater than or equal to the fundamental frequency F_0. This condition can be expressed as $\beta F_s / F_0 \leqslant M$. It follows that the window size M should be such that $M \geqslant \beta F_s / F_0$.

The ratio F_s / F_0 is the number of samples in one period. Thus the window size must be a multiple of the period (expressed in samples). The factor β depends on the type of window. For a Hamming window, it is equal to 4. As a general rule, for phase vocoder applications, the window size is taken to 4 or 5 times the period. If the sound is not periodic, the window size is determined by the distance between the closest frequency components that one wishes to separate. In practice the window size is increased until the output sounds satisfying.

Unfortunately increasing the window so that all the partials are resolved decreases the time resolution of the short-time spectrum. When the window is enlarged only one spectrum is computed for a large section of time, even if the sound is not stable within the section. The temporal variations that are inside the section are transformed into constant frequencies. Therefore at the time of synthesis the temporal variations inside one analysis frame will not be restored. On the other hand, if the window size is reduced so that time variability is saved, frequency resolution is affected. A compromise is necessary, which depends on the nature of the sound.

Figure 14 shows the resynthesized version of a cello sound. The modification is a very small time-stretch of a factor of 1.01 (see section on time-stretching). The modified version exhibits an amplitude envelope slightly different from the

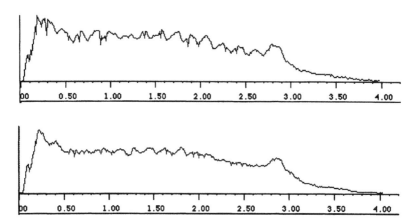

Figure 14. Cello sound envelope. Above: Original. Below: Modified version with large window size (0.11 s).

original. This is due to the analysis window size, which is too large relatively to the temporal variations of the sound; which implies a smoothing of the amplitude envelope.

The analysis of the attack portion of many instrumental sounds is a challenge because it requires a high frequency resolution, which is impossible given their short durations. Furthermore the sinusoidal model underlying the Fourier decomposition is not adapted to transients and noisy partials (Serra 1989).

The FFT size

If the window size is set as a function of the period, it is not necessarily equal to a power of two. If the window is enlarged to a power of two, we lose control over the frequency/time resolution tradeoff. To resolve this problem, a window size is initially chosen (as a function of the period, for example), and then is padded with enough samples with value zero so that the next-highest power of two is attained. Therefore the FFT size N is always greater or equal to the window size M. Zero-padding has the advantage of increasing the frequency definition of the spectrum (given by the analysis frequency F_s/N). It also allows filtering of the input sequence (here the windowed sequence) because the spectrum is oversampled ($N \geqslant M$).

Step size

The need for overlapping windows can be intuitively explained. In order to reduce spectral leakage, commonly used windows (such as Hamming, Hanning, and Blackman) attenuate the signal at their boundaries. This implies that part of the data has been lost. If the analysis frames were not overlapped, the events happening near the boundaries would be missed. Overlapping allows recovery of the lost samples. It is then implicit that the overlapping factor should be such that the overlapping windows add to a constant, so that there is no amplitude modulation of the input samples.

A more precise formulation (Allen 1977; Rabiner 1978) of this problem is how to choose the rate at which the STFT $S(rI, k)$ is sampled in time, so that it gives a valid representation of the input signal. According to the sampling theorem, a signal must be sampled at a rate greater than or equal to twice its bandwidth. Since for a given frequency the short-time spectrum $S(rI, k)$ is bandlimited by the window's Fourier transform (the bandwidth is approximated by β/M, M being the window length), it is sufficient to sample it while fullfilling the sampling conditions. Therefore the step size I should be less than or equal to M/β. β is called the *overlap factor*. For the Hamming window, where $\beta = 4$, the step size should be at least one-fourth the window size (the overlap factor is greater than or equal to 4). Because the window is not truly bandlimited, overlap factors are generally above the minimum required (twice the minimum for instance), which is 8 in the Hamming case. (In the Ircam phase vocoder the default overlap factor is 8 for Hamming, Hanning, and Blackman–Harris windows.)

Another approach allows deriving the minimum overlap factor (Allen 1977) by looking at the standard overlap-add synthesis equation (9). To retrieve the input signal, when no modification is made to the STFT, the sum of the window shifted by rI samples must equal a constant:

$$\sum_r w(rI - m) = 1.$$

It can be shown (Allen 1977; Rabiner 1978) that this is the case when the window $w(m)$ is sampled at a sufficiently dense rate. For the Hamming window the minimum rate is one-fourth the window length.

The use of a step size that is smaller than the required minimum is a means for improving the time resolution of the short-time spectral representation. As the step size shrinks, it becomes easier to see the details in the evolution of the spectrum.

Modulus, phase, and instantaneous frequency

For a given frequency bin k, and for a given frame r, the modulus $|S(rI, k)|$ and the phase $\theta(rI, k)$ of the short-time Fourier transform represent the amplitude and phase of the sinusoidal partial with frequency $f_k = kF_s/N$ and at time rI. The phase value is computed relative to the position rI of the window. On the next frame, another pair of values $|S((r+1)I, k)|$ and $\theta((r+1)I, k)$ is computed. The difference in phase between two adjacent frames $(r-1)I$ and rI, divided by the time interval I between two frames, gives the phase derivative of the signal at frequency f_k and at frame r. It is also called the instantaneous frequency $\bar{f}_{k,r}$:

$$\bar{f}_{k,r} = \frac{\theta(rI, k) - \theta((r-1)I, k)}{I}.$$

To understand the significance of the instantaneous frequency, it is convenient to consider the short-time Fourier transform $S(rI, k)$ as the output of a bank of bandpass filters (Allen and Rabiner 1977; Dolson 1983). If N is the FFT size, there are N filters with center frequencies $f_k = kF_s/N$; the index k corresponds to the filter number (or channel number). The output values of the filters are given every rI samples. The instantaneous frequency $\bar{f}_{k,r}$ corresponds to the frequency deviation of the filtered signal within a particular channel from the center frequency of the channel f_k. If the instantaneous frequency in the channel is zero, the signal in channel k has frequency f_k. If the instantaneous frequency is constant in time, the signal in channel k has a fixed frequency equal to f_k plus the instantaneous frequency $\bar{f}_{k,r}$.

The evaluation of the frequencies and amplitudes of the partials in the phase vocoder is not the same as in the additive/synthesis method (Serra 1989; Depalle 1993). In the phase vocoder the frequencies and amplitudes are measured with fixed and equally-spaced filters. For additive synthesis, the analysis starts with the computation of the STFT, but it is followed by a peak-search algorithm and by the evaluation of trajectories for amplitudes and frequencies (Serra 1989). At this stage a pitch-detection algorithm is needed. This difference implies that the two systems cannot be controlled in the same way.

Sound modifications

With the STFT the musician can achieve modifications that alter either time-dependent or frequency-dependent information. The temporal modifications consist of expanding or contracting the time-scale of the Fourier representation, therefore inducing a change in the speed and duration of a sound, without altering the spectra themselves. Frequency modifications alter the composition of a spectrum at a given moment. Filtering, the result of the multiplication of the signals spectrum by the transfer function of a filter, creates variations in the

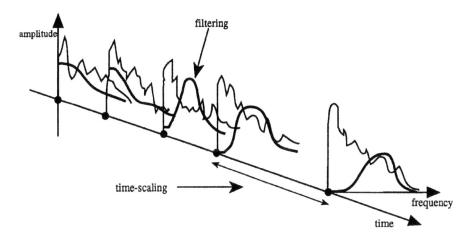

Figure 15. Time-scaling and filtering with the short-time Fourier transform.

frequency content of the sound, and thus variations in timbre can be achieved (Figure 15). When the filter corresponds to the spectrum of a sound, the modification thus consists of applying the spectro-temporal properties of one sound to another. This later operation is a special kind of cross-synthesis. Other frequency alterations are possible by modifying the values of the frequency bins at synthesis (Dolson 1986) or the instantanous frequencies of the partials. In the latter case limited transposition can be preformed as well.

In addition to the established repertoire of phase vocoder techniques, there is the possibility of combining the spectral information of two sounds, resulting in cross-synthesis. Fairly complex combinations of two sounds can thus be created, which is particularly useful from the musical standpoint.

Time compression and expansion

Time expansion and compression change the rate at which events occur, for an aesthetic effect. One can change the duration of a sound while retaining its spectral character, or change both speed and duration simultaneously.

Changing the speed at which a sound evolves makes it easier to perceive the details of the sound wave. The expansion of a piano sound, for example, makes it possible to isolate the striking of the hammer on the strings from the resonance of the vibrating string. In the same way, slowing down a recording of speech makes it easier to examine the articulation of the phonemes. This type of processing provides a useful effect by deforming the timescale of the micro-events that make up a sound.

Changing the duration of a sound is sometimes necessary when attempting to synchronize digital sounds, or when one needs to insert a sound of a predetermined duration into a piece of music. Since it is impractical, and sometimes impossible to sample a sound of exactly the desired duration (whether the sampling is done from a recording, or from a live player), one must be able to change this duration arbitrarily, without degrading the quality of the sound too much.

With the phase vocoder, time-scaling is accomplished by modification of the step size at the synthesis stage. Expansion (stretching) is obtained by increasing the step size. During synthesis, each DFT frame is converted to a buffer of N samples as in the normal case, but because the overlap of the buffers is decreased, the total number of samples in the ouput increases. In the opposite case, when the step size is reduced, the overlap increases, and the total number of samples in the output decreases.

Different factors must be taken under consideration so that the time-stretching does not distort the input signal. As noted in the previous section, the analysis step size must meet the constraint that the STFT $S(rI, k)$ is correctly sampled in time. If the step size is above the maximum limit β/M, which can be the case when the sound is stretched, the synthesized sound will be distorted. Some output samples will not be weighted equally by the synthesis window, resulting in an amplitude modulation of the signal. To overcome this problem, once the stretching factor is given, the analysis step size is taken to be the nominal size divided by the stretching factor, so that at the synthesis stage, the adjusted step size ensures a good synthesis.

The frequency resolution of the analysis, determined by the window type and size, is a key to the quality of the time-stretched version of the input sound. Indeed, if the phases $\theta(rI, k)$, are not well evaluated, there will be significant changes in the timbre. This is due to the phase correction that is performed to compensate the effect of time-scaling. Indeed, when the step size is modified, the speed at which the phases change is different from the speed in the input signal. Because frequency is proportional to the rate of change of phase with respect to time, a modification in this rate causes a frequency shift. Time expansion (similar to slowing down the playback of an analog tape recorder) will thus lower frequencies, and time compression will transpose a sound to higher frequencies. In order to correct for this transposition, the phase vocoder must apply a compensating operation. For example, if a sound is expanded by a factor of two, the phase values will change twice as fast. This compensating action should be invisible to the user. However, it is important to know this, since artefacts can appear, especially if the spectral analysis is lacking in resolution.

If the window size is too small, the phase measurements will not be reliable (because a filter may correspond to more than one partial). In this case the corrected phase value corresponds to the phase of a composite signal made up of two or more partials. These partials will be resynthesized with the same phase value, corrected for time-stretching. As a result, if the window is not large enough to resolve the partials, the synthesized signal will contain artificial frequencies.This phenomenon is clearly heard if the sound of a whispered voice is expanded with an insufficient window size. The synthesized voice becomes metallic, artificial harmonics appear, and an effect similar to flanging occurs.

Generally speaking, it is easy to time-stretch smooth and stable sounds, as long as the window size is adjusted to the pitch. Difficulties occur when stretching noisy or unstable sounds. Thus, it often happens that the attack portions of instrumental sounds do not lend themselves easily to time-stretching. Because they are short and unstable, it is very difficult or even impossible to find a compromise between time and frequency resolution. One way of stretching an instrumental sound is to apply a stretch after the end of the attack, when the sound's waveform is relatively stable. (This is possible in the Ircam phase vocoder, SVP, which implements time-varying time-stretching.)

Some algorithms perform time-scaling in the time-domain, by operating directly on sound samples. Examples are found in programs such as GRM Tools by INA-GRM (Vinet 1994), Sound Designer by Digidesign, Cloud Generator (Roads and Alexander 1996), and in real-time applications as Max on the Ircam Signal Processing Workstation. In contrast to techniques that work in the time domain, the phase vocoder performs time-scaling on the short-time Fourier representation. The phase vocoder is a more robust technique that is more independent of the type of input sound. Furthermore there is no theoretical limit on the amount of stretching that can be obtained.

Example 1: Double bassoon

Let us consider a sound sample of double bassoon with pitch F1 (A4 = 440 Hz). The frequency is 46.25 Hz. The figures shows several periods of the sound (Figure 16a), and the amplitude spectrum of this section (Figure 16b) computed via the FFT algorithm (the DFT size equals the duration of the section).

The time-stretching of this sound requires a window size equal to at least 4 times its period, which corresponds to 0.086 s, or 3814 samples if the sample rate is 44100 samples per second. The window size is quite long because the frequency of the sound is low. A time-stretching factor of two (the duration is doubled) is performed with different window sizes ranging from 512 samples to

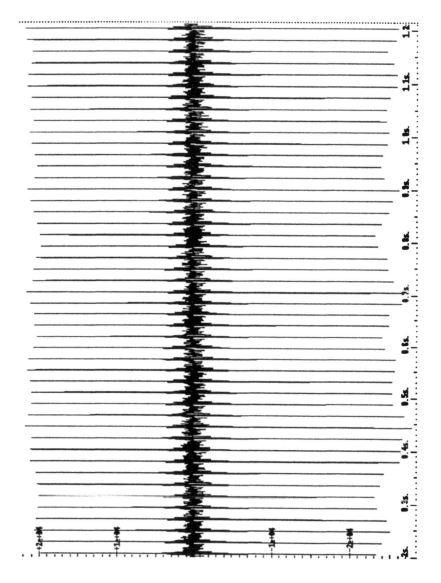

Figure 16a. Double-bassoon. Amplitude versus time, between 0.2 and 1.2 s.

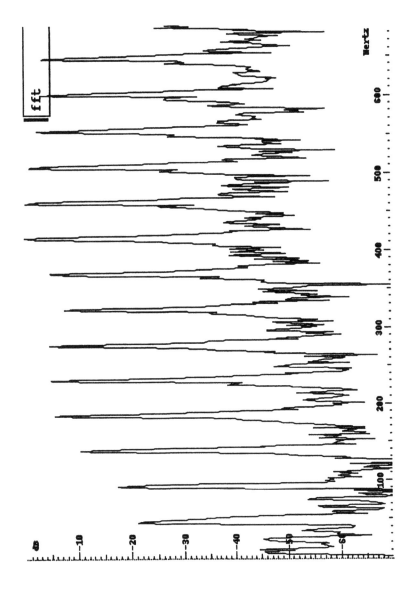

Figure 16b. Amplitude spectrum of the double-bassoon, details between 0 and 700 Hz, pitch 46.25 Hz.

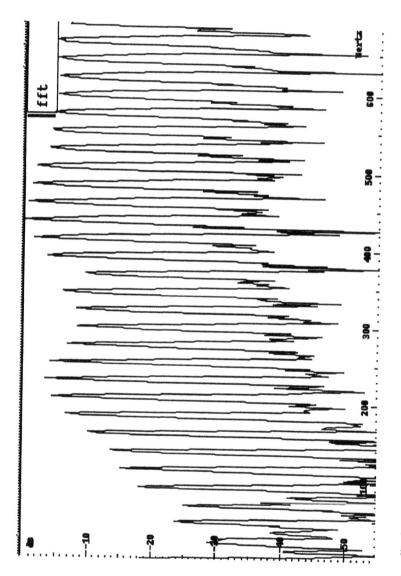

Figure 17a. Amplitude spectrum of the time-stretched double-bassoon, with a window size of 512 samples (0.011 s at 44.1 kHz), detail between 0 and 700 Hz.

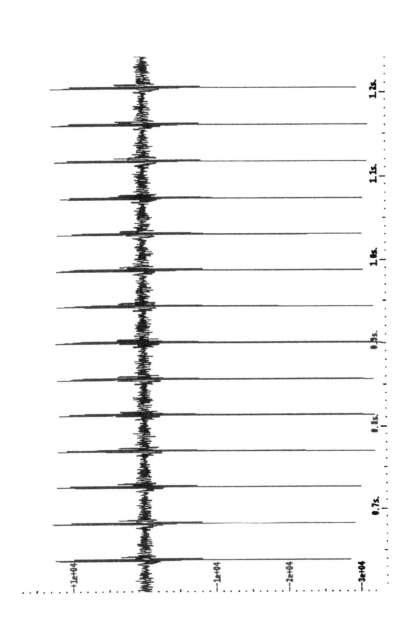

Figure 17b. Time-stretched double-bassoon with a window size of 512 samples (0.011 s at 44.1 kHz), detail between 0.2 and 1.2 s.

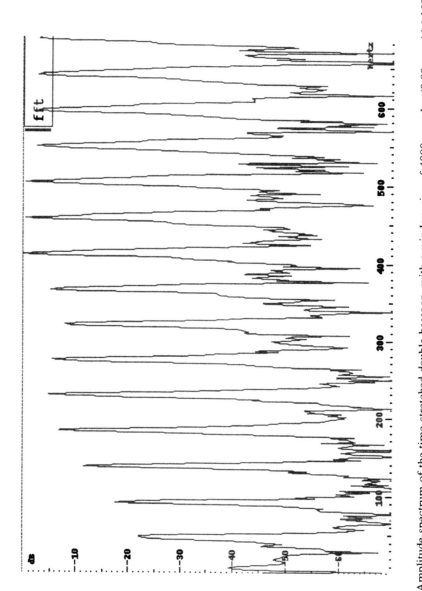

Figure 17c. Amplitude spectrum of the time-stretched double-bassoon, with a window size of 4000 samples (0.09 s at 44.1 kHz), detail between 0 and 700 Hz.

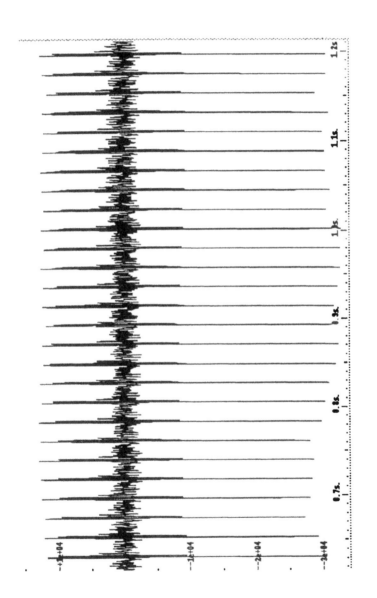

Figure 17d. Time-stretched double-bassoon with a window size of 4000 samples (0.09 s at 44.1 kHz), detail between 0.2 and 1.2 s.

4000 samples. With the 512 samples window, the output sound has a different timbre. A low frequency vibration, below the initial pitch, and heard as a series of pulses is superimposed to the input sound. Figures 17a–d portrays the spectrum of the output sound.

This low-frequency phenomenon starts to disappear when the window size becomes greater than 2500 points. With a window size of 4000 samples, the output sounds like the input, but with double its duration.

When the window size is too small (512 samples), the appearance in the output of a lower frequency component equal to half the pitch of the input sound can be explained as follows. The analysis does not see the fundamental frequency (because the window does not cover enough periods, or because the frequency resolution is not high enough). At the synthesis stage the initial pulses are separated with a time interval that is doubled, and are heard an octave below.

Example 2: Cymbal

Let us now consider the case of a cymbal sound that is time-expanded so that its total duration equals a given value. Because of the noisy nature of this type of sound, the window should be large enough for separating correctly the partials. But then the reconstruction of the attack is defective. To be able to resynthesize the sound with no distortion, time-stretching is performed after the end of the attack, when the sound becomes stable (Figures 18a–b). Three window sizes have been tried: of 512, 2000, and 4000 samples. With the smaller size, the time-stretched section contains artificial partials and does not connect properly to the untransformed section. This is because the phase matching between the two regions is not correct (the phases have changed in the dilated section). With a window size of 2000 samples, the connection between the two regions is better, and the dilated section contains less artifacts. With a window size of 4000 samples all the artifacts have disappeared and the output sounds natural.

In this example a time-varying time-stretching is applied. The STFT time-scale is left identical until the beginning of the dilation. Time must be allocated for the transition between non-stretched to stretched. More generally, when time-varying time-stretching is allowed, special care must be taken for the change of the dilation factor. If not, discontinuities in the output signal may appear, due to the phase mismatching between regions processed with different coefficients. This problem can be easily solved using linear interpolation of the dilation factor (Depalle 1993).

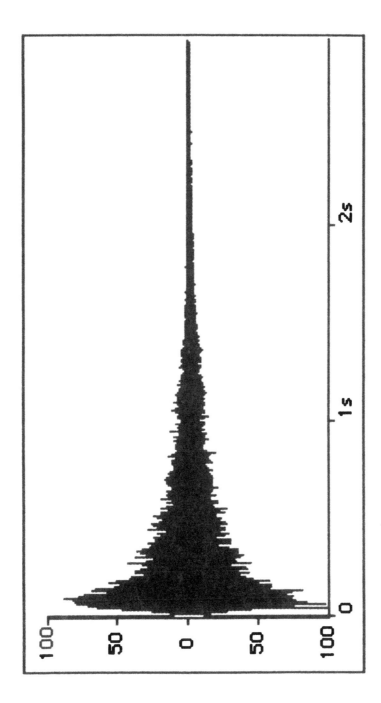

Figure 18a. Cymbal waveform.

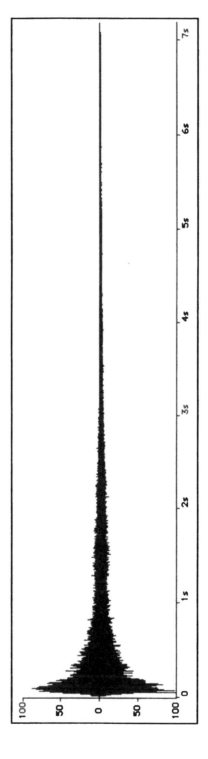

Figure 18b. Time-stretched cymbal, applied from 0.83 s with an expansion factor of 3.

Filtering

Filtering is the operation of multiplying the complex spectrum of the input sound by the transfer function of a filter (Smith 1985a, 1985b; Strawn 1985). Because it is a multiplication between complex numbers, the sound amplitude spectrum and the amplitude response of the filter are multiplied, while the sound phase spectrum and the filter phase response are added.

As the STFT analysis gives a time-varying spectrum, the amplitudes $A(rI, k)$ and phases $\theta(rI, k)$ of the partials can be modified with a time-varying filter. In such a case the filter response must be specified for each frame. Generally the user specifies only different states of the filter at different times, and the intermediate states are computed through linear interpolation (Depalle 1993).

Time-varying filtering is very attractive for achieving timbre variations. It is also a tool for creating rhythmic effects by alternating different filter configurations. For example, a rapid alternation between lowpass and highpass filters on a noisy input sound imposes on the sound a rhythm determined by the speed of the alternation.

Example 3: Gong

Figure 19a shows the amplitude envelope of a gong, while Figure 19b shows the result of a filtering made by a lowpass and highpass filter. The rhythm of the changes between the two filters is clearly depicted. Quick changes at the beginning are followed by a decelerando.

The size of the analysis window as well as the FFT size are crucial for the quality of the filtered sound. The first one determines the separation of the partials, and the second one gives the frequency resolution. As an example, let us consider the filtering of a flute sound. The sound has a pitch of C4 (261.63 Hz) and contains noisy partials that come from the blowing air. The presence of a tremolo is clearly depicted on the amplitude-time representation (Figure 20a). Figure 20b shows the amplitude spectrum computed on a large temporal section (between 3 and 5 s). The figure reveals the existence of a small vibrato as each harmonic oscillates. A very narrow bandpass filter is applied around the second harmonic; the filter center frequency is approximatively 523.26 Hz (261.63×2). In the first test, the filtering is done with a window size and a FFT size of 1024 samples (23 ms at 44.1 kHz); all the partials have disappeared except the second harmonic (Figure 20c). The vibrato is still visible in the amplitude spectrum. In the second test, the window size is increased to 3000 samples (68 ms at 44.1 kHz), and the FFT size to 4096 points. The oscillations due to the vibrato have disappeared (Figure 20d).

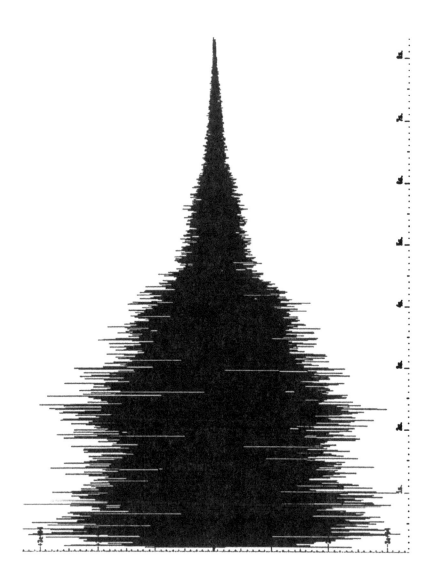

Figure 19a. Gong.

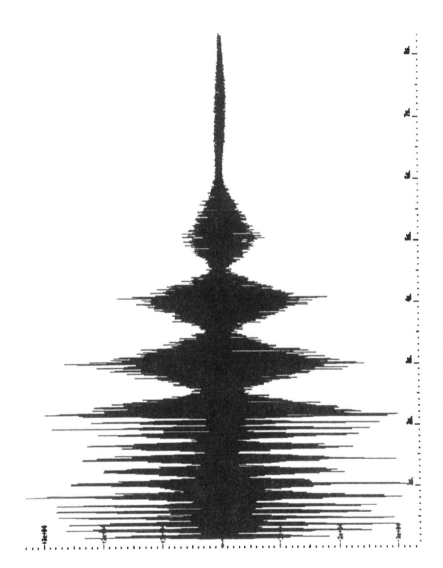

Figure 19b. Gong filtered with a rhythmic alternation of a lowpass and a highpass filter.

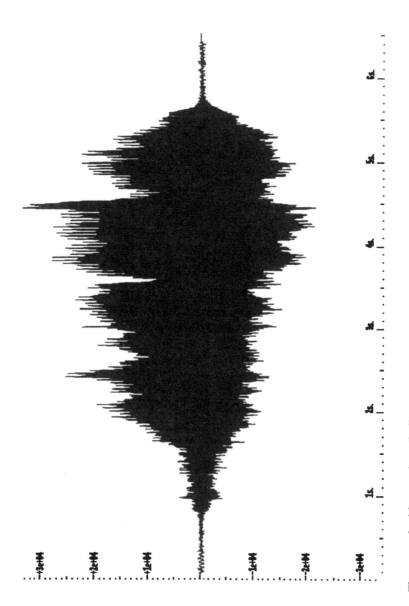

Figure 20a. Flute sound with tremolo and vibrato.

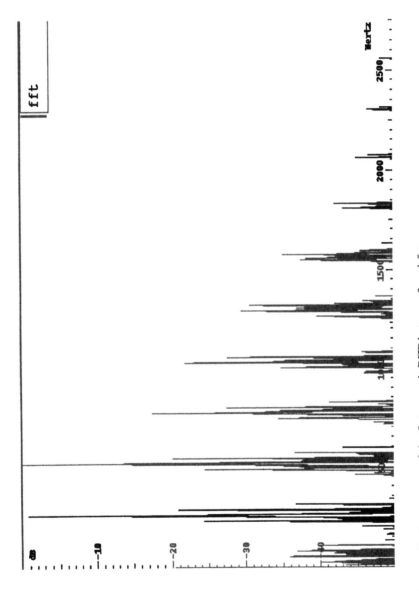

Figure 20b. Amplitude spectrum of the flute sound, DFT between 3 and 5 s.

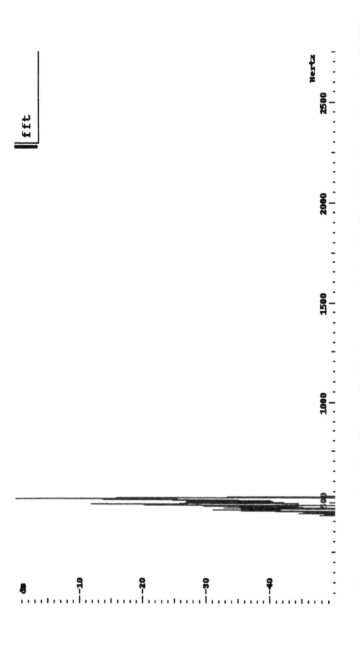

Figure 20c. Amplitude spectrum of the filtered flute. Filtering is performed after a STFT analysis with a window size of 1024 samples (23 ms at 44.1 kHz).

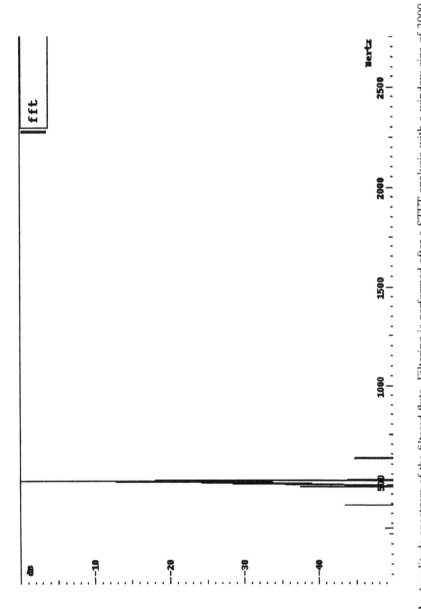

Figure 20d. Amplitude spectrum of the filtered flute. Filtering is performed after a STFT analysis with a window size of 3000 samples (68 ms at 44.1 kHz) and a FFT size of 4096.

Once an appropriate window size is found (such that the partials are correctly separated), the FFT size can be increased, so that the filtering operates on more points.

The phase φ_{nk} can be modified by applying a filter whose phase response is nonlinear. It is then possible to produce spectral distortion in the signal (for example, limited transposition of a sound). It does not, however, allow arbitrary transposition to be performed since the amount of frequency variation is limited to the window spectral bandwidth.

Cross-synthesis

Cross-synthesis (Figure 21) combines two sounds to produce a single composite sound. There are different methods for cross-synthesis depending on the nature of the data on which the combination is performed. Cross-synthesis can be done on the STFT representations of the two sounds. It can also be done with the data provided by additive analysis (Serra 1994; Tellman 1994). The two methods will not produce the same results.

The Ircam phase vocoder accepts two input channels and can generate the STFT representations of the two input sounds. If the the step size and the FFT size are the same, the two STFT representations have the same time-scale and frequency resolution (the number of points in the spectrum is the same). The STFT of the output sound is built on each frame and then converted to a buffer of samples with the inverse Fourier transform.

In the Ircam phase vocoder SVP, the most general cross-synthesis is made by combining the amplitude spectra and the instantaneous frequency spectra. Let $A_1(r, k)$ and $\bar{f}_1(r, k)$ be the amplitude and instantaneous frequency spectra for frame r for the first sound and $A_2(r, k)$ and $\bar{f}_2(r, k)$, the amplitude and instantaneous frequency spectra for the second sound on the same frame. The amplitude and instantaneous frequency spectra of the output sound on frame r are obtained using the following formula:

$$A(r, k) = E_1(r)A_1(r, k) + E_2(r)A_2(r, k) + q(r)A_1(r, k)A_2(r, k),$$
$$\bar{f}(r, k) = F_1(r)\bar{f}_1(r, k) + F_2(r)\bar{f}_2(r, k),$$

where $E_1(r)$, $E_2(r)$, $q(r)$, $F_1(r)$ and $F_2(r)$ are arbitrary constant or time-varying functions.

For a given frame r, the amplitude spectrum of the output is a linear combination of the amplitude spectra of the inputs, augmented by a multiplicative factor. Similarly at given frame r, the instantaneous frequency spectrum of the

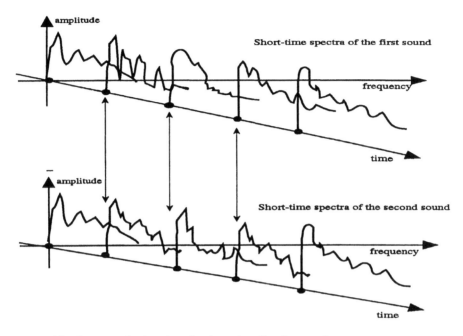

Figure 21. Cross-synthesis using the short-time Fourier transform.

output sound is a linear combination of the instantaneous frequency spectra of the inputs. This type of "hybridization" of two sounds gives independent control over the amplitudes and instantaneous frequencies of the partials in each analysis channel. It yields the possibility of altering the frequencies of a sounds partials without changing their amplitudes, and vice versa. With the combination $(E_1 = 1, E_2 = 0, F_1 = 0, F_2 = 1, q = 0)$ the instaneous frequency spectrum of the second sound is applied to first sound. With the combination $(E_1 = 0, E_2 = 1, F_1 = 1, F_2 = 0, q = 0)$ the amplitude spectrum of the second sound is applied to the first sound.

As an example we consider the cross-synthesis of a bass clarinet with a cymbal. The amplitude spectrum of each sound is shown in the Figures 22a and 22b, and has been computed by taking one DFT of one second in the middle of the sustain parts of the tones. Figures 22c and 22d show the output amplitude spectrum for two different types of cross-synthesis. Figure 22c illustrates the combination of the amplitude spectrum of the clarinet with the instantaneous frequency spectrum of the cymbal, and Figure 22d shows the effect of combining the amplitude spectrum of the cymbal with the instantaneous frequency spectrum of the clarinet.

These combinations lead to different hybrids of the two timbres. In the first one the sound is heard as a noisy and reverberated clarinet. In the second one

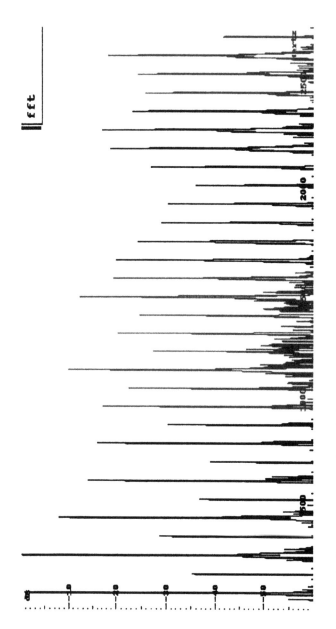

Figure 22a. Amplitude spectrum of the bass-clarinet.

Figure 22b. Amplitude spectrum of the cymbal.

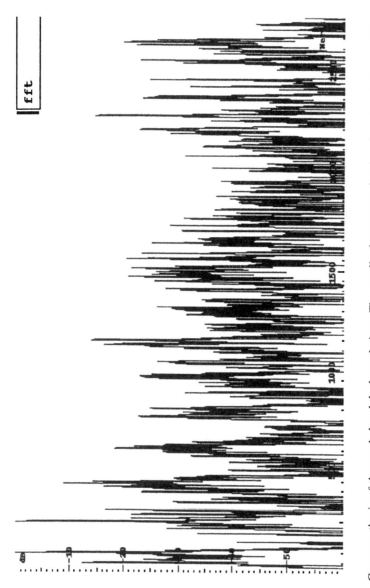

Figure 22c. Cross-synthesis of the cymbal and the bass clarinet. The amplitude spectrum is taken from the clarinet and the instantaneous frequency spectrum is taken from the cymbal.

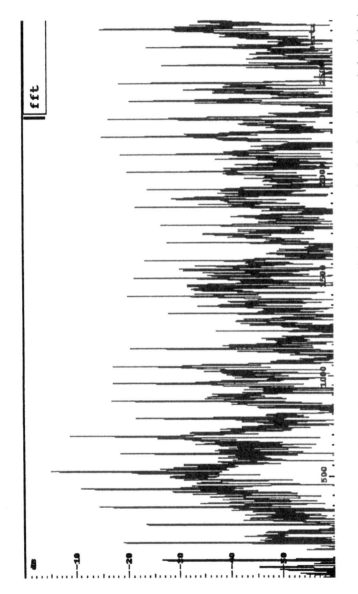

Figure 22d. Cross-synthesis of the cymbal and the bass clarinet. The amplitude spectrum is taken from the cymbal and the instantaneous frequency spectrum is taken from the bass clarinet.

the cymbal is proeminent, but because its partials are "organized" on the clarinet model, the timbre is less "chaotic."

The multiplication of the two amplitude spectra $q(r) \times A_1(r, k) \times A_2(r, k)$ is a rather delicate matter. When this operation is used alone (E_1 and E_2 are zero), the resultant spectrum may be zero if the two spectra are complementary; that is, when their spectra do not overlap at all. Furthermore, the multiplication of two amplitude spectra often results in a strong attenuation of high frequencies, because generally the input sounds have a spectrum with a decreasing amplitude/frequency slope. Thus this operation is often preceded by a preemphasis, which boosts high frequencies before processing the sound.

Generalized cross-synthesis is also a means of doing a "spectral crossfading" between two sounds, by applying sloping envelopes on the amplitude and instantaneous spectra. For instance the amplitudes envelopes $E_1(r)$ and $E_2(r)$ and can be taken as two opposite ramps, as well as the frequency envelopes $F_1(r)$ and $F_2(r)$. The effect of multiplying the spectra by opposite envelopes will lead to a progressive exchange between the two sounds. The exchange of instantaneous frequency spectra will induce progressive frequency changes that are difficult to control, because it is not a direct control of the frequency of the partials. The result of the spectral crossfading becomes more easily controlable if the input sounds have partials in common. If the STFT were not converted to amplitude and instantanous frequency, the result of spectral crossfading would be theoretically equivalent to a simple mixing between the two sounds. With spectral crossfading, timbral interpolation between two different types of sounds, like, for example, a pitched sound and a noise sound, is especially interesting.

As an example we consider the spectral crossfading of white noise with a double-bassoon. Figures 23a–d shows the amplitude spectrum of a section of the white noise, the amplitude spectrum of a section of the double-bassoon, the spectral crossfading between white noise and the double-bassoon, and the amplitude spectrum of a section of the output sound in the middle of the spectral crossfade.

Source-filter cross-synthesis is based on the combination of the STFT of one sound with the spectral envelope of the other. The computation of the spectral envelope can be done by using a *linear predictive coding* (LPC) algorithm (Markhoul 1975), or with a breakpoint approximation (Serra 1994). At the end of the analysis, two spectral representations are obtained, one is a series of short-time Fourier spectra, the other a series of spectral envelopes. The spectral representations are combined by pairwise multiplication of the Fourier spectra by the spectral envelopes. This multiplication serves to filter one sound by the spectral envelope of the other, a technique which is close to standard source-filter synthesis (Depalle 1991).

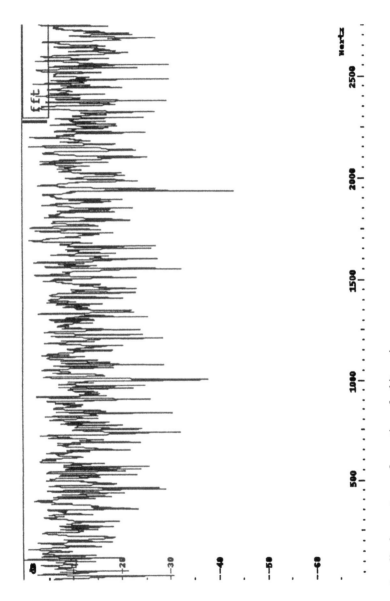

Figure 23a. Amplitude spectrum of a section of white noise.

MARIE-HÉLÈNE SERRA

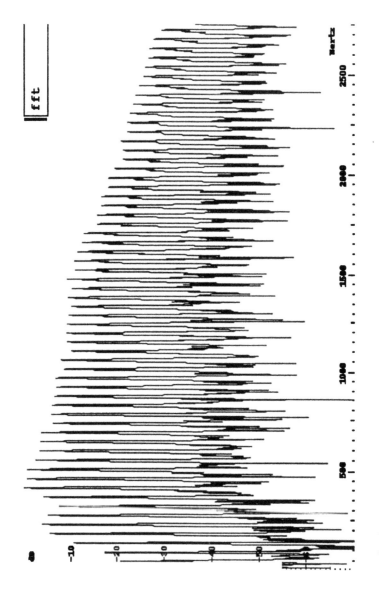

Figure 23b. Amplitude spectrum of a section of double-bassoon.

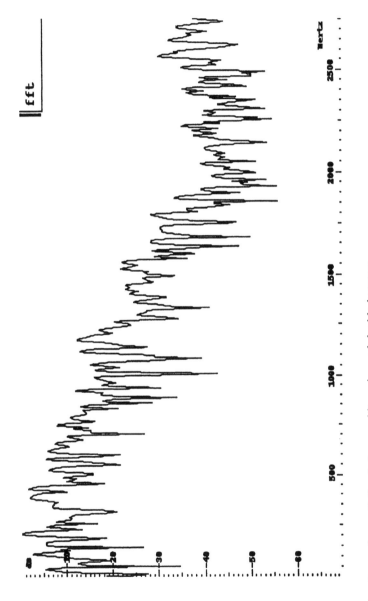

Figure 23c. Spectral crossfading between white noise and double bassoon.

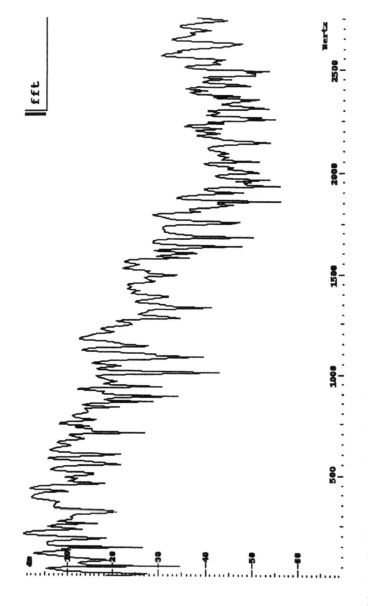

Figure 23d. Amplitude spectrum of a section of the spectral crossfading between white noise and double bassoon.

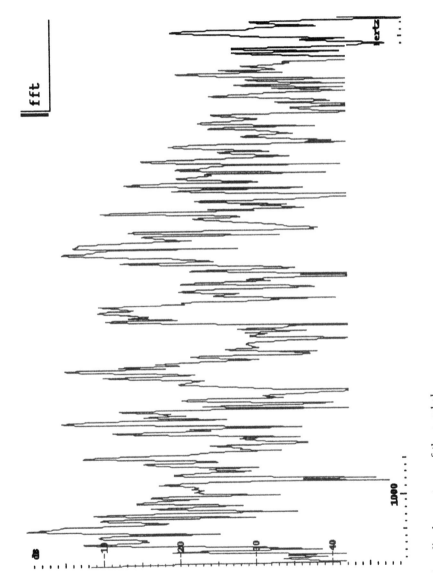

Figure 24a. Amplitude spectrum of the cymbal.

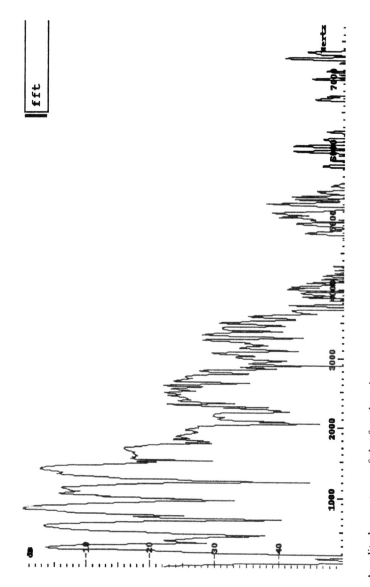

Figure 24b. Amplitude spectrum of the female voice.

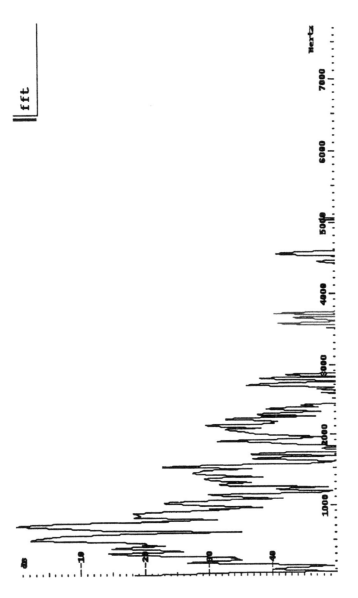

Figure 24c. Amplitude spectrum of the source-filter cross-synthesis, with the cymbal as the source and the voice as the filter.

Source-filter synthesis is useful for voice simulation, where the glottis is the source and the vocal tract is a time-varying filter. The source signal corresponds to an excitation, and the linear filter to a resonator. The source signal can be either a periodic impulse train, or a noise source. The resonator is characterized by its resonant frequencies, also called *formants*. The resulting sound spectrum is the product of the spectrum of the source signal (harmonic or noise spectrum) with the frequency response curve of the resonator (curve corresponding to the set of formants). With cross-synthesis the signal source is a sound, and the resonator is another sound.

LPC analysis is a means of estimating a spectral envelope (Rabiner 1977). The transfer function of the filter that represents the resonator is defined by a set of poles, which go by pair. Each pair of conjugate poles represents a formant in the spectral envelope. The number of poles (should be equal to twice the number of formants), controls the smoothness of the curve.

The applications of source-filter cross synthesis are numerous, and are, in general, quite interesting. One example, now commonplace, is the filtering of an instrumental sound by speech, or the inverse. In the first case, one hears the instrumental sound filtered by the vocal tract, shaped, as it were, by the phonemes of speech. The instruments timbre is deformed by the vocal formants. In the second case, the vocal impulse passes through the resonating instrument body. The vocal timbre is determined by the instruments coloration. The figures show the amplitude spectrum of a section in the sustain part of a cymbal (Figure 24a), a female voice (Figure 24b), and the amplitude spectrum of the source-filter cross-synthesis (Figure 24c), where the cymbal has been filtered by the spectral envelope of the voice.

References

Allen, J.B. 1977. "Short term spectral analysis, synthesis, and modification by discrete Fourier transform." *IEEE Transactions on Acoustics, Speech, and Signal Processing* ASSP-25: 235–238.

Allen, J.B and R. Rabiner. 1977. "A unified approach to short-time Fourier analysis and synthesis." *Proceedings of the IEEE* 65(1): 1558–1564.

Arfib, D. 1991. "Analysis, transformation and resynthesis of musical sounds with the help of a time-frequency representation." In G. De Poli, A. Piccialli, and C. Roads, eds. *Representation of Musical Signals*. Cambridge, Massachusetts: The MIT Press, pp. 87–118.

Beauchamp, J. 1969. "A computer system for time-invariant harmonic analysis and synthesis of musical tones." In H. Von Foerster and J. Beauchamp, eds. *Music by Computers*. New York: Wiley, pp. 19–62.

Crochiere, R.E. 1980. "A weighted overlapp-add method of short-time Fourier analysis/synthesis." *IEEE Transactions on Acoustics, Speech, and Signal Processing* ASSP-28(1).

Depalle, P. and G. Poirot. 1991. "SVP: A modular system for analysis, processing and synthesis of sound signals." In *Proceedings of the 1991 International Computer Music Conference*. San Francisco: International Computer Music Association.

Depalle, P. 1991. "Analyse, modélisation et synthèse des sons basées sur le modèle source-filtre." Doctoral thesis, Académie de Nantes, Université du Maine.

Dolson, M. 1986. "The phase vocoder: a tutorial." *Computer Music Journal* 10(4): 14–27.

Dolson, M. 1983. "A tracking phase vocoder and its use in the analysis of ensemble sounds." PhD thesis. Pasedena: California Institute of Technology.

Erbe, T. 1994. *SoundHack Documentation.* Lebanon, New Hampshire: Frog Peak Music.

Griffin, D.W. and J.S. Lim. 1984. "Signal estimation from modified short-time Fourier transform." *IEEE Transactions on Acoustics, Speech, and Signal Processing* ASSP-32(2).

Gordon, J.W. and J. Strawn. 1985. "An introduction to the phase vocoder." In J. Strawn, ed. *Digital Audio Signal Processing, An Anthology.* Madison: A-R Editions, pp. 221–270.

Harris, F.J. 1978. "On the use of windows for harmonic analysis with the discrete Fourier transform. *Proceedings of the IEEE* 65(1): 51–83.

Jaffe, D. 1987. "Spectrum analysis tutorial, part 1: the discrete Fourier transform." *Computer Music Journal* 11(2): 9–24.

Markhoul, J. 1975. "Linear prediction: a tutorial review." *Proceedings of the IEEE* 63: 561–580.

Moore, F.R. 1985. "An introduction to the mathematics of digital signal processing." In J. Strawn, ed. *Digital Audio Signal Processing. An Anthology.* Madison: A-R Editions, pp. 1–67.

Moore, F.R. 1990. *Elements of Computer Music.* Englewood Cliffs: Prentice Hall.

Moorer, J.A. 1978. "The use of the phase vocoder in computer music applications." *Journal of Audio Engineering Society* 27(3): 134–140.

Moorer, J.A. 1985. "Signal processing aspects of computer music: a survey." In J. Strawn, ed. *Digital Audio Signal Processing, An Anthology.* Madison: A-R Editions, pp. 149–220.

Moulines, E. 1990. "Algorithmes de codage et de modification des paramètres prosodiques pour la synthèse de parole à partir du texte." Thèse. Paris: Telecom.

Nuttal, A.H. 1981. "Some window with very good sidelobe behavior." *IEEE Transactions on Acoustics, Speech, and Signal Processing* ASSP-29(1): 84–91.

Oppenheim, A.V. and R. Shafer. 1975. *Digital Signal Processing.* Englewood Cliffs: Prentice Hall.

Portnoff, M.R. 1976. "Implementation of the digital phase vocoder using the fast Fourier transform." *IEEE Transactions on Acoustics, Speech, and Signal Processing* ASSP-24(3): 243–248.

Portnoff, M.R. 1980. "Time-Frequency representation of digital signals and systems based on short-time Fourier analysis." *IEEE Transactions on Acoustics, Speech, and Signal Processing* ASSP-28: 55–69.

Portnoff, M.R. 1981. "Time-scale modification of speech signal based on short-time Fourier analysis." *IEEE Transactions on Acoustics, Speech, and Signal Processing* ASSP-29(3): 364–373.

Puckette, M. 1991. "Combining event and signal processing in the MAX graphical programming environment." *Computer Music Journal* 15(3).

Rabiner, L.R and Shafer, R.W. 1987. *Digital Processing of Speech Signals.* Englewood Cliffs: Prentice Hall.

Risset, J.C. 1966. "Computer study of trumpet tones." Murray Hill: Bell Laboratories.

Risset, J.C. 1993. "Synthèse et matériau musical." *Les cahiers de l'Ircam* 2.

Roads, C., ed. 1985. *Composers and the Computer.* Madison: A-R Editions.

Roads, C. and J. Alexander. 1996. *Cloud Generator Manual.* Paris: Les Ateliers UPIC.

Rodet, X. 1980. "Time-domain formant-wave-function synthesis." In J.G. Simon, ed. *Spoken Language Generation and Understanding.* Dordrecht: Reidel. Reprinted in *Computer Music Journal* 8(3): 9–14, 1984.

Rodet, X., Y. Potard, and J.-B. Barrière. 1984. "The CHANT project: from synthesis of the singing voice to synthesis in general." *Computer Music Journal* 8(3): 15–31. Reprinted in C. Roads, ed. 1989. *The Music Machine.* Cambridge, Massachusetts: The MIT Press, pp. 449–466.

Saariaho, K. 1993. "Entretien avec Kaija Saariaho." *Les cahiers de l'Ircam* 2.

Serra, X. 1989. "A system for sound analysis/transformations/synthesis based on a deterministic plus stochastic decomposition." Stanford: Center for Computer Research in Music and Acoustics.

Serra, X. 1994. "Sound hybridization based on a deterministic plus stochastic decomposition model." In *Proceedings of the 1994 International Computer Music Conference.* San Francisco: International Computer Music Association, pp. 348–351.

Settle, Z. and C. Lippe. 1994. "Real-time musical applications using FFT-based resynthesis." In *Proceedings of the 1994 International Computer Music Conference*. San Francisco: International Computer Music Association, pp. 338–343.

Smith, J. 1985a. "Fundamentals of digital filter theory." *Computer Music Journal* 9(3): 13–23. Reprinted in C. Roads, ed. 1989. *The Music Machine*. Cambridge, Massachusetts: The MIT Press, pp. 509–520.

Smith, J. 1985b. "An introduction to digital filter theory." In J. Strawn, ed. *Digital Audio Signal Processing. An Anthology*. Madison: A-R Editions, pp. 69–135.

Strawn J., ed. 1985. *Digital Audio Signal Processing. An Anthology*. Madison: A-R Editions.

Tellman, E., L. Haken, and B. Holloway. 1994. "Timbre morphing using the Lemur representation." In *Proceedings of the 1994 International Computer Music Conference*. San Francisco: International Computer Music Association, pp. 329–330.

Vinet, H. 1994. *GRM Tools User Manual*. Paris: Institut National de l'Audio-visuel/Groupe de Recherches Musicale.

3

Musical sound modeling with sinusoids plus noise

Xavier Serra

When generating musical sound on a digital computer, it is important to have a model of sound whose parameters provide a rich source of meaningful transformations. Three basic types of models are in use today for musical sound generation: *instrument models, spectrum models*, and *abstract models*. Instrument models (or *physical models*) attempt to characterize sound parameters at their mechanical/acoustical source, such as the parts of a violin, clarinet, or vocal tract (see Chapter 7). Spectrum models could be seen as characterizing sound parameters at the basilar membrane of the ear, discarding whatever information the ear seems to discard in the spectrum (see Chapter 2). Abstract models, such as frequency modulation (FM, see Chapter 1), attempt to provide musically useful parameters in an abstract formula.

This article addresses the second category of synthesis techniques: spectrum modeling. The main advantage of this group of techniques is the existence of analysis procedures that extract the synthesis parameters out of real sounds, thus making it possible to reproduce and modify actual sounds. Our particular approach is based on modeling sounds as stable sinusoids (*partials*) plus noise (*the residual component*). The analysis procedure detects partials by studying the time-varying spectral characteristics of a sound and represents them with time-varying sinusoids. These partials are then subtracted from the original sound and the remaining residual is represented as a time-varying filtered white noise component. The synthesis procedure is a combination of additive synthesis for the sinusoidal part, and subtractive synthesis for the noise part.

This analysis/synthesis strategy can be used for either generating sounds (synthesis) or transforming pre-existing ones (sound processing). To synthesize sounds we generally want to model an entire timbre family, that is, an instrument. This can be done by analyzing single tones and isolated note transitions performed on an instrument, and building a database that characterizes the whole instrument or any desired timbre family, from which new sounds are synthesized. In the case of the sound processing application the goal is to manipulate any given sound, that is, not being restricted to isolated tones and not requiring a previously built database of analyzed data.

Some of the intermediate results from this analysis/synthesis scheme, and some of the techniques developed for it, can also be applied to other music related problems, for example, sound compression, sound source separation, musical acoustics, music perception, and performance analysis, but a discussion of these topics is beyond the current presentation.

Background on spectrum modeling

Additive synthesis is the original spectrum modeling technique. It is rooted in Fourier's theorem, which states that any periodic waveform can be modeled as a sum of sinusoids at various amplitudes and harmonic frequencies. Additive synthesis was among the first synthesis techniques in computer music. Indeed, it was described extensively in the first article of the first issue of *Computer Music Journal* (Moorer 1977).

In the early 1970s, Andy Moorer developed a series of analysis programs to support additive synthesis. He first used the *heterodyne filter* to measure the instantaneous amplitude and frequency of individual sinusoids (Moorer 1973). The heterodyne filter implements a single frequency bin of the *discrete Fourier transform* (DFT), using the rectangular window. The magnitude and phase derivative of the complex numbers produced by the sliding DFT provided instantaneous amplitude and frequency estimates. The next implementation (Moorer 1978) was based on the *digital phase vocoder* (Portnoff 1976). In this system, the *fast Fourier transform* (FFT) provided, effectively, a heterodyne filter at each harmonic of the fundamental frequency. The use of a non-rectangular window gave better isolation among the spectral components.

The main problem with the phase vocoder was that inharmonic sounds, or sounds with time-varying frequency characteristics, were difficult to analyze. The FFT can be regarded as a fixed filter bank or "graphic equalizer": If the size of the FFT is N, then there are N narrow bandpass filters, slightly overlapping, equally spaced between 0 Hz and the sampling rate. In the phase vocoder, the instantaneous amplitude and frequency are computed only for each *channel filter* or *bin*. A consequence of using a fixed-frequency filter bank is that the frequency of each sinusoid is not normally allowed to vary outside the bandwidth of its channel, unless one is willing to combine channels in some fashion which requires extra work. (The channel bandwidth is nominally the sampling rate divided by the FFT size.) Also, the analysis system was really set up for harmonic signals—you could analyze a piano if you had to, but the progressive sharpening of the partials meant that there would be frequencies where a sinusoid would be in the crack between two adjacent FFT bins. This was not an insurmountable condition (the adjacent bins could be combined intelligently to provide accurate amplitude and frequency envelopes), but it was inconvenient and outside the original scope of the analysis framework of the phase vocoder.

In the mid-1980s Julius Smith developed the program PARSHL for the purpose of handling inharmonic and pitch-changing sounds (Smith and Serra 1987). PARSHL was a simple application of FFT peak-tracking technology commonly used in the Navy signal processing community (General Electric 1977; Wolcin 1980a, 1980b; Smith and Friedlander 1984). As in the phase vocoder, a series of FFT frames is computed by PARSHL. However, instead of writing out the magnitude and phase derivative of each bin, the FFT is searched for peaks, and the largest peaks are "tracked" from frame to frame. The principal difference in the analysis is the replacement of the phase derivative in each FFT bin by interpolated magnitude peaks across FFT bins. This approach is better suited for analysis of inharmonic sounds and pseudo-harmonic sounds with important frequency variation in time.

Independently at about the same time, Quatieri and McAulay developed a technique similar to PARSHL for analyzing speech (McAulay and Quatieri 1984, 1986). Both systems were built on top of the short-time Fourier transform (Allen 1977).

The PARSHL program worked well for most sounds created by simple physical vibrations or driven periodic oscillations. It went beyond the phase vocoder to support spectral modeling of inharmonic sounds. A problem with PARSHL, however, is that it was unwieldy to represent noise-like signals such as the attack of many instrumental sounds. Using sinusoids to simulate noise is extremely expensive because, in principle, noise consists of sinusoids at every frequency within the band limits. Also, modeling noise with sinusoids does not yield a flexible sound representation useful for music applications. Therefore the next natural step to take in spectral modeling of musical sounds was to represent sinusoids and noise as two separate components (Serra 1989; Serra and Smith 1990).

The deterministic plus stochastic model

A sound model assumes certain characteristics of the sound waveform or the sound generation mechanism. In general, every analysis/synthesis system has an underlying model. The sounds produced by musical instruments, or by any physical system, can be modeled as the sum of a set of sinusoids plus a noise residual. The sinusoidal, or deterministic, component normally corresponds to the main modes of vibration of the system. The residual comprises the energy produced by the excitation mechanism which is not transformed by the system into stationary vibrations plus any other energy component that is not sinusoidal in nature. For example, in the sound of wind-driven instruments, the deterministic signal is the result of the self-sustained oscillations produced inside the bore and the residual is a noise signal that is generated by the turbulent streaming that takes place when the air from the player passes through the narrow slit. In the case of bowed strings the stable sinusoids are the result of the main modes of vibration of the strings and the noise is generated by the sliding of the bow against the string, plus by other nonlinear behavior of the bow-string-resonator system. This type of separation can also be applied to vocal sounds, percussion instruments and even to environmental sounds produced in nature.

A deterministic signal is traditionally defined as anything that is not noise (i.e., an analytic signal, or perfectly predictable part, predictable from measurements over any continuous interval). However, in the present discussion the class of deterministic signals considered is restricted to sums of quasi-sinusoidal components (sinusoids with slowly varying amplitude and frequency). Each sinusoid models a narrowband component of the original sound and is described by an amplitude and a frequency function.

A stochastic, or noise, signal is fully described by its *power spectral density*, which gives the expected signal power versus frequency. When a signal is assumed to be stochastic, it is not necessary to preserve either the instantaneous phase or the exact magnitude details of individual FFT frames. Therefore, the input sound $s(t)$ is modeled by

$$s(t) = \sum_{r=1}^{R} A_r(t) \cos[\theta_r(t)] + e(t),$$

where $A_r(t)$ and $\theta_r(t)$ are the instantaneous amplitude and phase of the rth sinusoid, respectively, and $e(t)$ is the noise component at time t (in seconds).

The model assumes that the sinusoids are stable partials of the sound and that each one has a slowly changing amplitude and frequency. The instantaneous phase is then taken to be the integral of the instantaneous frequency $\omega_r(t)$, and therefore satisfies

$$\theta_r(t) = \int_0^t \omega_r(\tau)d\tau,$$

where $\omega(t)$ is the frequency in radians, and r is the sinusoid number.

By assuming that $e(t)$ is a stochastic signal, it can be described as filtered white noise,

$$e(t) = \int_0^t h(t, \tau)u(\tau)d\tau,$$

where $u(t)$ is white noise and $h(t, \tau)$ is the response of a time varying filter to an impulse at time t. That is, the residual is modeled by the convolution of white noise with a time-varying frequency-shaping filter.

This model has problems with sounds that include "noisy partials" (for example, produced by a modulation). We have found this type of component, which is in between a deterministic and a stochastic signal, in the higher partials of vocal sounds, in some string sounds, specially when they have vibrato, and in the sound of metal plates, like a crashed cymbal. Due to these problems, the assumed separation between deterministic and stochastic components of a sound is rarely a clear one and the implementation of this process should be flexible enough to give the user some control over how it is done.

General diagram of the analysis/synthesis process

The deterministic plus stochastic model has many possible implementations. We will present a general scheme while giving indications on variations that have been proposed. Both the analysis and synthesis are frame-based processes with the computation done one frame at a time. Throughout this description we will consider that we have already processed a few frames of the sound and we are ready to compute the next one.

Figure 1 shows the block diagram for the analysis. First, we prepare the next section of the sound to be analyzed by multiplying it by an appropriate analysis window (Figure 2). We obtain its spectrum by applying the FFT. The

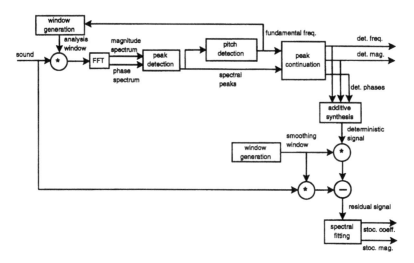

Figure 1. Block diagram of the analysis process.

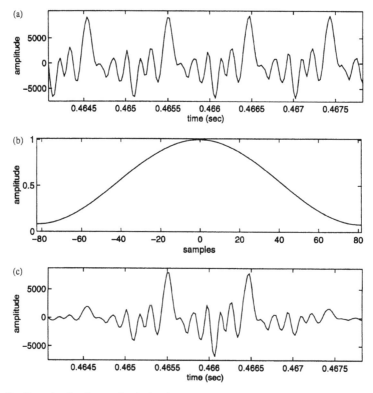

Figure 2. Sound selection and windowing. (a) Portion of a violin sound to be used in the analysis of the current frame. (b) Hamming window. (c) Windowed sound.

prominent spectral peaks are detected and incorporated into the existing partial trajectories by means of a *peak continuation algorithm.* This algorithm detects the magnitude, frequency, and phase of the partials present in the original sound (the deterministic component). When the sound is pseudo-harmonic, a pitch detection step can improve the analysis by using the fundamental frequency information in the peak continuation algorithm and in choosing the size of the analysis window. (This is called *pitch-synchronous analysis.*)

The stochastic component of the current frame is calculated by first generating the deterministic signal with additive synthesis, and then subtracting it from the original waveform in the time domain. This is possible because the phases of the original sound are matched and therefore the shape of the time-domain waveform preserved. The stochastic representation is then obtained by performing a spectral fitting of the residual signal.

Figure 3 presents a block diagram of the synthesis process. The deterministic signal, that is, the sinusoidal component, results from the magnitude and frequency trajectories, or their transformation, by generating a sine wave for each trajectory (i.e., additive synthesis). This can either be implemented in the time domain with the traditional *oscillator bank* method or in the frequency domain using the *inverse-FFT* approach.

The synthesized stochastic signal is the result of generating a noise signal with the time-varying spectral shape obtained in the analysis (i.e., subtractive synthesis). As with the deterministic synthesis, it can be implemented in the time domain by a convolution or in the frequency domain by creating a complex

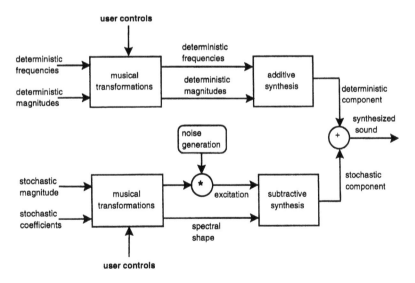

Figure 3. Block diagram of the synthesis process.

spectrum (i.e., magnitude and phase spectra) for every spectral envelope of the residual and performing an inverse-FFT.

Magnitude and phase spectra computation

The computation of the magnitude and phase spectra of the current frame is the first step in the analysis. It is in these spectra that the sinusoids are tracked and the decision takes place as to whether a part of the signal is considered deterministic or noise. The computation of the spectra is carried out by the *short-time Fourier transform* (STFT) technique (Allen 1977; Serra 1989).

The control parameters for the STFT (*window-size, window-type, FFT-size,* and *frame-rate*) have to be set in accordance with the sound to be processed. First of all, a high resolution spectrum is needed since the process that tracks the partials has to be able to identify the peaks that correspond to the deterministic component. Also the phase information is particularly important for subtracting the deterministic component to find the residual. We should use an odd-length analysis window (Figure 4) and the windowed data should be centered in the FFT-buffer at the origin in order to obtain the phase spectrum free of the linear phase trend induced by the window (this is called *zero-phase windowing*). A discussion on windows is beyond the scope of this article; see Harris (1978) for an introduction to this topic.

Since the synthesis process is completely independent from the analysis, the restrictions imposed by the STFT when the inverse transform is also performed, that is, that the analysis windows add to a constant, are unnecessary here. The STFT parameters are more flexible, and we can vary them during the course of the analysis, if that is required to improve the detection of partials.

The time-frequency compromise of the STFT has to be well understood. For deterministic analysis it is important to have enough frequency resolution to resolve the partials of the sound. For the stochastic analysis the frequency resolution is not that important, since we are not interested in particular frequency components, and we are more concerned with high time resolution. This can be accomplished by using different parameters for the deterministic and the stochastic analysis.

In stable sounds we should use long windows (several periods) with a good sidelobe rejection (for example, Blackman–Harris 92 dB) for the deterministic analysis. This gives a good frequency resolution, therefore an accurate measure of the frequencies of the partials; but these settings will not work for most sounds, thus a compromise is required. In the case of harmonic sounds the actual size of the window will change as pitch changes, in order to assure a

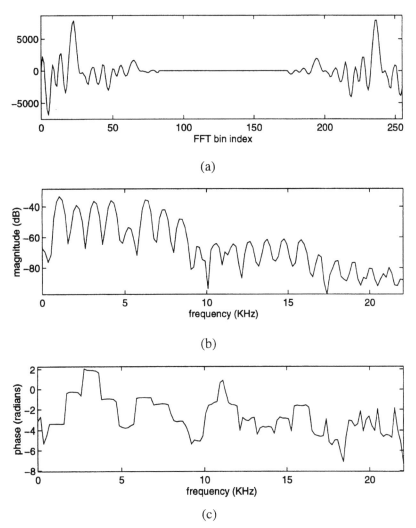

Figure 4. Computing the FFT. (a) Packing of the sound into the FFT buffer for a zero phase spectrum. (b) Magnitude spectrum. (c) Phase spectrum.

constant time-frequency tradeoff for the whole sound. In the case of inharmonic sounds we should set the window-size depending on the minimum frequency difference that exists between partials.

Peak detection

Once the spectrum of the current frame is computed, the next step is to detect its prominent magnitude peaks (Figure 5). Theoretically, a sinusoid that is stable

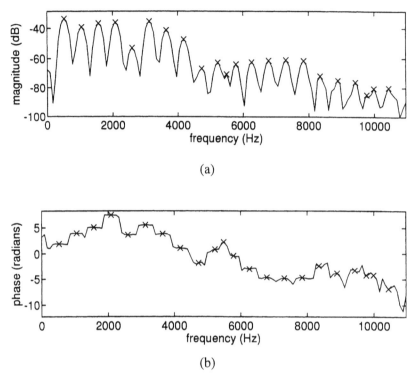

Figure 5. Peak detection. (a) Peaks in the magnitude spectrum. (b) Peaks in the phase spectrum.

both in amplitude and in frequency (a partial) has a well defined frequency representation: the transform of the analysis window used to compute the Fourier transform. It should be possible to take advantage of this characteristic to distinguish partials from other frequency components. However, in practice this is rarely the case, since most natural sounds are not perfectly periodic and do not have nicely spaced and clearly defined peaks in the frequency domain. There are interactions between the different components, and the shapes of the spectral peaks cannot be detected without tolerating some mismatch. Only some instrumental sounds (e.g., the steady-state part of an oboe sound) are periodic enough and sufficiently free from prominent noise components that the frequency representation of a stable sinusoid can be recognized easily in a single spectrum. A practical solution is to detect as many peaks as possible and delay the decision of what is a deterministic, or "well behaved" partial, to the next step in the analysis: the peak continuation algorithm.

A *peak* is defined as a local maximum in the magnitude spectrum, and the only practical constraints to be made in the peak search are to have a frequency range and a magnitude threshold. In fact, we should detect more than what we hear and obtain as many sample bits as possible from the original sound, ideally more than 16. The measurement of very soft partials, sometimes more than 80 dB below maximum amplitude, will be hard and they will have little resolution. These peak measurements are very sensitive to transformations because as soon as modifications are applied to the analysis data, parts of the sound that could not be heard in the original can become audible. The original sound should be as clean as possible and have the maximum dynamic range, then the magnitude threshold can be set to the amplitude of the background noise floor. To obtain better resolution in higher frequencies, preemphasis can be applied before the analysis, which is then deemphasized during the resynthesis.

Due to the sampled nature of the spectra returned by the FFT, each peak is accurate only to within half a sample. A spectral sample represents a frequency interval of f_s/N Hz, where f_s is the sampling rate and N is the FFT size. Zero-padding in the time domain increases the number of spectral samples per Hz and thus increases the accuracy of the simple peak detection. However, to obtain frequency accuracy on the level of 0.1% of the distance from the top of an ideal peak to its first zero crossing (in the case of a Rectangular window), the zero-padding factor required is 1000. A more efficient spectral interpolation scheme is to zero-pad only enough so that quadratic (or other simple) spectral interpolation, using only samples immediately surrounding the maximum-magnitude sample, suffices to refine the estimate to 0.1% accuracy.

Although we cannot rely on the exact shape of the peak to decide whether it is a partial or not, it is sometimes useful to have a measure of how close its shape is to the ideal sinusoidal peak. This measure can be obtained by calculating the difference from the samples of the measured peak to the samples of the analysis window transform centered at the measured frequency and scaled to the measured magnitude. This information, plus the frequency, magnitude, and phase of the peak, can help in the peak continuation process.

Pitch detection

Before continuing a set of peak trajectories through the current frame it is useful to search for a possible fundamental frequency, that is, for periodicity. If it exists, we will have more information to work with, and it will simplify and improve the tracking of partials. This fundamental frequency can also be used to set the size of the analysis window, in order to maintain constant the number of periods to be analyzed at each frame and to get the best time-frequency trade-off possible. This is called pitch-synchronous analysis. (See Chapter 5.)

Given a set of spectral peaks, with magnitude and frequency values for each one, there are many possible fundamental detection strategies (Piszczalski and Galler 1979; Terhardt *et al.* 1982; Hess 1983; Doval and Rodet 1993; Maher and Beauchamp 1994). For this presentation we restrict ourselves to single-source sounds and assume that a fundamental peak or one of its first few partials exists. With these two constraints, plus the fact that there is some number of buffered frames, the algorithm can be quite simple.

The fundamental frequency can be defined as the common divisor of the harmonic series that best explains the spectral peaks found in the current frame. The first step is to find the possible candidates inside a given range. This can be done by stepping through the range by small increments, or by only considering as candidates the frequencies of the measured spectral peaks and frequencies related to them by simple integer ratios (e.g., 1/2, 1/3, 1/4) that lie inside the range. This last approach simplifies our search enormously.

Once the possible candidates have been chosen we need a way to measure the "goodness" of the resulting harmonic series compared with the actual spectral peaks. A suitable error measure (Maher and Beauchamp 1994) is based on the weighted differences between the measured peaks and the ideal harmonic series (predicted peaks).

The predicted to measured error is defined as:

$$
\begin{aligned}
Err_{p \to m} &= \sum_{n=1}^{N} E_{\omega}\left(\Delta f_n, f_n, a_n, A_{\max}\right) \\
&= \sum_{n=1}^{N} \Delta f_n \cdot (f_n)^{-p} + \left(\frac{a_n}{A_{\max}}\right) \times \left[q \Delta f_n \cdot (f_n)^{-p} - r\right],
\end{aligned}
$$

where Δf_n is the difference between a predicted and its closest measured peak, f_n and a_n are the frequency and magnitude of the predicted peaks, and $A_{\max}$ is maximum peak magnitude.

The measured to predicted error is defined as:

$$
\begin{aligned}
Err_{m \to p} &= \sum_{k=1}^{K} E_{w}\left(\Delta f_k, f_k, a_k, A_{\max}\right) \\
&= \sum_{k=1}^{K} \Delta f_k \cdot (f_k)^{-p} + \left(\frac{a_k}{A_{\max}}\right) \times \left[q \Delta f_k \cdot (f_k)^{-p} - r\right],
\end{aligned}
$$

where Δf_k is the difference between a measured and its closest predicted peak, f_k and a_k are the frequency and magnitude of the measured peaks, and $A_{\max}$ is maximum peak magnitude.

The total error is:

$$Err_{\text{total}} = Err_{p \to m}/N + \rho Err_{m \to p}/K.$$

Maher and Beauchamp propose to use $p = 0.5$, $q = 1.4$, $r = 0.5$ and $\rho = 0.33$. The harmonic series with the smallest error is chosen, and since there is a certain frame memory, the preferred fundamental in a given frame will be compared with the fundamentals found in the previous ones. If the new fundamental is very different from the preceding ones, it is possible that something is wrong. Either we are in the middle of a note transition or the new fundamental is not a real one. When this new fundamental value does not prevail for a few frames it will not be accepted and the frame will be considered as containing only stochastic data. After a few frames, once it is clear that we were in a note transition and that we are now in a new note, we can re-analyze the previous frames by setting the window-size according to the fundamental of the new note. This will improve the measurements in the preceding frames and their time-frequency trade-off. We can also set the window-size for the next frame according to it.

Peak continuation

Once the spectral peaks of the current frame have been detected, the peak continuation algorithm adds them to the incoming peak trajectories. The schemes used in PARSHL (Smith and Serra 1987) and in the sinusoidal model (McAulay and Quatieri 1984, 1986) find peak trajectories both in the noise and deterministic parts of a waveform, thus obtaining a sinusoidal representation for the whole sound. These schemes are unsuitable when we want the trajectories to follow just the partials. For example, when the partials change in frequency substantially from one frame to the next, these algorithms easily switch from the partial that they were tracking to another one which at that point is closer.

   The algorithm described here is intended to track partials in a variety of sounds, although the behavior of a partial, and therefore the way to track it, varies depending on the signal. Whether we have speech, a harmonic instrumental tone, a gong sound, a sound of an animal, or any other, the time progression of the component partials varies. Thus, the algorithm requires some knowledge about the characteristics of the sound that is being analyzed. In the current algorithm there is no attempt to make the process completely automatic and some of the characteristics of the sound are specified through a set of parameters, described in the documentation supplied with the software package (see the section "Note to the reader").

The basic idea of the algorithm is that a set of *guides* advances in time through the spectral peaks, looking for the appropriate ones (according to the specified constraints) and forming trajectories out of them (Figure 6). Thus, a guide is an abstract entity which is used by the algorithm to create the trajectories and the trajectories are the actual result of the peak continuation process. The instantaneous state of the guides, their frequency and magnitude, are continuously updated as the guides are turned on, advanced, and finally turned off. For the case of harmonic sounds these guides are created at the beginning of the analysis, setting their frequencies according to the harmonic series of the first fundamental found, and for inharmonic sounds each guide is created when it finds the first available peak.

When a fundamental has been found in the current frame, the guides can use this information to update their values. Also the guides can be modified depending on the last peak incorporated. Therefore by using the current fundamental and the previous peak we control the adaptation of the guides to the instantaneous changes in the sound. For a very harmonic sound, since all the harmonics evolve together, the fundamental should be the main control, but when the sound is not very harmonic, or the harmonics are not locked to each other and we cannot rely on the fundamental as a strong reference for all the harmonics, the information of the previous peak should have a bigger weight.

Each peak is assigned to the guide that is closest to it and that is within a given frequency deviation. If a guide does not find a match it is assumed that the corresponding trajectory must "turn off". In inharmonic sounds, if a guide has not found a continuation peak for a given amount of time, the guide is killed. New guides, and therefore new trajectories, are created from the peaks of the current frame that are not incorporated into trajectories by the existing guides. If there are killed or unused guides, a new guide can be started. A guide is created by searching through the "unclaimed" peaks of the frame for the one with the highest magnitude. Once the trajectories have been continued for a few frames, the short ones can be deleted and trajectories with small gaps can be filled by interpolating the edges of the gaps.

The attack portion of most sounds is quite "noisy", and the search for partials is harder in such rich spectra. A useful modification to the analysis is to perform it backwards in time. The tracking process encounters the end of the sound first, and since this is a very stable part in most instrumental sounds, the algorithm finds a very clear definition of the partials. When the guides arrive at the attack, they are already tracking the main partials and can reject non-relevant peaks appropriately, or at least evaluate them with some acquired knowledge.

The peak continuation algorithm presented is only one approach to the peak continuation problem. The creation of trajectories from the spectral peaks is

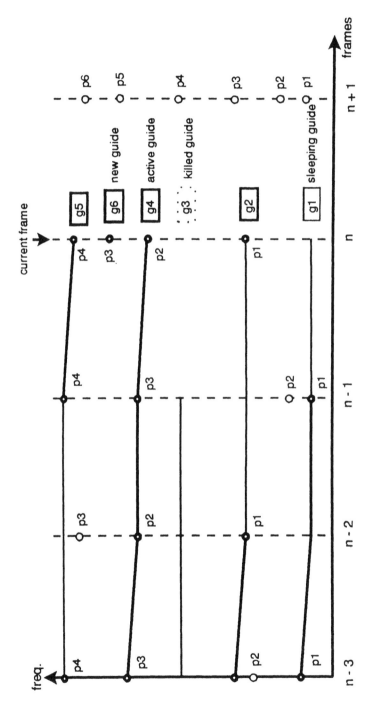

Figure 6. Peak continuation process. The variable g represent the guides and p the spectral peaks.

compatible with very different strategies and algorithms; for example, hidden Markov models have been applied (Garcia 1992; Depalle, Garcia, and Rodet 1993). An N Markov model provides a probability distribution for a parameter in the current frame as a function of its value across the past N frames. With a hidden Markov model we are able to optimize groups of trajectories according to a defined criteria, such as frequency continuity. This type of approach might be very valuable for tracking partials in polyphonic sounds and complex inharmonic tones. In particular, the notion of "momentum" is introduced, helping to properly resolve crossing fundamental frequencies.

Stochastic analysis

The deterministic component is subtracted from the original sound either in the time domain or in the frequency domain. This results in a residual sound on which the stochastic approximation is performed. It is useful to study this residual in order to check how well the deterministic component has been properly subtracted and therefore analyzed. If partials remain in the residual, the stochastic analysis models them as filtered noise and it will not sound good. In this case we should re-analyze the sound until we get a good enough residual, free of deterministic components. Ideally the resulting residual should be as close as possible to a stochastic signal. If the sound was not recorded in the ideal situation, the residual will also contain more than just the stochastic part of the sound, such as reverberation or background noise.

To model the stochastic part of sounds, such as the attacks of most percussion instrument, the bow noise in string instruments, or the breath noise in wind instruments, we need a good time resolution and we can give up some frequency resolution. The deterministic component cannot maintain the sharpness of the attacks, because, even if a high frame-rate is used we are forced to use a long enough window, and this size determines most of the time resolution. When the deterministic subtraction is done in the time domain, the time resolution in the stochastic analysis can be improved by redefining the analysis window. The frequency domain approach implies that the subtraction is done in the spectra computed for the deterministic analysis, thus the STFT parameters cannot be changed (Serra 1989).

In order to be able to perform a time domain subtraction, the phases of the original sound have to be preserved, this is the reason for calculating the phase of each spectral peak. But to generate a deterministic signal that preserves phases is computationally very expensive, as will be shown later. If we stay in the frequency domain, phases are not required and the subtraction of the spectral peaks from the original spectra, the ones that belong to partials, is simple. While the time domain subtraction is more expensive, the results are sufficiently better to to favor this method. This is done by first synthesizing one frame of the deterministic component which is then subtracted from the original sound in the time domain. The magnitude spectrum of this residual is then computed and approximated with an envelope. The more coefficients we use, the better the modeling of the frequency characteristics will be.

Since it is the deterministic signal that is subtracted from the original sound, measured from long windows, the resulting residual signal might have the sharp attacks smeared. To improve the stochastic analysis, we can "fix" this residual so that the sharpness of the attacks of the original sound are preserved. The resulting residual is compared with the original waveform and its amplitude re-scaled whenever the residual has a greater energy than the original waveform. Then the stochastic analysis is performed on this scaled residual. Thus, the smaller the window the better time resolution we will get in the residual. We can also compare the synthesized deterministic signal with the original sound and whenever this signal has a greater energy than the original waveform it means that a smearing of the deterministic component has been produced. This can be fixed a bit by scaling the amplitudes of the deterministic analysis in the corresponding frame by the difference between original sound and deterministic signal.

Most of the problems with the residual, thus with the stochastic analysis, is in the low frequencies. In general there is more energy measured at low frequencies than there should be. Since most of the stochastic components of musical sounds mainly contain energy at high frequencies, a fix to this problems is to apply a high-pass filter to the residual before the stochastic approximation is done.

Once the analysis is finished we can still do some post-processing to improve the data. For example, if we had a "perfect" recording and a "perfect" analysis, in percussive or plucked sounds there should be no stochastic signal after the attack. Due to errors in the analysis or to background noise, the stochastic analysis might have detected some signal after this attack. We can delete or reduce this stochastic signal appropriately after the attack.

Next we describe the two main steps involved in the stochastic analysis; the synthesis and subtraction of the deterministic signal from the original sound, and the modeling of the residual signal.

Deterministic subtraction

The output of the peak continuation algorithm is a set of peak trajectories up-dated for the current frame. From these trajectories a series of sinusoids can

XAVIER SERRA

be synthesized which reproduce the instantaneous phase and amplitude of the partials of the original sound. Thus, it is possible to subtract the synthesized sinusoids from the original sound and obtain a residual which is substantially free of the deterministic part (Figure 7).

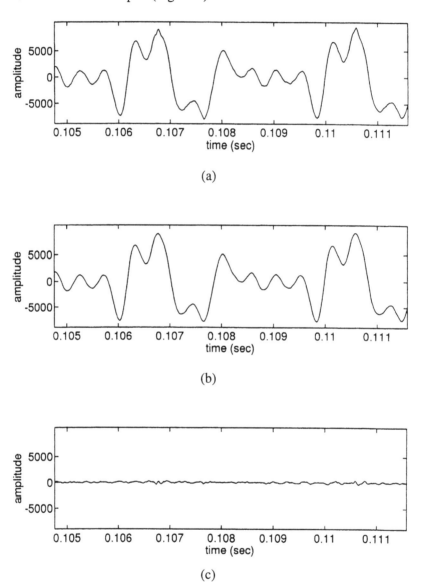

Figure 7. Deterministic subtraction. (a) Original sound. (b) Deterministic synthesis. (c) Residual sound.

One frame of the deterministic part of the sound, $d(m)$, is generated by

$$d(m) = \sum_{r=1}^{R} \hat{A}_r \cos\left[m\hat{\omega}_r + \hat{\varphi}_r\right], \quad m = 0, 1, 2, \ldots, S - 1,$$

where R is the number of trajectories present in the current frame and S is the length of the frame. To avoid "clicks" at the frame boundaries, the parameters $(\hat{A}_r, \hat{\omega}_r, \hat{\varphi}_r)$ are smoothly interpolated from frame to frame.

Let $(\hat{A}_r^{(l-1)}, \hat{\omega}_r^{(l-1)}, \hat{\varphi}_r^{(l-1)})$ and $(\hat{A}_r^l, \hat{\omega}_r^l, \hat{\varphi}_r^l)$ denote the sets of parameters at frames $l-1$ and l for the rth frequency trajectory (we will simplify the notation by omitting the subscript r). These parameters are taken to represent the state of the signal at time S (the left endpoint) of the frame.

The instantaneous amplitude $\hat{A}(m)$ is easily obtained by linear interpolation,

$$\hat{A}(m) = \hat{A}^{l-1} + \frac{\left(\hat{A}^l - \hat{A}^{l-1}\right)}{S} m,$$

where $m = 0, 1, \ldots, S - 1$ is the time sample into the lth frame.

Frequency and phase values are tied together (frequency is the phase derivative), and both control the instantaneous phase $\hat{\theta}(m)$, defined as

$$\hat{\theta}(m) = m\hat{\omega} + \hat{\varphi}.$$

Given that four variables affect the instantaneous phase: $\hat{\omega}^{(l-1)}, \hat{\varphi}^{(l-1)}, \hat{\omega}$, and $\hat{\varphi}$, we need three degrees of freedom for its control, but linear interpolation gives only one. Therefore, we need a cubic polynomial as an interpolation function,

$$\hat{\theta}(m) = \xi + \kappa m + \eta m^2 + \iota m^3.$$

It is unnecessary to go into the details of solving this equation since they are described by McAulay and Quatieri (McAulay and Quatieri 1986). The result is

$$\hat{\theta}(m) = \hat{\varphi}^{l-1} + \hat{\omega}^{(l-1)}m + \eta m^2 + \iota m^3,$$

where η and ι are calculated using the end conditions at the frame boundaries,

$$\eta = \frac{3}{S^2}\left(\hat{\varphi}^l - \hat{\varphi}^{l-1} - \hat{\omega}^{l-1}S + 2\pi M\right) - \frac{1}{S}\left(\hat{\omega}^l - \hat{\omega}^{l-1}\right),$$

$$\iota = -\frac{2}{S^3}\left(\hat{\varphi}^l - \hat{\varphi}^{l-1} - \hat{\omega}^{l-1}S + 2\pi M\right) - \frac{1}{S^2}\left(\hat{\omega}^l - \hat{\omega}^{l-1}\right).$$

This gives a set of interpolating functions depending on the value of M, among which we select the maximally smooth function. This is done by choosing M to be the integer closest to x, where x is

$$x = \frac{1}{2\pi}\left[(\hat{\varphi}^{l-1} + \hat{\omega}^{l-1}S - \hat{\varphi}^{l}) + \frac{S}{2}(\hat{\omega}^{l} - \hat{\omega}^{l-1}) \right].$$

Finally, the synthesis equation for frame l becomes

$$d^{l}(m) = \sum_{r=1}^{R^{l}} \hat{A}_{r}^{l}(m) \cos\left[\hat{\theta}_{r}^{l}(m) \right],$$

which goes smoothly from the previous to the current frame with each sinusoid accounting for both the rapid phase changes (frequency) and the slowly varying phase changes.

The synthesized deterministic component can be subtracted from the original sound in the time domain by

$$e(n) = w(n) \times \big(s(n) - d(n)\big), \quad n = 0, 1, \ldots, N - 1,$$

where $e(n)$ is the residual, $w(n)$ a smoothing window, $s(n)$ the original sound, $d(n)$ the deterministic component, and N the size of the window. We already have mentioned that it is desirable to set N smaller than the window-size used in the deterministic analysis in order to improve the time resolution of the residual signal. While in the deterministic analysis the window-size was chosen large enough to obtain a good partial separation in the frequency domain, in the deterministic subtraction we are especially looking for good time resolution. This is particularly important in the attacks of percussion instruments.

Tests on this residual can be performed to check whether the deterministic plus stochastic decomposition has been successful (Serra 1994a). Ideally the resulting residual should be as close as possible to a stochastic signal. Since the autocorrelation function of white noise is an impulse, a measure of correlation relative to total power could be a good measure of how close we are to white noise,

$$c = \frac{\displaystyle\sum_{l=0}^{L-1} |r(l)|}{(L-1)r(0)},$$

where $r(l)$ is the autocorrelation estimate for L lags of the residual, and c will be close to 0 when the signal is stochastic. A problem with this measure is that it does not behave well when partials are still left in the signal; for example, it does not always decrease as we progressively subtract partials from a sound. A simpler and sometimes better indication of the quality of the residual is to measure the energy of the residual as a percentage of the total sound energy. Although a problem with this measure is that it cannot distinguish subtracting partials from subtracting noise, and its value will always decrease as long as we subtract some energy, it is still a practical measure for choosing the best analysis parameters.

This sound decomposition is useful in itself for a number of applications. The deterministic component is a set of partials, and the residual includes noise and very unstable components of the sound. This technique has been used to study bow noise in string instruments and breath noise in wind instruments (Chafe 1990; Schumacher and Chafe 1990). In general, this decomposition strategy can give a lot of insight into the makeup of sounds.

The residual component is the part of the instrumental sounds that the existing synthesis techniques have a harder time reproducing, and it is especially important during the attack. A practical application would be to add these residuals to synthesized sounds in order to make them more realistic. Since these residuals remain largely invariant throughout most of the instrumental range, only a few residuals would be necessary to cover all the sounds of a single instrument.

Stochastic approximation

One of the underlying assumptions of the current model is that the residual is a stochastic signal. Such an assumption implies that the residual is fully described by its amplitude and its general frequency characteristics. It is unnecessary to keep either the instantaneous phase or the exact spectral shape information. Based on this, a frame of the stochastic residual can be completely characterized by a filter. This filter encodes the amplitude and general frequency characteristics of the residual. The representation of the residual for the overall sound will be a sequence of these filters, that is, a time-varying filter.

The filter design problem is generally solved by performing some sort of curve fitting in the magnitude spectrum of the current frame (Strawn 1980; Sedgewick 1988). Standard techniques are: spline interpolation (Cox 1971), the method of least squares (Sedgewick 1988), or straight line approximations (Phillips 1968). For our purpose a simple line-segment approximation to the log-magnitude spectrum is accurate enough and gives the desired flexibility (Figure 8).

One way to carry out the line-segment approximation is to step through the magnitude spectrum and find local maxima in each of several defined sections,

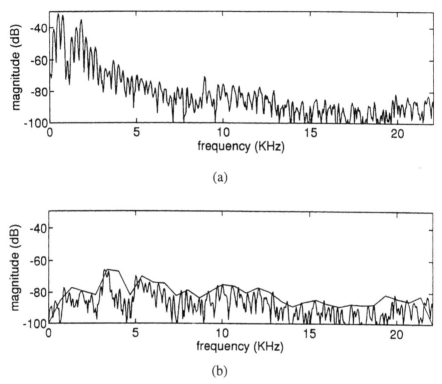

(a)

(b)

Figure 8. Stochastic approximation from the sound in Figure 7. (a) Original spectrum. (b) Residual spectrum and its line-segment approximation.

thus giving equally spaced points in the spectrum that are connected by straight lines to create the spectral envelope. The accuracy of the fit is given by the number of points, and that can be set depending on the sound complexity. Other options are to have unequally spaced points, for example, logarithmically spaced, or spaced according to perceptual criteria.

Another practical alternative is to use a type of least squares approximation called *linear predictive coding* (LPC) (Chapter 1; Makhoul 1975; Markel and Gray 1976). LPC is a popular technique used in speech research for fitting an *n*th-order polynomial to a magnitude spectrum. For our purposes, the line-segment approach is more flexible than LPC, and although LPC results in less analysis points, the flexibility is considered more important.

Representation of the analysis data

The output of the deterministic analysis is a set of amplitude and frequency functions with one breakpoint for every frame (Figure 9). From these functions

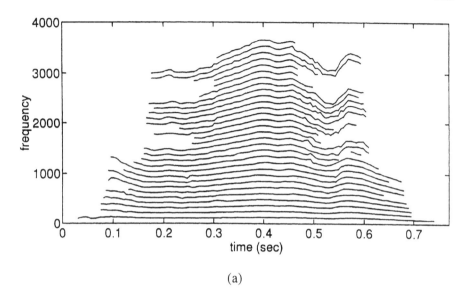

(a)

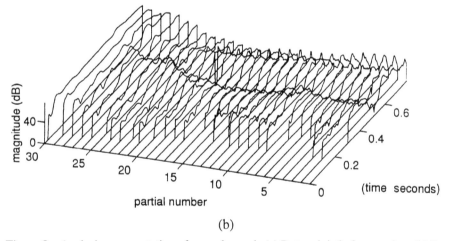

(b)

Figure 9. Analysis representation of a vocal sound. (a) Deterministic frequencies. (b) Deterministic magnitudes.

a series of sinusoids can be synthesized that reproduce the deterministic part of the sound. The phase trajectories are not kept because they are unnecessary in the final synthesis, they are perceptually irrelevant in most cases, and they make it harder to perform modifications. However, we have found some situations in which the preservation of phase data has made a difference in the quality of the resynthesis. These are: badly analyzed sounds, very low instrumental tones, and some vocal sounds. In the case of badly analyzed sounds, some of the trajectories may actually be tracking non-deterministic parts of the signal, in which case the phase of the corresponding peaks is important to recover the noisy characteristics of the signal. In the case when the analyzed sound has a very low fundamental, maybe lower than 30 Hz, and the partials are phase-locked to the fundamental, the period is perceived as a pulse and the phase of the partials is required to maintain this perceptual effect. Also in the case of some vocal sounds, the higher partials have a high degree of modulation that cannot be completely recovered from the frequency and magnitude information of the partials, but that seems to be maintained when we add the phases of the peaks.

The resulting amplitude and frequency functions can be further processed to achieve a data reduction of the representation or to smooth the functions.

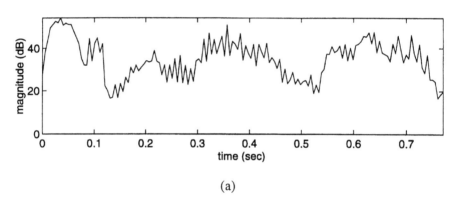

(a)

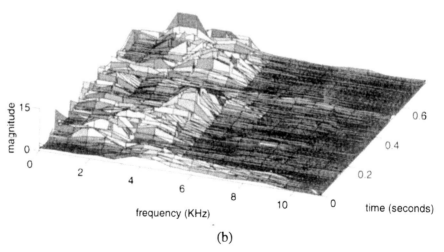

(b)

Figure 10. Analysis representation of a vocal sound. (a) Stochastic magnitude. (b) Stochastic coefficients.

A data reduction strategy is to perform a line-segment approximation on each function, thus reducing the number of breakpoints (Grey 1975; Strawn 1980). For the purpose of easy manipulation of the representation it is useful to have equally spaced points along each function, and thus it may be better to keep one breakpoint per frame as returned by the analysis, unless data reduction is a priority. Another alternative for data reduction is to combine groups of similar functions into a single one, thus reducing the number of functions (Laughlin et al. 1990).

The stochastic analysis returns an envelope for every frame (Figure 10). These envelopes can either be interpreted as a series of envelopes or frequency-shaping filters, one per frame, or as time-varying, equally spaced bandpass filters, each one centered at each breakpoint. It is convenient to normalize these envelopes by dividing them by their average magnitude so that we can control the spectral shape of the noise independently of its time-varying magnitude.

Modifications of the analysis data

One of the main considerations in setting the analysis parameters is the potential for manipulating the resulting representation. For this goal, we would like to have a representation with a small number of partials and stochastic coefficients, and each of the functions (amplitudes and frequencies for the partials, gain and coefficients for the noise) should be as smooth as possible. In most cases there will be a compromise between perceptual identity from the original sound versus flexibility of the representation. Depending on the transformation desired this will be more or less critical. If we only want to stretch the sound a small percentage or transpose it a few hertz, this is not a major issue. But when drastic changes are applied, details that were not heard in the straight resynthesis will become prominent and many of them will be perceived as distortion. For example, whenever the amplitude of a very soft partial is increased or its frequency transposed, since its measurements where not very accurate, the measurement errors that were not heard in the straight resynthesis, will probably come out.

The representation resulting from the analysis is very suitable for modification purposes, permitting a great number of sound transformations. For example, time-scale modifications are accomplished by resampling the analysis points in time and results in slowing down or speeding up the sound while maintaining pitch and formant structure. Due to the stochastic and deterministic separation, this representation is more successful in time-scale modifications than other spectral representations. With it, the noise part of the sound remains "noise" no matter how much the sound is stretched, which is not true with a sinusoidal representation. In the deterministic representation each function pair, amplitude and frequency, accounts for a partial of the original sound. The manipulation of these functions is easy and musically intuitive. All kinds of frequency and magnitude transformations are possible. For example, the partials can be transposed in frequency, with different values for every partial and varying during the sound. It is also possible to decouple the sinusoidal frequencies from their amplitude, obtaining effects such as changing pitch while maintaining formant structure.

The stochastic representation is modified by changing the shape of each of the envelopes and the time-varying magnitude, or gain. Changing the envelope shape corresponds to a filtering of the stochastic signal. Their manipulation is much simpler and more intuitive than the manipulation of a set of allpole filters, such as those resulting from an LPC analysis.

Interesting effects are accomplished by changing the relative amplitude of the two components, thus emphasizing one or the other at different moments in time. However we have to realize that the characterization of a single sound by two different representations, which are not completely independent, might cause problems. When different transformations are applied to each representation it is easy to create a sound in which the two components, deterministic and stochastic, do not fuse into a single entity. This may be desirable for some musical applications, but in general it is avoided, and requires some practical experimentation with the actual representations.

One of the most impressive transformations that can be done is by interpolating the data from two or more analysis files, creating the effect of "sound morphs" or "hybrids" (Serra 1994b). This is most successful when the analysis of the different sounds to be hybridized where done as harmonic and all the functions are very smooth. By controlling how the interpolation process is done on the different parts of the representation and in time, a large number of new sounds will result. This type of sound processing has been traditionally called *cross-synthesis,* nevertheless a more appropriate term would be sound hybridization. With this spectral modeling method we can actually explore the timbre space created by a set of sounds and define paths to go from one sound to another.

The best analysis/synthesis computation is generally considered the one that results in the best perceptual identity with respect to the original sound. Once this is accomplished, transformations are performed on the corresponding representation. For musical applications, however, this may not be always desirable. Very interesting effects result from purposely setting the analysis parameters "wrong". We may, for example, set the parameters such that the deterministic analysis only captures partials in a specific frequency range, leaving the rest to be considered stochastic. The result is a sound with a much stronger noise component.

Although this representation is powerful and many musically useful transformations are possible, we can still go further in the direction of a musically

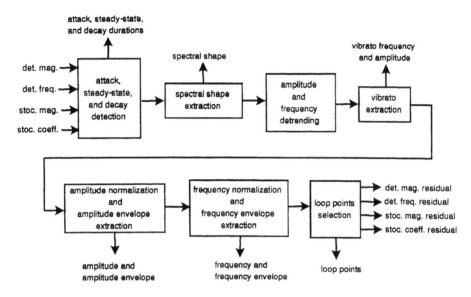

Figure 11. Extraction of musical parameters from the analysis representation of a single note of an instrument.

powerful representation based on analysis. The goal is to be able to control the perceptually relevant musical parameters of a sound, and the current representation is still far from that. Steps in this direction consist on extracting parameters, such as spectral shape, vibrato, overall amplitude and frequency evolution, from the current representation. These parameters can be extracted, modified and added back into the analysis data before the synthesis is done, without any degradation of the resulting sound. This process is easily implemented when the input sound is a single note, in which case the musical parametrization can be quite complete. Figure 11 shows a block diagram of the steps that should be done, but a discussion of the details involved in each of the steps is beyond the scope of this presentation.

Deterministic synthesis

The deterministic component is generated with additive synthesis, similar to the sinusoidal synthesis that was part of the analysis, with the difference that now the phase trajectories are discarded. By not considering phase, this synthesis can either be done in the time domain or in the frequency domain. We will first present the more traditional time domain implementation.

The instantaneous amplitude $\hat{A}(m)$ of a particular partial is obtained by linear interpolation,

$$\hat{A}(m) = \hat{A}^{l-1} + \frac{(\hat{A}^l - \hat{A}^{l-1})}{S} m,$$

where $m = 0, 1, \ldots, S - 1$ is the time sample in the lth frame.

The instantaneous phase is taken to be the integral of the instantaneous frequency, where the instantaneous radian frequency $\hat{\omega}(m)$ is obtained by linear interpolation,

$$\hat{\omega}(m) = \hat{\omega}^{l-1} + \frac{(\hat{\omega}^l - \hat{\omega}^{l-1})}{S} m,$$

and the instantaneous phase for the rth partial is

$$\hat{\theta}_r(m) = \hat{\theta}_r(l - 1) + \hat{\omega}_r(m).$$

Finally, the synthesis equation becomes

$$d^l(m) = \sum_{r=1}^{R^l} \hat{A}_r^l(m) \cos\left[\hat{\theta}_r^l(m)\right],$$

where $\hat{A}(m)$ and $\hat{\theta}(m)$ are the calculated instantaneous amplitude and phase.

A very efficient implementation of additive synthesis, when the instantaneous phase is not preserved, is based on the inverse FFT (Rodet and Depalle 1992; Goodwin and Rodet 1994). While this approach loses some of the flexibility of the traditional oscillator bank implementation, especially the instantaneous control of frequency and magnitude, the gain in speed is significant. This gain is based on the fact that a sinusoid in the frequency domain is a sinc-type function, the transform of the window used, and on these functions not all the samples carry the same weight. To generate a sinusoid in the spectral domain it is sufficient to calculate the samples of the main lobe of the window transform, with the appropriate magnitude, frequency, and phase values. We can then synthesize as many sinusoids as we want by adding these main lobes in the FFT buffer and performing an IFFT to obtain the resulting time-domain signal. By an overlap-add process we then obtain the time-varying characteristics of the sound.

The synthesis frame rate is completely independent of the analysis one. In the implementation using the IFFT we want to have a high frame rate, so that there is no need to interpolate the frequencies and magnitudes inside a frame. As in all short-time based processes we have the problem of having to make a compromise between time and frequency resolution. The window transform should have the fewest possible significant bins since this will be the number of points to generate per sinusoid. A good window choice is the Blackman–Harris 92 dB because its main lobe includes most of the energy. However the problem is that such a window does not overlap perfectly to a constant in the time domain. A solution to this problem is to undo the effect of the window by dividing by it in the time domain and applying a triangular window before performing the overlap-add process (Rodet and Depalle 1992). This will result in a good time-frequency compromise.

Stochastic synthesis

The synthesis of the stochastic component can be understood as the generation of a noise signal that has the frequency and amplitude characteristics described by the spectral envelopes of the stochastic representation. The intuitive operation is to filter white noise with these frequency envelopes, that is, perform a time-varying filtering of white noise, which is generally implemented by the time-domain convolution of white noise with the impulse response of the filter. But in practice, the easiest and most flexible implementation is to generate the stochastic signal by an inverse-FFT of the spectral envelopes. As in the deterministic synthesis, we can then get the time-varying characteristics of the stochastic signal by an overlap-add process.

Before the inverse-FFT is performed, a complex spectrum (i.e., magnitude and phase spectra), has to be obtained from each frequency envelope. The magnitude spectrum is generated by linear interpolating the spectral envelope to a curve of length $N/2$, where N is the FFT-size, and multiplying it by the average magnitude gain that was extracted in the analysis. There is no phase information in the stochastic representation, but since the phase spectrum of noise is a random signal, the phase spectrum can be created with a random number generator. To avoid a periodicity at the frame rate, new values are generated at every frame.

By using the IFFT method for both the deterministic and the stochastic synthesis it could be possible to use a single IFFT to generate both components. That is, adding the two spectra in the frequency domain and computing the IFFT once per frame. The problem to be solved is that in the noise spectrum there has not been any window applied and in the deterministic synthesis we have used a Blackman–Harris 92 dB. Therefore we should apply this window in the noise spectrum before adding it to the deterministic spectrum. This would imply to convolve the transform of the Blackman–Harris 92 dB by the noise spectrum, but with this operation there is no speed gain compared with performing the two IFFT separate and adding the deterministic and stochastic components in the time domain. This could be simplified by only convolving the most significant bins of the window transform.

Conclusions

Modeling sounds by their time-varying spectral characteristics is a well known and powerful tool. But only a few of the possible approaches are musically useful. Our discussion has been focused by the musical goal of creating a general and intuitive sound representation based on analysis, from which we can manipulate musical parameters while maintaining the perceptual identity with the original sound when no transformations are made. The sinusoids plus noise, or deterministic plus stochastic, model gives us a powerful starting point in this direction with many musical applications and possibilities for further development. In this chapter we have presented the basic concepts involved in obtaining this representation and we have discussed ways to transform and synthesize sounds from the analyzed data.

An interesting direction in which to continue the work on spectral modeling using the sinusoids plus noise model is to go beyond the representation of single sounds and towards the modeling of entire timbre families—such as all the sounds generated with an acoustic instrument—thus being able to represent their common characteristics by a common set of data and keeping separate only the perceptual differences. As part of this process it is also important to model the articulation between notes, so that we can generate expressive phrasing based also on analysis. The result is a powerful synthesis technique that has both the sound identity properties of sampling and the flexibility of FM.

Note to the reader

A software package running on different computer platforms that implements most of the technique presented in this article is publicly available on the Internet at <http://www.iua.upf.es/eng/recerca/ mit/sms>. The package includes programs for analysis, synthesis, transformation, printing, displaying, cleaning of analysis files, modification of analysis files, resampling analysis files, and reversing analysis files. It also includes examples, documentation and tips for effective use of the programs.

References

Allen, J.B. 1977. "Short term spectral analysis, synthesis, and modification by discrete fourier transform." *IEEE Transactions on Acoustics, Speech, and Signal Processing* 25(3): 235–238.

Chafe, C. 1990. "Pulsed noise in self-sustained oscillations of musical instruments." In *Proceedings of the IEEE International Conference on Acoustics, Speech, and Signal Processing*. New York: IEEE.

Cox, M.G. 1971. "An algorithm for approximating convex functions by means of first-degree splines." *Computer Journal* 14: 272–275.

Depalle, Ph., G. Garcia, and X. Rodet. 1993. "Analysis of sound for additive synthesis: tracking of partials using hidden markov models." In *Proceedings of the 1993 International Computer Music Conference*. San Francisco: International Computer Music Association.

Doval, B. and X. Rodet. 1993. "Fundamental frequency estimation and tracking using maximum likelihood harmonic matching and HMMs." In *Proceedings of the ICASSP '93*. New York: IEEE, pp. 221–224.

Garcia, G. 1992. "Analyse des signaux sonores en termes de partiels et de bruit. extraction automatique des trajets fréquentiels par des modèles de markov cachés." Mèmoire de DEA en Automatique et Traitement du Signal. Orsay: Université Paris-Sud.

General Electric Co. 1977. "ADEC subroutine description." Report 13201. Syracuse: Heavy Military Electronics Department.

Goodwin, M. and X. Rodet. 1994. "Efficient Fourier synthesis of nonstationary sinusoids." In *Proceedings of the 1994 International Computer Music Conference*. San Francisco: International Computer Music Association.

Grey, J.M. 1975. "An exploration of musical timbre." PhD Dissertation. Stanford: Stanford University.

Harris, F.J. 1978. "On the use of windows for harmonic analysis with the discrete Fourier transform." *Proceedings of the IEEE* 66: 51–83.

Hess, W. 1983. *Pitch Determination of Speech Signals*. New York: Springer-Verlag.

Laughlin, R., B. Truax, and B. Funt. 1990. "Synthesis of acoustic timbres using principal component analysis." In *Proceedings of the 1990 International Computer Music Conference*. San Francisco: International Computer Music Association.

Maher, R.C. and J.W. Beauchamp. 1994. "Fundamental frequency estimation of musical signals using a two-way mismatch procedure." *Journal of the Acoustical Society of America* 95(4): 2254–2263.

Makhoul, J. 1975. "Linear prediction: a tutorial review." *Proceedings of the IEEE* 63: 561–580.

Markel, J.D. and A.H. Gray. 1976. *Linear Prediction of Speech*. New York: Springer-Verlag.

McAulay, R.J. and T.F. Quatieri. 1984. "Magnitude-only reconstruction using a sinusoidal speech model." In *Proceedings of the 1984 IEEE International Conference on Acoustics, Speech, and Signal Processing*. New York: IEEE Press.

McAulay, R.J. and T.F. Quatieri. 1986. "Speech analysis/synthesis based on a sinusoidal representation." *IEEE Transactions on Acoustics, Speech, and Signal Processing* 34(4): 744–754.

Moorer, J.A. 1973. "The hetrodyne filter as a tool for analysis of transient waveforms." Stanford Artificial Intelligence Laboratory Memo AIM-208. Stanford: Stanford University.

Moorer, J.A. 1977. "Signal processing aspects of computer music." *Proceeding of the IEEE* 65(8): 1108–1137. Reprinted in *Computer Music Journal* 1(1): 4–37 and in J. Strawn, ed. 1985. *Digital Audio Signal Processing: An Anthology*. Madison: A-R Editions, pp. 149–220.

Moorer, J.A. 1978. "The use of the phase vocoder in computer music applications." *Journal of the Audio Engineering Society* 26(1/2): 42–45.

Phillips, G.M. 1968. "Algorithms for piecewise straight line approximation." *Computer Journal* 11: 211–212.

Piszczalski, M. and B.A. Galler. 1979. "Predicting musical pitch from component frequency ratios." *Journal of the Acoustical Society of America* 66(3): 710–720.

Portnoff, M.R. 1976. "Implementation of the digital phase vocoder using the fast Fourier transform." *IEEE Transactions on Acoustics, Speech, and Signal Processing* 24(3): 243–248.

Rodet, X. and P. Depalle. 1992. "Spectral envelopes and inverse FFT synthesis." In *93rd Convention of the Audio Engineering Society*. New York: Audio Engineering Society.

Schumacher, R.T. and C. Chafe. 1990. "Detection of aperiodicity in nearly periodic signals." In *Proceedings of the IEEE International Conference on Acoustics, Speech, and Signal Processing*. New York: IEEE.

Sedgewick, R. 1988. *Algorithms*. Reading, Massachusetts: Addison-Wesley.

Serra, X. 1989. "A system for sound analysis/transformation/synthesis based on a deterministic plus stochastic decomposition." PhD Dissertation. Stanford: Stanford University.

Serra, X. and J. Smith. 1990. "Spectral modeling synthesis: a sound analysis/synthesis system based on a deterministic plus stochastic decomposition." *Computer Music Journal* 14(4): 12–24.

Serra, X. 1994a. "Residual minimization in a musical signal model based on a deterministic plus stochastic decomposition." *Journal of the Acoustical Society of America* 95(5-2): 2958–2959.

Serra, X. 1994b. "Sound hybridization techniques based on a deterministic plus stochastic decomposition model." In *Proceedings of the 1994 International Computer Music Conference*. San Francisco: Computer Music Association.

Smith, J.O. and B. Friedlander. 1984. "High resolution spectrum analysis programs." Technical Memo 5466-05. Palo Alto: Systems Control Technology.

Smith, J.O. and X. Serra. 1987. "PARSHL: an analysis/synthesis program for non-harmonic sounds based on a sinusoidal representation." In *Proceedings of the 1987 International Computer Music Conference*. San Francisco: International Computer Music Association.

Strawn, J. 1980. "Approximation and syntactic analysis of amplitude and frequency functions for digital sound synthesis." *Computer Music Journal* 4(3): 3–24.

Terhardt, E., G. Stoll, and M. Seewann. 1982. "Algorithm for extraction of pitch and pitch salience from complex tonal signals." *Journal of the Acoustical Society of America* 71(3): 679–688.

Wolcin, J.J. 1980. "Maximum a posteriori line extraction: a computer program." Technical Memo 801042. Connecticut: Naval Underwater Systems Center.

Wolcin, J.J. 1980. "Maximum a posteriori estimation of narrowband signal parameters." Technical Memo 791115. Connecticut: Naval Underwater Systems Center. Also in *Journal of the Acoustical Society of America* 68(1): 174–178.

Part II

Innovations in
musical signal processing

Part II

Overview

Giovanni De Poli

Since the introduction of neumatic notation in Gregorian chant, music has used a bidimensional representation of sounds to describe the distribution of frequency energy along a time axis. During the centuries this representation and the abstract conception of music that it suggests has further evolved. Musicians today naturally think about music in terms of the two parameters of time and frequency. Not surprisingly, Dennis Gabor and other researchers were inspired by this representation of music when they laid the foundations of modern time-frequency representations, which are now the main reference tools in the theory of signals and all its myriad applications.

The classical sound analysis techniques described in Chapter 1 are commonly used in computer music practice. They are based on a time-frequency representation formalized in the framework of the short-time Fourier transform. As Part II shows, researchers and musicians have recently been led to other methods that can open new and interesting perspectives in music applications.

One of these new methods is the *wavelet transform*. It can be seen as a generalization of the classical time-frequency representation methods, and for this reason it has drawn the attention of researchers in many scientific fields. It is interesting to notice that one of the primal stimuli leading to its conception was to overcome the limitations of Fourier transform by taking into account the perceptual mechanisms, in particular auditory perception. In Chapter 4 Gianpaolo

Evangelista presents a tutorial on wavelet transform in music, with special reference to new results that are most relevant to analysis, synthesis, and manipulation of musical sounds.

Granular synthesis models complex sounds as a combination of many short acoustic events. This has turned out to be quite a general purpose model. Initially, users were overwhelmed by the complexity of control, but now that its properties have been better understood, it may also be possible to use it as a method of organizing the macrostructure. In Chapter 5, Sergio Cavaliere and Aldo Piccialli review the granular approach with special reference to *pitch-synchronous granular synthesis*. They describe an analysis methodology that extracts grains from quasi-periodic and stochastic parts of musical signals, and present examples of sound analysis and transformation based on this approach.

Musical signals demonstrate certain characteristics that are not detected by classical time-frequency analysis methods. In the signals produced by real instruments, for instance, the nonlinear dynamics of the exciter often results in turbulence during the evolution of the sound, or nonperiodic sounds such as the multiphonics. Moreover, synthesis control signals that evolve on a slow time scale are not well interpreted in the frequency domain. The fractal signal model often can be applied for signals used for spectral and expressive control. In Chapter 6, Angelo Bernardi, Gian-Paolo Bugna, and Giovanni De Poli survey analysis methods based on *chaos theory* to study the relevant properties both of the signal and its production mechanisms.

Just five years ago, *synthesis by physical models* was practiced only in a handful of research laboratories. Today it has been commercialized in a number of music synthesizers and has gained great popularity. This technique is based on simulation of the sound production mechanism of traditional musical instruments, rather than simulation of the sound itself. The basic advantage is that the model is naturally dynamic with a behavior that is similar to the acoustic instrument. Moreover, the control parameters have a physical interpretation (blowing pressure, reed stiffness, etc.). Under ideal circumstances, performers have the same type of interaction with the synthetic instrument that they have with a real instrument. Although simulation models have been designed for many years in musical acoustics field, the classical algorithms are very heavy from a computational point of view and thus not useful for real time synthesis of complex models. The approach by *digital waveguides* developed by Julius O. Smith is characterized by very efficient algorithms. In Chapter 7 Smith presents, in a tutorial way, the digital waveguide techique with some significant examples of models for musical instruments.

4

Wavelet representations of musical signals

Gianpaolo Evangelista

Thanks to the ever increasing number of contributions of many scientists, wavelet theory has become a mature field. Along with the extension of the theory, several interesting applications have emerged, shedding new light on the relevance of the transform in signal processing. This renovated interest has led me to write the present tutorial in which I have tried to include a number of novel perspectives. The paper is intended as an introductory tutorial for the non-specialist reader. Due to the vastness of the subject, I have chosen to present, in informal style, only those results that, in my opinion, are most relevant to the analysis, synthesis and manipulation of sound. For more general overviews, rigorous and extensive presentations of the results, the reader is referred to the tutorials and original papers cited in the—necessarily partial—bibliography.

The wavelet transform provides a time-scale representation of sound patterns (Kronland-Martinet, Morlet, and Grossmann 1987; Kronland-Martinet 1988; Daubechies 1990; Evangelista 1991a, b). The need for a two-dimensional representation of the signal, which could overcome the limitations offered by the Fourier transform, had long been recognized. Several time–frequency representations have been proposed, such as the short-time Fourier transform (Chapter 2; Allen and Rabiner 1977; Portnoff 1980, 1981), the tracking phase vocoder (Chapter 3; Dolson 1986), the Wigner distribution (Claasen and Mecklenbräuker 1980) and so on. Since time and scale, as well as time and frequency, are conjugated variables, the resolution of the representation may not be chosen at will and is subject to the uncertainty principle. The wavelet transform allows for a multiresolution representation (Mallat 1989) with constant quality factor $Q = \Delta f / f$, a concept pioneered in (Gambardella 1971), in which the uncertainty product $\Delta f \cdot \Delta t$ is kept constant (Meyer 1985) and a higher frequency resolution Δf is achieved at lower frequencies, corresponding to a higher time resolution Δt at higher frequencies. This feature is coherent with our understanding of auditory perception and critical band models.

Another common characteristic of these representations is their redundancy, which allows for sampling the transform domain (Jerri 1977). It is well-known that the Fourier transform of time-limited signals may be sampled i.e., the signal can be reconstructed from the knowledge of its Fourier transform evaluated on a countable number of frequency points. Similarly, any finite energy signal can be reconstructed from the knowledge of its wavelet transform on a discrete grid of points. Reducing information to the essential is important from the point of view of both data-compression and sound synthesis. Sampling the transform domain of the wavelet transforms leads to wavelet series expansion (Daubechies, Grossmann, and Meyer 1986; Daubechies 1988; Daubechies 1992) just as sampling of the short-time Fourier transform domain leads to generalized Gabor series expansion (Gabor 1946; Bastiaans 1980, 1985). All these concepts have a discrete-time counterpart, making them applicable to digital sound processing. A subclass of the known transforms may be set to operate synchronously to the pitch of the sound. We may exploit this feature in processing pseudo-periodic signals recorded from harmonic instruments.

The choice of the most appropriate representation for the application at hand is sometimes a matter of faith or taste. However, the power of a given representation is bound to the physical or perceptual meaning that we can ascribe to its elements. It is desirable that distinct components of sound, such as the bow noise and the harmonic resonant part of a violin tone, or fricative noise and voice in voiced consonants, be represented by means of separate, *orthogonal*, elements. Much like a vector in a two-dimensional space can be represented as the sum of its cartesian X-Y components obtained by orthogonally projecting the vector onto the coordinate axes, any sound can be represented as the sum of a number of components obtained by orthogonally projecting the signal onto a suitable orthogonal basis in an infinite-dimension space. Provided that a perceptual meaning can be attached to the basis functions, truncation of the representation can be performed on a perceptual basis and superposition of distinct components pertaining to two or more instruments allows for *cross-synthesis*. Components can be processed separately rendering time, pitch scaling and other manipulations more accurate and physical modeling easier.

Classic wavelets

In this section, I will briefly review the definitions and some of the basic properties of the wavelet transforms in their various forms: the integral wavelet transform, wavelet series, the discrete wavelet transform and discrete wavelet series.

The integral wavelet transform

The integral wavelet transform of a finite energy signal $s(t)$, with respect to an analyzing wavelet $\psi(t)$, is defined (Grossmann and Morlet 1984; Heil and Walnut 1989; Daubechies 1992; Rioul and Vetterli 1991) as the following function of two variables:

$$S(a, \tau) = \frac{1}{\sqrt{a}} \int_{-\infty}^{+\infty} dt \, s(t) \psi^* \left(\frac{t - \tau}{a} \right). \tag{1}$$

The variables $a > 0$ and τ in (1) respectively represent scale and time in the transform domain. The scale parameter controls the stretching of the wavelet, as shown in Figure 1. The analyzing wavelet plays the same role as the modulated window in the short-time Fourier transform. However, the frequency parameter is replaced by the scale variable a. To small values of a, there correspond short analysis windows. If the wavelet is an oscillating function that is amplitude modulated by a time envelope, the number of oscillations remains constant while their period changes as we vary a. This is to be compared to the short-time Fourier transform in which the number of oscillations varies according to the frequency parameter. The wavelet transform is obtained by convolving the signal with the time-reversed and scaled wavelet:

$$S(a, \tau) = s(\tau) * \frac{1}{\sqrt{a}} \psi^* \left(\frac{-\tau}{a} \right) = \sqrt{a} \mathfrak{I}^{-1} \left[S(f) \Psi^*(af) \right], \tag{2}$$

where $S(f)$ and $\Psi(f)$ respectively are the Fourier transforms of $s(t)$ and $\psi(t)$, the symbol $*$ denotes convolution and $\mathfrak{I}^{-1}[\ ]$ denotes the inverse Fourier transform of its argument. Wavelet transforming is equivalent to filtering the signal

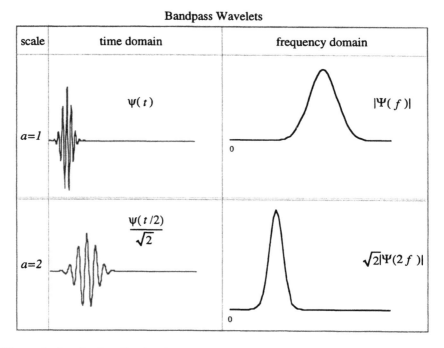

Figure 1. Result of scaling bandpass wavelets.

through—infinitely many—filters whose frequency responses are obtained from a single frequency response by means of a stretching operation. If the analyzing wavelet is a bandpass function, to different values of a correspond distinct—overlapping with each other—frequency bands. Both center frequency and bandwidth decrease as the scale is increased, leaving the quality factor $Q = \Delta f/f$ unchanged. In this respect, scale is reciprocal of frequency. On the other hand, since the variable a scales the analysis time, that is, the time interval in which the wavelet is essentially different from zero, to each scale corresponds a different time resolution.

Both the wavelet and the short-time Fourier transform project the time signal onto the time-frequency plane. To each fixed value of time and scale or time and frequency corresponds an uncertainty rectangle, as shown in Figure 2. Since the time-bandwidth product $\Delta f \cdot \Delta t$ of the wavelets, as well as the modulated window, is independent of scale, the area of these rectangles is independent of time and center frequency in both transforms. The sides of the rectangles are independent of center frequency in the short-time Fourier transform, obtaining uniform frequency resolution. In the wavelet transform, the time side of the rectangles grows with the center frequency and, correspondingly, the frequency side narrows as the center frequency is increased, that is, as the scale is decreased.

Time-frequency domain

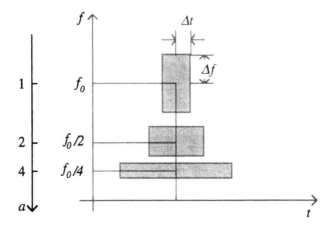

Figure 2. Time-frequency uncertainty rectangles of wavelets vs. center frequency and scale.

The inverse wavelet transform is obtained as follows:

$$s(t) = \frac{1}{C_\psi} \int_0^\infty \frac{da}{a^2} \int_{-\infty}^{+\infty} d\tau \, S(a, \tau) \frac{1}{\sqrt{a}} \psi\left(\frac{t - \tau}{a}\right), \tag{3}$$

where C_ψ is a constant that depends on ψ. The signal is reconstructed by means of a weighted superposition of convolutions of the wavelet transform with scaled wavelets. Again, the frequency domain counterpart of (3) is perhaps more illuminating:

$$S(f) = \frac{1}{C_\psi} \int_0^\infty \frac{da}{\sqrt{a^3}} \, \check{S}(a, f) \Psi(af), \tag{4}$$

where

$$\check{S}(a, f) = \mathfrak{I}[S(a, \tau)] = \sqrt{a} S(f) \Psi^*(af), \tag{5}$$

is the Fourier transform of the wavelet transform of $s(t)$ with respect to the time variable τ. Notice that by substituting (5) in (4) we obtain:

$$S(f) = S(f) + \frac{1}{C_\psi} \int_0^\infty \frac{da}{a} \left|\Psi(af)\right|^2, \tag{6}$$

showing that the transform is invertible provided that

$$C_\psi = \int_0^\infty \frac{da}{a} \left| \Psi(af) \right|^2 < \infty, \tag{7}$$

which implies that $\Psi(f)$ must have a zero at zero frequency and a reasonable decay at infinity. Bandpass wavelets clearly satisfy this requirement.

The integral wavelet transform (1) is both redundant and not directly suitable for digital implementations. By sampling the transform we eliminate the redundancy and obtain complete wavelet sets that are useful to expand continuous-time signals (Daubechies, Grossmann, and Meyer 1986; Daubechies 1988; Mallat 1989). These are the counterpart of Gabor sets for the short-time Fourier transform. On the other hand, by assuming that the signal is bandlimited, we may sample the time variable according to Shannon's theorem and obtain a wavelet transform that operates on discrete-time signals and provides a function of two variables. By sampling both the transform and the signal we obtain complete discrete-time wavelet sets (Evangelista 1989b, 1990; Rioul and Vetterli 1991; Rioul and Duhamel 1992), useful for the representation of digital signals.

Wavelet series

Sampling the wavelet transform is best understood if we perform the change of variables $a = e^\sigma$ and $\tau = e^\sigma \vartheta$ (Strang 1989; Shensa 1992). With this substitution, the wavelet transform (1) and its inverse (3), respectively, assume the following form:

$$\mathfrak{S}(\sigma, \vartheta) = S(e^\sigma, e^\sigma \vartheta) = e^{-\sigma/2} \int_{-\infty}^\infty dt \, s(t) \psi^*(e^{-\sigma} t - \vartheta), \tag{8}$$

and

$$s(t) = \frac{1}{C_\psi} \int_{-\infty}^\infty d\sigma \int_{-\infty}^\infty d\vartheta \, \mathfrak{S}(s, \vartheta) e^{-\sigma/2} \psi(e^{-\sigma} t - \vartheta). \tag{9}$$

The transform may be sampled if we are able to determine a grid of points $\{\sigma_n, \vartheta_m\}$ of the (σ, ϑ) plane such that, at least for a specific class of wavelets, the double integral in (9) may be replaced by the double sum:

$$s(t) = \sum_n \sum_m \mathfrak{S}(\sigma_n, \vartheta_m) e^{-\sigma_n/2} \psi(e^{-\sigma_n} t - \vartheta_m), \tag{10}$$

where

$$\mathfrak{S}(\sigma_n, \vartheta_m) = e^{-\sigma_n/2} \int_{-\infty}^{\infty} \mathrm{d}t \, s(t) \psi^*(e^{-\sigma_n}t - \vartheta_m). \tag{11}$$

Equations (10) and (11) represent the expansion of the signal over the complete and orthogonal set of functions $\psi_{n,m}(t) = e^{-\sigma_n/2}\psi(e^{-\sigma_n}t - \vartheta_m)$. This set

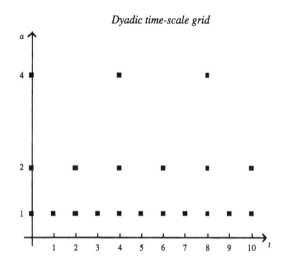

Figure 3. The dyadic sampling grid.

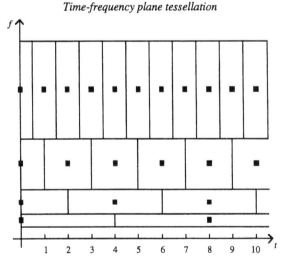

Figure 4. Covering the time-frequency plane by means of wavelets on the dyadic sampling grid.

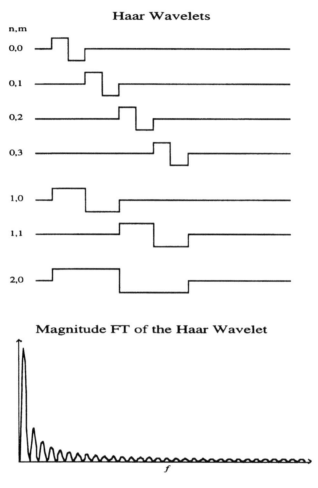

Figure 5. The Haar wavelet set.

is obtained by stretching and shifting a unique wavelet over the given grid. We
will not enter into the details of how a class of wavelets may be determined or
generated in order that (10) and (11) are valid for a given sampling grid. We
limit ourselves to point out that complete sets of wavelets have been generated
for the class of rational grids where $e^{\sigma_n} = r^n$, $\vartheta_m = m$, m integer and r a
rational number, of which the dyadic grid ($r = 2$)—shown in Figure 3—is the
simplest example (Vetterli and Herley 1990; Evangelista and Piccialli 1991; Blu
1993). Sampling the wavelet transform on the dyadic grid corresponds to the
tessellation of the time-frequency plane shown in Figure 4. The simplest wavelet
set on this grid is given by the Haar set shown in Figure 5.

Discrete wavelet transform and wavelet sets

The wavelet transform of bandlimited signals is obtained by substituting in (8) the sampling expansion of the signal:

$$s(t) = \sum_n s(k)\,\text{sinc}(t - k), \qquad (12)$$

yielding the following couple of discrete-time wavelet transform and inverse:

$$\mathfrak{S}(\sigma, \vartheta) = \sum_k s(k)\lambda^*_{\sigma,\vartheta}(k), \qquad (13)$$

and

$$s(k) = \frac{1}{C_\psi} \int_{-\infty}^{+\infty} d\sigma \int_{-\infty}^{+\infty} d\vartheta \, \mathfrak{S}(\sigma, \vartheta)\lambda_{\sigma,\vartheta}(k), \qquad (14)$$

where

$$\lambda_{\sigma,\vartheta}(k) = e^{-\sigma/2} \int_{-\infty}^{+\infty} dt \, \text{sinc}(t - k)\psi(e^{-\sigma}t - \vartheta), \qquad (15)$$

are aliased samples of the continuous-time wavelet. Notice from equation (5) that, as a function of the time variable ϑ, the wavelet transform of a bandlimited signal is itself bandlimited and it may be sampled. As for the continuous-time case, the discrete-time wavelet transform may be fully sampled provided that we determine a sampling grid $\{\sigma_n, \vartheta_m\}$ and a complete set of orthogonal wavelets $\psi_{n,m}(k) = \lambda_{\sigma_n,\vartheta_m}(k)$ over that grid. Over the dyadic grid we may generate sets of complete and orthogonal wavelets satisfying $\psi_{n,m}(k) = \psi_{n,0}(k - 2^n m)$, $n = 1, 2, \ldots$ and m integer. This corresponds to a simultaneous sampling of the scale variable and downsampling of the time variable ϑ. We obtain the following wavelet series expansion for any finite energy discrete-time signal $s(k)$:

$$s(k) = \sum_{n=1}^{\infty} \sum_m S_{n,m}\psi_{n,m}(k), \qquad (16)$$

where

$$S_{n,m} = \sum_k s(k)\psi^*_{n,m}(k). \qquad (17)$$

In principle, the expansion can be implemented in an infinite depth tree-structured multirate filterbank (Mallat 1989; Vaidyanathan 1990; Rioul and Duhamel 1992). However, practical implementation can only accommodate finite scale level expansions. Considering a depth N analysis and synthesis filterbank one has the following expansion of the input signal $s(k)$:

$$s(k) = \sum_{n=1}^{N} \sum_{m} S_{n,m} \psi_{n,m}(k) + r_N(k), \tag{18}$$

where the coefficients $S_{n,m}$ are given as in (17) and the sequence $r_N(k)$ represents the residue of the truncated expansion over the wavelet set. Equation (18) formally denotes the expansion of a signal over an orthogonal set of discrete wavelets truncated at a finite scale N. This widely used version of the wavelet transform is the one which is most suited for digital implementation. One can show that, associated to any set of discrete wavelets, there is a set of scaling sequences $\phi_{n,m}(k)$ having the following property:

$$r_N(k) = \sum_{m} b_{N,m} \phi_{N,m}(k), \tag{19}$$

where

$$b_{N,m} = \sum_{k} s(k) \phi_{N,m}^{*}(k), \tag{20}$$

are the scaling coefficients. The scaling sequences are orthogonal to all the wavelets. Thus, appending the scaling set to the set of finite-scale wavelets one obtains a complete and orthogonal set.

Dyadic wavelets may be generated from a pair of *quadrature mirror (QMF) transfer functions* $\{H(z), G(z)\}$ (Vaidyanathan 1987; Smith and Barnwell 1989; Evangelista 1989a; Rioul and Duhamel 1992; Herley and Vetterli 1993). QMF transfer functions are power complementary:

$$|H(f)|^2 + |G(f)|^2 = 2, \tag{21}$$

as shown in Figure 6, and they satisfy the constraint

$$H(f)H^{*}\left(f + \frac{1}{2}\right) + G(f)G^{*}\left(f + \frac{1}{2}\right) = 0, \tag{22}$$

which guarantees the orthogonality of the expansion.

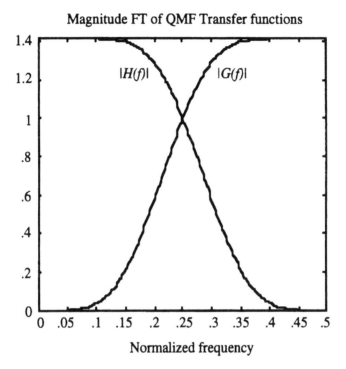

Figure 6. QMF transfer functions: lowpass $H(f)$ (starts at upper left) and highpass $G(f)$ (starts at lower left).

The finite-scale wavelet expansion (18) may be computed by means of the multirate filterbank reported in Figure 7. In ordinary wavelet expansions, the wavelets are bandpass sequences and the corresponding scaling sequences are lowpass, as shown in Figure 8. Therefore, the sequence $r_N(k)$ represents the lowpass residue reproducing the trend of the signal and approaching the DC component as N grows (see Figure 9). However, a peculiarity of discrete wavelet expansions is that comb–multiple frequency band–wavelets are admissible (Evangelista 1994a, b). As a final remark we point out that in all the forms of wavelet transform that we considered we assumed equal analysis and synthesis wavelets. However, with minor formal modifications, one may allow these wavelets to differ, for example, leading to biorthogonal (Daubechies, Grossmann, and Meyer 1986; Evangelista and Barnes 1990) rather than orthogonal wavelet sets. Biorthogonal wavelet sets allow for a more flexible design of the analysis filterbank since constraints (21) and (22) are replaced by constraints on the four analysis and synthesis transfer functions. Spline-like wavelets are an example of biorthogonal wavelets.

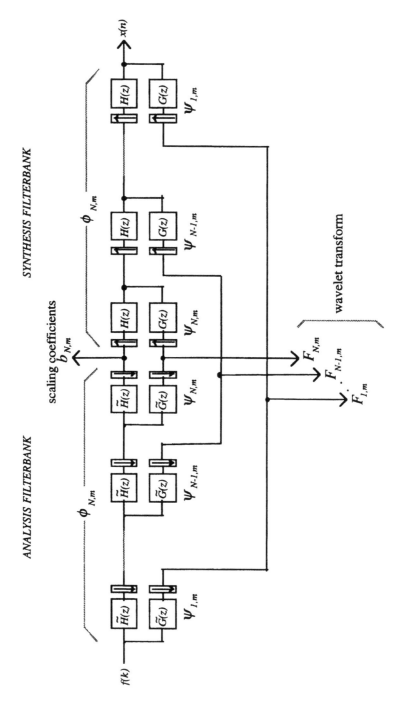

Figure 7. Multirate analysis and synthesis filterbanks implementing a discrete wavelet expansion.

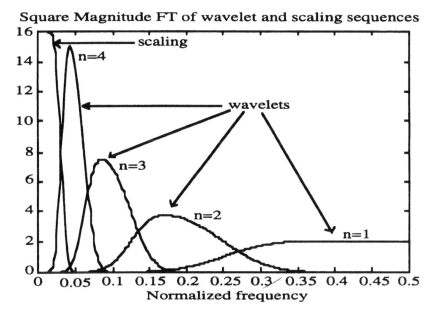

Figure 8. Frequency spectra of ordinary wavelets and scaling sequence.

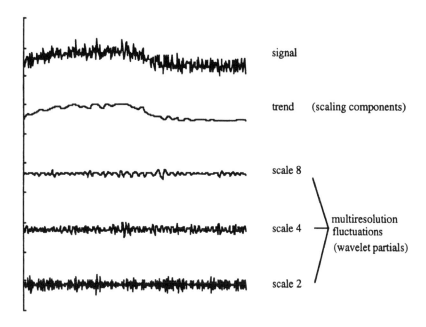

Figure 9. Trend plus fluctuations decomposition of a signal via wavelet transform.

Wavelet representations of music signals: applications and examples

The human ear is able to perceive both large scale quantities, such as pitch, and small scale events, such as short transients. These may appear as conflicting characteristics unless we postulate the ability for multiresolution analysis. The logarithmic characteristic of many musical scales specifically reflect this behavior. The wavelet transform provides a representation of sounds in which both non-uniform frequency resolution and impulsive characteristics are taken into account. The underlying assumption in these representations is that time resolution is sharper at higher frequencies just as frequency resolution is sharper at lower frequencies. These features may be exploited in auditory models (Yang *et al.* 1992), sound analysis, synthesis, coding and processing, although the actual behavior of the ear may be much more involved. In complete wavelet expansions, time and frequency resolutions are quantized according to a specific sampling grid. The dyadic grid provides an octave-band decomposition in which the time resolution doubles at each octave. Other trade-offs may be achieved by means of rational sampling grids. In this section we will consider a few examples of wavelet transform applied to music. We will confine ourselves to finite scale discrete wavelet expansions, which are most attractive from a computational point of view allowing for digital processing of sampled sounds.

For small depth N, the sequence of scaling coefficients of bandpass discrete wavelet expansion is simultaneously a frequency multiplied and time-compressed version of the input. In fact, this sequence is obtained as a result of non-ideal—but perfect reconstruction—lowpass downsampling. The ensemble of wavelet coefficients contains the information that is lost in this operation. As N grows, the scaling residue will essentially contain information on the trend of the signal. It is convenient to consider wavelet and scaling grains given by the wavelet and scaling sequence, respectively, multiplied by the expansion coefficient. Referring to (16), the signal is obtained as a double superposition of wavelet grains $s_{n,m}(k) = S_{n,m} \psi_{n,m}(k)$ plus the residue or scaling grains $r_{N,m}(k) = b_{N,m} \phi_{N,m}(k)$ at the same sampling rate as that of the signal. Each grain represents the contribution of the signal to a certain frequency band in the time interval given by the time support of the wavelet. Grains may be relevant for transient analysis and detection. In sound restoration we may attempt to remove or reduce the grains pertaining to impulsive noise. The superposition of the wavelet grains at a certain scale provides the corresponding wavelet component:

$$s_n(k) = \sum_m S_{n,m} \psi_{n,m}(k). \tag{23}$$

If we disregard the aliasing that may be present, these components are time domain signals that represent the contribution of the overall signal to a certain frequency band given by the frequency support of the wavelets. Hearing one of these components separately is equivalent to lowering all the sliders of a graphic equalizer except for one. Component-wise, that is, subband processing and coding may be convenient. Time-varying filters may be realized by multiplying the coefficients $S_{n,m}$ by time signals.

An important feature of wavelet transforms lies in their ability of separating trends from variations at several scales. For example, consider the phase-amplitude representation of a musical tone $s(k)$:

$$s(k) = a(k) \cos \theta(k), \tag{24}$$

where $a(k)$ and $\theta(k)$ respectively are the amplitude envelope and the instantaneous phase. These sequences may be computed by means of the Hilbert transform. Without affecting the signal, the phase can be unwrapped to an increasing sequence that we shall continue to denote by $\theta(k)$. The amplitude envelope $a(k)$ is a positive sequence that is generally not smooth since the oscillating part of a broad-band signal may leak in the magnitude extracted via the Hilbert transform. The envelope may be expanded over a set of real and orthogonal wavelets (Evangelista 1991b):

$$a(k) = \sum_{n=1}^{N} a_{n,m} \psi_{n,m}(k) + r_N(k). \tag{25}$$

The residue $r_N(k)$ is a lowpass sequence which represents an average of $a(k)$ at the scale indexed by N. If N is large enough the residue $r_N(k)$ is smooth and slowly varying and it represents the trend of $a(k)$. The residue and some of the wavelet components of the amplitude envelope extracted from a violin tone are shown in Figure 10. The components of the wavelet expansion of the envelope represent the variations from the trend, seen at different scales. These fluctuations become more and more refined at smaller scales. This feature may prove useful for envelope extraction and smoothing. The sharp fluctuations may be brought back to the phase sequence where they belong. The procedure may reduce the influence of the ripple of the extracted envelope in changing the duration of a tone.

Similarly, one can consider the truncated wavelet expansion of the unwrapped phase:

$$\theta(k) = \sum_{n=1}^{N} \theta_{n,m} \psi_{n,m}(k) + s_N(k). \tag{26}$$

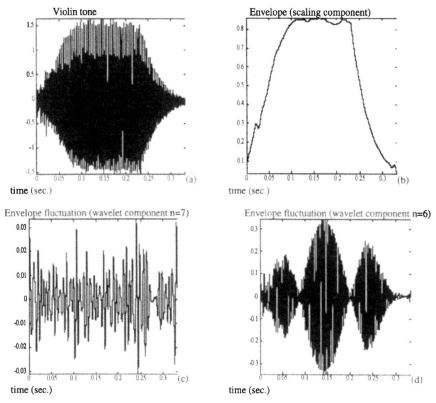

Figure 10. (a) Violin tone; (b) trend of the amplitude envelope (scaling component); (c) and (d) envelope fluctuations (wavelet components).

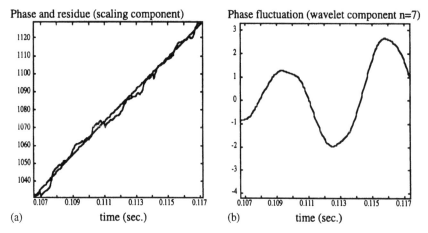

Figure 11. Zoom of (a) phase (solid line) and phase trend (scaling component) and (b) large scale fluctuation (wavelet component).

In this case, the residue $s_N(k)$ represents a slowly varying phase carrier. From the smoothed phase carrier we may extract the instantaneous frequency. The wavelet components represent modulations at different time scales. A zoom of the phase of the violin tone of Figure 10, together with the smooth residue (in overlay) and some of the wavelet modulants are shown in Figure 11. The last examples shows that the trend plus fluctuations feature of the wavelet expansion can be exploited for frequency modulation (FM) parameter estimation. A continuous-time counterpart of the procedure shown may be found in (Delprat *et al.* 1992). A different, energy approach to AM-FM estimation is proposed in (Bovik, Maragos, and Quatieri 1993).

New results in wavelet theory

Most musical signals from natural instruments are oscillatory in nature, although they are not exactly periodic in a strict mathematical sense. Although a possibly time-varying pitch can be assigned to them, in the time evolution we can identify a number of *periods* which almost never identically reproduce themselves, due to amplitude, frequency modulations and intrinsic randomness. We shall denote this behavior as *pseudo-periodic*. Most of the failures of fixed waveform synthesis methods are to be ascribed to this dynamic feature of sound. The ear is sensitive to transients and dynamic changes up to a certain time-resolution. Deprived of their fluctuations from the periodic behavior, musical signals sound quite "unnatural" and we are induced to think that a lot of information is contained in these variations. Fluctuations may occur at different proper scales: slow amplitude envelopes have a longer duration than fast modulations or transients.

The "harmonics plus fluctuations" model

In two recent papers (Evangelista 1993, 1994a), I introduced a new family of transforms, namely the comb, multiplexed and pitch-synchronous wavelet transforms. These transforms allow for separation of the period-to-period variations of signals at several scales from the average periodic behavior. The resulting representation is particularly suited to the analysis and synthesis of musical sounds since each component adds dynamics to the sound and its relevance may be perceptually evaluated. Ordinary finite-scale discrete wavelet expansions lead to a decomposition of the signal into a lowpass trend plus fluctuations at several scales. In the new family of transforms, signals are decomposed into an asymptotically periodic trend and aperiodic fluctuations at several scales.

Feature extraction such as separation of harmonic oscillations from inharmonic information is easily performed by means of partial wavelet expansions. Inharmonic components may be modeled as a superposition of independent stochastic processes, each representing a fluctuation from periodicity at a different scale. This is particularly relevant to data-rate reduction coding and pitch or time-scale alteration of music sounds.

The comb wavelet expansion can be realized by using multiple band comb quadrature mirror filters, tuned to the pitch of the signal, for generating wavelets. As already observed, this is a possibility that is not ruled out in discrete wavelet transforms. The multiplexed wavelet transform is defined by means of an intermediate pitch-synchronous vector signal representation. The input samples are demultiplexed over several channels, the number of channels being equal to the local pitch period of the signal. Each channel is individually wavelet transformed, obtaining a representation in terms of averages and fluctuations of the signal samples that fall one period apart. The number of multiplexing channels may be adaptively selected in order to take into account the fluctuations of the pitch. This may be achieved by controlling the demultiplexer by means of a pitch-detector. The transform reverts to the ordinary wavelet transform over totally aperiodic signal segments whose pitch period is equal to a single sample.

Comb, multiplexed and pitch-synchronous wavelet representations

The representation discussed in this section is based on the pitch information which can be extracted from signals, following one of the several methods for pitch detection that have been proposed (Ross *et al.* 1974; Rabiner *et al.* 1976; Hess, 1983). For the purpose of illustrating the gist of the method, suppose that the period T of a continuous-time signal $s(t)$ is constant. We can form the following two-dimensional signal:

$$s'(k, t) = s(t + kT), \quad 0 \leqslant t \leqslant T, \quad k = \text{truncate } (t/T) \qquad (27)$$

where truncate denotes truncation to integer. The discrete-time signal obtained by holding τ fixed in (27) represents the time history of a specific point in the period, which we shall refer to as the τ-section of the signal. If the signal is exactly periodic each section is constant. As already observed, natural harmonic sounds are pseudo-periodic so that sections are slowly varying signals. This characteristic is reflected in the frequency domain by the fact that the Fourier transform of a pseudo-periodic signal contains peaks that are centered on harmonically related frequencies. The more the signal is periodic, the narrower the peaks. By filtering the signal through a comb filter tuned to its pitch, we might introduce only minor distortions where transients and deviations from periodicity occur. The filtered signal has a reduced total bandwidth taken as the sum of the individual bandwidths of the multiple bands of the comb filter. A non-classical sampling theorem may be then applied in order to downsample the signal. Equivalently, Shannon's theorem applies to smooth signal sections and we may downsample these components individually. It is quite natural to apply ordinary discrete wavelet transforms in order to represent each section in terms of its trend and fluctuations at several scales. The collection of wavelet transforms of the sections forms the multiplexed wavelet transform. An alternate method is to represent the signal by means of tuned comb wavelets. It turns out that the multiplexed wavelet transform is more flexible than the comb wavelet transforms in terms of adaptation to the pitch.

The procedure described above can be applied to sampled signals as well, provided that we approximate the period to an integer multiple of the sampling rate. We will discuss the general case in which the pitch is not constant. Suppose that a sequence $P(k)$ of integer local pitch periods of a sampled signal $s(n)$ is available. We can store each period-length segment in a variable length vector $\boldsymbol{v}(k) = [v_0(k), \; v_1(k), \dots, v_{P(k)-1}(k)]^T$ (Mathews, Miller, and David 1961). Aperiodic segments are represented by a sequence of scalars, that is, length 1 vectors, while constant period P pseudo-periodic segments are represented by a sequence of length P vectors. The vector components can be expressed in terms of the signal as follows:

$$v_q(k) = s(q + M(k)) = \sum_r s(r)\delta(r - q - M(k)), \tag{28}$$
$$q = 0, 1, \dots, P(k) - 1,$$

where

$$M(k) = \sum_{r=0}^{k-1} P(r), \tag{29}$$

and

$$\delta(k) = \begin{cases} 1 & \text{if } k = 0 \\ 0 & \text{otherwise.} \end{cases}$$

The pitch-synchronous wavelet transform is obtained by expanding the sections $v_q(i)$ over a set of finite-scale, orthogonal discrete wavelets $\psi_{n,m}(k)$, $n = 1, 2, \dots, N$, $m = 0, 1, \dots$, with level N scaling sequences $\phi_{N,m}(k)$, $m =$

$0, 1, \ldots$. By defining the pitch-synchronous wavelets and scaling sequences, respectively, as the following sets of sequences:

$$\zeta_{n,m,q}(r) = \sum_k \delta(r - q - M(k))\psi_{n,m}(k)\chi_q(k),$$

$$n = 1, 2, \ldots, \quad m \text{ integer}, \quad q = 0, 1, \ldots, \tag{30}$$

and

$$\vartheta_{n,m,q}(r) = \sum_k \delta(r - q - M(k))\phi_{n,m}(k)\chi_q(k),$$

$$n = 1, 2, \ldots, \quad m \text{ integer}, \quad q = 0, 1, \ldots, \tag{31}$$

where

$$\chi_q(k) = \begin{cases} 1 & q = 0, 1, \ldots, P(k) - 1 \\ 0 & \text{otherwise}, \end{cases}$$

we obtain the following orthogonal expansion:

$$s(k) = \sum_{m,q} \left(\sum_{n=1}^{N} S_{n,m,q}\zeta_{n,m,q}(k) + \sigma_{N,m,q}\vartheta_{N,m,q}(k) \right), \tag{32}$$

where

$$S_{n,m,q} = \sum_r s(r)\zeta_{n,m,q}^*(r), \tag{33}$$

and

$$\sigma_{N,m,q} = \sum_r s(r)\vartheta_{N,m,q}^*(r). \tag{34}$$

Notice that the wavelet $\zeta_{n,m,q}$ is obtained from the product $\psi_{n,m}(k) \, \chi_q(k)$ by inserting $P(k) - 1$ zeros between the samples k and $k + 1$ and shifting by q. Multiplication by $\chi_q(k)$ annihilates the samples of $\psi_{n,m}(k)$ when q ranges outside the local period.

The scaling residue:

$$r_N(k) = \sum_{m,q} \sigma_{N,m,q}\vartheta_{N,m,q}(k),$$

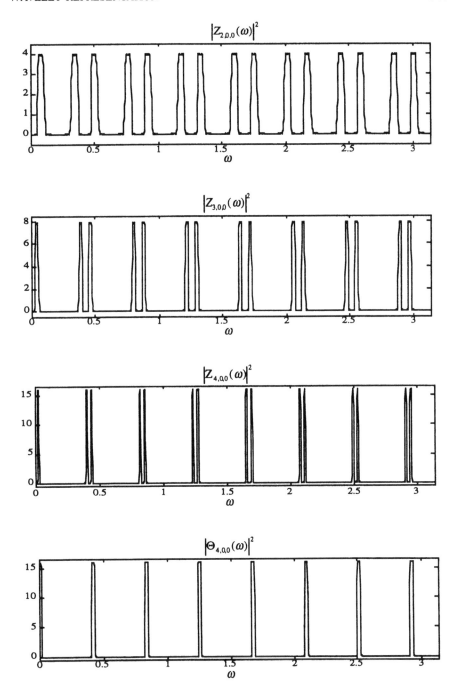

Figure 12. Spectra of multiplexed wavelets and scaling sequence.

represents the average harmonic behavior while each wavelet component:

$$w_n(k) = \sum_{m,q} S_{n,m,q} \zeta_{N,m,q}(k),$$

represents the fluctuation at scale 2^n local periods. The sum of these contributions equals the signal. Over stationary pitch sequences, the basis sequences have the comb-like frequency spectrum shown in Figure 12. In fact, the Fourier transform of the multiplexed scaling sequence, obtained from the pitch-synchronous scaling sequence when the pitch is held constant, is:

$$\Theta_{n,m,q}(\omega) = e^{j(q+2^n m)\omega} \Phi_{n,0}(P\omega),$$

where $\Phi_{n,0}(\omega)$ is the Fourier transform of the lowpass scaling function associated to ordinary wavelets. The frequency spectrum consists of multiple frequency bands that are centered on the harmonics at

$$\omega_p = \frac{2p}{P} p, \ \ p = 0, 1, \ldots, \left\lfloor \frac{P}{2} \right\rfloor.$$

As n grows, these bands narrow. Similarly, the Fourier transform of the multiplexed wavelet is:

$$Z_{n,m,q}(\omega) = e^{j(q+2^n m)\omega} \Psi_{n,0}(P\omega).$$

The frequency spectra of the constant pitch multiplexed wavelets have a multiple band structure consisting of sidebands of the harmonics. As n grows these bands narrow and get closer to the harmonics. The pitch-synchronous wavelets adapt to the pitch of the signal and have the spectral structure of the multiplexed wavelets over voiced segments and the structure of ordinary wavelets over aperiodic segments. This leads to a representation of pseudo-periodic signals in terms of a regularized oscillatory component plus period-to-period fluctuations.

Applications and examples

The wavelet transform leads to a trend-plus-fluctuation representation of signals. The principal difference between ordinary and pitch-synchronous wavelet transforms lies in the way the trend is formed. In ordinary wavelet transforms the trend is a running mean of the signal, that is a lowpass signal locally representing the mean value of the original signal. In pitch-synchronous wavelet transforms the trend is taken as an asymptotically periodic signal—the running mean period—locally representing the harmonic information contained in the original signal. Slow amplitude fluctuations correspond to narrow sidebands of the harmonics and are represented by wavelets with large scale indices. Faster fluctuations and transients correspond to wider bands which lie in between the harmonics and are represented by wavelets with a small scale index. These features of the representation may be best illustrated with an example. In Figure 13, a violin tone is decomposed by means of multiplexed wavelet expansion. The residue represents the most stationary structure of the signal, while the wavelet components represent fluctuations over this behavior. Low scale level fluctuations are mostly due to the friction of the bow over the string. By grouping these fluctuations one can isolate the bow noise from the harmonic components of the signal. The analysis of other musical instruments, like guitar, trumpet and harpsichord, and voice provides similar results. Transients, noise and the slowly-varying harmonic structure are represented by distinct components. Interesting cross-synthesis examples may be obtained by mixing the components obtained from different instruments.

Another application of the pitch-synchronous wavelet transform is in pitch alteration. The scaling coefficients of the pitch-synchronous wavelet expansion may be rearranged into a sequence that is a time-compressed version of the input

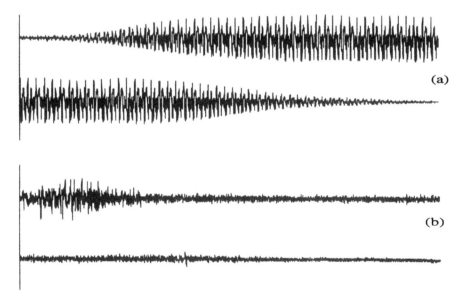

Figure 13. Pitch-synchronous wavelet decomposition of a violin tone in (a) regularized harmonic component (scaling residue) and (b) bow noise (superposition of wavelet components).

signal. Over constant pitch segments the sequence

$$s_{2^N}(k) = \sum_{q=0}^{P-1} \sum_m \sigma_{N,m,q} \delta(k - q - mP),$$ (35)

formed by multiplexing the scaling coefficients, represents a time-compressed version of the input signal by a factor 2^N—or dyadic wavelets—when replayed at the input sampling rate. When replayed at a sampling rate 2^N times smaller we obtain a pitch reduction of N octaves. Other rates of pitch reduction may be obtained by means of pitch-synchronous wavelet expansions based on rational sampling grids. This method of pitch scaling tends to cancel the inharmonic components that are represented by the small-scale wavelet coefficients associated to the fluctuations over the harmonic behavior. In order to obtain a good pitch-scaling algorithm one need to model and properly scale these coefficients. Low scale level fluctuations are generally noise-like and are represented by high-rate signals. It may be advantageous to model the signal fluctuations as time-varying stochastic processes. In a parametric representation the fluctuations may be modeled as the outputs of time-varying filters driven by independent white noise inputs (Evangelista 1993). This method, which parallels a model devised by X. Serra (1989), may be particularly effective in pitch or time-scale alteration, cross-synthesis, and data-rate reduction coding (Evangelista 1994b).

Conclusions

Wavelet theory is a unifying framework for time-frequency representations based on linear transforms, generalizing the concepts of short-time Fourier transform and Gabor expansions. The multiresolution character of the representation lends itself to useful interpretations in the context of musical sound analysis, synthesis, manipulations, and auditory models. However, as in the case of the two-century old Fourier transform, the wavelet transform itself may not suffice to solve any specific problem; more algorithms based on the transform need to be developed. I pointed out a few applications of the wavelet transform, for example, as an amplitude envelope estimator and a phase modulation model.

A recent extension of the wavelet family, the pitch-synchronous wavelet transform, leads to a unique signal representation in which harmonic information is treated as a whole and fluctuations are classified in terms of their rate-of-change at several scales. A perceptual significance may be attached to each component of the representation. This property may be significant in rate-reduction coding, feature extraction, and cross-synthesis algorithms. Fluctuations may be modeled as a set of independent stochastic processes each acting at different scale, in order to improve data-rate reduction, pitch and time-scale modification by processing the main perceptual components of musical sounds separately.

References

Allen, J.B. and L.R. Rabiner. 1977. "A unified theory of short-time spectrum analysis and synthesis." *Proceedings of the IEEE* 65: 1558–1564.

Bastiaans, M.J. 1980. "Gabor's expansion of a signal into Gaussian elementary signals." *Proceedings of the IEEE* 68(4): 538–539.

Bastiaans, M.J. 1985. "On the sliding-window representation in digital signal processing." *IEEE Transactions on Acoustics, Speech, and Signal Processing* ASSP-33: 868–873.

Blu, T. 1993. "Iterated filter banks with rational rate changes. Connections with discrete wavelet transforms." *IEEE Transactions on Signal Processing* 41: 3232–3244.

Bovik, A.C., P. Maragos, and T.F. Quatieri. 1993. "AM-FM energy detection and separation in noise using multiband energy operators." *IEEE Transactions on Signal Processing* 41: 3245–3265.

Claasen, T.A.C.M. and W.F.G. Mecklenbräuker. 1980. "The Wigner distribution—a tool for time-frequency signal analysis." *Philips Journal of Research* 35: 217–250, 276–300, 372–389.

Delprat, N., *et al.* 1992. "Asymptotic wavelet and gabor analysis: extraction of instantaneous frequencies." *IEEE Transactions on Information Theory* 38(2). Part II: 644–665.

Daubechies, I. 1988. "Orthonormal bases of compactly supported wavelets." *Communications on Pure and Applied Mathematics* XLI (7): 909–996.

Daubechies, I. 1990. "The wavelet transform, time frequency localization and signal analysis." *IEEE Transactions on Information Theory* 36(5): 961–1005.

Daubechies, I. 1992. *Ten Lectures on Wavelets*, CBMS-NSF Reg. Conf. Series in Applied Mathematics, SIAM.

Daubechies, I., A. Grossmann, and Y. Meyer. 1986. "Painless nonorthogonal expansions." *Journal of Mathematical Physics* 27(5): 1271–1283.

Dolson, M. 1986. "The phase vocoder: a tutorial." *Computer Music Journal* 10(4): 14–27.

Evangelista, G. 1989a. "Wavelet transforms and wave digital filters." In Y. Meyer, ed. *Wavelets and Applications*. Berlin: Springer-Verlag, pp. 396–412.

Evangelista, G. 1989b. "Orthonormal wavelet transforms and filter banks." In *Proceedings of the 23rd Asilomar Conference*. New York: IEEE.

Evangelista, G. 1990. "Discrete-time wavelet transforms." PhD dissertation, University of California, Irvine.

Evangelista, G. 1991a. "Wavelet transforms that we can play." In G. De Poli, A. Piccialli, and C. Roads, eds. *Representations of Musical Signals*. Cambridge, Massachusetts: The MIT Press, pp. 119–136.

Evangelista, G. 1991b. "Time-scale representations of musical sounds." In *Processing of IX CIM*, Genova, Italy, pp. 303–313.

Evangelista, G. 1993. "Pitch-synchronous wavelet representations of speech and music signals." *IEEE Transactions on Signal Processing* 41(12): 3313–3330.

Evangelista, G. 1994a. "Comb and multiplexed wavelet transforms and their applications to signal processing." *IEEE Transactions on Signal Processing*, 42(2): 292–303.

Evangelista, G. 1994b. "The coding gain of multiplexed wavelet transforms." Submitted to *IEEE Transactions on Signal Processing*.

Evangelista, G. and C.W. Barnes. 1990. "Discrete-time wavelet transforms and their generalizations." In *Proceedings of the International Symposium on Circuits and System*. New York: IEEE.

Evangelista, G. and A. Piccialli. 1991. "Trasformate discrete tempo-scala." In *Proceedings of the XIX national meeting of AIA (Italian Society of Acoustics)*, Italy, pp. 401–407.

Gabor, D. 1946. "Theory of communication." *Journal of Institute of Electrical Engineers* 93: 429–459.

Gambardella, G. 1971. "A contribution to the theory of short-time spectral analysis with nonuniform bandwidth filters." *IEEE Transactions on Circuit Theory* 18: 455–460.

Grossmann, A. and J. Morlet. 1984. "Decomposition of Hardy functions into square integrable wavelets of constant shape." *SIAM Journal Mathematical Analysis* 15(4): 723–736.

Heil, C.E. and D.F. Walnut. 1989. "Continuous and discrete wavelet transforms." *SIAM Review* 31(4): 628–666.

Herley, C. and M. Vetterli. 1993. "Wavelets and recursive filter banks." *IEEE Transactions on Signal Processing* 41(8): 2536–2556.

Hess, W. 1983. *Pitch Determination of Speech Signals.* New York: Springer-Verlag.

Jerri, A.J. 1977. "The Shannon sampling theorem—its various extensions and applications: a tutorial review." *Proceedings of the IEEE* 65(11): 1565–1596.

Kronland-Martinet, R. 1988. "The wavelet transform for the analysis, synthesis and processing of speech and music sounds." *Computer Music Journal* 12(4): 11–20.

Kronland-Martinet, R., R.J. Morlet, and A. Grossmann. 1987. "Analysis of sound patterns through wavelet transform." *International Journal of Pattern Recognition and Artificial Intelligence* 1(2): 97–126.

Mallat, S. 1989. "A theory for multiresolution signal decomposition: the wavelet representation." *IEEE Transactions Pattern Analysis and Machine Intelligence* PAMI-11(7): 674–693.

Mathews, M.V., J.E. Miller, and E.E. David. 1961. "Pitch synchronous analysis of voiced sounds." *Journal of the Acoustical Society of America* 33: 179–186.

Meyer, Y. 1985. "Principe d'incertitude, bases Hilbertiennes et algèbre d'operatéurs." *Séminaire Bourbaki* 662.

Portnoff, M.R. 1980. "Representation of digital signals and systems based on the short-time Fourier transform." *IEEE Transactions on Acoustics, Speech, and Signal Processing* ASSP-28(2): 55–69.

Portnoff, M.R. 1981. "Short-time Fourier analysis of sampled speech." *IEEE Transactions on Acoustics, Speech, and Signal Processing* ASSP-29: 364–373.

Rabiner, L.R., M.J. Cheng, A.E. Rosenberg, and C.A. McGonegal. 1976. "A comparative study of several pitch detection algorithms." *IEEE Transactions on Acoustics, Speech, and Signal Processing* ASSP-24: 399–418.

Rioul, O. and P. Duhamel. 1992. "Fast algorithms for discrete and continuous wavelet transforms." *IEEE Transactions on Information Theory* 38(2). Part II: 569–586.

Rioul, O. and M. Vetterli. 1991. "Wavelets and signal processing." *IEEE Signal Processing Magazine* 8: 14–38.

Ross, M.J., H.L. Shaffer, A. Cohen, R. Freudberg, and H.J. Manley. 1974. "Average magnitude difference function pitch extractor." *IEEE Transactions on Acoustics, Speech, and Signal Processing* ASSP-22: 353–362.

Serra, X. 1989. "A system for sound analysis/transformation/synthesis based on a deterministic plus stochastic decomposition." Technical Report STAN-M-58. Stanford: Department of Music, Stanford University.

Shensa, M.J. 1992. "The discrete wavelet transform: wedding the à trous and Mallat algorithms." *IEEE Transactions on Signal Processing* 40(10): 2464–2482.

Smith, M.J.T. and T.P. Barnwell. 1986. "Exact reconstruction for tree-structured subband coders." *IEEE Transactions on Acoustics, Speech, and Signal Processing* ASSP-34: 434–441.

Strang, G. 1989. "Wavelets and dilation equations: a brief introduction." *SIAM Review* 31(4): 614–627.

Vaidyanathan, P.P. 1987. "Theory and design of M-Channel maximally decimated quadrature mirror filters with arbitrary M, having the perfect reconstruction property." *IEEE Transactions on Acoustics, Speech, and Signal Processing* ASSP-35(4): 476–492.

Vaidyanathan, P.P. 1990. "Multirate digital filters, filter banks, polyphase networks, and applications: a tutorial." *Proceedings of the IEEE* 78(1): 56–93.

Vetterli, M. 1987. "A theory of multirate filter banks." *IEEE Transactions Acoustics, Speech, and Signal Processing* ASSP-35(3): 356–372.

Vetterli, M. and C. Herley. 1990. "Wavelets and filter banks: relationships and new results." In *Proceedings of ICASSP*. New York: IEEE, pp. 2483–2486.

Yang, X., *et al.* 1992. "Auditory representations of acoustic signals." *IEEE Transactions on Information Theory* 38(2). Part II: 824–839.

5

Granular synthesis of musical signals

Sergio Cavaliere and Aldo Piccialli

The main goal of musical signal processing is to provide musicians with representations that let them modify natural and synthetic sounds in perceptually relevant ways. This desideratum explains the existence of a large variety of techniques for synthesis, often supported by associated analysis methods. In line with this goal, *granular synthesis* applies the concept of *sound atoms* or *grains*. This representation has the advantage of a suggesting a wide range of manipulations with very expressive and creative effects.

The granular representation originated in pioneering studies by Gabor (1946, 1947) who, drawing from quantum mechanics, introduced the notion of *sound quanta*. In his own words:

> *A new method of analyzing signals is presented in which time and frequency play symmetrical parts, and which contains time analysis and frequency analysis as special cases. It is shown that the information conveyed by a frequency band in a given time interval can be analyzed in various ways into the same number of elementary quanta of information.* (Gabor 1946).

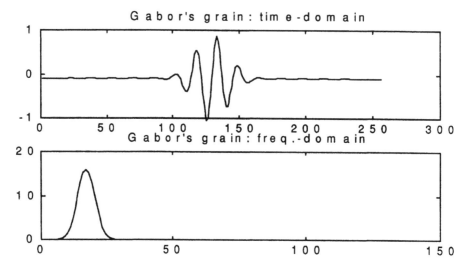

Figure 1. Gabor wavelet and spectrum.

Gabor's representation consisted of sinusoids windowed by a Gaussian enve-lope. The frequency of the sine wave controls the center frequency of the grain, whereas the width of the Gaussian envelope determines its duration and is, as well, inversely proportional to the frequency bandwidth of the grain. The choice of the envelope is connected to the property that with this envelope the resulting signal has a minimum area in the time-frequency plane (according to the uncer-tainty principle) (Figure 1). These "elementary signals" are the analyzing signal in terms of which any signal can be decomposed, thus defining *logons* in the time frequency plane.

Gabor's grains are wave-packets distributed both in time and frequency. Any composite sound can be regarded as a superposition of elementary grains hav-ing different center frequencies and times of occurrence. The resulting signal representation in the time-frequency plane is a collection of logons, each with its own amplitude, as shown in Figure 2.

The logons are related, in Gabor's scheme, to psychoacoustical criteria. He described them as "quanta of hearing" defined according to the limits of discrim-ination in time and frequency of the human ear. Gabor's ideas have stimulated a large field of research on time-frequency representation of signals. These devel-opments, suggested by the limitations of classical concepts when time-varying signals are concerned, benefit also of the growing computational resources pro-vided by the technology, which have rendered feasible time-frequency analysis.

Recently Gabor grains have been proposed in the field of computer music for analysis, modification, and synthesis of novel sounds, resulting in many fruitful experiments by Xenakis (1971, 1992) and Roads (1978, 1991). Later Truax

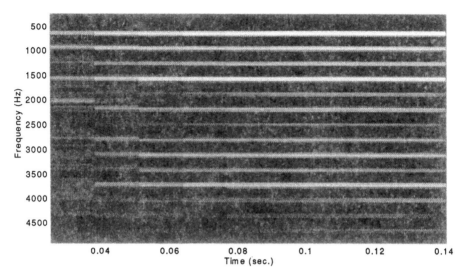

Figure 2. Gabor transform. The rectangular, constant intensity areas are Gabor's *logons* (Gabor 1946, 1947).

(1988), Jones and Parks (1988) and many others undertook this kind of work. Since the 1990s wide experimentation by many musicians has taken place.

It has sometimes been proposed that the grain is the shortest perceivable sonic event. In fact the time scale of the grain in the Gabor transform is entirely arbitrary. Psychoacoustic research has observed a scale relationship between the duration and frequency of perceived sound events, which has led to proposal such as the *constant Q transform* (Gambardella 1971) and the *wavelet transform* (Kronland-Martinet, Morlet, and Grossmann 1987).

In any case, in musical practice a wide range of grain durations have been employed, from less than 1 ms to more than 100 ms. In granular synthesis the basis grain waveform can be either an elementary sinusoid (as in the Gabor grains), a sampled waveform, or derived by model-based deconvolution.

From the viewpoint of signal processing, granular synthesis is a convolution technique and can be analyzed as such. Two basic forms of granular synthesis must be considered: *synchronous* or *asynchronous*. The former can be understood as a filtering technique: repeating sound grains at regular time intervals, then weighting the grains, is actually the result of the convolution of a periodic pulse train with the grain, used as the impulse response of a system. It can also be seen as a kind of subtractive synthesis since the grain or system response, is used to modify the frequency content of an initial wideband impulse.

Convolution also takes place in the asynchronous case where the pulses are not regularly emitted as an excitation function. In this case the filter interpretation does not give any insight into the analysis of the starting signal to be resynthesized or modified or the role of the grain itself, or even the final result of the elaboration. The analysis should be carried out with other means, taking into account psychoacoustical aspects.

In the synxhronous case, promising results can be obtained both for the resynthesis and modification of existing sounds. In the asynchronous case less regular but complex and interesting new sounds are produced. At the same time new aspects of existing sounds are detected and clearly displayed to the listener, which, hidden in the normal articulation of the sound structures, are revealed by granulation, time stretching, amplify, mainly from a perceptual point of view, some inner structures of the sounds and make them available to the listener (Roads 1991; Truax 1994).

As shown later, the waveshape of the grains has a certain degree of freedom, with the Gabor grains constituting only one example of a much larger class. In granular synthesis the basis grain waveform can be either sinousidal (such as a Gabor grain), sampled, or derived by deconvolution. It should be pointed out that for either artistic or practical purposes, the completeness of the representation is not necessarily a requirement. One can design grains to represent just a single sound. Then by varying the parameters of the representation one can generate a family of interesting sonic events.

In what follows we describe existing techniques for granular synthesis, showing the signal processing implications of these techniques. In particular, we focus on pitch-synchronous techniques on which our research is based, including methods of analysis, synthesis and parameter control, and finally implementation on signal-processing machines in terms of computational units programmed for optimal real-time synthesis.

Granular techniques

A variety of methods have been devised by both musicians and signal-processing engineers that can be grouped within the common paradigm of granular techniques, as pointed out in De Poli and Piccialli (1991). The grain waveform can be derived from natural sounds or from a description (the *model*) of a known sound-generating mechanism. Here we attempt a general classification of granular techniques:

- Grains à la Gabor, identified on the time-frequency plane as finite spots, perhaps related to psychoacoustic criteria, on the grounds of the "quantum of hearing" concept introduced by Gabor. These grains are chosen and controlled starting from musical ideas, perhaps sprayed graphically (Roads 1978, 1991). The resulting technique, called *asynchronous granular synthesis,* is fruitful when modeling sound effects such as *clouds* (explosions, water, wind, sparse rhythms, crackling textures). This approach could be formally described with a stochastic or also fractal evolution.

- Grains derived from the *short-time Fourier transform* (STFT). The grain in this case is the time-domain signal after proper windowing; synthesis in such case is carried on with the *overlap and add* (OLA) technique and is fruitful for *time-stretching* sounds (Crochiere 1980). When *pitch-synchronous* rectangular windows are used many advantages accrue: "deconvolution" on the basis of a model yields grains suitable for quality resynthesis and modification (De Poli and Piccialli 1991).

- Grains extracted from arbitrary natural sounds, which isolate musically interesting micro-textures. These micro-textures are combined as raw material to produce *sound clouds* (Roads 1991).

- Grains derived from models of instrumental or vocal sound production where formant regions in the spectrum can be isolated. An example is the *fonction d'onde formantique* or FOF method developed for voice synthesis (Rodet 1985), or derived by filter bank analysis as in Lienard (1987).

- Grains derived from time-scale techniques such as *wavelets* (Boyer and Kronland-Martinet 1989; Evangelista 1991, 1994). Certain time-scale approaches resemble perceptual features of human hearing.

This catalog of granular techniques is necessarily partial. Other techniques may also be interpreted within the framework of granular synthesis.

Extracting grains from natural sounds: pitch-synchronous techniques

We turn now to the technique known as *pitch-synchronous analysis and synthesis,* first developed at Bell Telephone Laboratories (Mathews, Miller, and David 1963; Pinson 1963). The starting idea is that, in the case of *periodic* or *pseudo-periodic* signals, pitch information enhances the spectrum analysis. Due to the periodicity, the analysis window can be pitch-synchronous and rectangular, therefore it does not add artifacts to the spectrum when evaluated at the pitch frequency and its multiples. In other words, in the periodic case the Fourier spectrum is a line spectrum (delta impulses coming from the Fourier series expansion). Windowing with any window, results in convolution in the frequency

domain, and therefore widens the lines of the source spectrum, spreading it to
the whole frequency axis.

If $s(t)$ is the signal and $w(t)$ the window, the resulting signal is:

$$y(t) = s(t)w(t),$$

and, in the frequency domain:

$$Y(\omega) = S(\omega) * W(\omega) = \int_{-\infty}^{\infty} S(\upsilon)W(\omega - \upsilon)\mathrm{d}\upsilon.$$

If the window is pitch-synchronous and rectangular, the unit value of the
central lobe picks the values of the line spectrum, while the zeros of the sidelobes, falling exactly on the lines of the spectrum clear the contribution from
other spectral lines. Therefore each line comes from the contribution of the
corresponding source spectrum line only (Figure 3). Figure 4 shows the non-
synchronous case: the contribution to the amplitude of the current spectral line
comes from all the harmonics. Figure 5 shows a simple case: a cosinusoidal
signal convolved with a non-pitch synchronous rectangular window, resulting in
spectral leakage, while with a synchronous window, a single spectral line would
result. In this case, if the cosinusoid has amplitude A:

$$Y(w) = \int_{-\infty}^{\infty} A\delta(\upsilon - \omega_0)W(\omega - \upsilon)\,\mathrm{d}\upsilon = W(\omega - \omega_0) \cdot A.$$

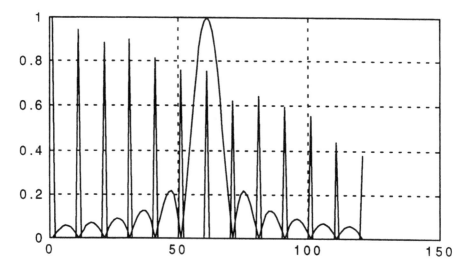

Figure 3. Convolution with a pitch-synchronous window.

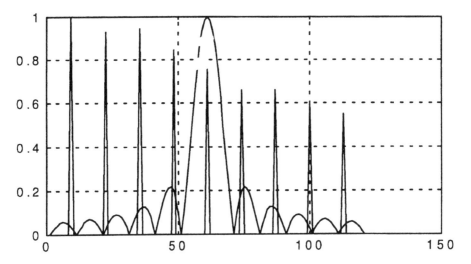

Figure 4. Convolution with a non-pitch-syncronous window.

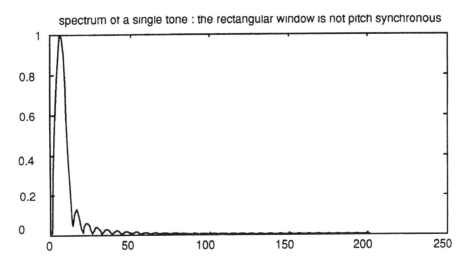

Figure 5. The spectral effect of imposing a square window on a single sinusoid.

In the case of a complex signal each spectral line spreads over the frequency axis, causing spectral leakage and distorting the original contributions. The pitch-synchronous analysis therefore lets one start from the "true" line spectra of the periodic sound, free of any artifacts. Later, we will benefit from this by applying deconvolution to obtain the impulse response. Therefore careful pitch detection is required at this stage.

Pitch extraction

Pitch-synchronous techniques for the extraction of grains apply periodicity detection in order to segment the signal into pitch periods. Many periodicity estimation algorithms have been proposed. These algorithms differ depending on whether one is interested in estimating the average period or the entire pitch envelope (local pitch). In most cases a previous coarse estimate of the pitch is needed. (This may not be a critical issue in offline analysis.) Coarse estimates can be implemented by finding peaks in the Fourier transform domain. This technique can be refined by looking for the particular harmonic spacing that traps most of the energy.

A time-domain technique for pitch extraction is to lowpass filter the signal and find the zero-crossing sequence. If the signal is properly filtered so that harmonics above the fundamental frequency are highly attenuated, then the interval between any two adjacent zero-crossing instants is a reasonable estimate of the actual pitch period. Clearly, in order to set the cutoff frequency of the lowpass filter, one has to have a coarse (within one-octave) estimate of the pitch itself. This may be achieved if the pitch-tracking algorithm relies upon the pitch estimate of the previous period. However, this technique has a tendency to fail on period intervals close to transients.

A different technique consists of computing the windowed autocorrelation of the signal and extracting its local maximum closest to lag zero (Rabiner 1977). The starting point is that a function of a periodic signal, the autocorrelation, is periodic and exhibits peaks at lags multiple of the period P. Picking the first peak in the autocorrelation usually detects the pitch. Since this measure is "local" and also time varying, proper windowing allows sharper peaks and less noisy detection. This method may produce reliable pitch estimates provided that thresholds on both the relative amplitude of the local maximum and the minimum signal energy level are properly set.

Connected to the autocorrelation analysis is the *average magnitude difference function* or AMDF (Ross 1973). This consists essentially in forming a difference signal obtained subtracting from the signal, delayed versions of the same at different delays; at each delay the absolute value of this difference signal is accumulated, thus forming the AMDF signal; it turns out that the latter exhibit nulls at multiple of the pitch period, thus allowing its detection and measure. Actually the AMDF signal is a measurement of the similarity between adjacent periods; in the limit if the signal is exactly periodic the AMDF signal for that value is null. Finally it turns out that the AMDF signal is in a relatively analytic relationship with the autocorrelation signal.

Other pitch-extraction techniques rely on the *short-time cepstrum* of the signal. The starting idea is processing in the domain of the logarithm of the spectrum

(Noll 1963; Oppenheim 1969). If the spectrum comes from a time domain convolution of an excitation and a source this convolution results in their product in the frequency domain. The logarithm results in the addition of two components. If these components occupy separate bands of the spectrum (namely the high part and the low part) they can be easily separated with a proper rectangular window. Going back through the inverse of logarithm (exponentation) and the IFFT we obtain a peaked signal showing clearly the period of the excitation. The pitch therefore is extracted by means of a peak tracking algorithm. The success of these methods depends on proper selection of the window width, which should be about three to four times the average period.

Pitch resolution can be improved by upsampling and interpolating the original signal (Medan and Yair, 1989). As shown by these authors, the low sampling rate sometimes used for speech synthesis (e.g., 8 kHz), causes errors that derive from an arbitrary sampling rate that is a noninteger multiple of the pitch period. In this case even a periodic continuous time signal becomes nonperiodic, and, when analyzed with a pitch-synchronous rectangular window, shows artifacts due to discontinuities at the ends of the interval. In the scheme proposed by Medan and Yair, resampling fits the sampling rate to an integer multiple of the pitch. In this procedure sophisticated filtering is performed for proper interpolation.

This method improves the pitch estimation, but it assumes perfect knowledge of the pitch period, which actually is not always well defined, and can be easily obscured in its precision by interference, amplitude and frequency modulation effects, or other sources of noise pollution.

Careful use of pitch estimation techniques allows one to reconstruct the pitch contour over time. This estimate can be be used to detect musical performance aspects like vibrato, or intonation (for vocal signals), thus enabling the reproduction of expressive features.

Period regularization

Real-world signals are never exactly periodic. Strong similarities among segments are found in voiced sounds and, generally, in pseudo-periodic signals, but superimposed on this periodicity we observe fluctuations, noise, small frequency variations and so on. These aperiodic components are due to different phenomena connected to the particular physical mechanism for the production of the specific class of sounds under analysis.

For example, in violin sounds, a noisy excitation due to the bow-string interaction is clearly superimposed to the periodic part of the sound. In the voice signal, during vocal sounds, the periodic part is due to the periodic glottal excitation, shaped by the resonances of the vocal tract; on this part, superimposed, we see noisy parts and non periodic components due to articulation of voice, transitions from vocal to consonants or from one vocal to the following; in this case we have also microvariations in the amplitude and pitch of the sound, which moreover confer naturalness and give expressivity to voice; intonation also represents a significant deviation from periodicity carrying also syntactical meaning. Another example of non periodicity is the beats between the piano strings allocated to the same piano key. Many other sources can contribute to these deviations from periodicity, which we can classify in three broad categories:

1. Noise due to the excitation.

2. Noise due to articulation between sounds.

3. Microvariations in amplitude and frequency of the signal.

Grains usually represent segments of the signal that extend beyond a single period. We can use them to synthesize relatively long sound segments, at least the steady-state part of the final sound. Thus noise, local transients, and fluctuations should be filtered out. On the grounds of these observations dealing with pseudo-stationary sounds we need to separate the two channels, the *quasi-harmonic part* from *transients and stochastic components.*

Another aspect remains to be taken into account: coexistence of these two channels can produce errors in the evaluation and extraction of pitch-synchronous segments, which carries severe errors in the identification of the channel features (Kroon and Atal 1991). Interpolation in the time domain and upsampling, as shown before for the purpose of proper pitch detection, can help to reduce the error in the identification and separation of the segments.

Various techniques for the separation of harmonic components of a signal from its stochastic parts have been developed during last years (Cavaliere, Ortosecco, and Piccialli 1992; Evangelista 1994; Chapter 3), leading to good results. Further analysis on a time scale basis should be carried out on noisy components, in order to characterize a large class of sounds, starting from the voice.

The proposed analysis carries out the following steps:

• Estimate the pitch period, if applicable.

• Separate pseudo-periodic components from inharmonic signals and noise.

• Set up a grid of addresses of the pitch-synchronous segments; this constitutes a matrix whose rows are the pitch-synchronous segments that characterize the dynamics of the quasi-stationary system.

Using this approach a pitch-synchronous representation of sounds can be derived, which accounts for both period-to-period similarities and slow changes (see Chapter 4). Single-frame Fourier analysis describes the evolution over time of each harmonic component. In the case of formant sounds, the resonant frequencies and bandwidths can be obtained at this level.

One method of separating aperiodic from periodic components is *period regularization,* which exploits period-to-period correlations. Separation may be achieved, for example, by averaging and subtracting adjacent periods of the signal. Clearly, replacing periods by their running averages yields a "more periodic" signal, while taking the difference between periods enhances the aperiodicity, if present. Thus, one can build a two-channel system, the output of one of the channels being a period-regularized version of the input, while the output of the other channel contains data on period-to-period fluctuations, transients, and noise. The aperiodic components correspond, for example, to articulation or voiced-unvoiced transitions in speech, or else, breath noise in some musical instruments. The procedure is equivalent to filtering with two comb filters, respectively, generated from lowpass and highpass filters. Chapter 4 presents a multiresolution version of this method, based on multiplexed wavelet transforms.

Computing the system impulse response: existing methods

After the extraction of pitch-synchronous segments, the next step is to compute the system impulse response. It is possible to estimate the impulse response for a general class of sounds, especially the voice, whose main feature is shape-invariant frequency response at different pitches. The purpose of this method is to model the original signal as the product of an excitation impulse plus a filter, which encompasses a relatively wide class of signals.

Many advantages accrue to this method as a tool for signal resynthesis. A very important benefit is that the impulse response methods grants phase continuity at any pitch in the resynthesis step. Another advantage is that perfect signal reconstruction is obtained when resynthesis is made at same pitch period; therefore this method is "exact". Last but not least, the implementation is not difficult.

In spite of the advantages in the synthesis phase, many simplifications must be made in order to reduce a complete sound event to this model. First of all, we must allow time-varying features both for the source and the excitation. A further simplification transfers all the information from the source to the filter, reducing the excitation impulse to a simple unit impulse. In practice, we can always convolve the excitation with the filter to obtain a filter response that incorporates spectral features of the source.

$$h_{\text{filter}} = h_{\text{impulse}} * h_{\text{filter}}.$$

If this model is properly identified in terms of its relevant parameters, more complex effects and dynamic features can be easily added (at least in the cases where this model is appropriate). Transformations are realized by varying the pitch of the excitation pulse train and its amplitude, or enveloping the amplitude of the signal. Dynamic variations can be implemented by interpolating between different grains to obtain spectral transitions.

Another problem to be solved occurs when the physical mechanism producing the sound is clearly made up of two phases: an *excitation phase,* and a *free oscillation phase.* This is the case of speech where the open glottis, closed glottis phases can be clearly identified and also seem to carry different informations (Parthasarathy and Tufts 1987; Miyoshi *et al.* 1987). The closed glottis phase shows a spectrum made up by the convolution of the glottal pulse and the cascaded filter, while the closed glottis is a sort of free system evolution dictated directly from the oral cavity and its resonances. By the way, this distinction can also be helpful when in complex system identification problems.

A *multipulse* excitation, as described in a moment, fills the gap with almost any secondary effect. It can also help from a numerical point of view, if we are able to detect an error or a deviation: it suffices, in this case, to encode the residual signal. Finally, a noisy channel can be added to simulate the effect of a continuous excitation, as in the case of violin, or also blown instruments. In all cases, fast amplitude envelopes can produce the typical rich spectra of the attack, or, in the case of voice, transitions to consonants.

In order to proceed to system identification and the computation of an overall system response, various strategies can be used. *Linear predictive coding* (LPC) is probably the most well-known technique that can be re-interpreted in the granular synthesis framework. In LPC the sound source is modeled as the output of a linear filter driven by a suitable excitation. The filter models the resonances that are found in the vocal tract or in the soundboard of many musical instruments. The filter coefficients may be estimated by minimizing the mean square error of the output versus the signal that we want to model. If the input excitation is modeled as white noise, the well-known normal equations may be established, which connect the output autocorrelation to the filter coefficients and may be solved for these. The filter may be an *all-pole* (AR), *all-zero* (MA) or both (ARMA).

The system attempts to predict the current signal sample, based on the knowledge of a number of past samples. Having obtained the resonant part (which may be time-varying), one may be interested in modeling the excitation in order to be able to manipulate the sound. In spite of the assumption of white noise input, when applied to voiced pseudo-periodic sounds, the resulting excitation (obtained by inverse filtering the sound source) is itself pseudo-periodic, and may be coarsely described as a train of short pulses. Schematically, if

$$x(t) = \sum_{k=0}^{\infty} a_k \delta(t - T_k),$$

is the input pulse train, with each pulse occurring at time t_k, and if $h(t)$ is the impulse response of the model filter, the resulting output is:

$$y(t) = \sum_{k=0}^{\infty} a_k h(t - T_k).$$

The latter may be interpreted as a superposition of grains, where the elementary grain is given by the impulse response $h(t)$. In this respect, LPC is a granular technique and as such can be used to extract grains (impulse response) from a segment of the signal. The LPC analysis can be carried synchronously with each pitch period, or only at proper time intervals, when significant spectral changes occur.

It can therefore provide the grains to be summed up at defined time intervals, with proper amplitudes, to reconstruct the signal. The pulses, as in all granular techniques, are not physically existent: they only define time intervals and amplitudes.

The traditional LPC technique, which has been applied primarily to vocal synthesis, suffers in general from a lack of naturalness in the resynthesis stage (El-Jaroudy and Makhoul 1991). Fortunately, this situation has been drastically improved by the use of a more complex excitation than simple impulses. One solution uses the *prediction residual,* obtained by inverse filtering the speech wave with the prediction filter. This residual can be decomposed into harmonics and then modified arbitrarily. In the simplest case, equal amplitudes and phases for all the harmonics generates a simple pulse excitation, while, on the opposite side, the original values can be left unmodified, thus reproducing the complete residual. Intermediate solutions can be evaluated both for naturalness and efficiency.

Another recent approach (Sukkar *et al.* 1989) decomposes the glottal excitation using a base set which, like a function to synthesize, is time-limited and pulse-type; using these ZINC functions, forming a complete orthogonal set built on the basis of the sinc function, the representation of time-limited pulses becomes more efficient then conventional Fourier representation.

More recently, in order to reduce error in the reconstruction, *multipulse excitation* has been successfully proposed (Singhal and Atal 1989). Compared to the ZINC solution, which requires many samples for the excitating pulse, multipulse excitation uses about 6–8 pulses, each of 10 ms. This method consists in the approximation of the error met with a single pulse, with another convolution, that is, using another pulse with proper amplitude and time position; repeating this procedure, one can find a limited number of pulses that approximates well the waveform to synthesize. The only limitation is that computing the pulse location and amplitudes requires a complex iterative optimization algorithm. Unlike the complex pulse excitation, which tries to reproduce the real-world excitation pulse, multipulse approach is based on a numerical approach.

In the case of granular synthesis a further degree of freedom can be allowed, however. The impulse responses do not necessarily have to derive from the responses of the LPC all-pole filter, but can be arbitrarily chosen grains.

In this case the multipulse approach can be also connected to a model of the producing mechanism: having different grains in different parts of the pitch period, is just a description of a time-varying system response. This is the case for some instruments, but mainly the voice. It has been shown (Parthasarathy and Tufts 1987) that, using two LPC models for the closed and open glottis phases of the pitch period, improves the acoustical results: translated in the granular synthesis paradigm this means using more than one grain for each pitch period, for improved quality.

Model-driven deconvolution

The grain extraction technique that we are going to present works best for sounds with a strong sense of pitch, such as instrumental tones. In the source excitation model the sound signal is approximated by the output of a, possibly time-varying, linear system whose input is a pulse train. The time scale of the variation of the system parameters is larger compared to the pitch period. In the simplest case where the impulse response is constant over time, the DFT of one pitch period is just a sampled version of the continuous-time Fourier transform of the system impulse response. In the time domain we have the convolution:

$$y(t) = h(t) * \sum_{k=-\infty}^{\infty} \delta(t - kP),$$

where P is the constant pitch period. Therefore, in the frequency domain we have the product:

$$Y(\omega) = H(\omega) \sum_{k=-\infty}^{\infty} \delta\left(\omega - \frac{2k\pi}{P}\right) = \sum_{k=-\infty}^{\infty} H\left(\frac{2k\pi}{P}\right)\delta\left(\omega - \frac{2k\pi}{P}\right),$$

which means sampling the frequency response $H(\omega)$ at intervals $\omega_k = 2k\pi(1/P)$.

From the knowledge of the samples of the original system frequency response, taken at multiples of the pitch frequency, we must recover the continuous frequency response, acting as a spectral envelope, to be used for reconstruction at arbitrary pitch periods. But, if we want to recover the continuous spectral envelope from known samples of it, we must interpolate these samples of the frequency response (Figure 6). Since any interpolation formula describes a moving average finite impulse response filter, we must filter the pulse sequence (in the frequency domain). This filtering operation is performed by convolution of the above pulse train having frequency transform $Y(\omega)$ and a proper interpolating function:

$$H'(\omega) = Y(\omega) * W(\omega).$$

Going back to the time domain, this interpolation results in multiplication of the time domain signal by the inverse Fourier transform of the interpolating function

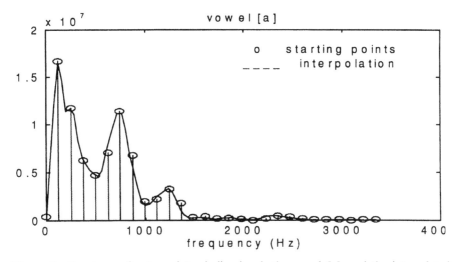

Figure 6. Spectrum of a (pseudo)periodic signal, the vowel [a], and the interpolated frequency response.

that we will call $w(t)$ and which is in fact a time window:

$$h'(t) = y(t)w(t).$$

Thus, by properly windowing the time-domain signal one can evaluate the system impulse response. It is clear therefore that the time-domain window embodies the features of the system and is related directly to the underlying model.

It must be pointed out that perfect reconstruction of the system impulse response is not possible, because aliasing in the time domain occurs. Equivalently, in the frequency domain it is not possible to recover the continuous frequency shape starting from samples of it taken at the pitch frequency. Here we must interchange the roles of time and frequency; in fact, in the usual case sampling in time, if sampling rate is not high enough, produces overlap of the responses in the frequency domain and makes it impossible to recover the original frequency response. Here instead we have frequency domain sampling and possible aliasing in the time domain. In the frequency domain we have sampling by multiplication with a periodic pulse train:

$$Y(\omega) = H(\omega) \cdot \sum_{k=-\infty}^{\infty} \delta\left(t - \frac{k}{T}\right),$$

while in the time domain we have convolution:

$$y(t) = h(t) * \sum_{k=-\infty}^{\infty} \delta(t - kT).$$

If the sampling interval in the frequency domain $1/T$ is low enough (less than the inverse of the duration of the impulse response), the frequency-domain convolution does not cause overlap. Therefore the rectangular window in time (equivalent to lowpass filtering in the usual case) allows one to isolate the frequency response. In Figure 7 the usual situation is shown, when aliasing (overlap) takes place. In the nonaliased case, multiplying by a rectangular window in the time domain is equivalent to convolving, in the frequency domain, the frequency samples with the sinc function coming from the Fourier transform of the window.

In the aliased case, the sampling theorems state that it is impossible to recover the frequency response from its samples, unless other information is available. Therefore, if we have more information on the system than that provided by sampling its frequency response at the pitch frequency, we may be able to evaluate the response. Usable information includes the resonances and bandwidths

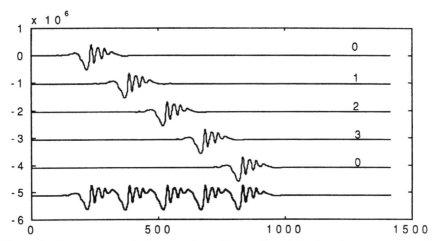

Figure 7. Time-domain aliasing: overlap of the replica of the impulse frequency at the pitch period.

of the underlying physical systems. In the case of vocal tones, for example, the formant structure can drive deconvolution. Each formant and its bandwidth can be associated with a pole in the transfer function, at least as a first approximation. Using error criteria an optimization procedure can lead to the determination of the poles or zero/pole structure of the system. System identification in this way leads to the time-domain impulse response to be used as basis grain for synthesis, as in the case of LPC.

If the sound does not have a formant structure, as in some instruments, the analysis can be done using the proper number of channels, instead than the few associated to known resonant frequencies, say the formants. In this case the grains are distributed over the entire frequency range, each having its own amplitude.

In some cases, a straightforward solution can be found if we consider, as mentioned before, that this deconvolution task equivalent to interpolation in the frequency domain or, more simply, in windowing the time domain signal. The latter has the advantage of easy real-time implementations. The problem in this case is to identify the proper window. In many situations a generic lowpass window works well (Lent 1989). Better results are obtained if the window is optimized on the basis of an error criterion, such as the error in the reconstruction of the sound for a relatively large number of periods. Eventually we derive a single grain which best approximates, by convolution with a pulse train, the sound to be reproduced, and which best characterizes the system. The number of periods to be analyzed depends on the degree of data compression desired.

We have found it efficient to use a simple parametric window shaped with a Gaussian curve, with only one parameter to optimize. The main advantage of this class of windows is that, unlike most windows, the transform of a Gaussian window does not exhibit an oscillatory tendency, but, on the contrary, decreases uniformly at both ends, thus showing only one lobe. The speed of decrease and therefore the equivalent width of the single lobe is controlled by the parameter. The lack of sidelobes in the transform prevents from the effects of large spectral leakage: in fact in the convolution due to windowing (see again Figure 4) the amplitude of any harmonic depends mostly on the corresponding harmonic of the source sound, while contributions from the contiguous harmonics may be neglected (for proper values of σ). In this circumstance, what happens is that, while interpolating between samples in the frequency domain, the interpolated curve crosses the starting samples at pitch periods or, at least, differs from them in a controllable amount.

Also with other windows, as a final stage, optimization of the grain in a discrete domain can improve the acoustical result; the error criterion is based on a spectral matching with the spectrum of a whole sound or speech segment.

As already pointed out, the grain in many musical instruments as well as in voice, is made up of two contributions: a source excitation and a quasi-stationary filter. The source excitation has a relatively simple and fast dynamic profile, while the latter exhibits slow variations when compared to the pitch period. In many cases, using techniques for inverse filtering it is possible to separate the individual constituents and in particular estimate parameters for the excitation; the total grain will be therefore determined by the convolution of the two different contributions, and will therefore allow more freedom in resynthesis or in modifications, which will result, in turn, in improved quality from a perceptual point of view. Thus convolution between grains may be useful to obtain more complex grains, embodying both steady state features and dynamical timbre changes.

With careful deconvolution the resulting grains are complete in the sense that they contain all information needed to reproduce the entire macrostructure. When they are used in conjunction with pitch and amplitude envelopes they may also include, in the case of spoken vowels, speaker-dependent features.

The microstructures (grains) so obtained are suitable to describe continuous sound from the point of view of timbre. At the same time, the musician can modify the parameters of the granular event in order to create expressive variations of the original sound.

Pitch-synchronous analysis–synthesis: an assessment

The pitch-synchronous analysis and synthesis model realizes the following hypotheses:

1. The signals under analysis are made of two distinct contributions: a *deterministic part* and a *stochastic part,* sometimes overlapping each other.

2. The deterministic component is assumed to be of the class "harmonic". This means that when the pitch period is determined, it is possible to extract pitch-synchronous segments. Both analysis and synthesis of this part of the signal is independent from the phase.

3. Phase. The model of the harmonic channel uses a source/excitation model; the input to the filter is a pulse train whose amplitude and pitch are modulated in time.

4. The stochastic part can be modeled both in the time domain and the frequency domain.

Under the assumptions made before, using properly selected and deconvolved grains enables one to recover the pseudo-harmonic part of the signal. An important feature is that while one grain may carry information on a long sound segment (also its expressive or intonation features), variations in dynamics and articulation are easily added with the use of multiple responses, or grains. In such case waveform interpolation uses a raised cosine weighting function or other proper nonlinear function. Interpolation breakpoints can be automatically detected on the base of spectrum distance criterion (see Serra, Rubine, and Dannenberg 1990; Horner *et al.* 1993). The spectral distance, or number of breakpoints to be used for synthesis, depends both on desired sound quality and requested coding gain. The most important criteria are derived from listening tests.

   In the resynthesis and modification, pitch and amplitude contours drive the synthesis, controlling the pulse amplitude and pitch. An advantage against other granular techniques is that phase problems never arise because the grains are not just overlapped one to the other, but a convolution takes place, even if in a very simple and efficient way. Pitch shifting of course most be done using extracted and selected grains, because for good acoustical results a grain extracted at a definite pitch can be used to synthesize a defined range of pitches, very close to the one at which the analyzed sound was produced.

   As regards the second channel of the sound, the nonperiodic or noisy part, see Chapter 3. Various techniques have been proposed for its analysis and synthesis, such as the impulse responses obtained by source sound granulation and also fractal waveforms. As an example, this approach has been successfully used in the synthesis of spoken fricatives. Source grains, properly selected and convolved with a Poisson pulse sequence, reproduce the original sound without perceptual distortion.

   The pulse train must satisfy the condition of no correlation in time between one pulse and the next. A straightforward choice, but not unique, is a Poisson pulse sequence. In this way the frequency spectrum is flat enough to avoid the perception of any pitch, even if we use a single grain. As far as regards the starting grain, which can be unique or also modified over time for improved spectral dynamics, it can be simply selected among sections of the starting signal for its similarity, in the frequency domain, with the whole sound to be synthesized. From a perceptual point of view, the results are almost indistinguishable from the original. In such a case, moreover, shortening or lengthening the source signal is straightforward, with the further advantage of providing a single mechanism both for vowel and consonant synthesis.

Finally, microvariations of the control parameters for amplitude and frequency are very relevant from a perceptual point of view. These are naturally coupled to pseudoperiodicity. These microvariations must be included in the synthesis model in order to enhance naturalness of the sounds. Stochastic or fractal techniques may be most efficient for modeling these fluctuations (Vettori 1995).

Resynthesis and modifications

Resynthesis is realized in two parallel paths. The signals generated by each path are added together to make up the final output signal. The first path is harmonic while the second is stochastic. The harmonic part is synthesized by convolution of a pulse train with the pulse sequences. The convolution is efficient since it can be reduced to a few adds, as shown later. Nonlinear interpolation between waveforms allows the transition from one grain to next. A database of grains supplies the raw material for synthesis. Using this approach a set of variations can be made, such as:

- Close reconstruction of the source signal.
- Reconstruction with altered pitches or introducing granularities (overlapping or convolution).
- Lengthening or shortening sounds without any modifications in its spectral content.
- Time-varying modifications of sounds using interpolation.
- Sub-band processing, allowing manipulations of the spectral content of the single grain and reconstruction of the same.
- *Cross-synthesis* using the grain as an impulse response allows one to modify a signal using the spectral content of another sound (see also Chapter 12).
- Synthesis of grains made up of more than one grain, with different features, by simple convolutions.

The complete algorithm

Before diving into the details, we present the overall flow of operations performed for our pitch-synchronous analysis and synthesis. Figure 8 presents the analysis/resynthesis algorithm without modifications, while Figure 9 shows the procedure used for resynthesis with transformation.

Figures 10 to 15 present some results of analysis-resynthesis operations for vocal sounds. Figure 10 displays a signal segment from the spoken vowel [a]: a pitch of 136 Hz was detected by pitch analysis. On this segment a pitch-synchronous Gaussian shaped window was applied on three periods of the segment, resulting in the signal of Figure 11. Figure 12 shows the frequency transform of the starting sound (taken over about 20 periods and using a generic Hanning window), and Figure 13 shows the frequency transform of the windowed signal of Figure 11. By inspection the overall frequency shape has been preserved, thus avoiding excessive spectral leakage and distortion. Numerical measurements confirm this assertion. Finally, the inverse transform provides the requested impulse response: as expected the response duration exceeds the pitch period but converges rapidly to zero. This frequency response is the grain to be used for resynthesis or modifications. In Figure 15 another grain is shown, resulting from a similar deconvolution, carried on a sound segment from vowel [i].

Implementation of single-pulse convolution

Single-pulse convolution takes advantage of the fact that one of the two sequences to be convolved—the excitation pulse—is different from zero only at pitch periods. Therefore very few multiplies need be carried out, resulting in a drastically reduced number of operations per output sample. If for example n_p is the number of samples in a pitch period and n_r is the length in samples of the pulse response to be convolved, the number of multiplies and adds is the minimum integer plus than or equal to n_p/n_r. In the case of vocal synthesis, at a pitch of $100 \rightarrow 200$ Hz and a sampling rate of 44.1 kHz, for a typical impulse response measured in tenths of a microsecond, say 100 μs, we have:

$$n_p = 400, \quad n_r = 4k(n_p/n_r) = 10.$$

Therefore ten multiplies and adds are required, instead than the 4 K required for a regular convolution with a 4 K impulse response. If, moreover, the convolution is made with a constant amplitude (unitary) pulse sequence, it requires only adds, while amplitude modulation is applied at the output of the convolution. As an alternative, amplitude modulation can be applied to the pulse sequence. In such

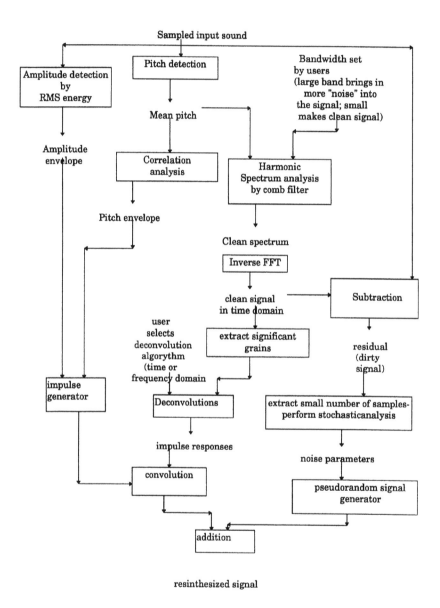

Figure 8. The analysis/resynthesis algorithm.

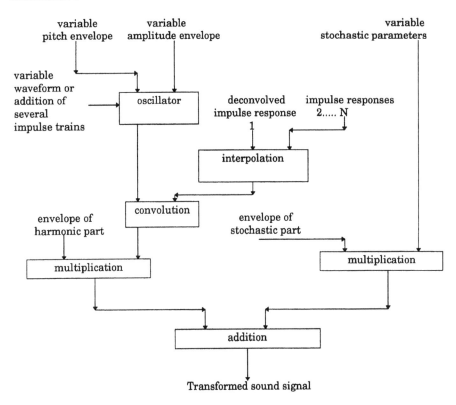

Figure 9. Resynthesis with transformation.

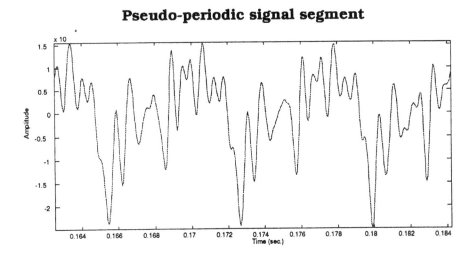

Figure 10. Pseudo-periodic signal segment.

Windowed signal segment

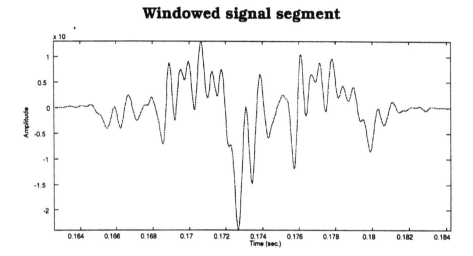

Figure 11. Windowed signal segment.

Magnitude FT of signal segment

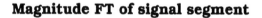
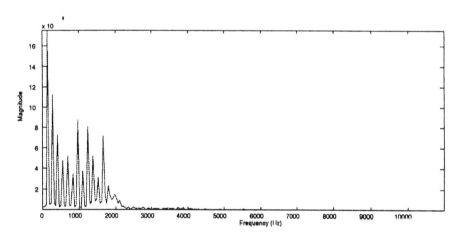

Figure 12. Magnitude Fourier transform of signal segment.

a case we can also take advantage of a reduced rate for the production of the amplitude modulation, which can be lowered down to the pitch of the excitation. Amplitude samples are needed only at pitch intervals.

The two models for amplitude modulation are not exactly equivalent. In case (a) fewer amplitude samples are used (and required), which are then interpolated

Magnitude FT of windowed signal segment

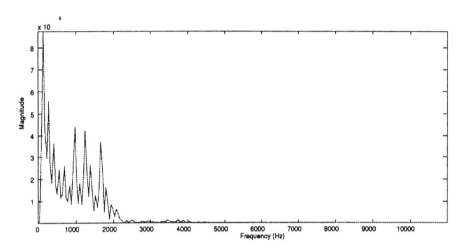

Figure 13. Magnitude Fourier transform of windowed signal segment.

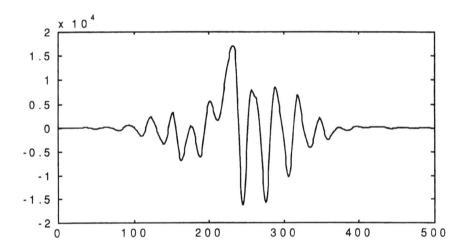

Figure 14. Extracted grain for the vowel [a].

by the convolution with the system pulse response. In case (b), interpolation between amplitude samples uses linear or higher order interpolation, independent from the above response. In any case, in smooth amplitude transitions the two mechanisms are quite equivalent. If the proper implementation is chosen for the convolution, multiple convolutions can be obtained just using the required number of simple convolutions.

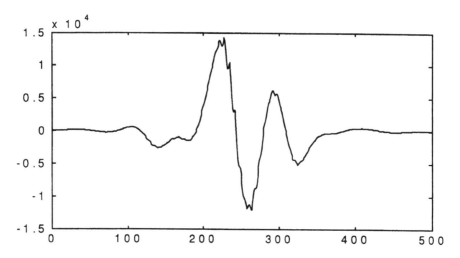

Figure 15. Extracted grain for the vowel [i].

As regards the simple convolution case, the time-domain situation is depicted in Figure 7. Here the convolution with a constant amplitude unit pulse sequence is simply the accumulation of independent lines, each containing a single replica of the impulse response. The implementation of the reduced convolution algorithms can be broken into several computational blocks, which can be implemented either in software or in a dedicated integrated circuit.

The pitch sequence is produced using a timer (mostly likely a ramp generator, with a type of overflow detection). Profiting from the overflow features of integer binary adders, the pitch sequence is periodic. Modulation of the slope of the ramp produces a variable pitch for the pulse sequence.

The pulse sequence triggers a single-shot oscillator, clearing the phase with which it is read out of a table. Reading from this table is done by addressing the table with the running phase and using proper overflow protect on the phase to read it only once.

This mechanism produces a number of nonoverlapping lines (as in Figure 7, lines 0–4–8...). If we produce also lines 1–5–9..., 2–6–10... and 3–7–11, adding these lines together we obtain the required convolution. The four time-domain signals thus far produced must have each a pitch period equal to four times the required pitch period and must also be in the proper phase relationship. They must be delayed by an amount of time equal to the final pitch period. Because of the time-domain correlation the mechanism to generate the various ramps must be unique.

A complete block diagram is shown in Figure 16. Here the base step of the time counter is one-fourth of the step pertaining to the desired pitch, while

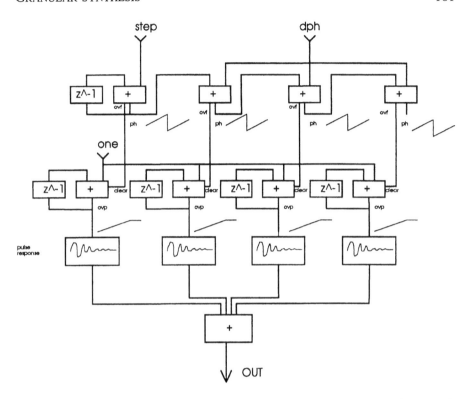

Figure 16. Patch for the resynthesis of pitch-synchronous granular sounds for a maximum overlap of four responses per period. From a single phase ramp four synchronous phase ramps are obtained. The *step* variable is 4 times the pitch period in sample number while *dph* is the constant offset 1/4. The overflows of these ramps clear (and thus synchronize) four ramps; one is the value needed to scan the whole grain table, sample after sample; also the ramps have an overflow protect feature, so that they begin scanning the grain table only when restarted by the clear signal.

the phase offset added at each stage is one-fourth of a complete 2π angle. This produces the proper time-domain correlation of the four lines to be accumulated.

A hardware realization requires a generator to produce efficiently the unit pulse sequences, as in Figure 17. This generator should take very few cycles of a microprogrammed architecture, or better a "clear on condition" instruction following the phase production, in order to realize a periodic restart of a single-shot oscillator (Figure 16). Finally also the generation of phase-correlated pulse sequences can be easily organized producing only one ramp and delaying it while adding a constant (Figure 16).

A VLSI circuit architecture could efficiently realize such convolutions with a minimum effort alongside a general-purpose processor or free-running oscilla-

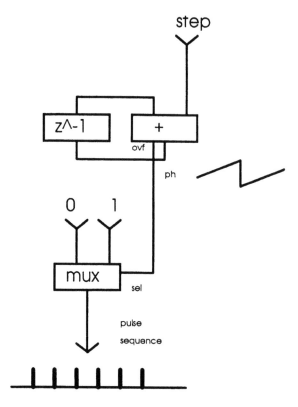

Figure 17. Patch for a simple pulse train generator. The *step* variable is the integer increment corresponding to the requested pitch period. The first ramp is used only to produce the *ovf* signal used to switch a multiplexer, which provides the non null pulse value at the requested frequency.

tors. Another possible implementation uses delay lines and a dual slope ramp generator, as in Figure 18. The MSBit out of the adder controls the selection of two different slopes: one is used to read all the samples of the pulse response, the other is used to realize a variable dead time. The resulting oscillator is periodic; if we delay this oscillator by one pitch period, a number of times, by proper correlation between delays and dead times, we can obtain, adding such independent lines, the required convolution.

If we then consider that delay lines are just tables where we write and read with the same address ramp, but with different offset, we realize that also in this case stored tables are needed, together with the properly offset ramps to read from it.

In order to test the algorithm, verify its quality, and experiment with real-time control issues, we have implemented it on the MARS workstation by IRIS.

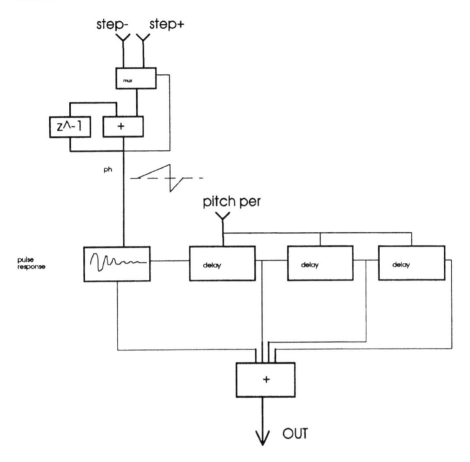

Figure 18. Patch for resynthesis using delays. The upper unit is a two slope ramp: the different slopes are chosen by the sign of the ramp. The first part of the ramp, with a constant increment value, reads, sample by sample, half a table where the grain is stored. The negative part, with an increment related to the desired pitch period, reads from the second part of the same table where zeros are written, thus providing the appropriate delay before the start of next grain. The resulting grain is then delayed for a pitch period, using random-access-memory read/write. Finally the outputs are added with the appropriate overlap factor. The *step* and *pitch per* variables are coupled and are stored in tables.

The computation "patch" was created using the EDIT20 program, a powerful patching program by IRIS researchers, based on a graphical icon approach, together with a large set of tools for editing parameters and waveforms. Finally the ORCHESTRA program in the same workstation was used to experiment with musical applications of the technique, in particular, sung vocal tones.

References

Ackroyd, M. 1970. "Instantaneous and time-varying spectra—an introduction." *The Radio and Electronic Engineer* 39(3): 145–151.

Ackroyd, M. 1973. "Time-dependent spectra: the unified approach." In J. Griffith, P. Stocklin, and C. Van Schooneveld, eds. *Signal Processing 1973*. New York: Academic Press.

Bastiaans, M. 1980. "Gabor's expansion of a signal into Gaussian elementary signals." *Proceedings of the IEEE* 68(4): 538–539.

Bastiaans, M. 1985. "Implementation of the digital phase vocoder using the fast Fourier transform." *IEEE Trans. Acoust. Speech Signal Process.* ASSP-33; 868–873.

Boyer, F. and R.Kronland-Martinet. 1989. "Granular resynthesis and transformation of sounds through wavelet transform analysis." In *Proceedings of the 1989 International Computer Music Conference*. San Francisco: Computer Music Association, pp. 51–54.

Cavaliere, S., G. Di Giugno, and E. Guarino. 1992. "Mars: the X20 device and SM1000 board." *Proceedings of the 1992 International Computer Music Conference*. San Francisco: International Computer Music Association, pp 348–351.

Cavaliere, S., I. Ortosecco, and A. Piccialli. 1992. "Modifications of natural sounds using a pitch-synchronous approach." In *Atti dell' International Workshop on Models and Representations of Musical Sounds*. Naples: University of Naples, pp. 5–9.

Cavaliere, S., I. Ortosecco, and A. Piccialli. 1993. "Analysis, synthesis and modifications of pseudo-periodic sound signals by means of pitch-synchronous techniques." In *Atti del X Colloquio di Informatica Musicale*. Milano, pp. 194–201.

Cheng, J. and D. O'Shaughnessy. 1989. "Automatic and reliable estimation of glottal closure instant and period." *IEEE Trans. Acoust. Speech Signal Process.* ASSP-37(12): 1805–1815.

Crochiere, R. 1980. "A weighted overlap-add method of short-time Fourier analysis/synthesis." *IEEE Trans. Acoust. Speech Signal Process.* ASSP-28: 99–102.

d'Alessandro, C. 1990. "Time-frequency speech transformation based on an elementary waveform representation." *Speech Communication* 9: 419–431.

De Mori, R. and M. Omologo. 1993. "Normalized correlation features for speech analysis and pitch extraction." In M. Cooke, S. Beet and M. Crawford, eds. *Visual Representations of Speech Signals*. New York: Wiley, pp.299–306.

De Poli, G. and A. Piccialli. 1991. "Pitch-synchronous granular synthesis." In G. De Poli, A. Piccialli, and C. Roads, eds. 1991. *Representations of Musical Signals*. Cambridge, Massachusetts: The MIT Press, pp. 391–412.

El-Jaroudi, A. and J.Makhoul. 1991. "Discrete all-pole modeling." *IEEE Trans. Signal Process.* 39(2): 411–423.

Evangelista, G. 1991. "Wavelet transforms we can play." In G. De Poli, A. Piccialli, and C. Roads, eds. *Representations of Musical Signals*. Cambridge, Massachusetts: The MIT Press, pp. 119–136.

Evangelista, G. 1994. "Comb and wavelet transforms and their application to signal processing." *IEEE Trans. Signal Process.* 42(2): 292–303.

Gabor, D. 1946. "Theory of communication." *Journal of the IEE* 93 (III): 429–457.

Gabor, D. 1947. "Acoustical quanta and the theory of hearing." *Nature* 4044: 591–594.

Gambardella, G. 1971. "A contribution to the theory of short-time spectral analysis with non uniform bandwidth filters."*IEEE Trans. Circuit Theory* 18: 455–460.

Helstrom, C. 1966. "An expansion of a signal in Gaussian elementary signals." *IEEE Trans. Inf. Theory* IT-12: 81–82.

Hermes, D. 1993. "Pitch analysis." In M. Cooke, S. Beet and M. Crawford, eds. *Visual Representations of Speech Signals*. New York: Wiley, pp. 3–26.

Hess, W. 1983. *Pitch Determination of Speech Signals*. Berlin: Springer-Verlag.

Horner, A., J. Beauchamp, and L. Haken. 1993. "Methods for multiple wavetable synthesis of musical instrument tones." *Journal of the Audio Engineering Society* 41(5): 336–354.

Janssen, A. 1984. "Gabor representation and wigner distribution of signals." In *Proceedings of the ICASSP* 41B.2.1–41B.2.4. New York: IEEE Press.

Jones, D. and T. Parks. 1988. "Generation and combination of grains for music synthesis." *Computer Music Journal* 12(2): 27–34.

Kronland-Martinet, R., R.J. Morlet, and A. Grossmann. 1987. "Analysis of sound pattern through the wavelet transform." *International Journal of Pattern Recognition and Artificial Intelligence* 1(2): 97–126.

Kroon, P. and B. Atal. 1991. "On the use of pitch predictor with high temporal resolution." *IEEE Trans. Signal Process.* 39(3): 733–735.

Krubsack, D. and R.Niederjohn. 1991. "An autocorrelation pitch detector and voicing decision with confidence measures developed for noise-corrupted speech." *IEEE Trans. Signal Process.* 39(2): 319–329.

Lent, K. 1989. "An efficient method for pitch shifting digitally sampled sounds." *Computer Music Journal* 13(4): 65–71.

Lienard, J. 1987. "Speech analysis and reconstruction using short-time, elementary waveforms." In *Proceedings of the ICASSP 1987.* New York: IEEE Press, pp. 948–951.

Mathews, M., J. Miller, and E.E. David Jr. 1963. "Pitch-synchronous analysis of voiced sounds." *Journal of the Acoustical Society of America* 35: 1264–1273.

McAulay, M. and T.F. Quatieri. 1986. "Speech analysis-synthesis based on a sinusoidal representation." *IEEE Trans. Acoust. Speech Signal Process.* ASSP-34(3): 744–754.

McAulay, R. and T.F. Quatieri. 1990. "Pitch estimation and voicing detection based on a Sinusoidal Model." In *Proceedings of the IEEE ICASSP.* New York: IEEE Press, pp. 249–252.

Medan, Y. and E. Yair. 1989. "Pitch-synchronous spectral analysis scheme for voiced speech." *IEEE Trans. Acoust. Speech Signal Process.* ASSP-37(9): 1321–1328.

Miyoshi, M., K. Yamato, R. Mizoguchi, M. Yanagida, and O. Kakusho. 1987. "Analysis of speech signals of short pitch period by a sample-selective linear prediction." *IEEE Trans. Acoust. Speech Signal Process.* ASSP-35(9): 1233–1240.

Montgomery, L. and I.S. Reed. 1967. "A generalization of the Gabor-Helstrom transform." *IEEE Trans. Inf. Theory* IT-13: 314–315.

Nathan, K., Y.T. Lee, and H.F. Silverman. 1991. "A Time varying analysis method for rapid transitions in speech." *IEEE Trans. Signal Process.* 39(4): 815–824.

Nehorai, A. and D. Starer. 1990. "Adaptive pole estimation." *IEEE Trans. Acoust. Speech Signal Process.* ASSP-38 (5): 825–838.

Nehorai, A. and B. Porat. 1986. "Adaptive comb filtering for harmonic signal enhancement." *IEEE Trans. Acoust. Speech Signal Processing* ASSP-34(5): 1124–1138.

Noll, A. 1967. "Cepstrum pitch determination." *Journal of the Acoustical Society of America* 41: 293–309.

Oppenheim, A. 1969. "Speech analysis-synthesis system based on homomorphic filtering." *Journal of the Acoustical Society of America* 45: 458–465.

Parthasarathy, S. and D. Tufts. 1987. "Excitation-synchronous modeling of voiced speech." *IEEE Trans. Acoust. Speech Signal Process.* ASSP-35(9): 1241–1249.

Picinbono, B. and W. Martin. 1983. "Reprèsentation des signaux par amplitude et phase instantanées." *Annales des Telecommunications* 38(5–6).

Pinson, E. 1963. "Pitch-synchronous time-domain estimation of formant frequencies and bandwidths."*Journal of the Acoustical Society of America* 35: 1264–1273.

Portnoff, M. 1976. "On the sliding-window representation in digital signal processing." *IEEE Trans. Acoust. Speech Signal Process.* ASSP-24: 243–246.

Quatieri, T., R.B. Dunn, and T.E. Hanna. 1993. "Time-scale modification of complex acoustic signals." In *Proc. Int. Conf. Acoustics, Speech, and Signal Processing.* New York: IEEE, pp. 1213–1216.

Quatieri, T. and R.J. McAulay. 1986. "Speech transformations based on a sinusoidal representation." *IEEE Trans. Acoust. Speech Signal Process.* ASSP-34(6): 1449–1464.

Quatieri, T. and R.J. McAuley. 1992. "Shape invariant time-scale and pitch modification of speech." *IEEE Trans. Signal Process.* 40(3): 497–510.

Rabiner, L. 1977. "On the use of autocorrelation analysis for pitch detection." *IEEE Trans. Acoust. Speech Signal Process.* ASSP-25: 24–33.

Rihaczek, A., 1968. "Signal energy distribution in time and frequency." *IEEE Trans. Inf. Theory* IT-14(3): 369–374.

Roads, C. 1978. "Automated granular synthesis of sound." *Computer Music Journal* 2(2): 61–62. Reprinted in C. Roads and J. Strawn, eds. 1985. *Foundation of Computer Music.* Cambridge, Massachusetts: The MIT Press, pp. 145–159.

Roads, C. 1991. "Asynchronous granular synthesis." In G. De Poli, A. Piccialli, and C. Roads, eds. *Representations of Musical Signals.* Cambridge, Massachusetts: The MIT Press, pp. 143–185.

Rodet, X. 1985. "Time-domain formant-wave-function synthesis." *Computer Music Journal* 8(3): 9–14.

Serra, M., D. Rubine, and R. Dannenberg. 1990. "Analysis and synthesis of tones by spectral interpolation." *Journal of the Audio Engineering Society* 38(3): 111–128.

Singhal, S. and B. Atal. 1989. "Amplitude optimization and pitch prediction in multipulse coders." *IEEE Trans. Acoust. Speech Signal Process.* ASSP-37(3): 317–327.

Sukkar, R., J. Lo Cicero, and J. Picone. 1989. "Decomposition of the LPC excitation using the ZINC basis function." *IEEE Trans. Acoust. Speech Signal Process.* ASSP-37(9): 1329–1341.

Truax, B. 1988. "Real-time granular synthesis with a digital signal processor." *Computer Music Journal* 12(2): 14–26.

Truax, B. 1994. "Discovering inner complexity: time shifting and transposition with a real time granulation technique." *Computer Music Journal* 18(2): 38–48.

Tsopanoglu, A., J. Mourjopoulos, and G. Kokkinakis. 1993. "Speech representation and analysis by the use of instantaneous frequency." In M. Cooke, S. Beet and M. Crawford, eds. *Visual Representations of Speech Signals.* New York: Wiley, pp. 341–346.

Vettori, P. 1995. "Fractional ARIMA modeling of microvariations in additive synthesis." In *Proccedings of XI Congresso Informatica Musicale.* Bologna: AIMI, pp. 81–84.

Ville, J. 1948. "Theorie et applications de la notion de signal analytique." *Cable et Transmission* 2: 61–74.

Xenakis, I. 1971. *Formalized Music.* Bloomington: Indiana University Press.

Xenakis, I. 1992. *Formalized Music.* Revised edition. New York: Pendragon Press.

6

Musical signal analysis with chaos

Angelo Bernardi, Gian-Paolo Bugna, and Giovanni De Poli

Certain characteristics of musical signals are not fully accounted for by the classical methods of time-frequency analysis. In the signals produced by acoustic instruments, for instance, the nonlinear dynamics of the exciter often causes turbulence during the evolution of the sound, or it may produce nonperiodic noises (such as multiphonics). This chapter investigates the possibility of using analysis methods based on chaos theory to study the relevant properties both of the signal and of its production mechanisms.

For a long time science purposely disregarded nonlinear phenomena or restricted their study to the most superficial and intuitive facets. The main cause of this attitude was a lack of analysis methods; as a matter of fact, nonlinear systems generally do not possess closed-form analytic solutions; consequently any study performed with classical techniques turns out to be impossible. Only of late have firm bases have been laid for the foundation of a new experimental science that studies and analyzes deterministic nonlinear systems, which was given the name of *chaos theory*. Beneath such an exotic name are profound reasons for the nonintuitive behavior of these complicated systems. In the past they were often described in terms of simple but incorrect extrapolations drawn from the theory of linear systems.

A chaotic nonlinear system can originate steady-state "irregular" but not divergent motions. The concept of "heavy dependence on the initial conditions" is maybe the most unforeseen finding of chaos theory. Previously, an apparent basic unpredictability within a deterministic system had been always ascribed to the effect of a variety of external random interferences. Among the results of chaos theory is the prediction that a nonlinear system, within a three-dimensional phase space, can have a Fourier spectrum spreading over the entire frequency range, while classical physics thought this a possible outcome only for systems with infinite degrees of freedom. Chaos physics proved deterministic equations were better suited to describing certain natural phenomena than what classical physics had established: the essential factor to be taken into account is the nonlinearity.

In dealing with the study of chaos, researchers have in recent years developed new instruments of analysis, more specific than those usually employed in the study of linear systems (that is, spectral analysis, correlation functions, and so on). *Fractal geometry,* in particular, turned out to be especially suitable for describing the typical features of chaos. Closely tied to that are the concepts of *self-similarity* and of *power scaling,* which showed at once their great correspondence to music.

Indeed, Voss and Clarke (1975, 1978) showed that the audio power and frequency fluctuations in common kinds of music have spectral densities that vary as $1/f$. This behavior implies a degree of correlation between these fluctuating quantities over all the times for which the spectral density is $1/f$. According to these scientists, music seems to possess the same blend of randomness and of predictability found in many other natural phenomena. Their results cleared the way for the use of fractal signals in the generation of melodies and of other musical features, even if an inadequate understanding of the theory often ended in applications limited to superficial simulations. In any case, concepts such as self-similarity and $1/f$ noise have become popular among many musicians.

Musical acoustics and sound synthesis by physical models have both showed the importance of nonlinearity in the production of sounds. Even though in the last century Helmholtz (1954) did recognize the fundamentally nonlinear behavior of self-sustaining musical instruments such as winds and strings, in musical acoustics (as well as in other fields of science) the basic role of nonlinearities has been misjudged for a long time. For practical reasons, studies focused on the linear part of the instruments (the resonator), and leading to the definition of measurements such as the input impedance or the resonance curve. The examination of phenomena like multiphonic sounds and wolf-notes was begun only recently, using tools derived from chaos physics. Biperiodic and chaotic steady states were discovered, which until then, had not been well understood. With the steady increase in computing power, it has become possible to build models of musical instruments in which the nonlinearities are taken into account. Nonlinearity and chaos are often linked; in the synthesis by physical models the concepts originated by chaos theory find many interesting applications.

After a brief review of the basic concepts of chaos theory, we introduce those analysis methods (chosen amongst many found in the literature) which have proven the most adequate in dealing with the study of musical signals and of the sound-generating physical systems. In particular, we will present a fractal model of sound signals, as well as analysis techniques of the local fractal dimension. Afterwards we introduce the reconstructed phase space, adopted here as the method to analyze the production mechanism of the steady-state portion of a sound.

The musical signal as a fractal (chaotic) signal

Time-frequency representations are the most commonly used signal models (Chapter 1). This belongs to a long tradition, which dates back to the very origins of musical notation. Its most recent and well developed versions are the *Fourier transform* (Chapters 2 and 3) and the *wavelet transform* (Chapter 4). The *source-filter* model has been widely used under the name of *subtractive synthesis*. Most notably, this latter model is one of the most frequently employed in speech coding, in which case it is called *linear predictive coding parametrization*. Recently, the signal processing community is exploring fractal (or chaotic) signal models. Chaotic signals are indeed interesting and important in experimental physics because of the wide range of actual processes that apparently give rise to chaotic behaviors. In particular, the physical systems interested by these signals are characterized by a strong nonlinearity and by a fractal dynamic nature. From the signal processing point of view, the detection, the analysis, and the characterization of such signals all present significant challenges, yet they offer an opportunity to explore and to develop completely new classes of signal processing algorithms.

Experimental evidence exists of musical signals characterized by a fractal nature: a first example is the sound produced by a nonlinear dynamics exciter with a chaotic behavior (Keefe and Laden 1991). Spectral density measurements of pitch variations in diverse types of music show a common link to the fractal world. Moreover, some kinds of computer-aided musical composition are coupled to the self-similarity property of an event-sequence generator. All the above theoretical considerations, together with experimental evidence, lead us to the use of fractals as the mathematical model for a study of musical signals.

The waveform of a musical signal can be studied by means of new analysis techniques based on the concepts of fractal geometry. The main purposes of this approach are to determine whether the structure of a musical signal can be regarded as self-similar and to quantify its degree of *fractal fluctuation*. The most important idea is the fractal dimension of a sound signal, because of its ability to quantify the fragmentation of the graph. If the starting hypothesis of dealing with a fractal signal is sufficiently true, then it becomes possible to extract the most significant properties of the musical signal. Moreover, with this new analysis method based on fractal geometry, we can obtain useful information for the characterization of a sound even if the signals is not closely related to a fractal.

Fractal signal models and local fractal dimension

To understand how fractal geometry and chaotic signals are related to musical signals, we can take a look at the basic concepts of exact self-similarity and of statistical self-similarity. The Von Koch curve is an example of exact self-similarity. Figure 1 illustrates a recursive procedure for building it up: a

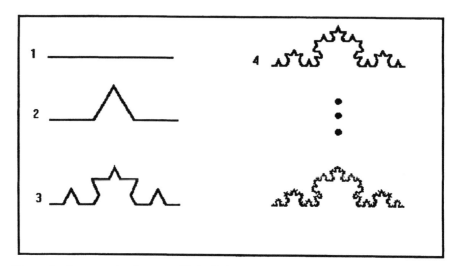

Figure 1. An example of exact self-similarity: the Von Koch curve. At each step of the construction, every segment is replaced by 4 segments whose length is 1/3 that of the original segment.

unit-length segment is first divided into three equal parts, and the central part is replaced by two other segments constituting the sides of an equilateral triangle; the next building step is accomplished by repeating the previous procedure over each of the resulting segments. With this simple procedure, recurrently applied infinitely many times, the Von Koch curve showed in Figure 1 (lower right corner) can be obtained. It is clear that the repeated iteration of simple construction rules can lead to profiles of a very complex nature, exhibiting interesting mathematical properties.

As it appears from the building process described above, the length of the Von Koch curve is increased by a 4/3 factor each step. As a consequence of the infinite recursion, the overall length of the curve diverges to infinity; on the other hand, from the properties of the geometric series, the subtended area can be easily shown to be finite. A further property of the curve is its being equally detailed at every scale factor: the more powerful the microscope with which one observes the curve, the more the details one can discover. More precisely, the curve can be said to possess a self-similarity property at any scale, that is, each small portion of the curve, if magnified, can exactly reproduce a larger portion. The curve is also said to be invariant under scale changes. These features of the curve can be epitomized by a parameter called *fractal dimension,* which provides useful clues about the geometrical structure of a fractal object.

Fractal dimension

The self-similarity property we have seen before is one of the fundamental concepts of fractal geometry, closely related to our intuitive notion of dimensionality. Any one-dimensional object, a segment for instance, can indeed be split into N suitably scaled replicas, each of them with a length ratio of $1/N$ to the original segment. Similarly, any two-dimensional object, like a square, can be cut into N replicas, each scaled down by a factor $r = 1/N^{1/2}$ (see Figure 2). The same holds for a three-dimensional object like a cube, for which the N smaller cubes are scaled by a factor $r = 1/N^{1/3}$.

Exploiting the self-similarity property peculiar to a fractal object, the previous procedure can be made more general, and a fractal dimension can be defined. We can assert that a self-similar object with fractal dimension D can be split into N smaller replicas of itself, each scaled by a factor $r = 1/N^{1/D}$. Thus, for a self-similar object whose N parts are scaled by a factor r, the fractal dimension can be determined as such:

$$D = \log(N)/\log(1/r). \tag{1}$$

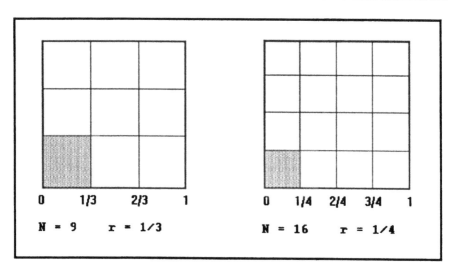

Figure 2. Relation of the concept of self-similarity and dimension.

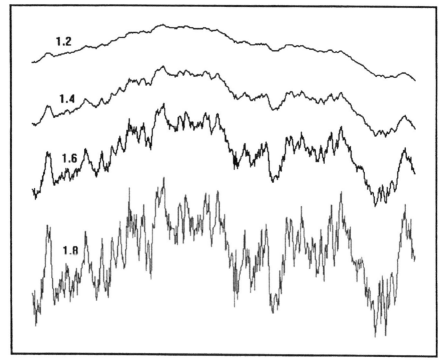

Figure 3. Examples of fractal curves, where an increase of the fluctuations corresponds to an increase of the fractal dimension D.

As opposed to the more familiar concept of Euclidean dimension, the fractal dimension need not be an integer. To the Von Koch curve, for instance, four new segments are added each step, each scaled by one-third with respect to the previous step; as a consequence the fractal dimension of the curve can be reckoned as such:

$$D = \log(4)/\log(3) = 1.2619\ldots. \tag{2}$$

This non-integer dimension (greater than 1 but less than 2) is the consequence of the non-standard properties of the curve. In fact the fractal curve "fills" more space than a simple line (with $D = 1$) and has thus an infinite length, yet it covers lesser space than an Euclidean plane ($D = 2$). Alongside with an increase of the fractal dimension from 1 to 2, the curve changes its starting line-like structure into an ever increasing covering of the Euclidean plane, with the entire plane as the limit for $D = 2$ (Figure 3). Even though its fractal dimension may be greater than one, the curve remains a "curve" in a topological sense, that is, with unit topological dimensionality; this can be seen by removing a single point of the curve, which splits it into two disjoint sets. The decimal portion of the fractal dimension only provides a measure of its geometrical irregularities.

Actual objects rarely exhibit exact self-similarity at any scale factor; however, when their smaller portions look like (but are not exactly like) a larger portion, they often possess the related property of *statistical self-similarity*. We can formally say that a signal is statistically self-similar if the stochastic description of the curve is invariant to changes of scale. Probably the most meaningful example to illustrate that propriety is a coast line: in this case, as well as in the case of the Von Koch curve, the closer the look at the unfoldings of the line, the more the details that can be tracked. Besides, considering a hypothetical measurement of the length of the line, taking faithfully into account the contributions of the smallest inlets makes the result larger: the greater the level of detail adopted, the longer the outcoming global length L. If the coast line is indeed self-similar, we will find a self-similarity power law relating L to the scale unit r employed in the measurement:

$$L(r) \propto 1/r^{D-1}. \tag{3}$$

In the plot of a given signal, the abscissa can be regarded as the time axis; it is then interesting to examine the spectral features of the fractal signal and their relationship with the fractal dimension. An unpredictably time-varying signal is called *noise;* its spectral density function gives an estimate of the mean square fluctuation at frequency f and, consequently, of the variations over a time scale of order $1/f$. From the results of signal theory one can verify the direct relationship between the fractal dimension and the logarithmic slope of the power spectral density function of a fractal signal (Voss 1985). A *fractional Brownian motion signal* (FBM) for instance (Mandelbrot 1982), with fractal dimension D, is characterized by a spectral density function proportional to $1/f^b$, where $b = (5 - 2D)$. One can exploit this feature to produce fractal signals with desired fractal dimension starting from a power spectrum. As an example, an FBM with given fractal dimension can be efficiently obtained by processing a Gaussian white noise signal through a filter whose frequency response is proportional to $1/f^{b/2}$. This can be accomplished by means of a filterbank (Corsini and Saletti 1988) or using FFT's. The *random midpoint displacement* (Carpenter 1982) is another effective method of generating fractal signals; it is also used to interpolate a given set of points employing fractal curves.

Local fractal dimension

The statistical self-similarity property considered above applies from arbitrarily large to arbitrarily small scales. With actual signals this property can be stated only over a finite range of scales. If we think back to the coast line, we can see that the upper bound for the range of scales is given by the size of the entire planet and that the lower bound is set by either the natural erosive smoothing or by the size of the single grains of sand or, eventually, by the atomic nature of particles.

With real signals, therefore, the hypothesis of statistical self-similarity can be maintained only for a finite range of time scales. Sound signals, for example, have all finite duration and, in the discrete time domain, they have also finite bandwidth. Although the fractal dimension should appear a constant over the entire scale range, actually it turns out to be a function of the time scale factor e, since real signals only approximately verify the hypothesis of self-similarity.

Various methods exist to define and to measure the fractal dimension (Grassberger and Procaccia 1983a, b); they all rely on quantities that can be extracted from the observed set and which vary according to a power law dependent on the scale of measures. One such quantity is the so-called *cover area*, a function of a linear unit scale factor. These quantities are generally displayed onto a log-log plot whose slope is measured. In the *box-counting method*, for instance, a square grid is superimposed on the plot of the fractal (Figure 4) and the number $N(r)$ of boxes touched by the plot is counted. This number is a function of the scale factor r, which is the spacing between the lines of the grid, and it is:

$$N(r) \propto 1/r^D. \tag{4}$$

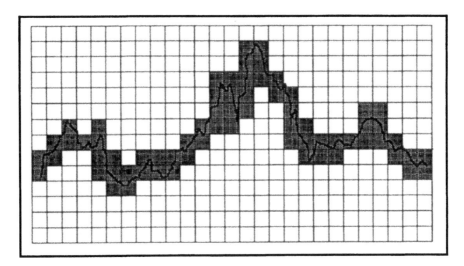

Figure 4. In the "box-counting" method a square grid is superimposed on the plot of the fractal and the number of boxes touched by the plot (dashed in the figure) is counted. This number is a function of the scale factor, which is the spacing between the lines of the grid.

As r becomes very small we find that $\log(N(r))/\log(1/r)$ converges to D, that is, to the fractal dimension. To sum up, the algorithm evaluates $N(r)$ for $r = 1, 2, \ldots$, plots the results onto logarithmic axes, and provides an estimate of the slope of the plotted graph. If the analyzed set is a pure fractal, the plot will display a perfectly linear shape; otherwise the local slope may vary widely. In these latter cases, the slope is measured in its average over a local interval around r. The outcome is then a measure of the slope, that is, of the fractal dimension, which depends on the observation scale r. Sometimes even the variability trend of the fractal dimension relative to the scale is a characterizing factor for the studied set, and it can be used to mark different phenomena. It has been used to distinguish between different textures in pictures for example, and the next sections present examples of musical sounds.

Musical signals admitting a description in terms of non-stationary processes display characteristics that vary as a function of time; the fractal dimension reflects this property. The average value of this variation, which is the estimate of the global fractal dimension, is anyway of little interest for the characterization of a sound. As a consequence, instead of the global dimension, we can better estimate a *local fractal dimension* (LFD), computed over a window which covers just a portion of the musical signal. Since the signal is generally non-stationary, the measurement made over distinct window placements will not be the same.

By shifting the window along the time course of the signal, we can mark several different behaviors at several different portions of the signal, all of which are characterized by a different fractal dimension.

The local fractal dimension is a function of time and of the scale factor, LFD(t, e). Note the similarity with the short-time Fourier transform (STFT) used to portray the local time/frequency variations of the signal, and remember the relationship between fractal dimension and spectral slope.

From the above considerations, it is clear that it is necessary to know how one quantity (the cover area) varies with regard to the scale factor in order to compute the FD. The diverse algorithms employed differ basically over the ways in which the covering of the signal is performed. In our following examples the cover area is computed by the efficient algorithm recently developed by Maragos (1991, 1993), which is based upon a morphological filtering of the time graph of the signal, and upon a method based on differences (Higuchi 1988; Bianchi, Bisello, and Bologna 1993).

LFD analysis of musical sounds

Fractal dimension as a function of the scale factor

Here are some fractal dimension analyses of instrumental sounds. Figure 5 shows the time behavior of a multiphonic oboe tone along with its fractal dimension versus the scale factor (Figure 6); the constancy of the fractal dimension proves the fractal model to be appropriate. On the other hand, as shown in Figures 7 and 8, when the graph does not exhibit self-similarity properties, the fractal dimension ceases to be constant with variations in the time scale. It appears that the absence of high-frequency fluctuations in the signal is a cause to small FD values for small scale values; for these scales, however, the estimate of the algorithm is less reliable. (Notice here how the fractal dimension is not representative of the analyzed instruments: the same instrument can indeed produce sounds with different dimensions.) After a large number of tests, we found that for quasi-periodic signals we could obtain the best results by using time windows spanning 1 or 2 periods of the signals.

Fractal analysis is not sensitive to amplitude scalings of the signal. For best results, anyway, we suggest a full range amplitude in order to gain a less sensitive dependency of the estimated dimension on quantization errors.

In the previous example we applied the fractal model to a basically quasi-periodic signal. To characterize turbulence better, we prefer to separate this latter component from the quasi-periodic part of the signal. The frequency and

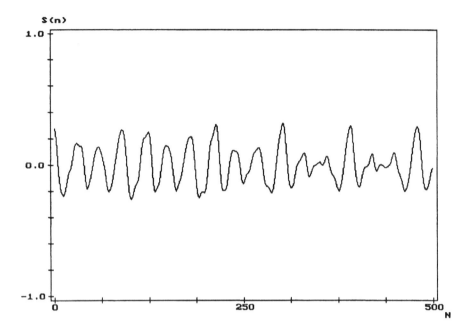

Figure 5. Time signal of a oboe multiphonic tone.

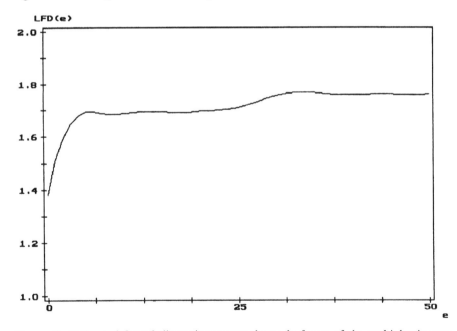

Figure 6. Estimated fractal dimension versus the scale factor of the multiphonic tone of Figure 5. The constancy of the fractal dimension proves the fractal model to be appropriate.

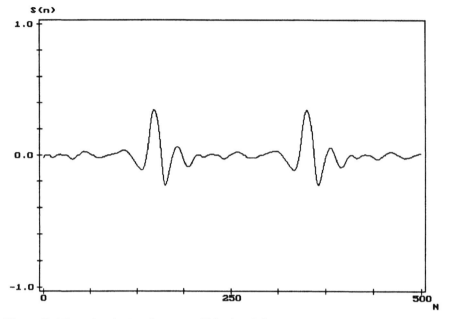

Figure 7. Time signal of a oboe tone. This signal does not exhibit self-similarity properties.

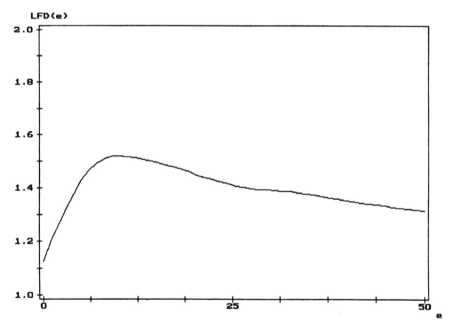

Figure 8. Estimated fractal dimension versus the scale factor of the oboe tone of Figure 7. Notice that the fractal dimension ceases to be constant with variations in the time scale factor.

amplitude deviations of the harmonics are extracted with the aid of a STFT analysis and then the fractal model is applied to them. Figures 9–12 show the estimated fractal dimension of the amplitude and frequency deviations of the first partial of a C4 played in the principal register by a pipe-organ. These fluctuations appear to have an approximate fractal dimension of 1.66 and 1.82 respectively. The following partials show similar behaviors. These pieces of evidence fully justify the use of fractal modeling for musical signals.

Many of the signals we analyzed maintain a sufficiently uniform local fractal dimension against variations of the scale factor e. Some signals do not satisfy this condition; some of them seem to stabilize very slowly into a steady fractal dimension while others never exhibit a stable fractal dimension, as is the case with reed-excited registers. Those musical signals are probably characterized by an absence of turbulence, so that the primary hypothesis of fractal modeling is not satisfied.

The information gained from the previous analysis could be employed in sound synthesis. One can think of an additive synthesis model in which the frequency and amplitude fluctuations of the partials are controlled by signals consistent with the fractal analysis. In the simpler cases a control signal with constant local fractal dimension should be sufficient. Fractal interpolation can

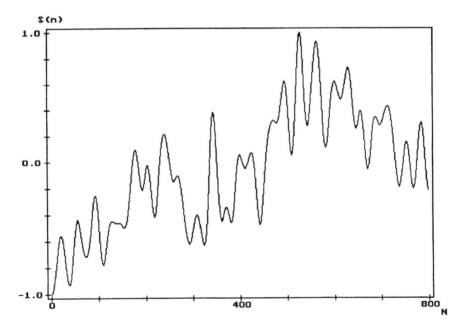

Figure 9. Amplitude variations of the first partial of an organ pipe (principal stop) during steady-state portion of the tone.

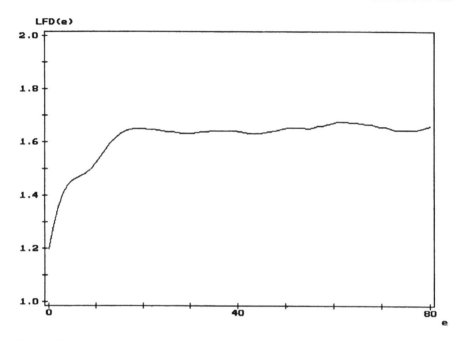

Figure 10. Estimated fractal dimension of amplitude variations of Figure 9.

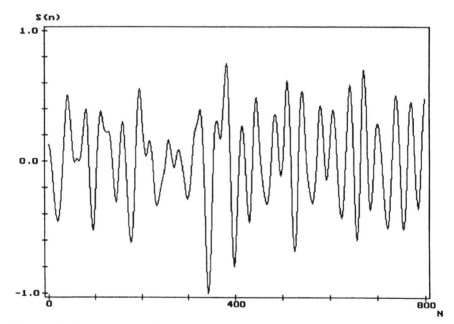

Figure 11. Frequency variations of the first partial of an organ pipe (principal stop) during steady state.

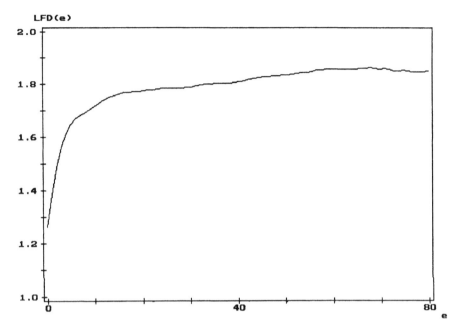

Figure 12. Estimated fractal dimension of frequency variations of Figure 11.

be used when a more general behavior is needed. Synthesis techniques could presumably be applied to obtain signals with varying local fractal dimension, the variation being ruled by a predefined function.

Fractal dimension as a function of time

The time-varying turbulence in the different phases of a sound can be pointed out by computing the variations of the fractal dimension as a function of time. This behavior is rendered evident by computing the value of the fractal dimension with a fixed scale factor, and by repeating this computation while the windows slides over the signal.

As an example, we show the analysis of a C4 tone played by a bass clarinet. Figure 13 displays the LFD(t) of the entire note while Figure 14 only a detail of the attack. Six different parts can be highlighted (A–E), and their time graphs are shown in Figures 15–20. Phase A portrays the ambient noise, which has a high fractal dimension; phase B marks the beginning of the player's air blowing, with dimension around 1.8 which is typical of reed-driven instruments. The small value of the LFD during phase C denotes a short, regular behavior; then, during phase D, oscillations start which are characterized by a decrease in the LFD down close to 1 (phase E); finally the dimension increases up to 1.1 where

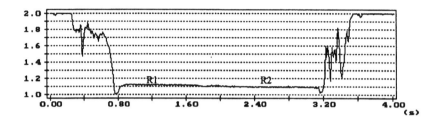

Figure 13. Local fractal dimension of a C4 tone of a bass clarinet.

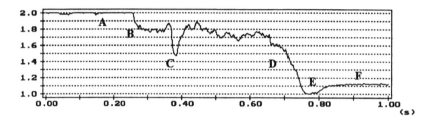

Figure 14. Detail of the LFD(*t*) during the attack of the tone of Figure 13.

Figure 15. Phase A of the signal that represents the ambient noise, which has a high fractal dimension.

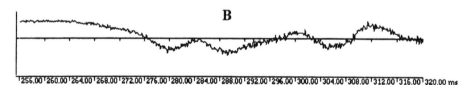

Figure 16. Phase B marks the beginning of the player's air blowing, with a dimension around 1.8.

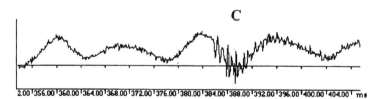

Figure 17. The small value of the LFD during phase C denotes a short, regular behavior, during the attack.

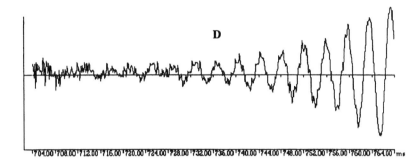

Figure 18. Detail of the attack: during phase D, oscillations start and the LFD decreases.

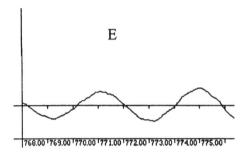

Figure 19. At low-amplitude oscillations, a quasi-sinusoidal sound is produced (phase E), characterized by a LFD value close to 1.

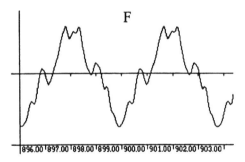

Figure 20. Phase F, regime: the tone richer in harmonics and is characterized by a LFD of approximatly 1.1.

it seems to gain stability (phase F). In fact, with low-amplitude oscillations, a quasi-sinusoidal sound is produced that becomes richer in harmonics. Notice from Figures 21, 22 that two distinct waveforms R1, R2 are detected by the LFD analys during the steady state part of the sound.

In general, after a transient where fluctuations may be noticeable, the fractal dimension of a pitched musical instrument sound shows a tendency to settle into

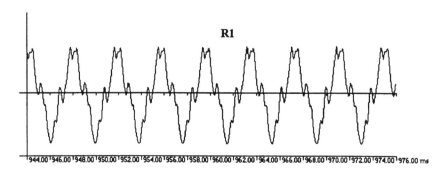

Figure 21. Signal during regime phase R1.

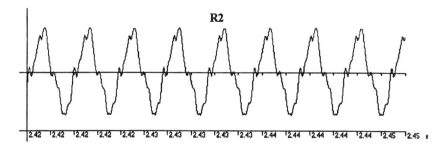

Figure 22. Signal during regime phase R2.

a constant value. Nevertheless, the previous pictures clearly show fluctuations of the fractal dimension during the attack and decay transients in sounds radiated by an actual instrument. Of course, this information could be usefully applied to the synthesis models to obtain a more natural synthesized sound.

Analysis of the generator dynamics in steady sounds

Apart from fractal modeling of signals, chaos theory contributes useful tools for the analysis of the sound generation mechanisms. Musical instruments are indeed a particular class of dissipative, nonlinear mechanical systems. With these tools, a representation of the dynamic evolution of the system is provided and a variety of phenomena become more easily visible.

This approach is particularly useful in musical acoustics to characterize steady states, also called the *attractors* of the physical system. The reconstruction of the attractor within a *time-delayed phase space* (Parker and Chua 1987; Lauterborn and Parlitz 1988) is the most important tool. The associated *Poincaré section* technique allows a one-dimension reduction in the description of the system. The method leaves system periodicities out, allowing an easier interpretation of

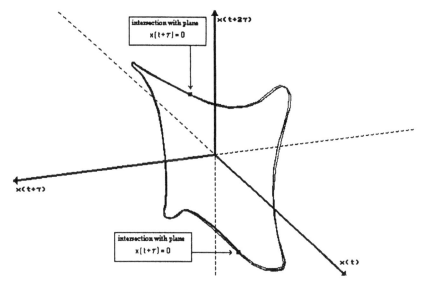

Figure 23a. A4 bassoon tone. Reconstructed attractor. The sound is periodic: the attractor is a closed curve.

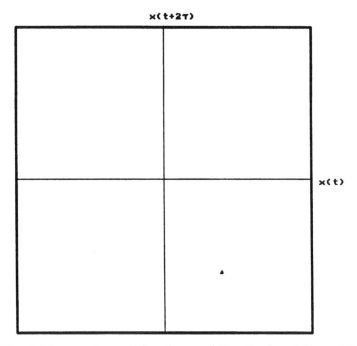

Figure 23b. A4 bassoon tone. Poincaré map of the attractor of Figure 23a. For a periodic sound the attractor is represented as a single point.

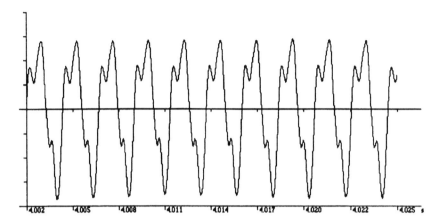

Figure 23c. A4 bassoon tone. Waveform of the bassoon tone.

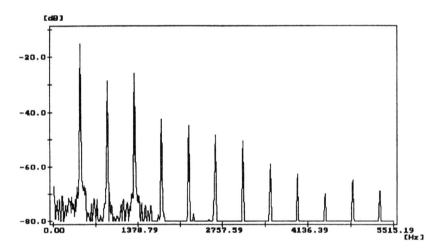

Figure 23d. A4 bassoon tone. Spectrum of the bassoon tone.

the signal properties. These tools complement the set of classical time-frequency analysis techniques, as they can reveal many aspects undetectable by a simple fast Fourier transform.

Figures 23–27 illustrate some types of attractor in instrumental musical sig nals. Figures 23a–d depict an A4 bassoon tone. In the reconstructed attractor (Figure 23a) a *limit cycle* can be detected, that is a closed curve corresponding to a single point in the Poincaré map (Figure 23b). Actually, the curve is not perfectly close because of noise and because of the small vibrato and tremolo effects that are unavoidably introduced by the player. Figures 23c displays a time analysis of the previous signal, while Figure 23d presents a frequency analysis.

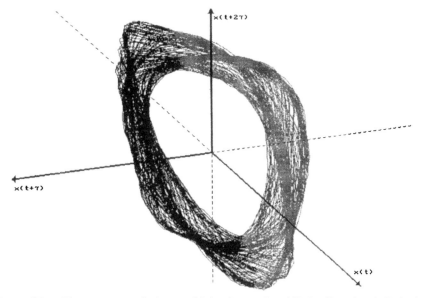

Figure 24a. Homogeneous clarinet multiphonic number 102 by Bartolozzi Garbarino showing a biperiodic attractor. Reconstructed attractor.

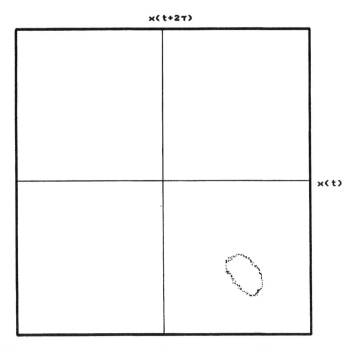

Figure 24b. Homogeneous clarinet multiphonic number 102 by Bartolozzi Garbarino showing a biperiodic attractor. Poincaré map.

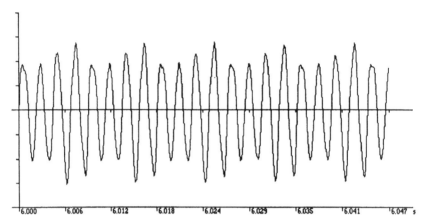

Figure 24c. Homogeneous clarinet multiphonic number 102 by Bartolozzi Garbarino showing a biperiodic attractor. Waveform.

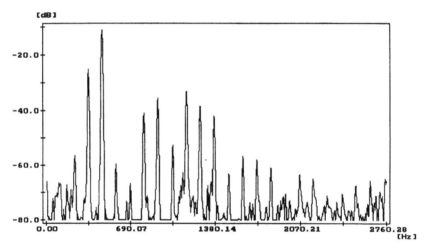

Figure 24d. Homogeneous clarinet multiphonic number 102 by Bartolozzi Garbarino showing a biperiodic attractor. Spectrum.

Both of these analyses confirm the information gained from the study of the phase space (note the lateral bands in the low-frequency components, an effect of tremolo and vibrato).

Figures 24a–d refer to the homogeneous clarinet multiphonic number 102 by Bartolozzi and Garbarino (1978). The waveform of the signal displays a slightly amplitude-modulated envelope, whereas the three-dimensional reconstruction and the Poincaré map show the attractor to be 2-periodic, that is, the system possesses spectral lines at frequencies $kf1 \pm jf2$. The trajectory of the signal in the phase space unfolds over the surface of a diffeomorphic replica

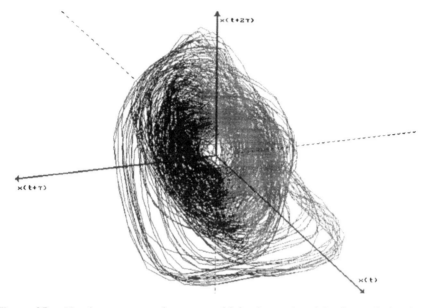

Figure 25a. Non-homogeneous bassoon multiphonic number 1 by Penazzi showing a chaotic attractor. Reconstructed attractor.

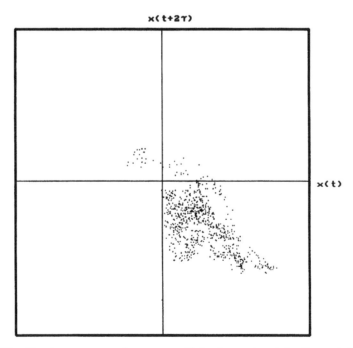

Figure 25b. Non-homogeneous bassoon multiphonic number 1 by Penazzi showing a chaotic attractor. Poincaré map.

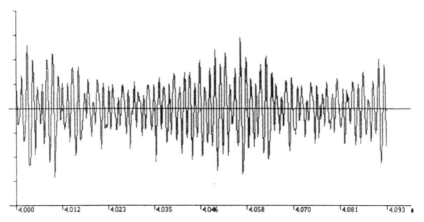

Figure 25c. Non-homogeneous bassoon multiphonic number 1 by Penazzi showing a chaotic attractor. Waveform.

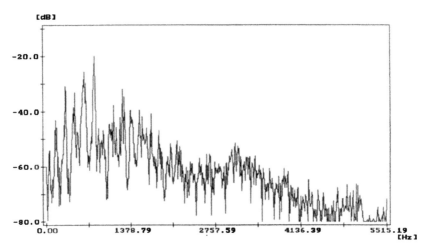

Figure 25d. Non-homogeneous bassoon multiphonic number 1 by Penazzi showing a chaotic attractor. Spectrum.

of a two-dimensional torus (see Figure 24a). We can see that the simple time-frequency analysis does not point out the peculiar nature of the attractor which instead appears clearly in the Poincaré map (Figure 24b); a subsequent examination of the signal spectrum allows an approximate estimate of the two basic frequencies.

Figures 25a–d refer to the nonhomogeneous bassoon multiphonic number 1 by Penazzi (1982). Here a strange (chaotic) attractor appears, which displays neither periodic nor non-periodic features. The trajectory is, in any case, restricted to a limited zone in the state space. In the frequency analysis this is portrayed by a spectral component spreading over the entire band and superimposing on the spectral lines.

For phase spaces, it should be noted that the reconstruction delay is a very critical factor in the pursuit of an expressive representation of phenomena, so that its choice needs to be considered carefully. With musical signals, good results can be obtained by selecting a zero (generally the first) of the autocorrelation function.

We have studied the steady states of some self-sustained musical instruments, with the aim of exploring the physical phenomena that underlie the mechanisms of sound production. Our analyses concerned oboe, clarinet, and recorder multiphonics, and double-bass wolf-notes. Measurements on the power spectra of multiphonic tones provided experimental evidence of chaos, confirmed by the reconstructed attractors in the phase space of the dynamical system.

The visual analysis of the locus spanned by the attractor in the phase space is completed by quantitative criteria for identifying the type of dynamics the system settles into. The fractal dimension of an attractor in the phase space provides a measure of the temporal and geometrical properties of the originating dynamic system. The estimated fractal dimension becomes a means of classifying the attractors; one should note the difference in meaning between this parameter and the LFD of the signal graph, which we saw before.

The fractal dimension of an attractor can be evaluated by embedding the time series into a space of higher dimensionality. It is convenient to use the correlation dimension D (Grassberger and Procaccia 1983a, b), measured by embedding a single time series into a higher dimensionality space in order to reconstruct the phase space of the dynamic system. The estimated dimension of the attractor sometimes shows the sound to possess the marks of chaotic dynamics, with a noninteger fractal dimension; at other times it reveals a behavior related to biperiodic spectra. The specific typology of the reconstructed attractor thus shows that the self-sustained musical instruments can be modeled by nonlinear dynamic systems with few degrees of freedom. Indeed, a phase-locked biperiodic spectrum is typical of chaotic attractors with small dimension which are found in mechanic or fluidodynamic systems. Specifically, the actual musical instruments analyzed appear to have behaviors similar to a quasi-periodic route to chaos.

As a complete example we report the analysis of the clarinet multiphonic number 33 (Bartolozzi 1974) in which three different kinds of steady-state behaviors were detected (Figures 26a–f). The attractor dimensions are 1.23 (like a periodic but slightly noisy sound), 3.24, and 3.82 respectively, suggesting a quasi-periodic route to chaos. The first state is quite different from the others, while a frequency analysis (and listening as well) provides similar outcomes in the second and the third case.

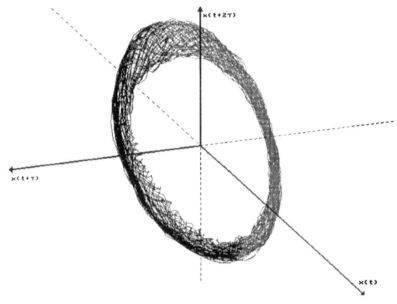

Figure 26a. Analysis of the clarinet multiphonic number 33 of Bartolozzi, in which three different kinds of steady state behaviors are detected. Reconstructed attractor of phase 1.

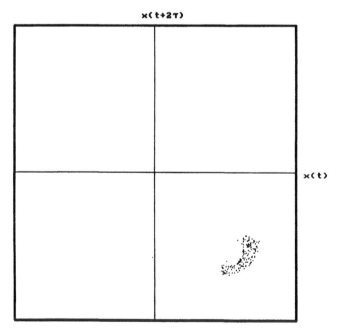

Figure 26b. Analysis of the clarinet multiphonic number 33 of Bartolozzi, in which three different kinds of steady state behaviors are detected. Poincaré map of phase 1.

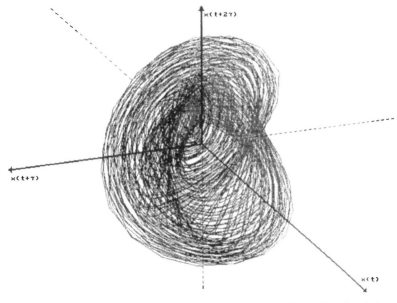

Figure 26c. Analysis of the clarinet multiphonic number 33 of Bartolozzi, in which three different kinds of steady state behaviors are detected. Reconstructed attractor of phase 2.

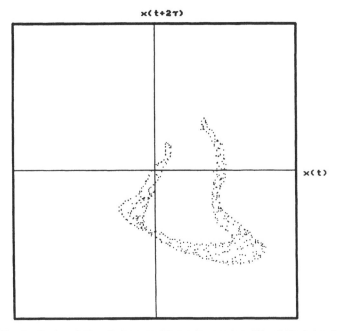

Figure 26d. Analysis of the clarinet multiphonic number 33 of Bartolozzi, in which three different kinds of steady state behaviors are detected. Poincaré map of phase 2.

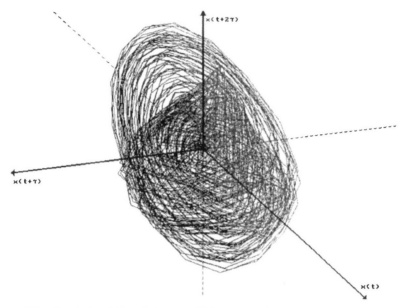

Figure 26e. Analysis of the clarinet multiphonic number 33 of Bartolozzi, in which three different kinds of steady state behaviors are detected. Reconstructed attractor of phase 3.

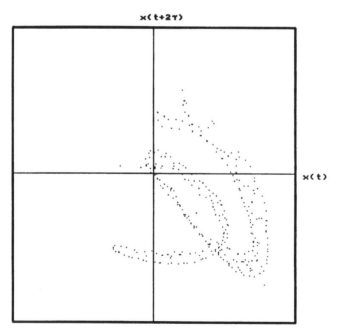

Figure 26f. Analysis of the clarinet multiphonic number 33 of Bartolozzi, in which three different kinds of steady state behaviors are detected. Poincaré map of phase 3.

A closer examination of the spectra (Figure 27a–c) completes the above information; in its first portion the multiphonic signal exhibits a behavior analogous to that reported by Backus (1978), that is, it is characterized by the presence of a small number of spectral components, which are related to the heterodyne

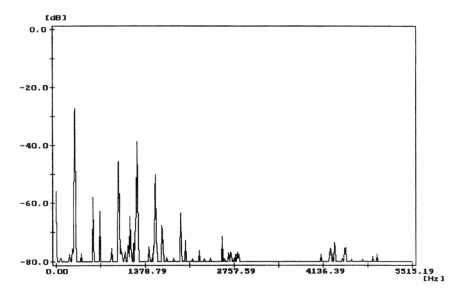

Figure 27a. Spectrum of the clarinet multiphonics number 33. Phase 1.

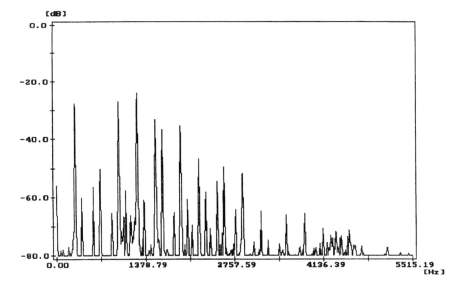

Figure 27b. Spectrum of the clarinet multiphonics number 33. Phase 2.

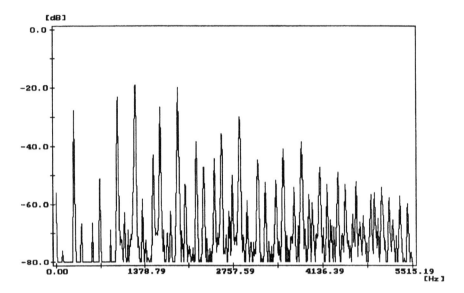

Figure 27c. Spectrum of the clarinet multiphonics number 33. Phase 3.

products of two basic frequencies, whose values are estimated as A = 287 Hz and B = 972 Hz. The spectral content gets much richer in the second portion of the signal, and moves closer to the spectrum described by Benade (1976), which possesses four principal components: $P = 287$ Hz, $Q = 685$ Hz, $R = 972$ Hz, and $S = 1259$ Hz. In the third portion the spectral content gets even richer: the spectral extension becomes wider while new distortion products are now easily seen, which were not detectable in the second portion. A spread spectral component is furthermore superimposed on the spectral lines.

The frequency analysis has then important points in common with both Backus's (first portion) and Benade's (second portion). No relevant discrepancy is present between the values of the heterodyne components in the first and in the second portion of the multiphonic tone. The frequency analysis in the second part substantially highlights a larger number of spectral components as new distortion products of the components of the first part. In the third part further distortion products are added, while the spectrum acquires a noisy character.

Bifurcation and routes to chaos

The behavior of a system depends on many parameters. With self-sustained wind musical instruments, two such parameters are the blowing pressure and the resonance frequency of the reed. The basic effect of these parameters lies in the modification of the equation that describes the system dynamics. If just one of the paramenters, the control parameter, is varied, and if measurements are correspondently taken, we may come to understand how the system modifies its steady-state behavior, that is, how it modifies its phase space attractor. If the attractor varies with changes in the control parameter, then a *bifurcation* is said to have taken place. Bifurcations belong to three basic typologies (Parker and Chua 1987): *Hopf bifurcation, saddle node bifurcation,* and *period doubling bifurcation.*

The best way to classify a given bifurcation is by experimentation, that is, by noticing that with the variation of the control parameter, the same type of bifurcation takes place repeatedly. This situation is referred to as a *peculiar bifurcation scenario;* categorizations exist for all the possible sequences of bifurcations to be encountered in actual situations, and they are known as *routes to chaos: quasi-periodic route to chaos, intermittent route to chaos, period-doubling route to chaos.*

The bifurcation diagram is another useful tool for the analysis of chaotic systems as it shows the evolution of the steady-state behavior as a function of a system parameter. Its foremost usefulness lies in the ability to sum up the features of the system over a wide range of variations for the selected control parameter. Even this tool can be employed in the synthesis by physical models; as McIntyre, Schumacher, and Woodhouse (1983) indeed pointed out, the dynamics of a musical oscillator, in their basic essence, can be reduced to an *iterative map* which, in each period, produces a reference amplitude as a function of the amplitude either of a portion of the period, or of the previous period. The behavior of this typical iterative map is well studied with the aid of bifurcation diagrams. Used in this way, this tool helps choose the correct parameter values in the physical model simulation. Moreover, this method shows the particular route to chaos of the model, which often turns out to be different from the route to chaos of the actual instrument. This points out a basic shortcoming of some physical models for sound synthesis, in which the global behavior (the route to chaos) of a real instrument sometimes cannot be obtained.

The analysis of a clarinet model to variations of a control parameter, as described by Schumacher (1981), is particularly meaningful. The bifurcation diagram shown in Figure 28 depicts the modification of the inner state of a clarinet when the blowing pressure *Pm* varies. It can be inferred from the diagram that small values for *Pm* result in limited oscillations inside the clarinet pipe, while with larger values the oscillations increase in amplitude (and, correspondently, the reed can be shown to be beating). Even though those "limit" behaviors correctly portray the working of a clarinet, the bifurcation diagram highlights a fundamental failure of Schumacher's model: the midpoint region in the bifurcation diagram shows a period-doubling route to chaos trend. This could not

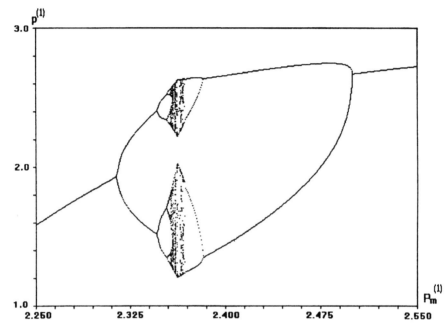

Figure 28. Bifurcation diagram of Schumacher's physical model of the clarinet. The control parameter is the blowing pressure. In the middle notice a period-doubling route to chaos.

occur in the real clarinet because the period-doubling process would lead to an octave-wide decrease in pitch, which is an effect no player has ever obtained. Further, the analyses performed by Benade (1976), Backus (1978), Gibiat (1988, 1990), Puaud (1991), and Bugna (1992) show that, under particular conditions, wind instruments exhibit quasi-periodic transitions which suggest a probable "quasi-periodic route to chaos" typical of fluidodynamic systems with few degrees of freedom. Yet no clarinet model is known to support, even partially, such behavior.

One should note that the bifurcation diagram represents dynamic variations as a function of a single parameter. If there are many significant parameters, the usefulness of the diagram diminishes, since the effect of multiple variations cannot be represented.

Conclusion

We have seen that tools derived from chaos theory provide useful parameters for the characterization of the dynamics of musical signals. These methods complement the classical techniques of time/frequency analysis presented in

Chapters 2, 3, 4, and 5. In particular, the notion of local fractal dimension provides a good description of the fluctuation of sound waveforms, exploiting the geometrical characteristics of its time graph. The local fractal dimension proves its usefulness in its scale- and time-varying formulation. We presented a set of diverse tools, mainly suitable to the study of the steady-state behavior of pitched musical instrument tones. These consistitute merely the first generation of chaos theory sound analyzers.

References

Backus, J. 1978. "Multiphonic tones in the woodwind instruments." *Journal of the Acoustical Society of America* 63(2): 591–599.

Bartolozzi, B. 1974. *Nuovi Suoni per i "Legni."* Milano: Edizioni Suvini Zerboni.

Bartolozzi, B. and G. Garbarino. 1978. *Nuova Tecnica per Strumenti a Fiato di Legno—Metodo per Clarinetto.* Milano: Edizioni Suvini Zerboni.

Benade, A.H. 1976. *Fundamentals of Musical Acoustics.* New York: Oxford University Press, chap. 25.

Bianchi, A., B. Bisello, and G. Bologna. 1993. "Estimation of fractal dimension of musical signals." *CSC Report.* Padua: University of Padua.

Bugna, G.P. 1992. "Analysis of musical signals in phase space using chaos theory." *CSC Report.* Padua: University of Padua.

Carpenter, L. 1982. "Computer rendering of stochastic models." *Communication of the ACM* 25: 371–384.

Corsini, G. and R. Saletti. 1988. "A $1/f$ power spectrum noise sequence generator." *IEEE Transactions on Instumentation Measurement* 37(12): 615–619.

Gibiat, V. 1988. "Phase space representations of acoustical musical signals." *Journal of Sound and Vibration* 123(3): 529–536.

Gibiat, V. 1990. "Chaos in musical sounds." *Proceedings of the Institute of Acoustics* 12(1): 511–518.

Grassberger, P. and I. Procaccia. 1983a. "Characterization of strange attractors." *Physical Review Letters* 50(5): 346–349.

Grassberger, P. and I. Procaccia. 1983b. "Measuring the strangeness of strange attractors." *Physica D* 9: 189–208.

Helmholtz, H.L.F. 1954. *Sensations of Tone.* New York: Dover.

Higuchi, T. 1988. "Approach to an irregular time series on the basis of the fractal theory." *Physica D* 31: 277–283.

Keefe, D.H. and B. Laden. 1991. "Correlation dimension of woodwind multiphonic tones." *Journal of the Acoustical Society of America* 90(4): 1754–1765.

Lauterborn, W. and U. Parlitz. 1988. "Methods of chaos physics and their application to acoustics." *Journal of the Acoustical Society of America* 84(6): 1975–1993.

Mandelbrot, B.B. 1982. *The Fractal Geometry of Nature.* New York: W.H. Freeman.

Maragos, P. 1991. "Fractal aspects of speech signals: dimension and interpolation." In *Proceedings of ICASSP.* New York: IEEE Press, pp. 417–420.

Maragos, P. and F.-K. Sun. 1993. "Measuring the fractal dimension of signals: morphological covers and iterative optimization." *IEEE Transactions on Signal Processing* 41(2): 108–121.

McIntyre, M.E., R.T. Schumacher, and J. Woodhouse. 1983. "On the oscillations of musical instruments." *Journal of the Acoustical Society of America* 74(5): 1325–1345.

Parker, T.S. and L.O. Chua. 1987. "Chaos: a tutorial for engineers." *Proceeding of the IEEE* 75(8): 982–1007.

Penazzi. 1982. *Il Fagotto—Altre Tecniche.* Milan: Ricordi.

Puaud, J., R. Caussé, and V. Gibiat. 1991. "Quasi-periodicity and bifurcations in wolf note." *Journal d'Acoustique* 4: 253–259.

Schumacher, R.T. 1981. "Ab initio calculations of the oscillations of a clarinet." *Acustica* 48: 72–85.

Voss, R.F. 1985. "Random fractal forgeries." In R.A. Earnshaw, ed. *Fundamental Algorithms for Computer Graphics*. Berlin: Springer-Verlag, pp. 805–835.

Voss, R.F. and J. Clarke. 1975. "1/f in music and speech." *Nature* 258: 317–318.

Voss, R.F. and J. Clarke. 1978. "1/f in music: music from 1/f noise." *Journal of the Acoustical Society of America* 63: 258–263.

7

Acoustic modeling using digital waveguides

Julius O. Smith III

This paper presents an introduction to music synthesis based on distributed ("waveguide") physical models of strings, horns, bores, and the like. Topics covered include digital waveguide models for ideal vibrating strings, damped strings, plucked and bowed strings, and the clarinet. The level of the article is tutorial, and much of the elementary theory is described in detail.

Techniques for physical modeling are generally quite mature. The basic goal is to use equations of physics describing a physical system to develop a numerical algorithm which solves the equations and/or simulates the system in a computer. Input signals are transformed by the numerical algorithm into simulated output signals. In the case of a musical instrument model, the inputs may come from performance sensors or from a compositional algorithm. From these inputs, the algorithm typically generates samples of acoustic pressure at a rate sufficiently high to control a loudspeaker. In this way, a mathematical model of a musical instrument becomes the instrument itself.

There are many fields from which we might draw in developing computational physical models for music applications. For example, structural engineers use detailed models of structures such as overpasses, bridges, and buildings to predict stresses throughout the structure under a variety of hypothesized loads. Earth-quakes are simulated numerically. Flight simulators are based on mathematical descriptions of flight dynamics and flight controls. Dynamic models of satellites are used in real-time state estimators running on ground-based computers.

For musical instrument modeling applications, we need *dynamic* system modeling techniques. This is because acoustic signals are generated by *vibrating* dynamic systems. Thus, we cannot readily use modeling techniques for static structures such as buildings and bridges or incompressible air models such as in flight analysis. On the other hand, a highly relevant field is that of *automatic control*. This is the field in which dynamic systems are modeled mathematically for the purpose of determining a control law which can be used to make the physical system behave as desired while maintaining stability and smoothness of response. As an extreme example, modern fighter jets are said to be impossible to fly in the absence of a stabilizing active control; the inherent instability of the uncompensated flight dynamics can be leveraged to provide extreme maneuverability in flight.

The general modeling scenario is depicted in Figure 1. Input signals are supplied to a model which processes them to produce output signals. For example, in a model of the clarinet, the input signals might be breath pressure, fingering, and some measurement of embouchure. The output can be sound pressure radiation at the first open tone hole, or it can consist of several tone-hole outputs, the bell, the register hole, and even the signal inside the bore (corresponding to having an internal microphone in the instrument).

When the physical details of the model are forgotten and the processing is characterized purely in terms of its abstract mathematical form (usually highly simplified), we enter the domain of *signal processing models*. Such models are quite classical in electrical engineering. When the signals are *sampled* in time, the model assumes an algorithmic form, and we have a model implemented via *digital* signal processing. Thus, to build physical models of dynamic systems, we may look to the fields of automatic control and digital signal processing for useful techniques.

In a signal processing model, there is rarely a physical interpretation of the diagram, except perhaps the input and output signals themselves (as samples of air pressure in an acoustic system, for example). This may happen because so many mathematical transformations have been applied to the processing that

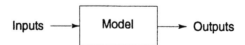

Figure 1. Input/output model of a dynamic system.

the physical interpretation is gone, or there may never have been a physical interpretation to begin with (as in standard digital filter theory and practice). This can be considered a disadvantage of a purely signal processing approach to musical instrument modeling.

Fortunately, certain signal processing structures do admit a precise physical interpretation, and these can be used as well understood building blocks for physical models. Furthermore, the more intuitive structures do not increase the cost of implementation. In fact, physical insights combined with properties of linear systems can lead to enormous reductions in the cost of implementation. These "physical signal processing" structures can be interfaced to any other type of physical model, so there is no loss of modeling generality. These are the essential properties of the digital waveguide approach.

The typical path to a computational model begins with the physical equations which describe the system. These equations are almost always combinations of three elementary relationships which we learn in first-year college physics:

$Force = mass \times acceleration$ (Newton's second law of motion),

$Force = spring\text{-}constant \times displacement$ (Hooke's spring law),

$Force = coefficient\text{-}of\text{-}friction \times velocity$ (Linearized friction model).

These three relations comprise the foundation for all *linear* dynamic systems. Sets of such equations can be called linear differential equations. Solving the differential equations gives functions which describe the behavior of the system over time. It is also possible to organize an Nth order differential equation into a single, vector, *first-order*, differential equation; this is the basis of the so-called *state space* model (Kailath 1980).

Physical modeling synthesis

Physical models used in music sound synthesis generally fall into two categories, *lumped* and *distributed*. Lumped models consist, in principle, of masses, springs, dampers, and nonlinear elements, and they can be used to approximate physical systems such as a brass player's lips, a singer's vocal folds, or a piano hammer.

One mass and one spring can be connected to create an elementary second-order resonator. In digital audio signal processing, a second-order resonator is implemented using a two-pole digital filter. As a result, lumped models are typically implemented using second-order digital filters as building blocks.

Distributed model implementations typically consist of delay lines (often called "digital waveguides" in the physical modeling context), digital filters, and nonlinear elements, and they model wave propagation in distributed media such as strings, bores, horns, plates, and acoustic spaces. In digital waveguide models, distributed losses and dispersion are still lumped at discrete points as low-order digital filters, separating out the pure delay-line which represents ideal propagation delay. Distributed waveguide models can be freely combined with lumped filter models; for example, a brass instrument model typically consists of a lumped model for the "lip reed" and a distributed waveguide model for the horn.

Summary

This tutorial gives an introduction to physical modeling synthesis based on digital waveguide models (Smith 1992). First, the theory of sampled traveling waves for the ideal vibrating string is discussed, since this is one of the simplest cases in practice. Next, various alternative choices of wave variables are discussed in order to make it clear how a variety of acoustic simulations can be constructed using digital waveguides. Then we introduce losses in the wave equation so that its solution becomes decaying traveling waves along the string. The important principle of *lumping* distributed losses is described. Finally, some applications examples are discussed, including the waveguide clarinet and bowed string.

The ideal vibrating string

The *wave equation* for the ideal (lossless, linear, flexible) vibrating string, depicted in Figure 2 is given by

$$Ky'' = \varepsilon \ddot{y}, \tag{1}$$

where

$$
\begin{aligned}
K &\triangleq \text{string tension} & y &\triangleq y(t, x), \\
\varepsilon &\triangleq \text{linear mass density} & \dot{y} &\triangleq \frac{\partial}{\partial t} y(t, x), \\
y &\triangleq \text{string displacement} & y' &\triangleq \frac{\partial}{\partial x} y(t, x),
\end{aligned} \tag{2}
$$

where "$\triangleq$" means "is defined as". The wave equation is fully derived in Morse (1981) and in most elementary textbooks on acoustics. It can be interpreted as a statement of Newton's second law, "*force = mass × acceleration*," on a

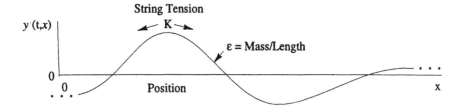

Figure 2. The ideal vibrating string.

microscopic scale. Since we are concerned with transverse vibrations on the string, the relevant restoring force (per unit length) is given by the string tension times the curvature of the string (Ky''); the restoring force is balanced at all times by the inertial force per unit length of the string which is equal to mass density times transverse acceleration ($\varepsilon \ddot{y}$).

The same wave equation applies to any perfectly elastic medium which is displaced along one dimension. For example, the air column of a clarinet or organ pipe can be modeled using the one-dimensional wave equation by substituting air-pressure deviation for string displacement, and longitudinal volume velocity for transverse string velocity. We refer to the general class of such media as *one-dimensional waveguides*. Extensions to two and three dimensions (and more, for the mathematically curious), are also possible (Van Duyne and Smith 1993, 1995).

For a physical string model, at least three coupled waveguide models should be considered, corresponding to the horizontal and vertical transverse wave polarizations, as well as longitudinal waves. For bowed strings, torsional waves should also be considered, since they affect bow-string dynamics (McIntyre, Schumacher, and Woodhouse 1983). In the piano, for key ranges in which the hammer strikes three strings simultaneously, nine coupled waveguides are required per key for a complete simulation (not including torsional waves); however, in a practical, high-quality, virtual piano, one waveguide per coupled string (modeling only the vertical, transverse plane) suffices quite well. It is difficult to get by with less than the correct number of strings, however, because their detuning determines the entire amplitude envelope as well as beating and aftersound effects (Weinreich 1979).

Traveling-wave solution

It can be readily checked that the lossless 1D wave equation $Ky'' = \varepsilon \ddot{y}$ is solved by any string shape which travels to the left or right with speed $c \triangleq \sqrt{K/\varepsilon}$. If we denote right-going traveling waves in general by $y_r(t - x/c)$ and left-going traveling waves by $y_l(t+x/c)$, where y_r and y_l are arbitrary twice-differentiable functions, then the general class of solutions to the lossless, one-dimensional, second-order wave equation can be expressed as

$$y(x, t) = y_r(t - x/c) + y_l(t + x/c). \tag{3}$$

Note that we have $\ddot{y}_r = c^2 y_r''$ and $\ddot{y}_l = c^2 y_l''$ showing that the wave equation is satisfied for all traveling wave shapes y_r and y_l. However, the derivation of the wave equation itself assumes the string slope is much less than 1 at all times and positions (Morse 1981). The traveling-wave solution of the wave equation was first published by d'Alembert in 1747.

Sampling the traveling waves

To carry the traveling-wave solution into the "digital domain," it is necessary to sample the traveling-wave amplitudes at intervals of T seconds, corresponding to a sampling rate $F_s \triangleq 1/T$ samples per second. For CD-quality audio, we have $F_s = 44.1$ kHz. The natural choice of *spatial sampling interval X* is the distance sound propagates in one temporal sampling interval T or $X \triangleq cT$ meters. In a lossless traveling-wave simulation, the whole wave moves left or right one spatial sample each time sample; hence, lossless simulation requires only digital delay lines. By lumping losses parsimoniously in a real acoustic model, most of the traveling-wave simulation can in fact be lossless even in a practical application.

For transverse waves on a string, the spatial sampling interval $X = cT = T\sqrt{K/\varepsilon}$ depends fundamentally on tension, density, and the temporal sampling rate chosen. Since $c = f_0 2L$, where f_0 is the fundamental frequency, and L is the string length, the spatial sampling interval can also be written as $X = L[f_0/(f_s/2)]$. A quick way to compute the number of spatial samples along a string is to divide half the sampling rate by the fundamental frequency, i.e., $L/X = (f_s/2)/f_0$. Note that this is also the total number of string overtones (when they are harmonics) retained in the digital representation. The number of harmonics is $(f_s/2)/f_0 = 22050/82.4 = 268$ for the low E string of a guitar and 67 for the high E. This equals the number of oscillators needed for an additive synthesis implementation, or the number of two-pole filters needed for a modal expansion implementation.

The spatial sampling interval for compact disc quality digital models of guitar strings ranges from about $X = Lf_0/(f_s/2) = L82.4/22050$, approximately 2.5 mm for the low E string (approximating the string length by 26 inches), up to around 10 mm for the high E string (two octaves higher and the same length). This means we have about 268 spatial samples along the low E string, and about 67 spatial samples along the high E string. While 67 samples may not seem like enough, they suffice because that's how many harmonics there are at 330 Hz (E above middle C) out to 22050 Hz (half the sampling rate).

In air, assuming the speed of sound to be 331 meters per second, we have $X = 331/44100 = 7.5$ mm for the spatial sampling interval, or a spatial sampling rate of 133 samples per meter. Thus, sound travels in air at a speed comparable to that of transverse waves on guitar strings, but faster than some strings and slower than others, depending on their tension and mass-density. Note, however, that sound travels much faster in most solids than in air, so longitudinal waves in strings travel much faster than the transverse waves (Askenfelt 1990).

Formally, sampling is carried out by the change of variables

$$x \rightarrow x_m = mX,$$
$$t \rightarrow t_n = nT.$$

Substituting into the traveling-wave solution of the wave equation gives

$$
\begin{aligned}
y(t_n, x_m) &= y_r\left(t_n - \frac{x_m}{c}\right) + y_l\left(t_n + \frac{x_m}{c}\right) \\
&= y_r\left(nT - \frac{mX}{c}\right) + y_l\left(nT + \frac{mX}{c}\right) \\
&= y_r[(n-m)T] + y_l[(n+m)T].
\end{aligned}
\tag{4}
$$

Since T multiplies all arguments, let us suppress it by defining

$$y^+(n) \triangleq y_r(nT), \quad y^-(n) \triangleq y_l(nT). \tag{5}$$

This new notation also introduces a "+" superscript to denote a traveling-wave component propagating to the right, and a "−" superscript to denote propagation to the left. This notation is similar to that used for acoustic tubes (Markel and Gray 1976).

The term $y_r[(n-m)T] = y^+(n-m)$ can be thought of as the output of an m-sample delay line whose input is $y^+(n)$. In general, subtracting a positive number m from a time argument n corresponds to *delaying* the waveform by m samples. Since y^+ is the right-going component, we draw its delay line with input $y^+(n)$ on the left and its output $y^+(n-m)$ on the right. This can be seen as the upper "rail" in Figure 3 for $m = 0, 1, 2, 3$. A C program implementing a plucked/struck string model in the form of Figure 3 is available on the Internet in:

ftp://ccrma-ftp.stanford.edu/pub/DSP/Tutorials/pluck.c.

Similarly, the term $y_l[(n+m)T] = y^-(n+m)$ can be thought of as the *input* to an m-sample delay line whose *output* is $y^-(n)$. (Adding m to the time argument n produces an m-sample waveform *advance*.) Since y^- is the left-going component, it makes sense to draw the delay line with its input $y^-(n+m)$ on the right and its output $y^-(n)$ on the left. This can be seen as the lower "rail" in Figure 3. Note that the position along the string, $x_m = mX = mcT$ meters, is laid out from left to right in the diagram for $m = 0, 1, 2, 3$ giving a physical interpretation to the horizontal direction in the diagram. Finally, the left- and right-going traveling waves must be summed to produce a physical output according to the formula

$$y(t_n, x_m) = y^+(n-m) + y^-(n+m). \tag{6}$$

We may compute the physical string displacement at any spatial sampling point x_m by simply adding the upper and lower rails together at position m along the delay-line pair. In Figure 3, "transverse displacement outputs" have been arbitrarily placed at $x = 0$ and $x = 3X$ ($m = 0$ and $m = 3$). The diagram is similar to that of well known ladder and lattice digital filter structures (Gray and Markel 1975), except for the delays along the upper rail, the absence of scattering junctions, and the direct physical interpretation. (A scattering junction implements partial reflection and partial transmission in the waveguide.)

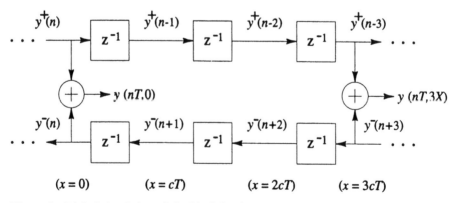

Figure 3. Digital simulation of the ideal, lossless waveguide with observation points at $x = 0$ and $x = 3X = 3cT$. The symbol z^{-1} denotes a one-sample delay.

We could proceed to ladder and lattice filters by (1) introducing a perfectly re-flecting (rigid or free) termination at the far right, and (2) commuting the delays rightward from the upper rail down to the lower rail (Smith 1987). The absence of scattering junctions is due to the fact that the string has a uniform wave impedance. In acoustic tube simulations, such as for voice (Gray and Markel 1976; Cook 1990) or wind instruments (Hirschman 1991), lossless scattering junctions are used at changes in cross-sectional tube area and lossy scattering junctions are used to implement tone holes. In waveguide bowed-string synthe-sis (discussed in a later section), the bow itself creates an active, time-varying, and nonlinear scattering junction on the string at the bowing point.

Any ideal, one-dimensional waveguide can be simulated in this way. It is important to note that the simulation is *exact* at the sampling instants, to within the numerical precision of the samples themselves. To avoid *aliasing* associated with sampling, we require all waveshapes traveling along the string to be ini-tially *bandlimited* to less than half the sampling frequency. In other words, the highest frequencies present in the signals $y_r(t)$ and $y_l(t)$ may not exceed half the temporal sampling frequency $f_s \triangleq 1/T$; equivalently, the highest *spatial* frequencies in the shapes $y_r(x/c)$ and $y_l(x/c)$ may not exceed half the spatial sampling frequency $\nu_s \triangleq 1/X$.

Digital waveguide interpolation

A more compact simulation diagram which stands for either sampled or contin-uous waveguide simulation is shown in Figure 4. The figure emphasizes that the ideal, lossless waveguide is simulated by a *bidirectional delay line,* and that ban-dlimited *spatial* interpolation may be used to construct a displacement output for an arbitrary x not a multiple of cT, as suggested by the output drawn in Figure 4

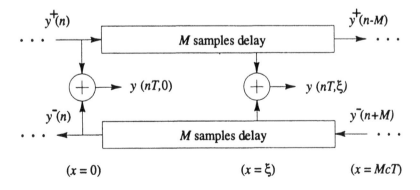

Figure 4. Simplified picture of ideal waveguide simulation.

at $x = \xi$. Similarly, bandlimited interpolation across time serves to evaluate the waveform at an arbitrary time not an integer multiple of T (Crochiere 1983; Smith and Gossett 1984; Laakso *et al.* 1996).

Ideally, bandlimited interpolation is carried out by convolving a continuous "sinc function" $\mathrm{sinc}(x) \triangleq \sin(x\pi)/x$ with the signal samples. Specifically, convolving a sampled signal $x(t_n)$ with $\mathrm{sinc}[(t_n - t_0)/T]$ "evaluates" the signal at an arbitrary continuous time t_0. The sinc function is the impulse response of the ideal lowpass filter that cuts off at half the sampling rate.

In practice, the interpolating sinc function must be *windowed* to a finite duration. This means the associated lowpass filter must be granted a "transition band" in which its frequency response is allowed to "roll off" to zero at half the sampling rate. The interpolation quality in the "pass band" can always be made perfect to within the resolution of human hearing by choosing a sufficiently large product of window-length times transition-bandwidth. Given "audibly perfect" quality in the pass band, increasing the transition bandwidth reduces the computational expense of the interpolation. In fact, they are approximately inversely proportional. This is one reason why *oversampling* at rates higher than twice the highest audio frequency is helpful. For example, at a 44.1 kHz sampling rate, the transition bandwidth above the nominal audio upper limit of 20 kHz is only 2.1 kHz, while at a 48 kHz sampling rate (used in DAT machines) the guard band is 4 kHz wide—nearly double. Since the required window length (impulse response duration) varies inversely with the provided transition bandwidth, we see that increasing the sampling rate by less than ten percent reduces the filter expense by almost fifty percent. Windowed-sinc interpolation is described further in (Smith and Gossett 1984). Many more techniques for digital resampling and delay-line interpolation are reviewed in (Laakso *et al.* 1996).

Alternative wave variables

We have thus far considered discrete-time simulation of transverse *displacement* y in the ideal string. It is equally valid to choose *velocity* $v \triangleq \dot{y}$, *acceleration* $a \triangleq \ddot{y}$, *slope* y', or perhaps some other derivative or integral of displacement

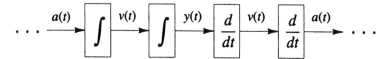

Figure 5. Conversions between various time derivatives of displacement: y = displacement, $v = \dot{y}$ = velocity, $a = \ddot{y}$ = acceleration, where $\dot{y}$ denotes dy/dt and $\ddot{y}$ denotes d^2y/dt^2.

with respect to time or position. Conversion between various time derivatives can be carried out by means of *integrators* and *differentiators,* as depicted in Figure 5. Since integration and differentiation are *linear* operators, and since the traveling wave arguments are in units of time, the conversion formulas relating y, v, and a hold also for the traveling wave *components* $y^\pm$, $v^\pm$, $a^\pm$.

Differentiation and integration have a simple form in the frequency domain. Denoting the *Laplace transform* of $y(t, x)$ by

$$Y(s, x) \triangleq \mathcal{L}_s\{y(\cdot, x)\} \triangleq \int_0^\infty y(t, x)e^{-st}\, dt, \tag{7}$$

where "$\cdot$" in the time argument means "for all time," we have, according to the *differentiation theorem* for Laplace transforms (LePage 1961),

$$\mathcal{L}_s\{v(\cdot, x)\} = sY(s, x) - y(0, x).$$

Similarly, $\mathcal{L}_s\{\dot{y}^+\} = sY^+(s) - y^+(0)$, and so on. Thus, in the frequency domain, the conversions between displacement, velocity, and acceleration appear as shown in Figure 6.

In discrete time, integration and differentiation can be accomplished using digital filters (Rabiner and Gold, 1975). Commonly used first-order approximations are shown in Figure 7.

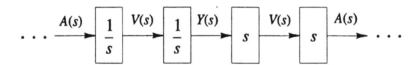

Figure 6. Conversions between various time derivatives of displacement in the frequency domain.

a) First-Order Difference   b) First-Order "Leaky" Integrator

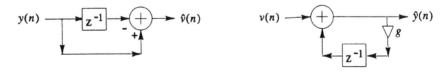

Figure 7. Simple approximate conversions between time derivatives in the discrete-time case: a) The first-order difference $\hat{v}(n) = y(n) - y(n - 1)$. b) The first-order "leaky" integrator $\hat{y}(n) = v(n) + g\hat{y}(n - 1)$ with loss factor g (slightly less than 1) used to avoid infinite DC build-up.

If discrete-time acceleration $a_d(n)$ is defined as the sampled version of continuous-time acceleration, that is, $a_d(n) \triangleq a(nT, x) = \ddot{y}(nT, x)$, for some fixed continuous position x that we suppress for simplicity of notation, then the frequency-domain form is given by the *z transform* (Strum and Kirk 1988).

$$A_d(z) \triangleq \sum_{n=0}^{\infty} a_d(n) z^{-n}.$$

The z transform plays the role of the Laplace transform for discrete-time systems. Setting $z = e^{sT}$, it can be seen as a sampled Laplace transform (divided by T), where the sampling is carried out by halting the limit of the rectangle width at T in the definition of a Reimann integral for the Laplace transform. An important difference between the two is that the frequency axis in the Laplace transform is the imaginary axis (the "$j\omega$ axis"), while the frequency axis in the z plane is on the unit circle $z = e^{j\omega T}$. As one would expect, the frequency axis for discrete-time systems has unique information only between frequencies $-\pi/T$ and π/T while the continuous-time frequency axis extends to plus and minus infinity.

These first-order approximations are accurate (though scaled by T) at low frequencies relative to half the sampling rate, but they are not "best" approximations in any sense other than being most like the definitions of integration and differentiation in continuous time. Much better approximations can be obtained by approaching the problem from a *digital filter design* viewpoint (Rabiner and Gold 1975; Parks and Burrus 1987; Loy 1988). Arbitrarily better approximations are possible using higher order digital filters. In principle, a *digital differentiator* is a filter whose frequency response $H(e^{j\omega T})$ optimally approximates $j\omega$ for ω between $-\pi/T$ and π/T. Similarly, a *digital integrator* must match $1/j\omega$ along the unit circle in the z plane. The reason an exact match is not possible is that the ideal frequency responses $j\omega$ and $1/j\omega$, when wrapped along the unit circle in the z plane (the frequency axis for discrete time systems), are not "smooth" functions any more. As a result, there is no filter with a rational transfer function (i.e., finite order) that can match the desired frequency response exactly. The frequency response for the ideal digital differentiator is shown in Figure 8.

The discontinuity at $z = -1$ alone is enough to ensure that no finite-order digital transfer function exists with the desired frequency response. As with bandlimited interpolation, it is good practice to reserve the top 10–20% of the spectrum as a "guard band," above the limits of human hearing, where digital filters are free to smoothly vary in whatever way gives the best performance across frequencies in the audible band at the lowest cost. Note that, as in filters used for bandlimited interpolation, a small increment in oversampling factor yields a much larger decrease in filter cost when the sampling rate is low.

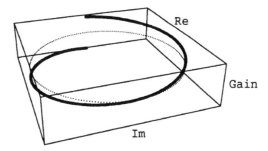

Figure 8. Imaginary part of the frequency response $H(e^{j\omega T}) = j\omega$ of the ideal digital differentiator plotted over the unit circle in the z plane (the real part being zero).

In the general case, digital filters can be designed to give arbitrarily accurate differentiation and integration by finding an optimal, complex, rational approximation to $H(e^{j\omega T}) = (j\omega)^k$ over the interval $-\omega_{max} \leqslant \omega \leqslant \omega_{max}$, where k is an integer corresponding to the degree of differentiation or integration, and $\omega_{max} < \pi$ is the upper limit of human hearing. For small guard bands $\delta \triangleq \frac{\pi}{T} - \omega_{max}$, the filter order required for a given error tolerance is approximately inversely proportional to δ (Rabiner and Gold 1975; Smith, Gutknecht, and Trefethen 1983; Parks and Burrus 1987; Beliczynski, Kale, and Cain 1992).

Spatial derivatives

In addition to time derivatives, we may apply any number of *spatial derivatives* to obtain yet more wave variables to choose from. The first spatial derivative of string displacement yields *slope waves*:

$$
\begin{aligned}
y'(t, x) &\triangleq \frac{\partial}{\partial x} y(t, x) \\
&= y_r'(t - x/c) + y_l'(t + x/c),
\end{aligned}
\tag{10}
$$

or, in discrete time,

$$
\begin{aligned}
y'(t_n, x_m) &\triangleq y'(nT, mX) \\
&= y_r'[(n - m)T] + y_l'[(n + m)T] \\
&\triangleq y'^{+}(n - m) + y'^{-}(n + m)
\end{aligned}
$$

$$= -\frac{1}{c}\dot{y}^{+}(n-m) + \frac{1}{c}\dot{y}^{-}(n+m)$$

$$\triangleq -\frac{1}{c}v^{+}(n-m) + \frac{1}{c}v^{-}(n+m) \tag{11}$$

$$= \frac{1}{c}[v^{-}(n+m) - v^{+}(n+m)].$$

From this we may conclude that $v^{-} = cy'^{-}$ and $v^{+} = -cy'^{+}$. That is, traveling slope waves can be computed from traveling velocity waves by dividing by c and negating in the right-going case. Physical string slope can thus be computed from a velocity-wave simulation in a digital waveguide by subtracting the upper rail from the lower rail and dividing by c. By the wave equation, *curvature waves*, $y'' = \ddot{y}/c^{2}$, are simply a scaling of acceleration waves.

In the field of acoustics, the state of a vibrating string at any instant of time t_0 is normally specified by the displacement $y(t_0, x)$ and velocity $\dot{y}(t_0, x)$ for all x (Morse 1981). Since displacement is the *sum* of the traveling displacement waves and velocity is proportional to the *difference* of the traveling displacement waves, one state description can be readily obtained from the other.

In summary, all traveling-wave variables can be computed from any one, as long as both the left- and right-going component waves are available. Alternatively, any two linearly independent *physical* variables, such as displacement and velocity, can be used to compute all other wave variables. Wave variable conversions requiring differentiation or integration are relatively expensive since a large-order digital filter is necessary to do it right. Slope and velocity waves can be computed from each other by simple scaling, and curvature waves are identical to acceleration waves to within a scale factor.

In the absence of factors dictating a specific choice, *velocity waves* are a good overall choice because (1) it is numerically easier to perform digital integration to get displacement than it is to differentiate displacement to get velocity, (2) slope waves are immediately computable from velocity waves. Slope waves are important because they are proportional to force waves.

Force waves

Referring to Figure 9, at an arbitrary point x along the string, the vertical force applied at time t to the the portion of string to the left of position x by the portion of string to the right of position x is given by

$$f_l(t, x) = K \sin(\theta) \approx K \tan(\theta) = K y'(t, x), \tag{12}$$

assuming $|y'(t, x)| \ll 1$, as is assumed in the derivation of the wave equation.

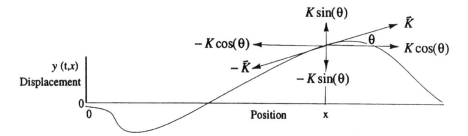

Figure 9. Transverse force propagation in the ideal string.

Similarly, the force applied *by* the portion to the left of position x *to* the portion to the right is given by

$$f_r(t, x) = -K \sin(\theta) \approx -K y'(t, x). \tag{13}$$

These forces must cancel since a nonzero net force on a massless point would produce infinite acceleration.

Vertical force waves propagate along the string like any other transverse wave variable (since they are just slope waves multiplied by tension K). We may choose either f_l or f_r as the string force wave variable, one being the negative of the other. It turns out that to make the description for vibrating strings look the same as that for air columns, we have to pick f_r, the one that *acts to the right*. This makes sense intuitively when one considers longitudinal pressure waves in an acoustic tube: a compression wave traveling to the right in the tube pushes the air in front of it and thus acts to the right. We therefore define the *force wave variable* to be

$$f(t, x) \triangleq f_r(t, x) = -K y'(t, x). \tag{14}$$

Note that a negative slope pulls *up* on the segment to the right. Using previous identities, we have

$$f(t, x) = \frac{K}{c} [\dot{y}_r(t - x/c) - \dot{y}_l(t + x/c)], \tag{15}$$

where $K/c \triangleq K/\sqrt{K/\varepsilon} = \sqrt{K\varepsilon}$. This is a fundamental quantity known as the *wave impedance* of the string (also called the *characteristic impedance*), denoted as

$$R \triangleq \sqrt{K\varepsilon} = \frac{K}{c} = \varepsilon c. \tag{16}$$

The wave impedance can be seen as the geometric mean of the two resistances to displacement: tension (spring force) and mass (inertial force).

The digitized traveling force-wave components become

$$
\begin{aligned}
f^+(n) &= \quad Rv^+(n), \\
f^-(n) &= -Rv^-(n),
\end{aligned}
\tag{17}
$$

which gives us that the right-going force wave equals the wave impedance times the right-going velocity wave, and the left-going force wave equals minus the wave impedance times the left-going velocity wave. Thus, in a traveling wave, force is always *in phase* with velocity (considering the minus sign in the left-going case to be associated with the direction of travel rather than a 180 degrees phase shift between force and velocity). Note also that if the left-going force wave were defined as the string force acting to the left, the minus sign would disappear. The fundamental relation $f^+ = Rv^+$ is sometimes referred to as the mechanical counterpart of *Ohm's law*, and R in c.g.s. units can be called *acoustical Ohms* (Kolsky 1963).

In the case of the *acoustic tube* (Morse 1981; Markel and Gray 1976), we have the analogous relations

$$
\begin{aligned}
p^+(n) &= \quad R_t u^+(n), \\
p^-(n) &= -R_t u^-(n),
\end{aligned}
\tag{18}
$$

where $p^+(n)$ is the right-going traveling *longitudinal pressure wave* component, $p^-(n)$ is the left-going pressure wave, and $u^\pm(n)$ are the left- and right-going *volume velocity waves*. In the acoustic tube context, the wave impedance is given by

$$
R_t = \frac{\rho c}{A} \quad \text{(acoustic tubes)},
\tag{19}
$$

where ρ is the mass per unit volume of air, c is sound speed in air, and A is the cross-sectional area of the tube (Morse and Ingard 1968). Note that if we had chosen *particle velocity* rather than volume velocity, the wave impedance would be $R_0 = \rho c$ instead, the wave impedance in open air. Particle velocity is appropriate in open air, while volume velocity is the conserved quantity in acoustic tubes or "ducts" of varying cross-sectional area (Morse and Ingard 1968).

Power waves

Basic courses in physics teach us that *power* is *work per unit time,* and *work* is a measure of *energy* which is typically defined as *force times distance.* Therefore, power is in physical units of force times distance per unit time, or force times velocity. It therefore should come as no surprise that *traveling power waves* are defined for strings as

$$
\begin{aligned}
\mathcal{P}^+(n) &\triangleq f^+(n)v^+(n), \\
\mathcal{P}^-(n) &\triangleq -f^-(n)v^-(n).
\end{aligned}
\tag{20}
$$

From the elementary relations $f^+ = Rv^+$ and $f^- = -Rv^-$, we also have

$$
\mathcal{P}^+(n) \triangleq R[v^+(n)]^2 = [f^+(n)]^2/R,
\tag{21}
$$

$$
\mathcal{P}^-(n) \triangleq R[v^-(n)]^2 = [f^-(n)]^2/R.
$$

Thus, both the left- and right-going components are *nonnegative*. The sum of the traveling powers at a point gives the total power at that point in the waveguide:

$$
\mathcal{P}(t_n, x_m) \triangleq \mathcal{P}^+(n-m) + \mathcal{P}^-(n+m).
\tag{22}
$$

If we had left out the minus sign in the definition of left-going power waves, the sum would instead be a net power flow.

Power waves are important because they correspond to the actual ability of the wave to do work on the outside world, such as on a violin bridge at the end of a string. Because energy is conserved in closed systems, power waves sometimes give a simpler, more fundamental view of wave phenomena, such as in conical acoustic tubes. Also, implementing nonlinear operations such as *rounding* and *saturation* in such a way that signal power is not increased, gives suppression of *limit cycles* and *overflow oscillations* (Smith 1986b).

Energy density waves

The vibrational energy per unit length along the string, or *wave energy density* (Morse 1981) is given by the sum of potential and kinetic energy densities:

$$
W(t, x) \triangleq \frac{1}{2}Ky'^2(t, x) + \frac{1}{2}\varepsilon \dot{y}^2(t, x).
\tag{23}
$$

Sampling across time and space, and substituting traveling wave components, one can show in a few lines of algebra that the *sampled* wave energy density is given by

$$W(t_n, x_m) \triangleq W^+(n-m) + W^-(n+m), \tag{24}$$

where

$$
\begin{aligned}
W^+(n) &= \mathcal{P}^+(n)/c = f^+(n)v^+(n)/c = \varepsilon[v^+(n)]^2 = [f^+(n)]^2/K, \\
W^-(n) &= \mathcal{P}^-(n)/c = f^-(n)v^-(n)/c = \varepsilon[v^-(n)]^2 = [f^-(n)]^2/K.
\end{aligned}
\tag{25}
$$

Thus, traveling power waves (energy per unit time) can be converted to energy density waves (energy per unit length) by simply dividing by c, the speed of propagation. Quite naturally, the *total wave energy* in the string is given by the integral along the string of the energy density:

$$\mathcal{E}(t) = \int_{x=-\infty}^{\infty} W(t, x)\, dx \cong \sum_{m=-\infty}^{\infty} W(t, x_m)X. \tag{26}$$

In practice, of course, the string length is finite, and the limits of integration are from the x coordinate of the left endpoint to that of the right endpoint, e.g., 0 to L.

Root-power waves

It is sometimes helpful to *normalize* the wave variables so that signal power is uniformly distributed numerically. This can be especially helpful in fixed-point implementations.

From equation (21), it is clear that power normalization is given by

$$
\begin{aligned}
\tilde{f}^+ &\triangleq f^+/\sqrt{R}, \quad \tilde{f}^- \triangleq f^-/\sqrt{R}, \\
\tilde{v}^+ &\triangleq v^+ \cdot \sqrt{R}, \quad \tilde{v}^- \triangleq v^- \cdot \sqrt{R},
\end{aligned}
\tag{27}
$$

where we have dropped the common time argument '(n)' for simplicity. As a result, we obtain

$$
\begin{aligned}
\mathcal{P}^+ &= f^+v^+ = \tilde{f}^+\tilde{v}^+ \\
&= R(v^+)^2 = (\tilde{v}^+)^2 \\
&= (f^+)^2/R = (\tilde{f}^+)^2,
\end{aligned}
\tag{28}
$$

and

$$
\begin{aligned}
\mathcal{P}^- &= -f^- v^- = -\tilde{f}^+ \tilde{v}^+ \\
&= R(v^-)^2 = (\tilde{v}^-)^2 \\
&= (f^-)^2/R = (\tilde{f}^-)^2.
\end{aligned}
\tag{29}
$$

The normalized wave variables $\tilde{f}^\pm$ and $\tilde{v}^\pm$ behave physically like force and velocity waves, respectively, but they are scaled such that either can be squared to obtain instantaneous signal power. Waveguide networks built using normalized waves have many desirable properties. One is the obvious numerical advantage of uniformly distributing signal power across available dynamic range in fixed-point implementations. Another is that only in the normalized case can the wave impedances be made *time varying* without modulating signal power (Gray and Markel 1975; Smith 1986). In other words, use of normalized waves eliminates "parametric amplification" effects; signal power is decoupled from parameter changes.

The lossy one-dimensional wave equation

In any real vibrating string, there are energy losses due to yielding terminations, drag by the surrounding air, and internal friction within the string. While losses in solids generally vary in a complicated way with frequency, they can usually be well approximated by a small number of odd-order terms added to the wave equation. In the simplest case, force is directly proportional to transverse string velocity, independent of frequency. If this proportionality constant is μ, we obtain the modified wave equation

$$
Ky'' = \varepsilon \ddot{y} + \mu \dot{y}.
\tag{30}
$$

Thus, the wave equation has been extended by a "first-order" term, that is, a term proportional to the first derivative of y with respect to time. More realistic loss approximations would append terms proportional to $\partial^3 y/\partial t^3$, $\partial^5 y/\partial t^5$, and so on, giving frequency-dependent losses.

It can be ascertained that for small displacements y and small loss coefficient μ, the following modified traveling wave solution satisfies the lossy wave equation:

$$
y(t, x) = e^{-(\mu/2\varepsilon)x/c} y_r(t - x/c) + e^{(\mu/2\varepsilon)x/c} y_l(t + x/c).
\tag{31}
$$

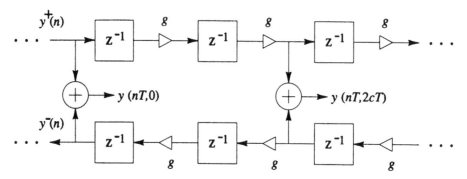

Figure 10. Discrete simulation of the ideal, lossy waveguide. The loss factor $g \triangleq e^{-\mu T/2\varepsilon}$ *summarizes* the distributed loss incurred in one sampling period.

The left-going and right-going traveling-wave components decay *exponentially* in their respective directions of travel.

Sampling these exponentially decaying traveling waves at intervals of T seconds (or $X = cT$ meters) gives

$$y(t_n, x_m) = g^m y^+(n - m) + g^{-m} y^-(n + m), \tag{32}$$

where $g \triangleq e^{-\mu T/2\varepsilon}$. The simulation diagram for the lossy digital waveguide is shown in Figure 10.

Again the discrete-time simulation of the decaying traveling-wave solution is an *exact* implementation of the continuous-time solution at the sampling positions and instants, even though losses are admitted in the wave equation. Note also that the losses which are *distributed* in the continuous solution have been consolidated, or *lumped*, at discrete intervals of cT meters in the simulation. The loss factor $g \triangleq e^{-\mu T/2\varepsilon}$ *summarizes* the distributed loss incurred in one sampling interval. The lumping of distributed losses does not introduce an approximation error at the sampling points. Furthermore, bandlimited interpolation can yield arbitrarily accurate reconstruction between samples. The only restriction is again that all initial conditions and excitations be bandlimited to below half the sampling rate.

Loss consolidation

In many applications, it is possible to realize vast computational savings in digital waveguide models by *commuting* losses out of unobserved and undriven sections of the medium and consolidating them at a minimum number of points. Because the digital simulation is linear and time invariant (given constant medium

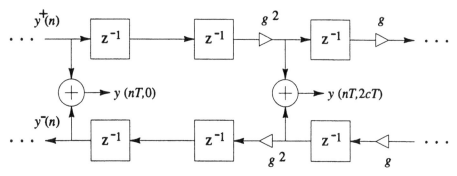

Figure 11. Discrete simulation of the ideal, lossy waveguide. Each per-sample loss factor g may be "pushed through" delay elements and combined with other loss factors until an input or output is encountered which inhibits further migration. If further consolidation is possible on the other side of a branching node, a loss factor can be pushed *through* the node by pushing a copy into each departing branch. If there are other *inputs* to the node, the *inverse* of the loss factor must appear on each of them. Similar remarks apply to pushing backwards through a node.

parameters K, ε, μ), and because linear, time-invariant elements commute, the diagram in Figure 11 is exactly equivalent (to within numerical precision) to the previous diagram in Figure 10.

Frequency-dependent losses

In nearly all natural wave phenomena, losses increase with frequency. Distributed losses due to air drag and internal bulk losses in the string tend to increase monotonically with frequency. Similarly, air absorption increases with frequency, adding loss for sound waves in acoustic tubes or open air (Morse and Ingard 1968).

The solution of a lossy wave equation containing higher odd-order derivatives with respect to time yields traveling waves which propagate with frequency-dependent attenuation. Instead of scalar factors g distributed throughout the diagram, we obtain lowpass filters having frequency-response per sample denoted by $G(\omega)$. If the wave equation (30) is modified by adding terms proportional to $\partial^3 y/\partial t^3$ and $\partial^5 y/\partial t^5$, for instance, then $G(\omega)$ is generally of the form

$$G(\omega) = g_0 + g_2\omega^2 + g_4\omega^4,$$

where the g_i are constants depending on the constant coefficients in the wave equation. These per-sample loss filters may also be consolidated at a minimum number of points in the waveguide without introducing an approximation error in the linear, time-invariant case.

In an efficient digital simulation, lumped loss factors of the form $G^k(\omega)$ are approximated by a rational frequency response $\widehat{G}_k(e^{j\omega T})$. In general, the coefficients of the optimal rational loss filter are obtained by minimizing $\|G^k(\omega) - \widehat{G}(e^{j\omega T})\|$ with respect to the filter coefficients or the poles and zeros of the filter. To avoid introducing frequency-dependent delay, the loss filter should be a *zero-phase, finite-impulse-response* (FIR) filter (Rabiner and Gold 1975). Restriction to zero phase requires the impulse response $\hat{g}_k(n)$ to be finite in length (i.e., an FIR filter) and it must be symmetric about time zero, i.e., $\hat{g}_k(-n) = \hat{g}_k(n)$. In most implementations, the zero-phase FIR filter can be converted into a causal, *linear phase* filter by reducing an adjacent delay line by half of the impulse-response duration.

Coupling to alternative physical models

The digital waveguide is a sampled, "distributed" acoustic model, as opposed to consisting of "lumped" elements. These terms refer to the nature of the basic physical constants in the model: In an ideal string, mass is uniformly distributed along the string, as is the springiness. A lumped model of the ideal string consists of a row of masses interconnected by springs, the so-called mass-spring chain (Morse and Ingard 1968). Lumped elements are most natural when the physical object being modeled behaves as a discrete mass, spring, or dashpot. Brass-players' lips are typically modeled as lumped mass-spring systems, as are models of the vocal folds in the human voice. Distributed models are more natural for media which support traveling-wave propagation such as strings, rods, bores, horns, membranes, plates, and acoustic spaces. In these cases, the digital waveguide formulation can be used to improve the speed and accuracy of the computation.

The universal interface to all types of physical models is by means of *ports* and *driving point impedances*. These concepts are fundamental in *classical network theory* (Belevitch 1968) which was developed to provide a general mathematical framework for electromagnetic circuits. It is important to understand that distributed and lumped models can be freely interconnected by means of port connections.

To connect a digital waveguide (distributed model) to a lumped model (such as a modal expansion using second-order resonators), it is convenient to formulate the lumped network as a *driving-point impedance*, i.e., the ratio of applied force to resulting velocity at each frequency. A lumped impedance attached to a waveguide gives rise to signal *scattering*, i.e., waves traveling into the impedance are partially reflected and partially transmitted similar to traveling waves encountering a discontinuity in wave impedance. However, a wave-impedance discontinuity results in constant reflection and transmission coefficients, while in the more general lumped impedance case, the reflection and transmission coefficients become digital filters. This topic is described further in (Smith 1987b, p. 125), and the constant-coefficient case is used extensively in speech modeling (Markel and Gray 1976; Smith 1987b).

We will now review selected applications in digital waveguide modeling. First, a few elementary illustrative examples are considered, such as the ideal plucked and struck strings, introduction of losses, and various related highlights. Second, two advanced applications are considered: single reed woodwinds (such as the clarinet), and bowed strings (such as the violin). In these applications, a sustained sound is synthesized by the interaction of the digital waveguide with a *nonlinear* junction causing spontaneous, self-sustaining oscillation in response to an applied mouth pressure or bow velocity, respectively. This nonlinear, self-sustaining oscillation method forms the basis of the Yamaha VL series of synthesizers ("VL" standing for "virtual lead").

Elementary applications

This section presents elementary applications of waveguide models, including rigid terminations of a string, the ideal plucked string, the ideal struck string, the externally excited string, the damped plucked string. We also consider the subject of frequency-dependent damping for more realistic simulation.

Rigid terminations

A *rigid termination* is the simplest case of a string termination. It imposes the constraint that the string cannot move at all at the termination. If we terminate a length L ideal string at $x = 0$ and $x = L$, we then have the "boundary conditions"

$$y(t, 0) \equiv 0, \quad y(t, L) \equiv 0,$$

where "$\equiv$" means "identically equal to", i.e., equal for all t.

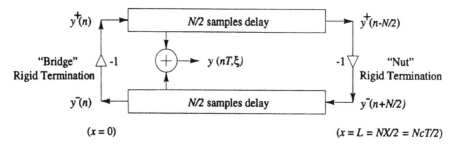

Figure 12. The rigidly terminated ideal string, with a position output indicated at $x = \xi$. Rigid terminations reflect traveling displacement, velocity, or acceleration waves with a sign inversion. Slope or force waves reflect with no sign inversion.

Since $y(t, 0) = y_r(t) + y_l(t) = y^+(t/T) + y^-(t/T)$ and $y(t, L) = y_r(t - L/c) + y_l(t + L/c)$, the constraints on the sampled traveling waves become

$$y^+(n) = -y^-(n), \tag{33}$$

$$y^-(n + N/2) = -y^+(n - N/2), \tag{34}$$

where $N \triangleq 2L/X$ is the time in samples to propagate from one end of the string to the other and back, or the total "string loop" delay. The loop delay is also equal to twice the number of spatial samples along the string. A digital simulation diagram for the rigidly terminated ideal string is shown in Figure 12. A virtual "pick-up" is shown at the arbitrary location $x = \xi$.

The total energy $\mathcal{E}$ in a rigidly terminated, freely vibrating string can be computed as

$$\mathcal{E}(t) \triangleq \int_0^L W(t, x)dx = \int_{t_0}^{t_0 + 2L/c} \mathcal{P}(\tau, x)d\tau,$$

for any $x \in [0, L]$. Since the energy never decays, t and t_0 are arbitrary. Thus, because free vibrations of a doubly terminated string must be *periodic* in time, the total energy equals the integral of power over any period at any point along the string.

The ideal plucked string

The ideal *plucked string* is defined as an initial string displacement and a zero initial velocity distribution (Morse 1981). More generally, the initial displacement along the string $y(0, x)$ and the initial velocity distribution $\dot{y}(0, x)$, for all x, fully determine the resulting motion in the absence of further excitation.

An example of the appearance of the traveling wave components and the resulting string shape shortly after plucking a doubly terminated string at a point one fourth along its length is shown in Figure 13. The negative traveling-wave portions can be thought of as inverted reflections of the incident waves, or as doubly flipped "images" which are coming from the other side of the terminations.

An example of an initial "pluck" excitation in a digital waveguide string model is shown in Figure 14. There is one fine point to note for the discrete-time case: We cannot admit a sharp corner in the string since that would have infinite bandwidth which would alias when sampled. Therefore, for the discrete-time case, we define the ideal pluck to consist of an arbitrary shape as in Figure 14 *lowpass filtered* to less than half the sampling rate. Alternatively, we can simply require the initial displacement shape to be bandlimited to spatial frequencies less than $f_s/2c$. Since all real strings have some degree of stiffness which prevents the formation of perfectly sharp corners, and since real plectra are never in

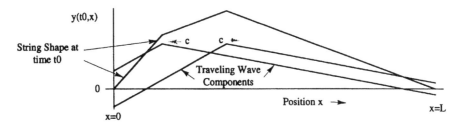

Figure 13. A doubly terminated string, "plucked" at one fourth its length.

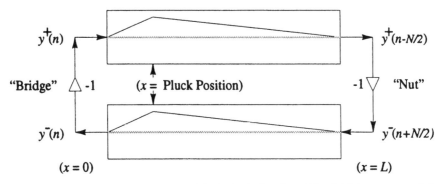

Figure 14. Initial conditions for the ideal plucked string. The initial contents of the sampled, traveling-wave delay lines are in effect *plotted* inside the delay-line boxes. The amplitude of each traveling-wave delay line is half the amplitude of the initial string displacement. The sum of the upper and lower delay lines gives the actual initial string displacement.

contact with the string at only one point, and since the frequencies we do allow span the full range of human hearing, the bandlimited restriction is not limiting in any practical sense.

Note that acceleration (or curvature) waves are a simple choice for plucked string simulation, since the ideal pluck corresponds to an initial *impulse* in the delay lines at the pluck point. Of course, since we require a bandlimited excitation, the initial acceleration distribution will be replaced by the impulse response of the anti-aliasing filter chosen. If the anti-aliasing filter chosen is the ideal lowpass filter cutting off at $f_s/2$, the initial acceleration $a(0, x) \triangleq \ddot{y}(0, x)$ for the ideal pluck becomes

$$a(0, x) = \frac{A}{X}\text{sinc}\left(\frac{x - x_p}{X}\right), \tag{35}$$

where A is amplitude, x_p is the pick position, and $\text{sinc}[(x - x_p)/X]$ is the ideal, bandlimited impulse, centered at x_p and having a rectangular spatial frequency response extending from $-\pi/X$ to π/X. (Recall that $\text{sinc}(\xi) \triangleq \sin(\pi\xi)/(\pi\xi)$.) Division by X normalizes the area under the initial shape curve. If x_p is chosen to lie exactly on a spatial sample $x_m = mX$, the initial conditions for the ideal plucked string are as shown in Figure 15 for the case of acceleration or curvature waves. All initial samples are zero except one in each delay line.

Aside from its obvious simplicity, there are two important benefits of obtaining an impulse-excited model: (1) an extremely efficient "commuted synthesis" algorithm can be readily defined (Karjalainen and Laine 1991; Smith 1993; Jaffe and Smith 1995), and (2) linear prediction (and its relatives) can be readily used to calibrate the model to recordings of normally played tones on the modeled

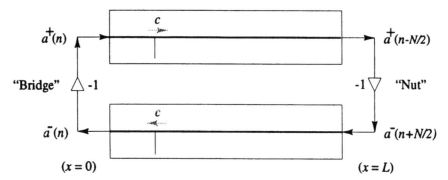

Figure 15. Initial conditions for the ideal plucked string when the wave variables are chosen to be proportional to acceleration or curvature. If the bandlimited ideal pluck position is centered on a spatial sample, there is only a single nonzero sample in each of the initial delay lines.

instrument. Linear Predictive Coding (LPC) has been used extensively in speech modeling (Atal and Hanauer 1971; Makhoul 1975; Markel and Gray 1976). LPC estimates the model filter coefficients under the assumption that the driving signal is *spectrally flat*. This assumption is valid when the input signal is (1) an impulse, or (2) white noise. In the basic LPC model for voiced speech, a periodic impulse train excites the model filter (which functions as the vocal tract), and for unvoiced speech, white noise is used as input.

In addition to plucked and struck strings, simplified *bowed strings* can be calibrated to recorded data as well using LPC (Smith 1983, 1993). In this simplified model, the bowed string is approximated as a periodically plucked string.

The ideal struck string

The ideal *struck string* (Morse 1981) involves a *zero* initial string displacement but a nonzero initial velocity distribution. In concept, a "hammer strike" transfers an "impulse" of momentum to the string at time 0 along the striking face of the hammer. An example of "struck" initial conditions is shown in Figure 16 for a striking hammer having a rectangular shape. Since $v^{\pm} = \pm f^{\pm}/R = \mp cy'^{\pm}$, the initial velocity distribution can be integrated with respect to x from $x = 0$, divided by c, and negated in the upper rail to obtain equivalent initial displacement waves (Morse 1981).

The hammer strike itself may be considered to take zero time in the ideal case. A finite spatial width must be admitted for the hammer, however, even in the ideal case, because a zero width and a nonzero momentum transfer sends one point of the string immediately to infinity under infinite acceleration. In a discrete-time simulation, one sample represents an entire sampling interval, so a one-sample hammer width is well defined.

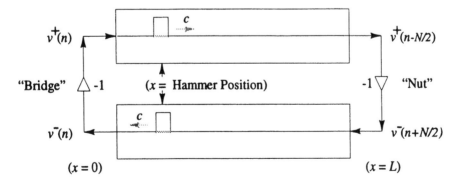

Figure 16. Initial conditions for the ideal struck string in a *velocity wave* simulation.

If the hammer velocity is v_h, the wave impedance force against the hammer is $-2Rv_h$. The factor of 2 arises because driving a point in the string's interior is equivalent to driving two string endpoints in "series," i.e., their reaction forces sum. If the hammer is itself a dynamic system which has been "thrown" into the string, the reaction force slows the hammer over time, and the interaction is not impulsive, but rather the momentum transfer takes place over a period of time. The momentum transferred is given by the integral of the contact force with respect to time.

The hammer-string collision is ideally *inelastic* since the string provides a reaction force that is equivalent to that of a dashpot. In the case of a pure mass striking a single point on the ideal string, the mass velocity decays exponentially, and an exponential wavefront emanates in both directions. In the musical acoustics literature for the piano, the hammer is often taken to be a nonlinear spring in series with a mass (Suzuki 1987). A waveguide piano using the Suzuki hammer-felt model is described in (Borin and De Poli 1989). A commuted waveguide piano model including a linearized piano hammer is described in (Smith and Van Duyne 1995; Van Duyne and Smith 1995). The more elaborate "wave digital hammer," which employs a traveling-wave formulation of a lumped model and therefore analogous to a wave digital filter (Fettweis 1986), is described in (Van Duyne, Pierce, and Smith 1994).

The externally excited string

The preceding two subsections illustrated plucking or striking the string by means of *initial conditions*: an initial displacement for plucking and an initial velocity for striking. Such a description parallels that found in textbooks on acoustics. However, if the string is already in motion, as it often is in normal usage, it is more natural to excite the string externally by the equivalent of a "pick" or "hammer" as is done in the real world instrument.

Figure 17 depicts a rigidly terminated string with an external excitation input. The wave variable w can be set to acceleration, velocity, or displacement, as appropriate. (Choosing force waves would require eliminating the sign inversions at the terminations.) The external input is denoted Δw to indicate that it is an additive incremental input, superimposing with the existing string state.

For idealized plucked strings, we may take $w = a$ (acceleration), and Δw can be a single nonzero sample, or impulse, at the plucking instant. As always, bandlimited interpolation can be used to provide a non-integer time or position. In the latter case, there would be two or more summers along both the upper and lower rails, separated by unit delays. More generally, the string may be plucked

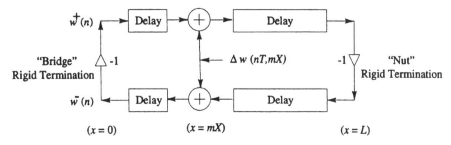

Figure 17. Discrete simulation of the rigidly terminated string with an external excitation.

by a *force distribution* $f_p(t_n, x_m)$. The applied force at a point can be translated to the corresponding velocity increment via the wave impedance R:

$$\Delta v = \frac{f_p}{2R},\tag{36}$$

where $R = \sqrt{K/\varepsilon}$ as before. The factor of two comes from the fact that two string endpoints are being driven in parallel. (Physically, they are in parallel, but as impedances, they are formally in series.)

Note that the force applied by a rigid, stationary pick or hammer varies with the state of a vibrating string. Also, when a pick or hammer makes contact with the string, it partially *terminates* the string, resulting in reflected waves in each direction. A simple model for the termination would be a mass affixed to the string at the excitation point. A more general model would be an arbitrary impedance and force source affixed to the string at the excitation point during the excitation event. In the waveguide model for bowed strings (discussed in the advanced applications section), the bow-string interface is modeled as a nonlinear scattering junction.

The damped plucked string

Without damping, the ideal plucked string sounds more like a cheap electronic organ than a string because the sound is perfectly periodic and never decays. Static spectra are very boring to the ear. The discrete Fourier transform (DFT) of the initial "string loop" contents gives the Fourier series coefficients for the periodic tone produced. Incorporating damping means we use *exponentially decaying traveling waves* instead of non-decaying waves. As discussed previously, it saves computation to *lump* the loss factors which implement damping in the waveguide in order to minimize computational cost and round-off error.

To illustrate how significant the computational savings can be, consider the simulation of a "damped guitar string" model in Figure 18. For simplicity, the length L string is rigidly terminated on both ends. Let the string be "plucked" by initial conditions so that we need not couple an input mechanism to the string. Also, let the output be simply the signal passing through a particular delay element rather than the more realistic summation of opposite elements in the bidirectional delay line. (A comb filter corresponding to output position can be added in series later.)

In this string simulator, there is a loop of delay containing $N = 2L/X = f_s/f_1$ samples where f_1 is the desired pitch of the string. Because there is no input/output coupling, we may lump *all* of the losses at a single point in the delay loop. Furthermore, the two reflecting terminations (gain factors of -1) may be commuted so as to cancel them. Finally, the right-going delay may be combined with the left-going delay to give a single, length N, delay line. The result of these inaudible simplifications is shown in Figure 19.

If the sampling rate is $f_s = 50$ kHz and the desired pitch is $f_1 = 100$ Hz, the loop delay equals $N = 500$ samples. Since delay lines are efficiently implemented as circular buffers, the cost of implementation is normally dominated by the loss factors, each one requiring a multiply every sample, in general. (Losses

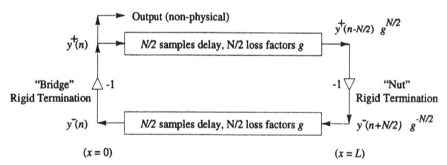

Figure 18. Discrete simulation of the rigidly terminated string with distributed resistive losses. The N loss factors g are embedded between the delay-line elements.

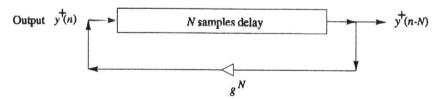

Figure 19. Discrete simulation of the rigidly terminated string with *consolidated* losses (frequency-independent). All N loss factors g have been "pushed" through delay elements and combined at a *single* point.

of the form $1 - 2^{-k}$, $1 - 2^{-k} - 2^{-l}$, etc., can be efficiently implemented using shifts and adds). Thus, the consolidation of loss factors has reduced computational complexity by *three orders of magnitude,* that is, by a factor of 500 in this case. However, the physical accuracy of the simulation has not been compromised. In fact, the *accuracy is improved* because the N round-off errors per period arising from repeated multiplication by g have been replaced by a single round-off error per period in the multiplication by g^N.

Frequency-dependent damping

As discussed previously, damping should increase with frequency for better realism. This means the loss factors g of the previous section should instead be digital filters having gains which decrease with frequency and never exceed 1 (for stability of the loop). These filters commute with delay elements because they are linear and time invariant. Thus, following the reasoning of the previous section, they can be lumped at a single point in the digital waveguide. Let $\widehat{G}(z)$ denote the resulting *string loop filter.* We have the stability (passivity) constraint $|\widehat{G}(e^{j\omega T})| \leqslant 1$, and making the filter linear phase (constant delay at all frequencies) will restrict consideration to symmetric FIR filters only.

In the simplest case of a *first-order* lowpass loss filter, $\widehat{G}(z) = b_0 + b_1 z^{-1}$, the linear-phase requirement imposes $b_0 = b_1$. Assuming the damping approaches zero at frequency zero implies $b_0 + b_1 = 1$. Thus, two equations in two unknowns uniquely determine the coefficients to be $b_0 = b_1 = 1/2$ which gives a string loop frequency response equal to $|\widehat{G}(e^{j\omega T})| = \cos(\omega T/2)$, $|\omega| \leqslant \pi f_s$.

The simulation diagram for the ideal string with the simplest frequency-dependent loss filter is shown in Figure 20. Readers of the computer music literature will recognize this as the structure of the *Karplus–Strong algorithm* (Karplus and Strong 1983; Jaffe and Smith 1983; Sullivan 1990).

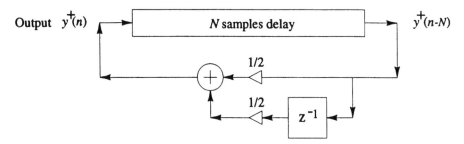

Figure 20. Rigidly terminated string with the simplest frequency-dependent loss filter. All N loss factors (possibly including losses due to yielding terminations) have been consolidated at a single point and replaced by a one-zero filter approximation.

The Karplus–Strong algorithm, per se, is obtained when the delay-line initial conditions used to "pluck" the string consist of random numbers, or "white noise". We know the initial *shape* of the string is obtained by *adding* the upper and lower delay lines of Figure 18, that is, $y(t_n, x_m) = y^+(n - m) + y^-(n + m)$. It was also noted earlier how the initial *velocity* distribution along the string is determined by the *difference* between the upper and lower delay lines. Thus, in the Karplus–Strong algorithm, the string is "plucked" by a *random initial displacement and initial velocity distribution*. This is a very energetic excitation, and usually in practice the white noise is lowpass filtered; the lowpass cutoff frequency gives an effective *dynamic level* control since natural stringed instruments are typically brighter at louder dynamic levels (Jaffe and Smith 1983).

Advanced examples

In this section, the clarinet and bowed string are considered as advanced examples of digital waveguide synthesis.

Single-reed instruments

Figure 21 shows a simplified model for a single-reed woodwind instrument. If the bore is cylindrical, as in the clarinet, it can be modeled quite simply using a bidirectional delay line. If the bore is conical, such as in a saxophone, it can still be modeled as a bidirectional delay line, but interfacing to it is slightly more complex, especially at the mouthpiece (Benade 1988; Agullo *et al.* 1988; Gilbert *et al.* 1990; Välimäki and Karjalainen 1995; Van Walstijn and De Bruin 1995; Välimäki 1995). Because the main control variable for the instrument is air pressure in the mouth at the reed, it is convenient to choose *pressure wave variables*.

To first order, the bell passes high frequencies and reflects low frequencies, where "high" and "low" frequencies are divided at the wavelength which equals

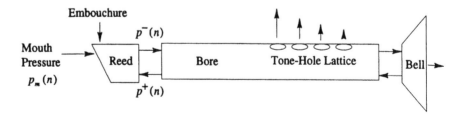

Figure 21. A schematic model for woodwind instruments.

the bell's diameter. Thus, the bell can be regarded as a simple "cross-over" network, as is used to split signal energy between a woofer and tweeter in a loudspeaker cabinet. For a clarinet bore, the nominal "cross-over frequency" is around 1500 Hz (Benade 1990). The flare of the bell lowers the cross-over frequency by decreasing the bore characteristic impedance toward the end in an approximately non-reflecting manner (Berners and Smith 1994). Bell flare can be considered analogous to a transmission-line *transformer.*

Tone holes can also be treated as simple cross-over networks. However, it is more accurate to utilize measurements of tone-hole acoustics in the musical acoustics literature (Keefe 1982), and convert their "transmission matrix" description to the traveling-wave formulation by a simple linear transformation. For typical fingerings, the first few open tone holes jointly provide a bore termination (Benade 1990). Either the individual tone holes can be modeled as (interpolated) scattering junctions, or the whole ensemble of terminating tone holes can be modeled in aggregate using a single reflection and transmission filter, like the bell model. Since the tone hole diameters are small compared with audio frequency wavelengths, the reflection and transmission coefficients can be implemented to a reasonable approximation as constants, as opposed to cross-over filters as in the bell. At a higher level of accuracy, adapting transmission-matrix parameters from the existing musical acoustics literature leads to first-order reflection and transmission filters. The individual tone-hole models can be simply lossy two-port junctions, to model only the internal bore loss characteristics, or as three-port junctions, when it is desired also to model accurately transmission characteristics to the outside air. The subject of tone-hole models is elaborated further in (Välimäki, Karjalainen, and Laakso 1993). For simplest practical implementation, the bell model can be used unchanged for all tunings, as if the bore were being cut to a new length for each note and the same bell were attached.

Since the length of the clarinet bore is only a quarter wavelength at the fundamental frequency, (in the lowest, or "chalumeau" register), and since the bell diameter is much smaller than the bore length, most of the sound energy traveling into the bell reflects back into the bore. The low-frequency energy that makes it out of the bore radiates in a fairly omnidirectional pattern. Very high-frequency traveling waves do not "see" the enclosing bell and pass right through it, radiating in a more directional beam. The directionality of the beam is proportional to how many wavelengths fit along the bell diameter; in fact, many wavelengths away from the bell, the radiation pattern is proportional to the two-dimensional spatial Fourier transform of the exit aperture (a disk at the end of the bell) (Morse and Ingard 1968).

The theory of the single reed is described in (McIntyre, Schumacher, and Woodhouse 1983). In the digital waveguide clarinet model described below

(Smith 1986), the reed is modeled as a signal- and embouchure-dependent *non-linear reflection coefficient* terminating the bore. Such a model is possible because the reed mass is neglected. The player's embouchure controls damping of the reed, reed aperture width, and other parameters, and these can be implemented as parameters on the contents of the lookup table or nonlinear function.

Single-reed implementation

A diagram of the basic clarinet model is shown in Figure 22. The delay-lines carry left-going and right-going *pressure* samples p_b^+ and p_b^- (respectively) which sample the traveling pressure-wave components within the bore.

The reflection filter at the right implements the bell or tone-hole losses as well as the round-trip attenuation losses from traveling back and forth in the bore. The bell output filter is highpass, and *power complementary* with respect to the bell reflection filter (Vaidyanathan 1993).

At the far left is the reed mouthpiece controlled by *mouth pressure* p_m. Another control is *embouchure,* changed in general by modifying the contents of the *reflection-coefficient* function $\rho(h_\Delta^+)$, where $h_\Delta^+ = p_m/2 - p_b^+$. A simple choice of embouchure control is an offset in the reed-table address. Since the main feature of the reed table is the pressure-drop where the reed begins to close, a simple embouchure offset can implement the effect of biting harder or softer on the reed, or changing the reed stiffness.

In the field of computer music, it is customary to use simple piecewise linear functions for functions other than signals at the audio sampling rate, for example, for amplitude envelopes, FM-index functions, and so on (Roads 1989; Roads and Strawn 1985; Roads 1996). Along these lines, good initial results were obtained

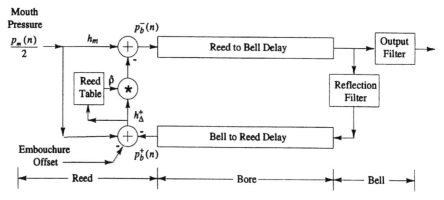

Figure 22. Waveguide model of a single-reed, cylindrical-bore woodwind, such as a clarinet.

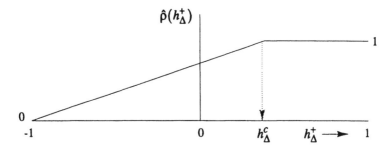

Figure 23. Simple, qualitatively chosen reed table for the digital waveguide clarinet.

(Smith 1986) using the simplified *qualitatively* chosen table

$$\hat{\rho}(h_\Delta^+) = \begin{cases} 1 - m(h_\Delta^c - h_\Delta^+), & -1 \leqslant h_\Delta^+ < h_\Delta^c, \\ 1, & h_\Delta^c \leqslant h_\Delta^+ \leqslant 1, \end{cases} \tag{37}$$

depicted in Figure 23 for $m = 1/(h_\Delta^c + 1)$. The corner point h_Δ^c is the smallest pressure difference giving reed closure. (For operation in fixed-point DSP chips, the independent variable $h_\Delta^+ \triangleq p_m/2 - p_b^+$ is generally confined to the interval $[-1, 1)$. Note that having the table go all the way to zero at the maximum negative pressure $h_\Delta^+ = -1$ is not physically reasonable (0.8 would be more reasonable), but it has the practical benefit that when the lookup-table input signal is about to clip, the reflection coefficient goes to zero, thereby opening the feedback loop. Embouchure and reed stiffness correspond to the choice of offset h_Δ^c and slope m. Brighter tones are obtained by increasing the curvature of the function as the reed begins to open; for example, one can use $\hat{\rho}^k(h_\Delta^+)$ for increasing $k \geqslant 1$.

Another variation is to replace the table-lookup contents by a piecewise polynomial approximation. While less general, good results have been obtained in practice (Cook 1992). For example, one of the SynthBuilder (Porcaro *et al.* 1995) clarinet patches employs this technique using a cubic polynomial.

An intermediate approach between table lookups and polynomial approximations is to use interpolated table lookups. Typically, linear interpolation is used, but higher order polynomial interpolation can also be considered (Schafer and Rabiner 1973; Smith and Gossett 1984; Välimäki 1995).

Practical details
To finish off the clarinet example, this section describes the remaining details of the SynthBuilder clarinet patch "Clarinet2.sb".

The input mouth pressure is summed with a small amount of white noise, corresponding to turbulence. For example, 0.1% is generally used as a minimum, and larger amounts are appropriate during the attack of a note. Ideally, the turbulence level should be computed automatically as a function of pressure drop p_Δ and reed opening geometry (Flanagan and Ishizaka 1976; Verge 1995). It should also be lowpass filtered as predicted by theory.

Referring to Figure 22, the reflection filter is a simple one-pole with transfer function

$$H(z) = \frac{1 + a_1(t)}{1 + a_1(t)z^{-1}}, \tag{38}$$

where $a_1(t) = v(t) - 0.642$, $v(t) = A_v \sin(2\pi f_v t)$, A_v is vibrato amplitude (e.g., 0.03), and f_v is vibrato frequency (e.g., 5 Hz). Further loop filtering occurs as a result of using simple linear interpolation of the delay line. (There is only one delay line in the actual implementation since the lower delay line of Figure 22 can be commuted with the reflection filter and combined with the upper delay line, ignoring the path to the output filter since a pure delay of less than a period in the final output sound is inconsequential.) There is no transmission filter or tone-hole modeling.

Legato note transitions are managed using two delay line taps and cross-fading from one to the other during a transition (Jaffe and Smith 1995; Smith 1996). In general, legato problems arise when the bore length is changed suddenly while sounding, corresponding to a new fingering. The reason is that really the model itself should be changed during a fingering change from that of a statically terminated bore to that of a bore with a new scattering junction appearing where each "finger" is lifting, and with disappearing scattering junctions where tone holes are being covered. In addition, if a hole is covered abruptly (especially when there are large mechanical caps, as in the saxophone), there will also be new signal energy injected in both directions on the bore in superposition with the signal scattering. As a result of this ideal picture, is difficult to get high quality legato performance using only a single delay line.

A reduced-cost, approximate solution for obtaining good sounding note transitions in a single delay-line model was proposed in (Jaffe and Smith 1995). In this technique, the bore delay line is "branched" during the transition, i.e., a second feedback loop is formed at the new loop delay, thus forming two delay lines sharing the same memory, one corresponding to the old pitch and the other corresponding to the new pitch. A cross-fade from the old-pitch delay to the new-pitch delay sounds good if the cross-fade time and duration are carefully chosen. Another way to look at this algorithm is in terms of "read pointers" and "write pointers." A normal delay line consists of a single write pointer followed by a single read pointer, delayed by one period. During a legato transition, we simply cross-fade from a read-pointer at the old-pitch delay to a read-pointer at the new-pitch delay. In this type of implementation, the write-pointer always traverses the full delay memory corresponding to the minimum supported pitch in order that read-pointers may be instantiated at any pitch-period delay at any time. Conceptually, this simplified model of note transitions can be derived from the more rigorous model by replacing the tone-hole scattering junction by a single reflection coefficient.

Bowed strings

A schematic block diagram for bowed strings is shown in Figure 24. The bow divides the string into two sections, so the bow model is a nonlinear two-port, in contrast with the reed which was a one-port terminating the bore at the mouthpiece. In the case of bowed strings, the primary control variable is bow velocity, so *velocity waves* are the natural choice for the delay lines.

The theory of bow-string interaction is described in (Friedlander 1953; Keller 1953; McIntyre and Woodhouse 1979; McIntyre, Schumacher, and Woodhouse 1983; Cremer 1984). The basic operation of the bow is to reconcile the bow-string friction curve with the string state and string wave impedance. In a bowed string simulation as in Figure 24, a velocity input (which is injected equally in the left- and right-going directions) must be found such that the transverse force of the bow against the string is balanced by the reaction force of the moving string. If bow-hair dynamics are neglected, the bow-string interaction can be simulated using a memoryless table lookup or segmented polynomial in a manner similar to single-reed woodwinds (Smith 1986).

Bowed-string implementation
A more detailed diagram of the digital waveguide implementation of the bowed-string instrument model is shown in Figure 25. The right delay-line pair carries left-going and right-going velocity waves samples $v_{s,r}^+$ and $v_{s,r}^-$, respectively, which sample the traveling-wave components within the string to the right of

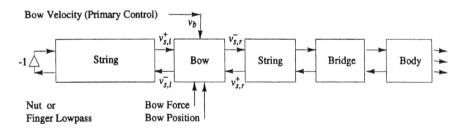

Figure 24. A schematic model for bowed-string instruments.

the bow, and similarly for the section of string to the left of the bow. The '+' superscript refers to waves traveling *into* the bow.

String velocity at any point is obtained by adding a left-going velocity sample to the right-going velocity sample immediately opposite in the other delay line, as indicated in Figure 25 at the bowing point. The reflection filter at the right implements the losses at the bridge, bow, nut or finger-terminations (when stopped), and the round-trip attenuation/dispersion from traveling back and forth on the string. To a very good degree of approximation, the nut reflects incoming velocity waves (with a sign inversion) at all audio wavelengths. The bridge behaves similarly to a first order, but there are additional (complex) losses due to the finite bridge driving-point impedance (necessary for transducing sound from the string into the resonating body).

Figure 25 is drawn for the case of the lowest note. For higher notes the delay lines between the bow and nut are shortened according to the distance between the bow and the finger termination. The bow-string interface is controlled by *differential velocity* v_Δ^+ which is defined as the bow velocity minus the total incoming string velocity. Other controls include *bow force* and *angle* which are changed by modifying the contents of the reflection-coefficient look-up table $\rho(v_\Delta^+)$. Bow position is changed by taking samples from one delay-line pair and appending them to the other delay-line pair. Delay-line interpolation can be used to provide continuous change of bow position (Laakso *et al.* 1996).

Figure 26 illustrates a simplified, piecewise linear bow table. The flat center portion corresponds to a fixed reflection coefficient "seen" by a traveling wave encountering the bow stuck against the string, and the outer sections of the curve give a smaller reflection coefficient corresponding to the reduced bow-string interaction force while the string is slipping under the bow. The notation v_Δ^c at the corner point denotes the capture or break-away differential velocity.

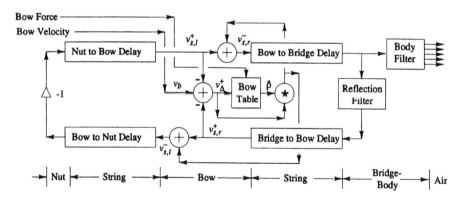

Figure 25. Waveguide model for a bowed string instrument, such as a violin.

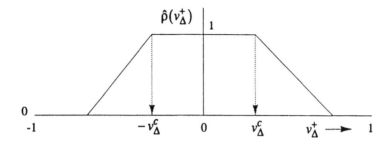

Figure 26. Simple, qualitatively chosen bow table for the digital waveguide violin.

Conclusions

Starting with the traveling-wave solution to the wave equation and sampling across time and space, we obtained an acoustic modeling framework known as the "digital waveguide" approach. Its main feature is computational economy for models of distributed media such as strings and bores. Successful computational models have been obtained for several musical instruments of the string, wind, brass, and percussion families, and more are on the way.

While physics-based synthesis can provide extremely high quality and expressivity in a very compact algorithm, new models must be developed for each new kind of instrument, and for many instruments, no sufficiently concise algorithm is known. Sampling/wavetable synthesis, on the other hand, is completely general since it involves only playing back and processing natural recorded sound. However, sampling synthesis demands huge quantities of memory for the highest quality and multidimensional control. It seems reasonable therefore to expect that many musical instrument categories now being implemented via sampling synthesis will ultimately be upgraded to parsimonious, computational models derived as signal processing style implementations of models from musical acoustics. As this evolution proceeds, the traditional instrument quality available from a given area of silicon can be expected to increase dramatically.

References

Agullo, J., A. Barjau, and J. Martinez. 1988. "Alternatives to the impulse response $h(t)$ to describe the acoustical behavior of conical ducts." *Journal of the Acoustical Society of America* 84: 1606–1627.

Amir, N., G. Rosenhouse, and U. Shimony. 1993. "Reconstructing the bore of brass instruments: Theory and experiment." In *Proceedings of the Stockholm Musical Acoustic Conference.* Stockholm: Royal Swedish Academy of Music, pp. 470–475.

Askenfelt, A. 1990. *Five Lectures on the Acoustics of the Piano.* Publication number 64. Sound example CD included. Stockholm: Royal Swedish Academy of Music.

Atal, B.S. and L.S. Hanauer. 1971. "Speech analysis and synthesis by linear prediction of the speech wave." *Journal of the Acoustical Society of America* 50: 637–655.

Belevitch, V. 1968. *Classical Network Theory*. San Francisco: Holden Day.

Beliczynski, B., I. Kale, and G.D. Cain. 1992. "Approximation of FIR by IIR digital filters: An algorithm based on balanced model reduction." *IEEE Transactions on Acoustics, Speech, and Signal Processing* 40: 532–542.

Benade, A.H. 1988. "Equivalent circuits for conical waveguides." *Journal of the Acoustical Society of America* 83: 1764–1769.

Benade, A. 1990. *Fundamentals of Musical Acoustics*. New York: Dover.

Berners, D.P. and J.O. Smith. 1994 "On the use of Schroeder's equation in the analytic determination of horn reflectance." In *Proceedings of the 1994 International Computer Music Conference*. San Francisco: International Computer Music Association, pp. 419–422.

Borin, G., G. De Poli, and A. Sarti. 1989. "A modular approach to excitator-resonator interaction in physical models synthesis." In *Proceedings of the 1989 International Computer Music Conference*. San Francisco: International Computer Music Association, pp. 46–50.

Caussé, R., J. Kergomard, and X. Lurton. 1984. "Input impedance of brass musical instruments-comparison between experiment and numerical models." *Journal of the Acoustical Society of America* 75: 241–254.

Chafe, C. 1990. "Pulsed noise in self-sustained oscillations of musical instruments." In *Proceedings of the International Conference on Acoustics, Speech, and Signal Processing*. New York: IEEE Press. Available as CCRMA Technical Report STAN-M-65, Music Dept., Stanford University.

Cook, P.R. 1990. "Identification of control parameters in an articulatory vocal tract model, with applications to the synthesis of singing". PhD thesis. Stanford: Stanford University Department of Electrical Engineering.

Cook, P.R. 1992. "A meta-wind-instrument physical model, and a meta-controller for real time performance control." In *Proceedings of the 1992 International Computer Music Conference*. San Francisco: International Computer Music Association, pp. 273–276.

Cremer, L. 1984. *The Physics of the Violin*. Cambridge, Massachusetts: The MIT Press.

Crochiere, R. and L.R. Rabiner. 1983. *Multirate Digital Signal Processing*. Englewood Cliffs, NJ: Prentice Hall.

Dietz, P.H. 1989. "Simulation of trumpet tones via physical modeling." CMU Report LASIP-89-07. Pittsburgh: Carnegie Mellon University, Department of Electrical Engineering and Computer Science.

Fettweis, A. 1986. "Wave digital filters: theory and practice." *Proceedings of the IEEE* 74: 270–327.

Flanagan, J.L. and K. Ishizaka. 1976. "Automatic generation of voiceless excitation in a vocal cord-vocal tract speech synthesizer." *IEEE Transactions on Acoustics, Speech, and Signal Processing* 24: 163–170.

Friedlander, F.G. 1953. "On the oscillations of the bowed string." *Proceedings of the Cambridge Philosophy Society* 49: 516–530.

Gilbert, J., J. Kergomard, and J.D. Polack. 1990. "On the reflection functions associated with discontinuities in conical bores." *Journal of the Acoustical Society of America* 87 (4): pp. 1773–1780.

Gray, A.H. 1980. "Passive cascaded lattice digital filters." *IEEE Transactions on Acoustics, Speech, and Signal Processing* 27(5): 337–344.

Gray, A.H. and J.D. Markel. 1975. "A normalized digital filter structure." *IEEE Transactions on Acoustics, Speech, and Signal Processing* 23(6): 268–277.

Hirschman, S. 1991. "Digital waveguide modelling and simulation of reed woodwind instruments." Engineer's thesis. Stanford: Stanford University, Electrical Engineering Department. Available as CCRMA Technical Report Stan-M-72. Stanford: Stanford University, Music Department.

Jaffe, D.A. and J.O. Smith. 1983. "Extensions of the Karplus–Strong plucked string algorithm." *Computer Music Journal* 7(2): 56–69.

Jaffe, D.A. and J.O. Smith. 1995. "Performance expression in commuted waveguide synthesis of bowed strings." In *Proceedings of the 1995 International Computer Music Conference*. San Francisco: International Computer Music Association, pp. 343–346.

Kailath, T. 1980. *Linear Systems*. Englewood Cliffs: Prentice Hall.

Karjalainen, M. and U.K. Laine. 1991. "A model for real-time sound synthesis of guitar on a floating-point signal processor." In *Proceedings of the International Conference on Acoustics, Speech, and Signal Processing.* New York: IEEE Press, pp. 3653–3656.

Karjalainen, M., U.K. Laine, T.I. Laakso, and V.Välimäki. 1991. "Transmission-line modeling and real-time synthesis of string and wind instruments." In *Proceedings of the 1991 Internation Computer Music Conference.* San Francisco: International Computer Music Association, pp. 293–296.

Karjalainen, M., J. Backman, and J. Pölkki. 1993. "Analysis, modeling, and real-time sound synthesis of the kantele, a traditional finnish string instrument." In *Proceedings of the International Conference Acoustics, Speech, and Signal Processing*, Minneapolis: IEEE Press, pp. 229–232.

Karjalainen, M., V. Välimäki, and Z. Jánosy. 1993. "Towards high-quality sound synthesis of the guitar and string instruments." In *Proceedings of the 1993 International Computer Music Conference.* San Francisco: International Computer Music Association, pp. 56–63.

Karplus, K. and A. Strong, 1983. "Digital synthesis of plucked string and drum timbres." *Computer Music Journal* 7(2): 43–55.

Keefe, D.H. 1982. "Theory of the single woodwind tone hole. Experiments on the single woodwind tone hole." *Journal Acoustical Society of America* 72(9): 676–699.

Keller, J.B. 1953. "Bowing of violin strings." *Communications Pure Applied Mathematics* 6: 483–495.

Kolsky, H. 1963. *Stress Waves in Solids.* New York: Dover.

Laakso, T.I., V. Välimäki, M. Karjalainen, and U. K. Laine. 1996. "Splitting the unit delay." *IEEE Signal Processing Magazine* 13(1): 30–60.

LePage, W.R. 1961. *Complex Variables and the Laplace Transform for Engineers.* New York: Dover.

Loy, N.J. 1988. *An Engineer's Guide to FIR Digital Filters.* Englewood Cliffs: Prentice Hall.

Makhoul, J. 1975. "Linear prediction: A tutorial review." *Proceedings of the IEEE* 63(4): 561–580.

Markel, J.D. and A.H. Gray. 1976. *Linear Prediction of Speech.* New York: Springer-Verlag.

McIntyre, M.E. and J. Woodhouse. 1979. "On the fundamentals of bowed string dynamics." *Acustica* 43(9): 93–108.

McIntyre, M.E., R.T. Schumacher, and J. Woodhouse. 1983. "On the oscillations of musical instruments." *Journal Acoustical Society of America* 74(11): 1325–1345.

Morse, P.M. 1981. *Vibration and Sound.* New York: American Institute of Physics, for the Acoustical Society of America. (1st ed. 1936, 4th ed. 1981).

Morse, P.M. and K.U. Ingard. 1968. *Theoretical Acoustics.* New York: McGraw-Hill.

Parks, T.W. and C.S. Burrus. 1987. *Digital Filter Design.* New York: Wiley.

Porcaro, N., P. Scandalis, J.O. Smith, D.A. Jaffe, and T. Stilson. 1995. "Synthbuilder—a graphical real-time synthesis, processing and performance system." In *Proceedings of the 1995 International Computer Music Conference.* International Computer Music Association, pp. 61–62. See http://www-leland.stanford.edu/group/OTL/SynthBuilder.html for information on how to obtain and run SynthBuilder. See also http://www-ccrma.stanford.edu for related information.

Rabiner, L.R. and B. Gold. 1975. *Theory and Application of Digital Signal Processing.* Englewood Cliffs: Prentice Hall.

Roads, C. ed. 1989. *The Music Machine.* Cambridge, Massachusetts: The MIT Press.

Roads, C. 1996. *The Computer Music Tutorial.* Cambridge, Massachusetts: The MIT Press.

Roads, C. and J. Strawn, eds. 1985. *Foundations of Computer Music.* Cambridge, Massachusetts: The MIT Press.

Rodet, X. 1993. "Flexible yet controllable physical models: A nonlinear dynamics approach." In *Proceedings of the 1993 International Computer Music Conference.* San Francisco: International Computer Music Association, pp. 10–15.

Schafer, R.W. and L.R. Rabiner. 1973. "A digital signal processing approach to interpolation." *Proceedings of the IEEE* 61(6): 692–702.

Smith, J.O. 1985. "A new approach to digital reverberation using closed waveguide net-works." In *Proceedings of the 1985 International Computer Music Conference.* Computer Music Association, pp. 47–53. Also available in (Smith 1987).

Smith, J. 1986a. "Efficient simulation of the reed-bore and bow-string mechanisms." In *Proceedings of the 1986 International Computer Music Conference*. San Francisco: International Computer Music Association, pp. 275–280. Also available in (Smith 1987a).

Smith, J. 1986b. "Elimination of limit cycles and overflow oscillations in time-varying lattice and ladder digital filters." Technical Report STAN-M-35, CCRMA, Music Department, Stanford University. Short version published in *Proceedings of the IEEE Conference on Circuits and Systems*, San Jose, 1986, pp. 197–200. Full version also available in (Smith 1987a).

Smith, J. 1987a. "Music applications of digital waveguides." Technical Report STAN-M-39. Stanford: CCRMA, Music Department, Stanford University. A compendium containing four related papers and presentation overheads on digital waveguide reverberation, synthesis, and filtering. CCRMA technical reports can be ordered by calling (415)723–4971 or by sending E-mail request to hmk@ccrma.stanford.edu.

Smith, J. 1987b. "Waveguide filter tutorial." In *Proceedings of the 1987 International Computer Music Conference*. San Francisco: International Computer Music Association, pp. 9–16.

Smith, J. 1991. "Waveguide simulation of non-cylindrical acoustic tubes." In *Proceedings of the 1991 International Computer Music Conference*. San Francisco: International Computer Music Association, pp. 304–307.

Smith, J. 1992. "Physical modeling using digital waveguides." *Computer Music Journal* 16(Winter): 74–91.

Smith, J. 1993. "Efficient synthesis of stringed musical instruments." In *Proceedings of the 1993 International Computer Music Conference*. San Francisco: International Computer Music Association, pp. 64–71.

Smith, J. 1996. "Physical modeling synthesis update." *Computer Music Journal* 20(2): 44–56.

Smith, J.O. and P. Gossett. 1984. "A flexible sampling-rate conversion method." In *Proceedings of the International Conference on Acoustics, Speech, and Signal Processing* 2(3): pp. 19.4.1– 19.4.2. New York: IEEE Press. An expanded tutorial based on this paper is available in the directory ftp://ccrma-ftp.stanford.edu/pub/DSP/Tutorials/, file BandlimitedInterpolation.eps.Z, as is C code for implementing the technique in directory ftp://ccrma-ftp.stanford.edu/pub/NeXT/, file resample-n.m.tar.Z, where n.m denotes the latest version number. Note that the C source code is included so it is easy to port it to any platform supporting the C language.

Smith, J.O. and S.A. Van Duyne. 1995. "Commuted piano synthesis." In *Proceedings of the 1995 International Computer Music Conference*. San Francisco: International Computer Music Association, pp. 319–326.

Smith, J.O., M. Gutknecht, and L.N. Trefethen. 1983. "The Caratheodory–Fejer (CF) method for recursive digital filter design." *IEEE Transactions on Acoustics, Speech, and Signal Processing* 31(6): 1417–1426.

Steiglitz, K. 1996. *A Digital Signal Processing Primer with Applications to Audio and Computer Music*. Reading: Addison-Wesley.

Stilson, T. 1995. "Forward-going wave extraction in acoustic tubes." In *Proceedings of the 1995 International Computer Music Conference*. San Francisco: International Computer Music Association, pp. 517–520.

Strum, R. and D.E. Kirk. 1988. *First Principles of Discrete Systems and Digital Signal Processing*. Reading: Addison-Wesley.

Sullivan, C. 1990. "Extending the Karplus–Strong algorithm to synthesize electric guitar timbres with distortion and feedback." *Computer Music Journal* 14(3): 26–37.

Suzuki, H. 1987. "Model analysis of a hammer-string interaction." *Journal of the Acoustical Society of America* 82: 1145–1151.

Vaidyanathan, P.P. 1993. *Multirate Systems and Filter Banks*. Englewood Cliffs, NJ: Prentice Hall.

Välimäki, V. 1995. "Discrete-time modeling of acoustic tubes using fractional delay filters." PhD thesis, Report no. 37. Espoo: Helsinki University of Technology, Faculty of Electrical Engineering, Laboratory of Acoustic and Audio Signal Processing.

Välimäki, V. and M. Karjalainen. 1994. "Digital waveguide modeling of wind instrument bores constructed of truncated cones." In *Proceedings of the 1994 International Computer Music Conference*. San Francisco: International Computer Music Association, pp. 423–430.

Välimäki, V. and M. Karjalainen. 1995. "Implementation of fractional delay waveguide models using allpass filters." In *Proceedings of the International Conference on Acoustics, Speech, and Signal Processing*. New York: IEEE Press, pp. 8–12.

Välimäki, V., M. Karjalainen, and T.I. Laakso. 1993. "Modeling of woodwind bores with finger holes." In *Proceedings of the 1993 International Computer Music Conference*. San Francisco: International Computer Music Association, pp. 32–39.

Välimäki, V., J. Huopaniemi, M. Karjalainen, and Z. Jánosy. 1996. "Physical modeling of plucked string instruments with application to real-time sound synthesis." *Journal of the Audio Engineering Society* 44(5).

Van Duyne, S.A. and J.O. Smith. 1993. "Physical modeling with the 2-D digital waveguide mesh." In *Proceedings of the 1993 International Computer Music Conference*. San Francisco: International Computer Music Association, pp. 40–47.

Van Duyne, S.A. and J.O. Smith. 1995. "Developments for the commuted piano." In *Proceedings of the 1995 International Computer Music Conference*. San Francisco: International Computer Music Association, pp. 335–343.

Van Duyne, S.A. and J.O. Smith. 1995. "The tetrahedral waveguide mesh: multiply-free computation of wave propagation in free space." In *Proceedings of the IEEE Workshop on Applications of Signal Processing to Audio and Acoustics*. New York: IEEE Press. See also in *Proceedings of the 1996 International Computer Music Conference*. San Francisco: International Computer Music Association.

Van Duyne, S.A., J.R. Pierce, and J.O. Smith. 1994. "Traveling-wave implementation of a lossless mode-coupling filter and the wave digital hammer." In *Proceedings of the 1994 International Computer Music Conference*. San Francisco: International Computer Music Association, pp. 411–418. Also presented at the conference of the Acoustical Society of America, November, 1994.

Van Walstijn, M. and G. de Bruin. 1995. "Conical waveguide filters." In *Proceedings of the International Conference on Acoustics and Musical Research*. Ferrara: CIARM, pp. 47–54.

Verge, M. 1995. "Aeroacoustics of confined jets with applications to the physical modeling of recorder-like instruments." PhD thesis. Eindhoven: Eindhoven University.

Wawrzynek, J. 1989. "VLSI models for sound sythesis." In M.V. Mathews and J.R. Pierce, eds. *Current Directions in Computer Music Research*. Cambridge, Massachusetts: The MIT Press, pp.113–148.

Weinreich, G. 1977. "Coupled piano strings." *Journal of the Acoustical Society of America* 62: 1474–1484. See also 1979. *Scientific American* 240: 94.

Part III

Musical signal
macrostructures

Part III

Overview

Stephen Travis Pope

As the title of this part indicates, Chapters 8, 9, and 10 examine how larger-scale, higher-level musical signals can be represented and manipulated. This part addresses various approaches to the description of musical data at several levels of scale. Why is this of interest? As Roger Dannenberg, Peter Desain, and Henkjan Honing state in the opening of their chapter (slightly paraphrased):

> *Music invites formal description. There are many obvious numerical and structural relationships in music, and countless representations and formalisms have been developed and reported in the literature. Computers are a great tool for this endeavor because of the precision they engender. A music formalism implemented as a computer program must be completely unambiguous, and implementing ideas about musical structure on a computer often leads to greater understanding and new insights into the underlying domain.*
>
> *Programming languages can be developed specifically for music. These languages support common musical concepts such as time, simultaneous behavior, and expressive control. At the same time, languages try to avoid pre-empting decisions by composers, theorists, and performers, who use the language to express very personal concepts. This leads language designers to think of musical problems in very abstract, almost universal, terms.*

The history of computer music software development is largely concerned with the evolution of music input languages, starting from the simple note-list formats used with the early "Music N" series of languages (still in widespread use today in their descendants), and leading up to today's grand frameworks for structure representation and computer-assisted algorithmic composition.

Two very different forces drive the development of formal music languages. The first is the need by composers to express their works to the computer in facile, succinct, and "musician-friendly" format. The second force is the music research issue of just how musical signals and disctete event structures can be formalized in a useful, expressive, compact, and manipulable way. The three contributions in this part address very different aspects of this topic.

Chapter 8, by Roger Dannnenberg, Peter Desain, and Henkjan Honing (acknowledged experts on the topic), introduces the fundamental issues in music representation formalisms and music description languages. The authors provide a survey of several of the design solutions found in the literature. They look at the novel demands that music representation places on programming language design, and at some of the interesting ways in which advanced computer science concepts can be applied to musical data. The authors then describe in some detail their two music representation languages—Nyquist (Dannenberg) and GTF (Desain and Honing)—and compare and contrast them in terms of the key concepts they introduce.

Over the past two decades there have been several attempts to use object-oriented (O-O) software techniques in a variety of programming languages (Lisp, Objective C, and Smalltalk, for example) to build music representations. Chapter 9, by Stephen Pope, introduces the basic notions of O-O software technology, and discusses how these might be useful for music representation. This chapter offers simple examples of using O-O languages for music representation, and then gives a detailed description of the Smalltalk music object kernel (Smoke) music representation language. Smoke facilitates the formal description of low-level musical data such as note events, and also of higher-level structures such as chord progressions and musical form "objects."

The topic of musical applications of artificial intelligence (AI) is addressed in the contribution by Antonio Camurri and Marc Leman. They present the requirements for music software systems based on AI, and assess the current state of the art in this area. Several issues are central to their considerations, such as the integration of multiple representational levels and reasoning mechanisms, the grounding of such systems in the music signal-processing environment, the importance of metaphors and analogies, and real-time requirements. An AI-based computer music tool developed by the authors and their colleagues—HARP—is then examined, and its integration with concrete musical applications is discussed.

All three of these chapters present unique and interesting solutions to well-known software engineering problems related to musical data representation, and all three describe the application of state-of-the-art computer science technology to music representation and manipulation. The four concrete systems presented here are, however, very different. The documentation of their designs and applications given here can serve as an in-depth introduction to the complex theoretical and practical issues related to the representation and processing of musical signal macrostructures.

The source code for all of the systems described here is available in the public domain on the Internet. Interested readers are referred to the World-Wide Web pages and ftp archives of *Computer Music Journal* and the International Computer Music Association.

8

Programming language design for music

Roger B. Dannenberg, Peter Desain, and Henkjan Honing

Music invites formal description. There are many obvious numerical and structural relationships in music, and countless representations and formalisms have been developed. Computers are a great tool for this endeavor because of the precision they demand. A music formalism implemented as a computer program must be completely unambiguous, and implementing ideas on a computer often leads to greater understanding and new insights into the underlying domain.

Programming languages can be developed specifically for music. These languages strive to support common musical concepts such as time, simultaneous behavior, and expressive control. At the same time, languages try to avoid pre-empting decisions by composers, theorists, and performers, who use the language to express very personal concepts. This leads language designers to think of musical problems in very abstract, almost universal, terms.

In this chapter we describe some of the general problems of music representation and music languages and describe several solutions that have been developed. The next section introduces a set of abstract concepts in musical terms. The following section on computing with music representations describes a number of computational issues related to music. Then, we begin to describe two languages we have developed that address these issues; the section on a shared framework of Nyquist and GTF introduces several important ideas that are common to our work and that of others. The section on the Nyquist language describes a language for sound synthesis and composition; that on the GTF representation language presents a music language emphasizing combination and transformation. The final section treats a number of implementation issues for music languages.

Representing music

The domain of music is full of wonderfully complex concepts whose precise meaning depends on the context of their use, their user (be it composer, performer, or musicologist), and the time in history of their usage. It is difficult to capture these meanings in clear, formal representations that can be treated mechanically, but still reflect as much as possible of the richness of the domain constructs and their interplay. Studying prototypical examples of musical concepts and their natural, intuitive behavior is a good starting point for the recognition of the properties that representations for music should exhibit. Once representations can be designed that on the one hand do not reduce music to simplistic and rigid constructs, but on the other hand can be defined clearly and formally such that their behavior is predictable and easy to grasp, then their use in composition systems, analysis tools and computational models of music perception and production will be quite natural.

Continuous versus discrete representations

One of the interesting representation problems in music is that musical information can be either discrete or continuous. Data is called discrete when it can take on a value or set of values that occur at some instant in time. For example, a musical note is often represented by a set of values for its attributes (pitch, loudness, instrument, duration, etc.) at a particular starting time. Data is said to be continuous if its value represents a function of time that has a well-defined value everywhere within some time interval or set of intervals. An example of this is a note whose pitch follows a contour evolving through time.

The distinction between continuous and discrete is not always clear-cut, and it may alternate between levels of representation; for example, a note may be represented by a discrete description at the specification level, a continuous audio signal at the realization level, and a discrete set of sample values at the signal-processing level. Sometimes the distinction is arbitrary. A trill, for example, can be described as one note with an alternating control function for its pitch, or it can be described as a discrete musical object consisting of several notes filling the duration of the trill. Both descriptions must add more elements (periods or notes) when stretched.

The drum roll or vibrato problem

A well-known problem called the *vibrato problem* occurs when a representation of a musical note with a continuously variable pitch is transformed. In Figure 1(a), such a continuous (control) function is shown. The difficulty is in how to obtain the proper shape or form of the pitch contour when it is used for a longer note, or, equivalently, when the note is stretched. In the case of its interpretation as a simple sinusoidal vibrato, some extra vibrato cycles should be added to the pitch envelope (see first frame in Figure 1(b)). When interpreted as an sinusoidal glissando, the pitch contour should be elasticity stretched (see second frame in Figure 1(b)). All kinds of intermediate and more complex behaviors should be expressible as well (see other examples in Figure 1(b)). A similar kind of control is needed with respect to the start time of a discrete object (Figure 1(c)); what should happen to the contour when it is used for an object at a different point in time, or, equivalently, when the note is shifted? Again a whole range of possible behaviors can be thought of, depending on the interpretation of the control function—the kind of musical knowledge it embodies. For instance, when multiple voices synchronize their vibrati, shifting a note may not alter the phase of the vibrato relative to global time.

The *drum roll problem* is the discrete analog to the vibrato problem—what happens when a drum roll is stretched? If the representation of the roll consists of audio samples, a simple resampling at a different rate will make the frequency spectrum lower and the drum strokes slower. If the roll is described in terms of drum stroke events only, each stroke can be easily made to sound roughly the same, but the strokes are slower. By convention, a stretched drum roll should maintain the same stroke rate and contain more strokes, so not only continuous data, like a vibrato control function, needs to embody musical knowledge, but also discrete musical objects, like a drum roll or a *trill*.

In more realistic situations, these continuous functions and discrete musical objects form layers of multiple, nested descriptions of continuous and discrete data (Honing 1993). For instance, Figure 2 illustrates the specification of an object with several alternating levels. One can imagine that stretching such an object is not equivalent to simply stretching the resulting waveform. Instead,

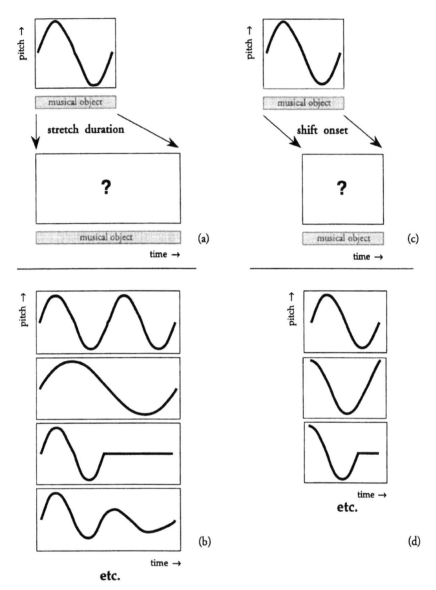

Figure 1. The vibrato problem—what should happen to the form of the contour of a continuous control function when used for a discrete musical object with a different length? For example, a sine wave control function is associated with the pitch attribute of a note in (a). In (b) possible pitch contours for the stretched note, depending on the interpretation of the original contour, are shown. Second, what should happen to the form of the pitch contour when used for a discrete musical object at a different point in time (c)? In (d) possible pitch contours for the shifted note are shown. There is, in principle, an infinite number of solutions depending on the type of musical knowledge embodied by the control function.

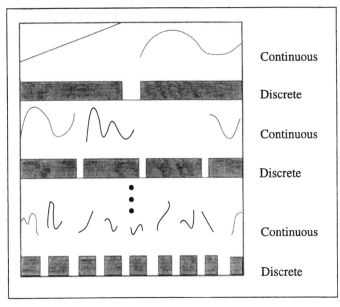

Figure 2. The specification of a musical object is shown here in the form of alternating layers of continuous and discrete representation, each with its own time-stretching and shifting behavior.

"to stretch" is some sort of abstract operation that involves more oscillations, changing amplitude contours, added cycles for the *vibrati*, and so on.

The necessity of planning and anticipation

Traditional music is full of examples where a simple hierarchical structure is not rich enough to give a full account of performance behavior. Ornaments which precede the starting time of a structure are a good example. In order to play a note on a downbeat with an attached grace note, one must anticipate the starting time slightly to allow time for the grace note.

In order for humans to perform ornaments and transitions, there must be some amount of anticipation and planning. At any given time, the actions are at least partly a function of what is coming next. Most computer systems make the simplifying assumption that processing for an event at time t can begin at time t. Since computers are often fast enough, usually this strategy works fine. However, the *anticipation problem* illustrates that processing must sometimes precede the starting time, i.e., it has to be anticipated.

Anticipation is necessary in other contexts as well. In a music performance, a performer will alter the way a note ends and the way the next note begins depending upon overall phrase markings and the nature of the two notes. An instrumentalist may separate two notes with a very slight pause if there is a large leap in pitch, or a singer may perform a *portamento* from one note to the next and alter the pronunciation of phonemes depending upon neighboring sounds. The *transition problem* characterizes the need for language constructs that support this type of information flow between musical objects.

Many synthesizers implement a portamento feature. It enables glissandi between pitches to be produced on a keyboard. But the glide can only be started after its direction and amount is known, i.e., when a new key is pressed. This is different from, for instance, a singer who can anticipate and plan a portamento to land in time on the new pitch. Modeling the latter process faithfully can only be done when representations of musical data are, to a limited extent, accessible ahead of time to allow for this planning.

Even for a simple isolated note, the perceptual onset time may occur well after the actual (physical) onset. This is especially true if the note has a slow attack. To compensate, the note must be started early. Here again, some anticipation is required.

The complex nature of structural descriptions

Discrete structural descriptions in music form a rich class of constructs. Structural descriptions of various kinds (phrase, meter, voice, harmony, ornamentation, etc.) can be imagined that overlay the surface material (the notes) in an entangled, web-like way. Let us consider *part-of* relations, with which compound musical objects can be decomposed into their elements. Such a decomposition can take place on several levels, giving rise to nested structural units, for example, a hierarchy of phrases and sub-phrases. Sometimes these substructures behave almost homogeneously, at least for a portion of the hierarchy. Then the behavior at one level resembles behavior on a higher level closely and a recursive description is quite natural, for example, in defining the timing patterns linked to the levels of the metrical subdivision. Sometimes structural descriptions can be ambiguous, for instance, when different analyses of the same piece are available—an ambiguity that may be kept intact and even communicated in a performance. Even more difficult to deal with formally are part-of relations that do not form a strict hierarchy, as is the case in two phrases that overlap, the end of the first being the beginning of the second. Part-of relations of various kinds are in general mutually incompatible, too—a phrase may end in the middle of a bar.

Next to part-of relations, some parts can be considered more essential than others that are more of an *ornamental* nature. Some musicological analyses and, conversely, some regularities found in performance are based on ornamental distinctions. Another structural coupling between parts is the *associative* link between, for example, a theme and its variation.

There are other kinds of links than structural ones that can be made between concrete sets of events in a piece. Between abstract musical concepts—such as between an A minor chord, a chord and a cluster—there is a complex system of dependencies that can be modeled to a reasonable degree of accuracy with a set of *is-a* definitions and refinements thereof.

Context dependency

Once musical structural descriptions are set up, the further specification of their attributes depends upon the context in which they are placed. Take for instance the loudness of a musical ensemble. The use of dynamics of an individual player cannot really be specified in isolation because the net result will depend on what the other players are doing as well. To give a more technical example, an audio compressor is a device that reduces the dynamic range of a signal by boosting low amplitude levels and cutting high amplitude levels. Now, imagine a software compressor operation that can transform the total amplitude of a set of notes, by adjusting their individual amplitude contours. This flow of information from parts to whole and back to parts is difficult to represent elegantly. We will refer to it as the *compressor problem*.

A comparable example is the *intonation problem*, where a similar type of communication is needed to describe how parallel voices (i.e., singers in a choir) adjust their intonation dynamically with respect to one another (Ashley 1992).

The relation between sounds and instruments

Composers may think about notes as independent sounds or as directives for a single performer. In a pointillistic passage notes are distinct, and whether two notes emerge from the same clarinet or two is not important. The main entity here is the note. In contrast, a legato solo phrase of ten notes could not be played by ten violins, each playing one note. The main entity here is the solo violin. In most cases, composers think about both notes and instruments, and the existence of both entities is important. Thus, the note has a dual nature; it is both an independent entity and an instrument control signal. The *instrument problem* refers to the challenge of modeling sound-producing resources (instruments) and their relationship to sound instances (notes).

The general problem is not restricted to a two-level hierarchy of notes and instruments. Consider that a violin note can be played on a choice of strings, and violins may be organized into sections. Other instruments also exhibit complex structures; a piano has a separate hammer for each string but a single damper pedal. A polyphonic synthesizer has a limited degree of polyphony, and modulation controls often apply to all notes. In the new physical modeling approach to sound synthesis (Smith 1992), finding general ways to represent these issues becomes a major challenge (Morrison and Adrien 1993).

Computing with music representations

We have presented a number of specific problems in music representation. In this section we will discuss how representations can be manipulated computationally, solving some of these problems. A few central constructs from computer science will turn out to be useful in describing the appropriate behavior.

Behavioral abstraction or context-sensitive polymorphism

In order to get the desired isomorphism (strict correspondence) between the representation and the reality of musical sounds, a music representation language needs to support a property that we will call "context-sensitive polymorphism" or "behavioral abstraction" (we cannot agree on a single term). "Polymorph" refers to the fact that the result of an operation (like stretching) depends on its argument type, e.g., a vibrato time function behaves differently under a stretch transformation than a glissando time function. "Context-sensitive" indicates that an operation is also dependent on its lexical context. As an example of the latter, interpret the situation in Figure 1(c) as two notes that occur in parallel with one note starting a bit later than the other. The behavior of this musical object under transformation is now also dependent on whether a particular control function is linked to the object as a whole (i.e., to describe synchronized vibrati; see second frame in Figure 1(d)), or whether it is associated with the individual notes (e.g., an independent vibrato; see first frame in Figure 1(d)). Specific language constructs are needed to made a distinction between these different behaviors.

The term "behavioral abstraction" refers to the process of taking a specific behavior (anything that varies as a function of time) and abstracting it—providing a single representation for a multitude of possible instances. An abstract behavior (such as vibrato) is abstract in two senses—first, it regards certain properties as separate from the rest, e.g., the duration and starting time of vibrato may be considered to be particular details of vibrato. Second, a behavioral abstraction draws a distinction between a concept and any particular instance or realization.

Note that the vibrato problem is in fact a general issue in temporal knowledge representation—an issue not restricted to music. In animation, for example, we could use similar representation formalisms. Think, for instance, of a scene in which a comic strip character walks from point A to point B in a particular way. When one wants to use this specific behavior for a walk over a longer distance, should the character make more steps (as in vibrato) or larger steps, or should it start running?

In-time, out-of-time, and real-time

Music representations are intimately connected with time. Borrowing the terminology of Xenakis (1971), time-based computation can be *in-time,* meaning that computation proceeds in time order, or *out-of-time,* meaning that computation operates upon temporal representations, but not necessarily in time order. When in-time computations are performed fast enough, the program is said to be *real-time*—the physical time delay in responding and communicating musical data has become so small that is not noticeable.

An example of in-time data is a MIDI data stream. Since MIDI messages represent events and state changes to be acted upon immediately, MIDI data does not contain time stamps, and MIDI data arrives in time order. When the computers, programs and synthesizers are fast enough (such that MIDI never overflows) a MIDI setup can be considered *real-time.* An example of out-of-time data is the MIDI representation used in a MIDI sequencer, which allows for data to be scrolled forward and backward in time and to be edited in an arbitrary time order.

"Out-of-time" languages are less restricted, hence more general, but "in-time" languages can potentially run in real time and sometimes require less space to run because information is processed or generated incrementally in time order.

Programs that execute strictly in time order are said to obey *causality* because there is never a need for knowledge of the future. This concept is especially important when modeling music perception processes and interactive systems that have to respond to some signal that is yet unknown—for example, a machine for automatic accompaniment of live performance.

The situation may become quite complicated when there is out-of-time information about the future available from one source, whereas for the other source strict in-time processing is required, such as in a score-following application where the full score is known beforehand, but the performer's timing and errors only become available at the time when they are made (Dannenberg 1989a).

Another confusing situation arises when a system designed or claimed to calculate in-time cannot run in real-time because of hardware limitations, and is developed using a simulation of its working by presenting its input out-of-time. Strict discipline of the developer is then needed to maintain causality and refrain from introducing any kind of "listen-ahead."

Discrete representations

Discrete information comes in many forms. One of these is discrete data such as notes, which are often represented as a data structure with a start time and various attributes. Other sorts of discrete data include cue points, time signatures, music notation symbols, and aggregate structures such as note sequences. The term "discrete" can also be applied to actions and transitions.

A step or action taken in the execution of a program is discrete. In music-oriented languages, an instance of a procedure or function application is often associated with a particular time point, so, like discrete static data, a procedure invocation can consist of a set of values (parameters) and a starting time point. The use of procedure invocation to model discrete musical events is most effective for *in-time* computation, such as in real-time interactive music systems, or for algorithmic music generation. This representation is less effective for complex reasoning about music structures and their interrelationships, because these relationships may exist across time, while procedure invocation happens only at one particular instant.

Another sort of discrete action is the instantiation or termination of a process or other on-going computation. The distinction between discrete and continuous is often a matter of perspective. "Phone home" is a discrete command, but it gives rise to continuous action. Similarly, starting or stopping a process is discrete, but the process may generate continuous information.

Discrete data often takes the form of an object, especially in object-oriented programming languages. An object encapsulates some state (parameters, attributes, values) and offers a set of operations to access and change the state. Unlike procedure invocations, an object has some persistence over time. Typically, however, the state of the object does not change except in response to discrete operations.

Object-based representations are effective for *out-of-time* music processing because the state of objects persists across time. It is therefore possible to decouple the order of computation from the order of music time. For example, it is possible to adjust the durations of notes in a sequence to satisfy a constraint on overall duration.

Even within an object-based representation system, there is computation, and computation normally takes place in discrete steps, actions, or state transitions. Object updates, for example the so-called *message passing* of object-oriented programming languages, is another form of discrete event. Often, in music processing languages, object updates are associated with discrete time points, adding a temporal component to the operation.

As we have seen, the term "discrete" can apply to many things: data, program execution, state transitions, objects, and messages. It is helpful to have a generic term for all of these, so we will use the term *discrete event* or simply *event* when nothing more specific is intended.

Continuous representations

Continuous data is used to represent audio signals, control information such as filter coefficients or amplitude envelopes, and other time-varying values such as tempo. Continuous data can be a "first-class" data type, an attachment to discrete data, or an even more restricted special type of data.

The most general possibility is to treat continuous data as a "first class" data type or class of object. For example, in the Nyquist language (which will be described in more detail below), continuous data is a data type that can be used for audio signals, control signals, or other time-varying values. In the GTF representation (see below), continuous data may exist as attachments to discrete structures at any level. Several language systems have been constructed where continuous functions serve strictly as transformations in time and in other controls. For example, tempo curves are continuous functions that provide a transformation from beat time to real time. Functions in Formula (Anderson and Kuivila 1986) provide tempo, duration, and other variables as a way to control expressive timing, articulation, and phrasing. The power of continuous representations is well illustrated by the fact that one composition system (Mathews and Moore 1970) embraced this format as its one and only representation of musical signals.

Anticipation

Representing transitions well is difficult because it requires that independent behaviors be joined in some way. FORMES (Cointe and Rodet 1984; Rodet and Cointe 1984) was perhaps the best example of a system that has specific mechanisms for transitions. In FORMES, a transition behavior is achieved by modifying the start and end times of the behaviors involved in the transition and interpolating between the behaviors. In FORMES, behaviors are implemented by objects organized in a tree structure, and the transition behavior requires several passes over the object tree, including some non-causal look-ahead. Language support for a more real-time "anticipation window" to support ornaments and transitions is an interesting area for future research.

With respect to ornaments, this is either non-causal (e.g., because we need to go back in time from the downbeat to the time of the grace note), or we need to complicate matters at some other level by designating the starting time of the pair of notes as before the downbeat. Many computer systems compute information with a time advance in order to achieve more accurate timing (Vercoe 1985; Anderson and Kuivila 1986) but it is unusual to allow observation of future events in order to modify current behavior (Loyall and Bates 1993).

Context dependency

Why is modeling a compressor difficult? The problem is that a global amplitude function must depend upon local amplitude functions, and these local functions in turn depend upon starting times and durations (just as in the case of vibrato). It may not be possible to determine the amplitude of a note without instantiating the note in context, and even then, it may not be possible to identify and extract an envelope. Furthermore, in some languages, information can flow from a global function to a sequence of nested notes, but information cannot flow from a note attribute to a global function. (Note that this type of transformation can only be realized when musical objects are available after definition, e.g., when they are accessible data structures.)

One area where the distinction between causal and non-causal programming is the most obvious is the handling of duration. The problem with duration is that it is often nice to know in advance how long a note will last; the shape of the amplitude envelope, the exact frequency of vibrato, the dynamic level, and many other details may depend upon the length of a note. In a non-causal system, notes can be manipulated as abstract objects. For example, notes may be shifted, stretched and reorganized. After the organization is in place and durations are fixed, the details can be added with full knowledge of the note duration.

In the causal case, duration can be determined in various ways. In the simplest case, the duration may be specified at the time the note is started. This would be typical in a programming language where evaluation proceeds top-down from high-level procedures to the innermost low-level procedures. High-level procedures compute the details of each note including starting time, pitch, and duration. Even in this case, the duration of a phrase is the sum of the durations of its components, and all of these durations may not be known when the phrase begins.

Portamento is intimately connected to duration. Advanced knowledge of duration enables the anticipation of the ending time of a note, and anticipation allows the portamento to begin before the end of the note. Otherwise the portamento will be late.

Abstract musical structure versus instrument structure

The resource-instance model (Dannenberg, Rubine, and Neuendorffer 1991) makes a distinction based on how discrete data or events are handled. In the first case, discrete information (either a data object or a function application as described above) denotes a new instance of some class of behaviors or objects. In the Music N family of languages (Mathews 1969) for example, each note in the score language denotes an instance (a copy) of an instrument computation described in the orchestra language.

In the second case, discrete information is directed to a resource (e.g., an instrument), where the information is used to modify the behavior of the resource. For example, a pitch-bend message in MIDI is directed to a channel resource, affecting the tuning of all notes sounding on that channel (either now or in the future).

A language or representation may be either instance-based, resource-based, or some combination of the two. In the combined case, discrete information is used to designate the instantiation (creation or allocation) of new resources. (This supports the instance model.) Once instantiated, a resource may receive updates that modify the behavior or instantiate sub-behaviors. (This supports the resource model.)

In the resource-instance model, one might create and play a virtual guitar by first instantiating a guitar resource. Next, updates are sent to this guitar resource, requesting the instantiation of six strings. Finally, updates are sent to stop the strings at particular frets and to strum the strings, making sound. The ability to instantiate new resources and to update the state of existing resources is very powerful because it provides a natural representation for addressing the instrument problem defined above.

The resource-instance model also provides flexibility. A composer can choose to instantiate a guitar for each note, to share the guitar but instantiate a new string for each note, or to play every note on the same string. These choices give rise to different sounds, and the model helps to clarify the available choices.

Structure

Music representations and languages support varying degrees and types of structure, ranging from unstructured (flat structure) note-lists to complex recursive
hierarchical (tree-like) and heterarchical (many-rooted) structures.

Two-level structure

A simple two-level structure is found in the Music *N* languages such as Music
V (Mathews 1969), Csound (Vercoe 1986), and cmusic (Moore 1990). In these
languages, there is a "flat" unstructured list of notes expressed in the score
language. Each note in the score language gives rise to an instance of an
instrument, as defined in the orchestra language. Instruments are defined using
a "flat" list of signal generating and processing operations. Thus, there is a
one-level score description and a one-level instrument description, giving a total
of two levels of structure in this class of language.

The Adagio language in the CMU MIDI Toolkit (Dannenberg 1986a, 1993a)
and the score file representation used in the NeXT Music Kit (Jaffe and Boynton
1989) are other examples of one-level score languages. These languages are
intended to be simple representations that can be read and written easily by
humans and machines. When the lack of structure is a problem, it is common to
use another programming language to generate the score. This same approach
is common with the score languages in Music *N* systems.

Nested discrete structures

Rather than resort to yet another language to generate scores, it is possible to
augment the score language with additional structure so that a separate language
is not necessary. Typically, functions (or macros, or procedures) represent musical behaviors or collections of musical events. By invoking the function in
multiple places, several instances of the behavior can be obtained, and by using
nested functions, a hierarchical structure can be described. The section "shared
framework of Nyquist and GTF" (below) will explore this idea further.

Recursive structures

In addition to nested, hierarchical structures, languages can support true recursion. Consider the following prescription for a drum roll, "to play a drum roll,
play a stroke, and if you are not finished, play a drum roll." This is a recursive definition because the definition of "drum roll" is defined using the "drum
roll" concept itself. This definition makes perfectly good sense in spite of the
circularity or recursion. Recursion is useful for expressing many structures.

Non-hierarchical structures

It is often not at all clear how specific knowledge about a particular kind of music should be represented, and "wiring-in" assumptions at a low level of the representation language can make it useless for applications for which the assumptions do not hold. When there is need for a general "part-of" relation between structural units, without the usual restriction to single strict hierarchical structure (e.g., representing overlapping phrases), it is important to represent this capability on a low level, with as little knowledge about music as possible, not relying on ad-hoc opinions about specific musical concepts. A solution that supports a general part-of relation with names that function as "hooks" to link in specific musical knowledge proved successful in POCO (Honing 1990), a workbench for research on expressive timing. Non-hierarchical structures are also found in representation work by Brinkman (1985) and Dannenberg (1986b).

Ornamental relations

Ornaments often have their specific behavior under transformation, for example, a grace note does not have to be played longer when a piece is performed slower. In a calculus for expressive timing (Desain and Honing 1991) and in Expresso, a system based on that formalism (Honing 1992), ornamental structures of different kinds are formalized such that they maintain consistency automatically under transformations of expression (for instance, lowering the tempo or exaggerating the depth of a rubato). In this application one cannot avoid incorporating some musical knowledge about these ornaments and one has to introduce, for example, the basic distinction between *acciacatura* and *appogiatura* (time-taking and timeless ornaments).

Shared framework of Nyquist and GTF

We can now present more concrete proposals for representation and programming languages for music that are aimed at addressing the issues introduced above. One formalism (referred to as ACF, for "Arctic, Canon and Fugue") evolved in a family of composition languages (in historic order, Arctic, Canon, Fugue, and Nyquist—Dannenberg 1984; Dannenberg, McAvinney, and Rubine 1986; Dannenberg 1989b; Dannenberg and Fraley 1989; Dannenberg, Fraley, and Velikonja 1991, 1992; Dannenberg 1992b, 1993b) and found its final form (to date) in the Nyquist system. The second formalism (called GTF, for "Generalized Time Functions") originated from the need to augment a composition system with continuous control (Desain and Honing 1988; Desain and Honing 1992a; Desain and Honing 1993). Their similarities and differences were discussed in Dannenberg

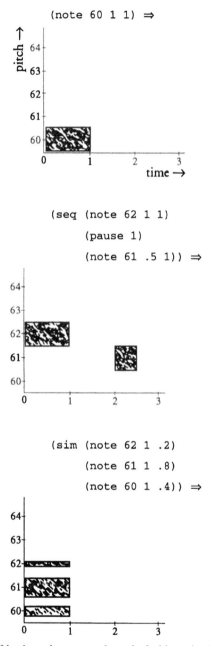

Figure 3. Examples of basic and compound musical objects in ACF and GTF are given in Lisp and graphical pitch-time notation. A note with MIDI pitch 60 = middle C, duration 1 (second or beat), and maximum amplitude (a), a sequence of a note, a rest and another, shorter note (b), and three notes in parallel, each with different pitches and amplitudes (c).

(1992a) and Honing (1995). Here we will first describe the set of musical objects, time functions and their transformation that is shared by the ACF and GTF systems. We use the Canon syntax (Dannenberg 1989b) for simplicity. The examples will be presented with their graphical output shown as pitch-time diagrams.

In general, both the ACF and GTF systems provide a set of primitive musical objects (in ACF these are referred to as "behaviors") and ways of combining them into more complex ones. Examples of basic musical objects are the note construct, with parameters for duration, pitch, amplitude and other arbitrary attributes (that depend on the synthesis method that is used), and pause, a rest with duration as its only parameter. (Note that, in our example code, pitches are given as MIDI key numbers, duration in seconds, and amplitude on a 0–1 scale). These basic musical objects can be combined into compound musical objects using the time structuring constructs named seq (for sequential ordering) and sim (for simultaneous or parallel ordering). Figure 3 presents examples.

New musical objects can be defined using the standard procedural abstraction (function definition) of the Lisp programming language, as in,

```
;; This is a comment in Lisp.
;; Define a function called ''melody.''
(defun melody ()
  ;; that produces a sequence
  ;; of three sequential notes.
  ;; note takes arguments pitch, dur, amp
  (seq (note 60 .5 1)
       (note 61 .5 1)
       (note 62 .5 1)))
```

Figure 4 shows an example of the use of the melody abstraction, playing it twice sequentially.

Both ACF and GTF provide a set of control functions or functions of time, and ways of combining them into more complex ones. We will give two examples of basic time functions: a linear interpolating ramp and an oscillator generating a sine wave.

There are several possible ways to pass time functions to musical objects. One method is to pass a function directly as an attribute of, for instance, the pitch parameter of a note (Figure 5). When using this parameterization method for building complex musical objects, it has to be known in advance which parameters can be controlled from the outside—the encapsulation of the musical

(seq (melody) (melody)) ⇒

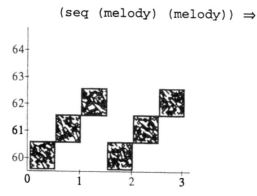

Figure 4. A sequence of a user-defined musical object (a melody) repeated twice.

(note (ramp 60 61) 1 1) ⇒

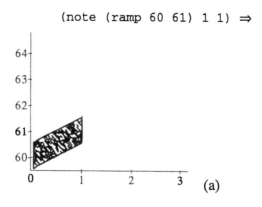

(a)

(note (oscillator 61 1 1) 1 1) ⇒

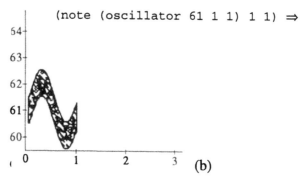

(b)

Figure 5. Two examples of notes with continuous pitch attribute are illustrated here. A interpolating linear ramp with start and end value as parameters is shown in (a), and a sine wave oscillator with offset, modulation frequency and amplitude as parameters is given in (b).

object needs to be parameterized. For example, when building a chord function it may be parametrized naturally by the pitch contour of the root, but it has to be known in advance whether at some time in the future we will want to de-tune one specific note of the chord. Once foreseen, it is easy to write a chord function with an extra parameter for this capability, but in general it is hard to decide on the appropriate amount of encapsulation in defining compound musical objects for general use. (This is also one of the reasons why we believe in composition systems in the form of general programming languages with their capabilities of abstraction; there are so many styles of music composition that any pre-wired choice of the designer of a composition system is doomed to be wrong for some composer at some time.)

An alternative method to specification by parameterization is to make a musical object with simple default values and to obtain the desired result by transformation. For instance, a transposition transformation applied to a simple note with constant pitch yields a note with a specific pitch envelope. When using this method for specifying a complex musical object the transformation is in principle applied to the whole object and cannot differentiate its behavior with regard to specific parts.

In one context the first method will be more appropriate, in another the latter. The following examples show the equivalence between specification by means of transformation and by parameterization (their output is as shown in Figures 5(a) and 5(b), respectively):

```
;; specification by parameterization
(note (ramp 60 61) 1 1))
;; specification by transformation
(trans (ramp 0 1) (note 60 1 1))

;; specification by parameterization
(note (oscillator 61 1 1) 1 1))
;; specification by transformation
(trans (oscillator 0 1 1) (note 61 1 1))
```

Finally, both systems support different types of transformations. As an example of a time transformation, stretch will be used (Figure 6(a)). This transformation scales the duration of a musical object (its second parameter) with a factor (its first parameter). As examples of attribute transformations we will use one for pitch (named trans), and one for amplitude (named loud). These transformations take constants (Figure 6(b), (c) and (d)) or time functions (see

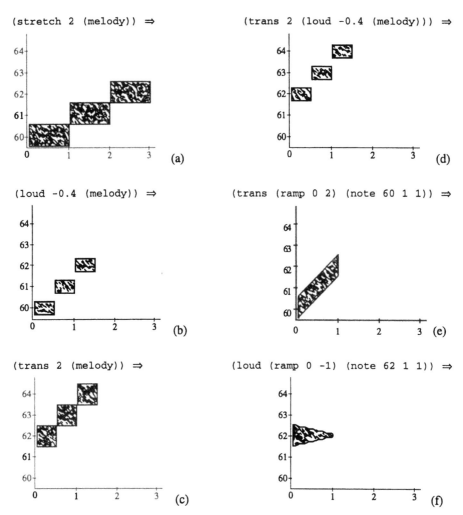

Figure 6. This figure shows several examples of transformations on musical objects: a stretch transformation (a), an amplitude transformation (b), a pitch transformation (c), a nesting of two transformations (d), a time-varying pitch transformation (e), and a time-varying amplitude transformation (f).

Figure 6(e) and (f)) as their first argument, and the object to be transformed as their second argument.

The Nyquist language

Nyquist is a language for sound synthesis and composition. There are many approaches that offer computer support for these tasks, so we should begin by explaining some advantages of a language approach. A key problem in sound synthesis is to provide detailed control of the many parameters that are typically required by modern digital sound synthesis techniques. As described above, it is very difficult to anticipate the needs of composers; often, the composer wants to fix a set of parameters and focus on the control of a few others. A programming language is ideal for describing customized instruments that have only the parameters of interest and that behave according to the composer's requirements. In other words, the composer can create his or her own language that is specific to the compositional task at hand.

Composition itself can benefit from a programming language model. Musical information processing can range from the automation of simple mechanical tasks all the way to computer-based composition where all aspects of a composition are determined by a program. Whatever the approach, it is a great advantage to have a close link between the compositional language and the synthesis language. With Nyquist, one language serves both composition and signal processing, and blurs the distinction between these tasks.

Nyquist is based on Lisp, which has several advantages for music. First, Lisp is a very high-level language, with many built-in functions and data types. Second, Lisp is a good language for symbol processing, which is a common task when manipulating musical information. Finally, Lisp provides an incremental, interpreted programming environment which is ideal for experimental and exploratory programming.

Nyquist adds a few capabilities to Lisp to make it more suitable for sound synthesis and music composition. First, Nyquist adds a new data type called SOUND, which efficiently represents audio and control signals. Second, Nyquist provides new control constructs that deal with time, including the sequential (seq) and parallel (sim) behaviors introduced above. Third, Nyquist supports various kinds of temporal and musical transformations such as transposition (trans), tempo change (stretch), and loudness (loud) control, that we defined above.

In the sections that follow, we will examine the new concepts and constructs that Nyquist adds to Lisp. It will be seen that a small number of new constructs are required to create a very flexible language for music.

The SOUND data type

A Nyquist SOUND is a time-varying signal. As is common in signal processing systems, the signal is represented by a sequence of samples denoting the value of the signal at regularly spaced instants in time. In addition to samples, a SOUND has a designated starting time and a fixed sample rate. Furthermore, a SOUND has a *logical stop time*, which indicates the starting time of the next sound in a sequence. (Sequences are described later in greater detail.)

Multi-channel signals are represented in Nyquist by arrays of SOUNDs. For example, a stereo pair is represented by an array of two SOUNDs, where the first element is the left channel, and the second element is the right channel. Nyquist operators are defined to allow multi-channel signals in a straightforward way, so we will not dwell on the details. For the remainder of this introduction, we will describe SOUNDs and operations on them without describing the multi-channel case.

A SOUND in Nyquist is immutable. That is, once created, a SOUND can never change. Rather than modify a SOUND, operators create and return new ones. This is consistent with the functional programming paradigm that Lisp supports. The functional programming paradigm and the immutable property of sounds is of central importance, so we will present some justifications and some implications of this aspect of Nyquist in the following paragraphs.

There are many advantages to this functional approach. First, no side-effects result from applying (or calling) functions. Programs that contain no side-effects are often simple to reason about because there are no hidden state changes to think about.

Another advantage has to do with data dependencies and incremental processing. Large signal processing operations are often performed incrementally, one sample block at a time. All blocks starting at a particular time are computed before the blocks in the next time increment. The order in which blocks are computed is important because the parameters of a function must be computed before the function is applied. In functional programs, once a parameter (in particular, a block of samples) is computed, no side effects can change the samples, so it is safe to apply the function. Thus, the implementation tends to have more options as to the order of evaluation, and the constraints on execution order are relatively simple to determine.

The functional style seems to be well-suited to many signal-processing tasks. Nested expressions that modify and combine signals provide a clear and parsimonious representation for signal processing.

The functional style has important implications for Nyquist. First, since there are no side-effects that can modify a SOUND, SOUNDs might as well be immutable. Immutable sounds can be reused by many functions with very little effort. Rather than copy the sound, all that is needed is to copy a reference (or pointer) to the sound. This saves computation time that would be required to copy data, and memory space that would be required to store the copy.

As described above, it is possible for the Nyquist implementation to reorder computation to be as efficient as possible. The main optimization here is to compute SOUNDs or parts of SOUNDs only when they are needed. This technique is called *lazy evaluation*.

In Nyquist, the SOUND data type represents continuous data, and most of the time the programmer can reason about SOUNDs as if they are truly continuous functions of time. A coercion operation allows access to the actual samples by copying the samples from the internal SOUND representation to a Lisp ARRAY type. ARRAYs, of course, are discrete structures by our definitions.

Functions as instruments and scores

In Nyquist, Lisp functions serve the roles of both instrument definitions and musical scores. Instruments are described by combining various sound operations; for example, (pwl 0.02 1 0.5 0.3 1.0) creates a piece-wise linear envelope, and (osc c4 1) creates a 1-second tone at pitch C4 using a table-lookup oscillator. These operations, along with the mult operator can be used to create a simple instrument, as in,

```
;; Define a simple instrument with an envelope.
(defun simple-instr (pitch dur)
   (mult (pwl 0.02 1 0.5 0.3 dur)
         (osc pitch dur)))
```

Scores can also be represented by functions using the seq and sim constructs described earlier. For example, the following example will play a short melody over a pedal tone in the bass,

```
;; Define a simple score function.
(defun simple-score ()
   ;; bass note
   (sim (simple-inst g2 8)
      ;; melody simultaneous with bass
      (seq (pause 1)
           (simple-inst b4 1)
           (simple-inst a4 2)
           (simple-inst e4 1)
           (simple-inst d4 3)))))
```

Nyquist also supports transformation functions for modifying pitch, duration, loudness, and other parameters. The functions are applied using special transformation operators. For example, the following expression would play simple-score transposed up a fifth seven half-steps and accelerated to 0.8 times the normal duration,

```
(trans 7 (stretch 0.8 (simple-score)))
```

Transformations may also be continuous functions of time, in which case a SOUND type is used to specify a function. All of the operators available for synthesis can also be used to specify transformation functions.

Behavioral abstraction

In Nyquist, a behavior is implemented by a function that returns a sound. Supporting the idea that abstract behaviors denote a class of actual behaviors, Nyquist behaviors take parameters. These parameters consist of both conventional function arguments of Lisp, and a set of implicit parameters called the *environment*. The environment contains transformation attributes that normally affect pitch, loudness, time, articulation, and tempo. The environment is dynamically scoped, meaning that the environment of a "parent" function is passed to each "child" function called. In normal usage, the environment is passed from top-level functions all the way down to the lowest-level built-in functions, which implement the transformations contained in the environment. A function can however override or modify the environment at any time to achieve behaviors that differ from the default.

The expression (osc c4) for example, is a simple behavior that computes a sinusoid lasting one second. The stretch operation normally affects the duration of a behavior, so that,

```
(stretch 2 (osc c4))
```

creates a two-second sinusoid. Suppose we wanted to create an "inelastic" behavior that did not stretch? The following will do the job,

```
(stretch-abs 1 (osc c4))
```

The stretch-abs operation modifies the environment by replacing the stretch factor by some value (in this case 1). In the following expression, the outer stretch has no effect, because it is overridden by the stretch-abs operation.

```
(stretch 2 (stretch-abs 1 (osc c4)))
```

Figure 7 illustrates the information flow in the interpretation of this expression. To give a more concrete example, imagine the problem of a short grace note of fixed length followed by a "stretchable" note. The sequence might be described as follows.

```
(seq (grace-note) (ordinary-note))
```

The implementation of **grace-note** will look something like,

```
(defun grace-note () (stretch-abs 0.1 (a-note)))
```

(To keep this definition as simple as possible, we have assumed the existence of a function called **a-note**, which in reality might consist of an elaborate specification of envelopes and wave forms.) Note how the knowledge of whether to stretch or not is encapsulated in the definition of **grace-note**. When a stretch is applied to this expression, as in,

```
(stretch 2 (seq (grace-note) (ordinary-note)))
```

the environment passed to **seq** and hence to **grace-note** will have a stretch value of 2, but within **grace-note**, the environment is modified as in Figure 7

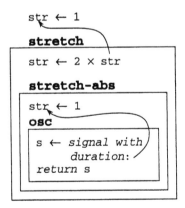

Figure 7. Information flow showing how Nyquist environments support behavioral abstraction. Only the stretch factor is shown. The outer stretch transformation alters the environment seen by the inner stretch-abs transformation. The stretch-abs overrides the outer environment and passes the modified environment on to the osc function. The actual duration is returned as a property of the sound computed by osc.

so that a-note gets a stretch value of 0.1, regardless of the outer environment. On the other hand, ordinary-note sees a stretch value of 2 and behaves accordingly.

In these examples, the grace note takes time and adds to the total duration. A stretch or stretch-abs applied to the preceding or succeeding note could compensate for this. Nyquist does not offer a general solution to the ornament problem (which could automatically place the grace note before the beat), or to the transition problem (which could terminate the preceding note early to allow time for the grace note).

In a real program, pitches and other information would probably be passed as ordinary parameters. Here is the previous example, modified with pitch parameters and using the note object with duration, pitch, and amplitude parameters,

```
;; Define and demonstrate a grace-note function.
(defun grace-note (pitch)
  (stretch-abs 0.1 (note 1 pitch 1)))

(stretch 2 (seq (grace-note c4) (note 1 d4 1)))
```

As these examples illustrate, information flow in Nyquist is top down from transformations to behaviors. The behaviors, implemented as functions, can observe the environment and produce the appropriate result, which may require overriding or modifying the environment seen by lower-level functions. This approach is essentially a one-pass causal operation—parameters and environments flow down to the lowest-level primitives, and signals and stop times flow back up as return values.

The next section describes the GTF representation language, after which we discuss implementation issues related to this kind of system.

The GTF representation language

GTF (Generalized Time Functions) is a representation language for music. The central aim of its development is to define constructs that make it easy to express musical knowledge. This would be very useful as the underlying mechanism for a composition system, but at the moment we are only using it for exploring new ideas about music representation. The system uses a mixed representation—some aspects are represented numerically by continuous control functions, and some aspects are represented symbolically by discrete objects. Together, these discrete musical objects and continuous control functions can form alternating layers of information. For example, a phrase can be associated with a continuous amplitude function, while consisting of notes associated with their own envelope function, which are in turn divided into small sections each with its specific amplitude behavior. The lowest layer could even be extended all the way down to the level of discrete sound samples (Figure 2).

With respect to the continuous aspects (e.g., the vibrato problem), control functions of multiple arguments are used—the so-called "time functions of multiple times" or *generalized time functions* (GTF). These are functions of the actual time, start time and duration (or variations thereof) and they can be linked to any attribute of a musical object to describe the value of that parameter as an envelope evolving over time.

If we ignore for the moment the dependence of time functions on absolute start time, they can be plotted as three-dimensional surfaces that show a control value for every point in time given a certain time interval, as in Figure 8. Similar plots could be made to show a surface dependent on start time. A specific surface describes the behavior under a specific time transformation (e.g., stretching the discrete object to which it is linked). In Figure 8, this surface is shown for a simple sinusoidal vibrato and a sinusoidal glissando. A vertical slice through such a surface describes the characteristic behavior for a certain time interval—the specific time function for a musical object of a certain duration (Figure 9).

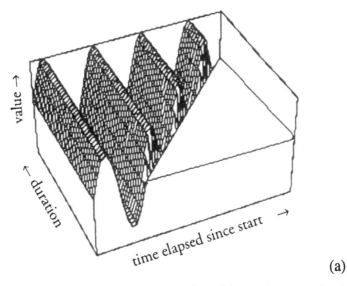

(a)

Figure 8. Two surfaces showing functions of elapsed time and note duration for different stretch behaviors are shown here. In the case of a sinusoidal vibrato, one needs to add more periods for longer durations (a), but a sinusoidal glissando stretches along with the duration parameter (b).

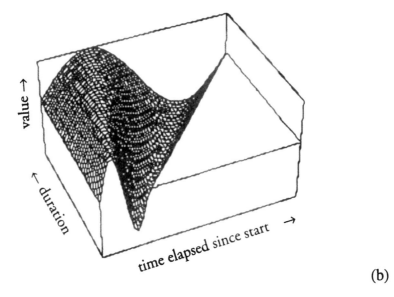

(b)

Figure 8. (Continued.)

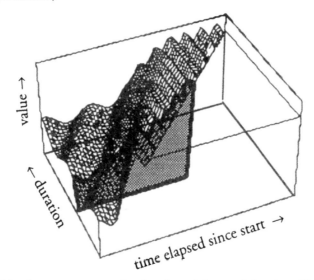

Figure 9. This shows a more complex function of time and duration. The appropriate control function to be used for an object of a certain duration is a vertical slice out of the surface.

Basic GTFs can be combined into more complex control functions using a set of operators—compose, concatenate, multiply, add, etc.—or by supplying GTFs as arguments to other GTFs. In these combinations the components retain their characteristic behavior. Several pre-defined discrete musical objects (such as note and pause) can be combined into compound ones (e.g., using the time structuring functions S and P, for sequential and parallel—similar to seq and sim in ACF).

All musical objects (like note, s, or p) are represented as functions that will be given information about the context in which they appear. The latter supports a pure functional description at this level using an environment for communicating context information (Henderson 1980). Musical objects can be freely transformed by means of function composition, without actually being calculated (see the "lazy evaluation" discussion below). These functions are only given information about their context at execution time, and return a data structure describing the musical object that, in turn, can be used as input to a musical performance or graphical rendering system.

To integrate these continuous and discrete aspects, the system provides facilities that support different kinds of communication between continuous control functions and discrete musical objects. They will be introduced next.

Passing control functions to attributes of musical objects

As presented above, there are at least two ways of passing time functions to musical objects. One method is to pass a function directly as an attribute to, for instance, the pitch parameter of a note—*specification by parameterization.* An alternative method is to make a musical object with simple default values and to obtain the desired result by transformation—*specification by transformation.* When using the parameterization method, a GTF is passed the start-time and the duration of the note that it is linked to as attribute. For the transformation method, a GTF used in a transformation is passed the start-time and the duration of the compound object it is applied to. Thus, to give it the same power as the transformation method, one needs a construct to "wrap" a control function "around" a whole musical object, and apply it as parameter to the different parts. The example below shows the natural use of the transformation style in applying an amplitude envelope to a compound musical object. It produces output as shown in Figure 10. Note that amplitude, s and p in GTF are similar to loud, seq and sim in ACF, respectively; keyword/value pairs are used to specify a note's parameters, as in (:duration 2).

```
;; Apply an amplitude envelope to a phrase of two notes.
(amplitude (ramp 0 1)
           (s (note :pitch 60 :duration 2 :amplitude 1)
              (note :pitch 61 :duration 1 :amplitude 1)))
```

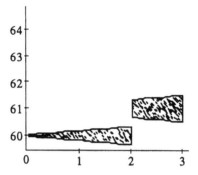

Figure 10. Continuous attributes of compound musical objects can be obtained either by transformation or parameterization (see text for the program code).

The next example shows the alternative specification (see the output in Figure 10). The construct `with-attached-gtfs` names the amplitude envelope for later reference in parts of a discrete compound musical object and links it (for the time behavior) to the whole object.

```
;; Attach an amplitude envelope to a phrase.
(with-attached-gtfs ((envelope (ramp 0 1)))
   (s (note :pitch 60 :duration 2 :amplitude envelope)
      (note :pitch 61 :duration 1 :amplitude envelope))
```

Passing control functions between musical objects

Once control functions are incorporated into musical objects as attributes, it is interesting to allow later access to them from other musical objects (i.e., the transition problem). The construct `with-attribute-gtfs` supports this notion, taking care that transformations on attributes of musical objects propagate their effects properly when outside reference to these attributes was made. Control functions are only defined for the duration of the object to which they are linked, but when they can be referred to from musical objects at other time positions, it is useful to be able to evaluate them at other times. This enables extrapolation, for instance, needed in describing what happens in a transition between notes. Figure 11 shows a simple example of such a transition transformation. It applies to two notes, derives the pitch control function from both, and calculates an interpolation between them (using the `cross-fade` GTF operator).

One should note that it is easy to write the example above using a "top-down" communication, defining the control functions in advance, before they (s (note-1) (pause :duration .75) (note-2)) ⇒

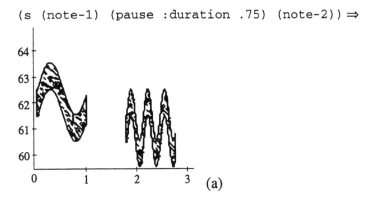

(a)

(transition (note-1) (note-2)) ⇒

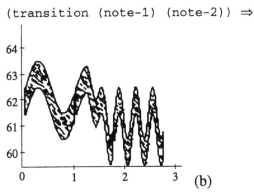

(b)

Figure 11. A sequence of two notes with continuous time functions associated with their pitch attributes can be seen in (a), and the result of applying a transition transformation in (b).

are referred to. However, this communication has to be planned, and general encapsulation of musical objects cannot always be maintained. In contrast, allowing access to attributes of musical objects after their instantiation does not discourage abstraction.

```
;; Define a transition to operate between two notes.
(defun transition (note-a note-b)
 (with-attribute-gtfs (((pitch-a :pitch) note-a)
                       ((pitch-b :pitch) note-b))
  (s note-a
     (note :duration .75 :pitch (cross-fade pitch-a pitch-b))
       note-b)))
```

```
(defun note-1 () (note :pitch (oscillator 62 1 1)))
(defun note-2 () (note :pitch (oscillator 61 3 1)))
```

Passing control functions upward

Sometimes a global transformation of an attribute needs to refer to the attribute values of the parts of a complex musical object to which it is applied. This "bottom-up" communication is needed, for instance, when one wants to compress the loudness of musical object (the compressor problem mentioned above). This is an amplitude transformation that needs access to the amplitude of the parts of the object. The total amplitude at any time depends on the sum of the amplitudes of parallel parts, so the amplitude transformation of a specific note relies on its parallel context. Figure 12 illustrates the type of communication

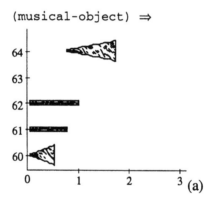

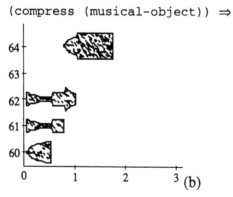

Figure 12. Two notes in parallel with different amplitude envelopes are shown in (a), and the result of applying a compressor transformation to this in (b).

that is needed to write a compressor transformation. The overall amplitude is
calculated by summing amplitude contours for parallel sub-structures and con-
catenating them for sequential ones. This resulting overall amplitude function
for the compound musical object can then be compressed—in this simple example by inverting it—and communicated down to each basic musical object by an
amplitude transformation.

```
;; Define an object that can be used with the compress
function.
(defun musical-object ()
  (p (note :amplitude .1 :pitch 62)
     (s (note :duration .75 :amplitude .1 :pitch 61)
        (note :amplitude (ramp 0 .8) :pitch 64))
        (note :amplitude (ramp 0 .8) :duration .5 :pitch 60)))


;; Define a dynamic range compressor.
(defun compress (musical-object)
  (with-attribute-gtfs
      (((amp :amplitude #' concatenator #'summer)
        musical-object))
      (amplitude (gtf-/ 1 amp) musical-object)))
```

Implementation issues

Unfortunately not all work is done when good representations and computational
ways of dealing with them are designed. Computer music systems, and especially real-time applications, put a heavy burden on computation resources, and
only a wise management of both computation time and memory can help a system that is formally correct to become practically useful too. Luckily, several
techniques have emerged for efficient implementation that do not destroy the
higher abstract levels of language constructs. These techniques allow the casual
user to ignore lower level implementation mechanisms.

Control and information flow

A subtle aspect of language design is the nature of control and information
flow. This is often critical to the design and implementation of a language and

a key to understanding its powers and limitations. We will consider a variety of possibilities.

Top-down information flow

As a first example, consider a typical procedural language such as C or Pascal, with a library of procedures that generate MIDI data. Program evaluation is performed in the usual manner, evaluating inner procedures as they are encountered, using a stack to save the intermediate state of outer (calling) procedures until the inner (called) procedure returns. If all parameters are passed by value (by copying values from the caller to the callee), and if no results are returned from functions, then the information flow is purely top-down. Control flow is depth-first; the structure implied by procedural nesting is traversed in a depth-first order. This means that the next program statement is not evaluated until the current program statement is fully evaluated, including all nested procedures.

Depth-first information flow

If functions return values, then the control flow remains depth-first, but the information flow is both top-down and bottom-up. Since information flows to a procedure instance when the procedure is called, and information flows out of the procedure only when it returns, there is essentially a one-pass information flow through the structure, as shown in Figure 13.

Lazy evaluation

While it is natural to organize a program to reflect musical structure, this does not always result in a natural order of execution. For example, if there are

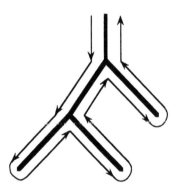

Figure 13. When nested procedures or functions are evaluated in the usual depth-first order, information is passed "down" through parameters and "up" through returned values. The information flow over the course of evaluation is diagrammed here. Note that in conventional stack-based language implementations, only portions of this tree would be present at any one instant of the computation.

two parallel behaviors, a melody and a harmony, a normal depth-first order of evaluation would compute one behavior in its entirety before executing the other behavior. Thus, the "natural" structure of a procedural program does not result in any parallel behavior. In non-real-time programs, this problem can be solved by sorting the output into time order. Alternatively, the procedures that output notes may insert them directly into a sorted note list structure or even into a digital audio sound file as in Cmix (Lansky 1987). The point is that the execution order may not correspond to the time order of the behaviors involved.

The fact that normal execution order and time order are not the same has some important consequences. First, it is not possible to build real-time programs if the execution does not proceed in time order. This limits procedural, normal execution order programs to "out of time" composition tasks. Second, information flow between parallel behaviors can be at best one-way (from the first behavior executed to the second). It is not possible to have two-way or ensemble-like communication because each behavior, for example each voice of an ensemble, is computed in sequence.

One way out of this dilemma is to resort to more elaborate programming models. For example, multiple processes can be used to perform concurrent computation. A good example of a process-based language is Formula (Anderson and Kuivila 1990). Programming with concurrent processes does however require special care if processes share data, communicate, and synchronize.

Alternatively, an *active object* approach can be used to perform interleaved computations. FORMES was an early example of the active object approach (Rodet and Cointe 1984). Active objects are simpler to use than a process-based approach, but still require sophisticated programming techniques.

Perhaps the simplest way to achieve concurrent behavior is with the approach used in Moxie, a language designed by Douglas Collinge (1985), Collinge and Scheidt (1988) and re-implemented in the CMU MIDI Toolkit (Dannenberg 1986a, 1993a). Here, procedure calls can be deferred to some time point in the future. A periodic process-like behavior results if a procedure performs an action and then calls itself with a delay. These procedural approaches to concurrency deserve a chapter of their own (in fact, many books are written about programming with processes), but we will leave this subject and return to more functional approaches.

An alternative to procedural approaches uses *lazy evaluation,* where computation proceeds according to the demand for data. Consider a nested expression: $(a \times b) + (c \times d)$, where a, b, c and d are signals. In the "normal" order of execution, we would multiply a and b in their entirety. Then we would multiply c and d. Finally, we would add the two products. Note that this order of operation would require space for the intermediate products and the final sum.

Since these are signals, the space could be quite large. For example, monaural 16-bit audio track at a 44.1 kHz sample rate requires 88.2 kbytes of memory per second of audio.

Alternatively, lazy evaluation delays the execution of expressions until the value is needed. This is accomplished by creating a "place-holder" for the expression that can be invoked later to produce the final value. In the case of $(a \times b)$, a structure (usually called a *suspension*) is created to "remember" the state of the operation—that a and b are to be multiplied. Lazy evaluation systems often support the incremental evaluation of expressions. This means that a signal could be computed one sample or one block of samples at a time, leaving the remainder of the computation in suspension.

The Nyquist implementation uses lazy evaluation. In Nyquist, all signals are represented using suspensions that are activated as needed to compute blocks of samples. The expression $(a \times b) + (c \times d)$, when first evaluated, creates the structure shown in Figure 14. If the beginning of the signal is needed, the "+" suspension requests a block from the first "$\times$" suspension. This suspension in turn requests a block from each of a and b, which may activate other suspensions. The blocks returned from a and b are multiplied and returned to the "+" suspension. Then, the second "$\times$" suspension is called to compute a block in a manner similar to the first one. The two product blocks are added and the sum is returned from the "+" suspension.

Lazy evaluation results in a computation order that is not simply one pass over the program structure. Instead, a pass is made over the structure of suspensions each time additional samples are required from the expression. This results in a time-ordered interleaving of a, b, c, and d. A similar technique is used in Music N languages so that samples will be computed in time order with a minimal use of memory for sample computation.

Neither Nyquist nor Music N languages require the programmer to think about data structures, suspensions, or even lazy evaluation. The programmer merely writes the expression, and the implementation automatically transforms

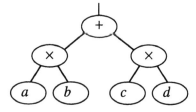

Figure 14. The expression $(a \times b) + (c \times d)$, when evaluated lazily, returns a suspension structure as shown here rather than actually performing the computation.

it into a lazy structure. This can lead to a very clean notation even though the run-time behavior is quite complex.

Lazy evaluation is a powerful and important technique for music systems because it can automatically convert from an execution order based on musical and program structure to an execution order that corresponds to the forward progress of time. Since the semantics are unchanged by the transformation, however, programming languages based on nested functions (such as Nyquist) still have the limitation that information flow is strictly top-down through parameters and bottom-up via results. To get around this one-pass restriction, more elaborate language semantics are required (the compressor problem).

Constraints, rules, and search

Because Nyquist and GTF are rooted in functional programming, most of our examples have considered information flow based on function semantics; information flows from actual to formal parameters and values are returned from a function to the function application site. This is adequate for many interesting problems, and the functional style can lead to elegant notation and simple semantics, but there are also many alternatives. One is procedural or object-oriented programming where data structures are modified as the program executes. Programs can follow links between data objects, resulting in almost arbitrary data flow and data dependencies. One of the main problems with this style, in fact, is the difficulty of maintaining intended relationships and invariant properties among data elements.

To illustrate the problem, consider computing the sum of two signals, A and B. Suppose that MA and MB are memory locations that store the current values of A and B. Computing the sum of A and B at the current time is implemented by computing $content(MA) + content(MB)$. The problem is knowing when the contents of MA and MB are current. If A depends upon several other variables, it may be inefficient to recompute MA every time one of the several variables changes. An alternative is to compute MA from the dependencies only when MA is required, but if there are several points in the program that require a value for MA, it is inefficient to recompute it upon every access. Furthermore, the values on which MA depends may not always be available.

A solution to this dilemma is the use of constraint-based programming (Levitt 1984). In this paradigm, the programmer expresses dependencies as constraints directly in the programming language and the underlying implementation maintains the constraints. For example, if the constraint $C = A + B$ is specified, then any access to C will yield the same value as $A + B$. The details that achieve this can largely be ignored by the programmer, and the implementor is able to use sophisticated algorithms to maintain constraints efficiently. Since the book-keeping is tedious, constraint-based systems can automate many programming details that would be necessary in procedural and object-oriented systems.

Another possibility for constraint-based systems is that constraints can be bidirectional. In the previous example, if C and A are given, then a system with bidirectional constraints can compute $B = C - A$. This is quite interesting because it means that information flow is determined by the problem instead of the programming language. This would be useful to us in computing durations. Sometimes a sequence must be of a certain duration, in which case the durations of the elements of the sequence are computed from the desired total duration. In other cases, the duration of the sequence is not specified and must be computed as the sum of the durations of the sequence components. This type of flexibility is difficult to achieve in most music programming languages without programming the dependencies and setting the direction of information flow in advance.

Another situation where information flow is extremely flexible is rule-based systems, where a set of *rules* are applied to a *working memory*. Rules are usually of the form,

if *condition* **then** *action*

where *condition* tests the working memory for some property and *action* performs some modification to the working memory. Rule-based systems are often used for expert systems and ill-structured problems where no straightforward step-by-step algorithm is known. The conventional wisdom is that rules encode units of knowledge about how to solve a problem. By iteratively applying rules, a solution can be found, even though the path to the solution is not known in advance by the programmer. In these situations, the information flow and dependencies between memory objects is very complex.

Both constraint-based systems and rule-based systems can use search techniques to find an evaluation order that solves the problem at hand. The search for a solution can be very costly, though. One of the drawbacks of constraint-based systems and rule-based systems is that they inevitably incur extra overhead relative to a functional program (where execution order is implied by the programming language semantics) or a procedural program (where execution order is given explicitly by the programmer). With constraints and rules, the implementation must compute what to do in addition to doing it. If the problem demands this flexibility, a constraint-based system or rule-based system can perform well, especially if the system has been carefully optimized.

Duration

The duration of a musical object does not always have to be represented explicitly in that object; the time when the object has to end could be specified by a separate stop event. MIDI, a real-time protocol, uses separate `note-on` and `note-off` messages to avoid specifying duration before it is known. If this approach is taken, the internal details of the note cannot depend upon the total duration, and some extra mechanisms are needed to decide which start-event has to be paired with a specific stop-event

Even when the duration of an object is handled explicitly, several approaches are possible. In a top-down approach, the duration of a musical object is *inherited* by the object—an object is instructed to last for a certain duration. In contrast, many musical objects have *intrinsic* or *synthesized* durations, including sound files and melodies. In that case the object can only be instructed to start at a specific time, and its duration only becomes available when the object is actually played to its end. A third possibility is to use representations of musical objects that pass durations "bottom up," so that each instance of a compound object computes a duration in terms of its components and returns it.

In Nyquist, durations are intrinsic to sounds. The sound data structure carries a marker indicating the *logical stop time* for the sound. When a sequence of behaviors is to be computed, the first behavior is instantiated to compute a sound. At the logical stop time of the first sound, the second behavior is instantiated. At the logical stop time of the second sound, the third behavior is instantiated, and so on. An interesting aspect of logical stop times in Nyquist is that high-level events such as the instantiation of a new behavior can depend upon very low-level signal processing behaviors. In contrast, many systems, especially real-time systems, try to separate the high-level control computation from the low-level signal computation. This is so that the high-level control can run at a coarser time granularity, allowing time-critical signal processing operations to proceed asynchronously with respect to control updates. Nyquist does not attempt this separation between control and signal processing. It is convenient to have intrinsic durations determine the start of the next element in a sequence, but this direction of information flow adds noticeable overhead to signal-processing computations.

In GTF, primitive musical objects can be given explicit durations. Compound musical objects constructed directly with the time ordering operations out of these primitive objects then calculate their durations bottom-up. It is possible, though, to write functions that expect a duration argument and construct a compound musical object with an arbitrary time structure—for example, elongating a *fermata* instead of slowing down the tempo as a way of making the melody have a longer duration.

Events as signals

Continuous signals usually carry information from a source to one or more
destinations. The output of an instrument may be connected to the input of a
mixer for example. In contrast, discrete data does not necessarily have a specific
source or destination. In Music N languages, discrete note events are listed in
the score language, so there is no specific note source. Each note denotes an
instance of an instrument computation, so there is no specific destination either.
We could say that the source is the score and the destination is the orchestra,
but since there is only one score and one orchestra, this is not very meaningful.

This Music N model, in which events denote an instance of a behavior, is
simple but limited. (Nyquist and GTF share this limitation.) Suppose, for
example, that we wish to model two MIDI streams, each one connected to a
different synthesizer. This is not so simple because each MIDI stream contains
indistinguishable note-on events, so there is no way to say which stream the
note-on comes from, and there is no destination other than a global behavior
named note-on.

On the other hand, signals do not pose similar problems. If we write a
reverberation function called `revb` in C, then we can apply reverberation to
several inputs as follows.

```
output_1 := revb(input_1);
output_2 := revb(input_2);
output_3 := revb(input_3);
```

This example contains the germ of an idea. By analogy, we should be able to
write

```
output_1 := synth(input_1);
output_2 := synth(input_2);
```

But in this case, `input_1` and `input_2` are MIDI streams, not signals.

Having seen the form of the solution, we need to find language semantics that
make this possible! A new data type is required to represent event streams (such
as MIDI in this example). The data type consists of a sequence of "events," each
consisting of a time, a function name, and a set of actual parameter values. Like
signals, event streams may be infinite. We call these *timed streams* to distinguish
them from streams in languages like Lucid (Ashcroft and Wadge 1977) where
events are accessed by position (first, second, third, . . .) rather than time.

It now makes sense to have event stream operators. For example, merge(E1, E2) computes the union of events in streams E1 and E2, and gate(S1, E1) acts as an "event switch" controlled by a Boolean function of time S1. When S1 is true, events pass through, and when S1 is false, events are discarded.

It must also be possible to define new operators involving both signals and event streams. We will not go into great detail here, but imagine something like an object-oriented language class definition. An instance of a user-defined operator on event streams is just an instance of this class, and each event is a message to the instance object. For example, here is C-style pseudocode for the merge operation that handles only note-on and note-off events.

```
merge(E1, E2) is [
  handle
    event E1.NoteOn(c, p, v)  is [send NoteOn(c, p, v)];
    event E1.NoteOff(c, p, v) is [send NoteOff(c, p, v)];
    event E2.NoteOn(c, p, v)  is [send NoteOn(c, p, v)];
    event E2.NoteOff(c, p, v) is [send NoteOff(c, p, v)];
]
```

Notice the send command, which places a message such as NoteOn(c, p, v) in the output event stream. Also notice that input "messages" come only from event stream parameters. This is markedly different from object-oriented programming systems where messages come from anywhere and message sends always specify a receiver object. Remember also that message streams are *values* that can be assigned to variables and passed as parameters (such as E1 and E2) to other operations.

The concept of timed streams is not a new one, although the concept has not been studied systematically. Many software systems for MIDI use a stream model for routing MIDI messages among application programs. The NeXT Music Kit (Jaffe 1989) and the programming language Max (Puckette 1991) also allow connections that carry discrete data between software objects. The approach outlined in this section is different in that event streams are immutable *values* just like signals.

Resource updates as signals

The idea of streams is relevant to the resource-instance model. In a pure instance model, every discrete event denotes an instantiation, so it is not necessary to have a specific source or target for the events. In the resource model, the resource (instrument) becomes a destination for a stream of updates, so the idea that discrete events are organized into streams is a natural one.

The event-stream concept is interesting and powerful, especially because many event-transforming operators are possible, including transposition, conditional selection, delay, stretching, and dynamic level changing. Treating events as elements of a stream also clarifies data dependencies (destinations depend upon sources), which in turn relates to the scheduling or ordering of computation.

Conclusion

We have surveyed a number of problems in music representation, including the vibrato problem, transitions and anticipation, continuous versus discrete data, and the link between descriptions of sounds and descriptions of instruments. These problems and the search for their solution influence the design of music representation and programming languages. Some of the language concepts motivated by musical concerns are: behavioral abstraction (or context-sensitive polymorphism); in- and out-of-time processing; various forms of discrete and continuous data; and hierarchical and heterarchical structure. The Nyquist and GTF languages are examples of languages that incorporate many of these concepts while remaining fairly broad in their application. As we have seen, a number of interesting implementation issues arise in music languages, including lazy evaluation, timed event streams, information flow, and duration.

Languages are a measure of our understanding. Our ability to design good languages for a particular domain (such as music) depends upon our ability to clearly describe the terms, conditions, and concepts of the domain. So far, we have mastered some of the concepts and provided good support for them in a number of music representation languages. Other concepts are not yet well understood, and are not well-supported by languages. The anticipation problem, for example, where current behavior is a function of both the current state and future *intensions*, is quite interesting. How does one represent and operate upon future plans?

These and other problems make clear that the representation of music still poses a major challenge to language design. We hope that this chapter will lead to a greater understanding of existing languages and will motivate others to find new solutions to the problems we have raised. Perhaps a greater awareness of these issues will also help other language designers to incorporate existing knowledge about language design for music.

Acknowledgments

This first author would like to thank the School of Computer Science at Carnegie Mellon for support in many forms. Part of this work was done during a visit of the last two authors at CCRMA, Stanford University on the kind invitation of Chris Chafe and John Chowning, supported by a travel grant of the Netherlands Organization for Scientific Research (NWO). Their research has been made possible by a fellowship of the Royal Netherlands Academy of Arts and Sciences (KNAW).

References

Anderson, D.P. and R. Kuivila. 1986. "Accurately timed generation of discrete musical events." *Computer Music Journal* 10(3): 49–56.

Anderson, D.P. and R. Kuivila. 1990. "A system for computer music performance." *ACM Transactions on Computer Systems* 8(1): 56–82.

Ashcroft, E.A. and W.W. Wadge. 1977. "Lucid, a nonprocedural language with iteration." *Communications of the ACM* 20(7): 519–526.

Ashley, R.D. 1992. "Modelling ensemble performance: dynamic just intonation." In *Proceedings of the 1992 International Computer Music Conference*. San Francisco: International Computer Music Association, pp. 38–41.

Brinkman, A. 1985. "A data structure for computer analysis of musical scores." In *Proceedings of the 1984 International Computer Music Conference*. San Francisco: International Computer Music Association, pp. 233–242.

Cointe, P. and X. Rodet. 1984. "Formes: an object and time oriented system for music composition and synthesis." In *1984 ACM Symposium on LISP and Functional Programming*. New York: Association for Computing Machinery, pp. 85–95.

Collinge, D.J. 1985. "MOXIE: a language for computer music performance." In *Proceedings of the 1984 International Computer Music Conference*. San Francisco: International Computer Music Association, pp. 217–220.

Collinge, D.J. and D.J. Scheidt. 1988. "MOXIE for the Atari ST." In *Proceedings of the 14th International Computer Music Conference*. San Francisco: International Computer Music Association, pp. 231–238.

Dannenberg, R.B. 1984. "Arctic: a functional language for real-time control." In *1984 ACM Symposium on LISP and Functional Programming*. New York: Association for Computing Machinery, pp. 96–103.

Dannenberg, R.B. 1986a. "The CMU MIDI Toolkit." In *Proceedings of the 1986 International Computer Music Conference*. San Francisco: International Computer Music Association, pp. 53–56.

Dannenberg, R.B. 1986b. "A structure for representing, displaying, and editing music." In *Proceedings of the 1986 International Computer Music Conference*. San Francisco: International Computer Music Association, pp. 130–160.

Dannenberg, R.B. 1989a. "Real-time scheduling and computer accompaniment." In M.V. Mathews and J.R. Pierce, eds. *Current Directions in Computer Music Research*. Cambridge, Massachusetts: The MIT Press, pp. 225–262.

Dannenberg, R.B. 1989b. "The Canon score language." *Computer Music Journal* 13(1): 47–56.

Dannenberg, R.B. 1992a. "Time functions." Letters. *Computer Music Journal* 16(3): 7–8.

Dannenberg, R.B. 1992b. "Real-time software synthesis on superscalar architectures." In *Proceedings of the 1992 International Computer Music Conference*. San Francisco: International Computer Music Association, pp. 174–177.

Dannenberg, R.B. 1993a. *The CMU MIDI Toolkit*. Software distribution. Pittsburgh, Pennsylvania: Carnegie Mellon University.

Dannenberg, R.B. 1993b. "The implementation of Nyquist, a sound synthesis language." In *Proceedings of the 1993 International Computer Music Conference*. San Francisco: International Computer Music Association, pp. 168–171.

Dannenberg, R.B. and C.L. Fraley. 1989. "Fugue: composition and sound synthesis with lazy evaluation and behavioral abstraction." In *Proceedings of the 1989 International Computer Music Conference*. San Francisco: International Computer Music Association, pp. 76–79.

Dannenberg, R.B., C.L. Fraley, and P. Velikonja. 1991. "Fugue: a functional language for sound synthesis." *IEEE Computer* 24(7): 36–42.

Dannenberg, R.B., C.L. Fraley, and P. Velikonja. 1992. "A functional language for sound synthesis with behavioral abstraction and lazy evaluation." In D. Baggi, ed. *Readings in Computer-Generated Music*. Los Alamitos: IEEE Computer Society Press, pp. 25–40.

Dannenberg, R.B., P. McAvinney, and D. Rubine. 1986. "Arctic: a functional language for real-time systems." *Computer Music Journal* 10(4): 67–78.

Dannenberg, R.B., D. Rubine, and T. Neuendorffer. 1991. "The resource-instance model of music representation." In *Proceedings of the 1991 International Computer Music Conference*. San Francisco: International Computer Music Association, pp. 428–432.

Desain, P. and H. Honing. 1988. "LOCO: a composition microworld in Logo." *Computer Music Journal* 12(3): 30–42.

Desain, P. and H. Honing. 1991. "Towards a calculus for expressive timing in music." *Computers in Music Research* 3: 43–120.

Desain, P. and H. Honing. 1992a. "Time functions function best as functions of multiple times." *Computer Music Journal* 16(2). Reprinted in P. Desain and H. Honing 1992b.

Desain, P. and H. Honing. 1992b. *Music, Mind and Machine, Studies in Computer Music, Music Cognition and Artificial Intelligence*. Amsterdam: Thesis Publishers.

Desain, P. and H. Honing. 1993. "On continuous musical control of discrete musical objects." In *Proceedings of the 1993 International Computer Music Conference*. San Francisco: International Computer Music Association, pp. 218–221.

Henderson, P. 1980. *Functional Programming: Application and Implementation*. London: Prentice Hall.

Honing, H. 1990. "POCO: an environment for analyzing, modifying, and generating expression in music." In *Proceedings of the 1990 International Computer Music Conference*. San Francisco: Computer Music Association, pp. 364–368.

Honing, H. 1992. "Expresso, a strong and small editor for expression." In *Proceedings of the 1992 International Computer Music Conference*. San Francisco: International Computer Music Association, pp. 215–218.

Honing, H. 1993. "Issues in the representation of time and structure in music." In I. Cross and I. Deliège, eds. "Music and the Cognitive Sciences." *Contemporary Music Review* 9: 221–239. Also in P. Desain and H. Honing 1992b.

Honing, H. 1995. "The vibrato problem, comparing two solutions." *Computer Music Journal* 19(3): 32–49.

Jaffe, D. and L. Boynton. 1989. "An overview of the Sound and Music Kit for the NeXT computer." *Computer Music Journal* 13(2): 48–55. Reprinted in S.T. Pope, ed. 1991. *The Well-Tempered Object: Musical Applications of Object-Oriented Software Technology*. Cambridge, Massachusetts: The MIT Press.

Lansky, P. 1987. *CMIX*. Software distribution. Princeton: Princeton University.

Levitt, D. 1984. "Machine tongues X: constraint languages." *Computer Music Journal* 8(1): 9–21.

Loyall, A.B. and J. Bates. 1993. "Real-time control of animated broad agents." In *Proceedings of the Fifteenth Annual Conference of the Cognitive Science Society*. Boulder, Colorado: Cognitive Science Society.

Mathews, M.V. 1969. *The Technology of Computer Music*. Cambridge, Massachusetts: The MIT Press.

Mathews, M.V. and F.R. Moore. 1970. "A program to compose, store, and edit functions of time." *Communications of the ACM* 13(12): 715–721.

Moore, F.R. 1990. *Elements of Computer Music*. Englewood Cliffs: Prentice Hall.

Morrison, J.D. and J.M. Adrien. 1993. "MOSAIC: a framework for modal synthesis." *Computer Music Journal* 17(1): 45–56.

Puckette, M. 1991. "Combining event and signal processing in the Max graphical programming environment." *Computer Music Journal* 15(3): 68–77.

Rodet, X. and P. Cointe. 1984. "FORMES: composition and scheduling of processes." *Computer Music Journal* 8(3): 32–50. Reprinted in S.T. Pope, ed. 1991. *The Well-Tempered Object: Musical Applications of Object-Oriented Software Technology*. Cambridge, Massachusetts: The MIT Press, pp. 64–82.

Smith, J.O. 1992. "Physical modeling using digital waveguides." *Computer Music Journal* 16(4): 74–91.

Vercoe, B. 1985. "The synthetic performer in the context of live performance." In *Proceedings of the 1984 International Computer Music Conference*. San Francisco: International Computer Music Association, pp. 199–200.

Vercoe, B. 1986. *Csound: A Manual for the Audio Processing System and Supporting Programs*. Cambridge, Massachusetts: MIT Media Laboratory.

Xenakis, I. 1971. *Formalized Music*. Bloomington: Indiana University Press.

9

Musical object representation

Stephen Travis Pope

This chapter introduces the basic notions of *object-oriented* (O-O) software technology, and investigates how these might be useful for music representation. Over the past decade several systems have applied O-O techniques to build music representations. These have been implemented in a variety of programming languages (Lisp, Objective C, or Smalltalk, for example). In some of these, O-O technology is hidden from the user, while in others, the O-O paradigm is quite obvious and becomes part of the user's conceptual model of the application.

We begin with a short introduction to the principles of object-oriented software technology, then discuss some issues in the design of O-O programming languages and systems. The topic of using O-O languages as the basis of music representation systems is then presented, followed by a detailed description of the Smalltalk music object kernel (Smoke) music representation language.

The intended audience for this discussion is programmers and musicians working with digital-technology-based multimedia tools who are interested in the design issues of music representations, and are familiar with the basic concepts of software engineering. Other documents (Pope 1993, 1995) describe the software environment within which Smoke has been implemented (the MODE).

Object-oriented software technology

Object-oriented (O-O) software technology has its roots both in structured software methods, and in simulation languages designed in the mid-1960s; it can be
said to be *evolutionary rather than revolutionary* in that it builds on and extends
earlier technologies rather than being a radical new idea in software engineering. O-O technology can be said to be the logical conclusion of the trend to
structured, modular software, and to more sophisticated software engineering
methodologies and tools of the 1970s and early 1980s.

O-O technology is based on a set of simple concepts that apply to many
facets of software engineering, ranging from analysis and design methodologies
to programming language design, databases, and operating systems. There is a
mature literature on each of these topics (see, for example, the *Proceedings of the
ACM Conferences on O-O Programming Systems, Languages, and Applications*
[OOPSLA], or any of the journals and magazines devoted to this technology,
such as *Journal of Object-Oriented Programming, Object Messenger, Object
Magazine* or the *Smalltalk Report*). This chapter focusses on O-O programming
methods and languages for musical applications.

There are several features that are generally recognized as constituting an
O-O technology: *encapsulation, inheritance,* and *polymorphism* are the most
frequently cited (Wegner 1987). I will define each of these in the sections
below. There are also several issues that arise when trying to provide a software
development environment for the rapid development of modern applications;
these can be divided into *methodology* issues, *library* issues, and *tool* issues. We
will not discuss these in detail here, but refer the interested reader to (Goldberg
and Pope 1989; Pope 1994).

Encapsulation

Every generation of software technology has had its own manner of packaging
software components—either into "jobs" or "modules" or other abstractions for
groups of functions and data elements. In traditional modular or structured technology, a *module* includes one or more—public or private—data types and also
the—public or private—functions related to these data items. In large systems,
the number of functions and the "visibility" of data types tended to be large,
leading to problems with managing data type and function names—which are
required to be unique in most structured programming languages.

Object-oriented software is based on the concept of *object encapsulation*
whereby every data type is strongly associated with the functions that operate on it. There is no such thing as a standalone data element or an unbound

function. Data and operations—*state* and *behavior* in O-O terms—are always encapsulated together. A data type—known as a *class*, of which individual objects are *instances*—has a definition of what data storage (state) is included in the instances. These are called *instance variables* in the Smalltalk family of languages (which includes several dialects). The class also defines the functions (behavior or *methods*) operate on instances of the class. Strict object encapsulation means that the internal state of an object is completely invisible to the outside and is accessible only through its behaviors.

Any object must be sent messages to determine its state, so that, for example, an object that represents a 2D point in Cartesian geometry would have x and y instance variables and methods named x and y for accessing them. The advantage of this strict separation of private state from public behavior is for example that another kind of geometrical point might store its data in polar

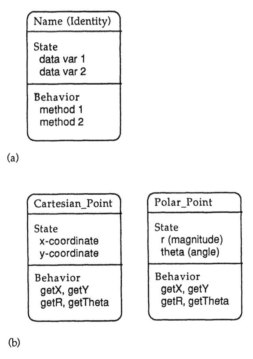

Figure 1. Object encapsulation. (a) The components of an object. The diagram shows that an object may have internal state (data storage) that is hidden from the outside, and provides a public interface in terms of its behaviors (functions). (b) Two kinds of point objects. Two different objects that represent geometrical points are shown here. Their behaviors are identical even though their internal storage formats differ. The external user (client) of these points has no way of telling from the outside which is which.

coordinates, with its angle and magnitude (r and Θ). It would be very good to be able to use these two kinds of points interchangeably, which is possible if I am only concerned with *what* they can do, and not with *how* they do it. Behaviorally, they are identical (ignoring performance for now); I can send them each messages such as "x" to get their x coordinate, without having to know whether it is cached or computed. Figure 1 shows these two kinds of point objects.

As an example from the musical domain, imagine an object that represents a musical event or "note." This object would have internal (strictly private) data to store its parameters—e.g., duration, pitch, loudness, timbre, and other properties—and would have methods for accessing these data and for "performing" itself on some medium such as a MIDI channel or note list file. Because the internal data of the object is strictly hidden (behind a behavioral interface), one can only access its state via behaviors, so that, if the note object understood messages for several kinds of pitch—e.g., `pitchInHz`, `pitchAsNoteNumber`, and `pitchAsNoteName`—then the user would not have to worry about how exactly the pitch was stored within the note. Figure 2 illustrates a possible note event object. The state versus behavior differentiation is related to what old-fashioned structured software technology calls *information hiding* or the separation of the *specification* (the *what*) from the *implementation* (the *how*). In *uniform* O-O languages (e.g., Smalltalk), this object encapsulation is strictly enforced, whereas it is weaker (or altogether optional) in *hybrid* O-O languages (such as C++).

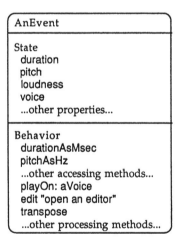

Figure 2. A musical event or "note" object. This exemplary note event object has state for its duration, pitch, loudness, and position, and behaviors for accessing its properties and for performing it.

Inheritance

Inheritance is a simple principle whereby classes can be defined as *refinements* or *specializations* of other classes, so that a collection of classes can form a tree-like specialization or *inheritance* hierarchy. At each level of this kind of subclass-superclass hierarchy, a class only needs to define how it differs from its superclass.

Examples of class hierarchies are well-known (and widely misunderstood) in the literature on O-O systems. The hierarchy of classes used to represent numbers makes a good starting example. If one had a class for objects that represented "units of measure"—often called *magnitudes* in the abstract sense— then it is easy to see that numbers would be one possible subclass (refinement) of it, and that the various types of numbers (integers, fractions, and floating-point numbers) might be further subclasses of the number class. There are also other possible magnitude classes that are not numbers, dates and times-of-day, for example. Figure 3 shows a possible hierarchy of magnitudes and numbers.

A musical example of this would be a system with several types of event parameters—different notations for pitches, durations, loudness values, etc. If there was a high-level ("abstract") class for representing musical pitches, then several possible pitch notations could be constructed as subclasses ("concrete classes") of it. Further examples of this kind of subclass-superclass hierarchy will be presented below. Remember that at each level, we are most interested in behavioral differences (rather than storage representations).

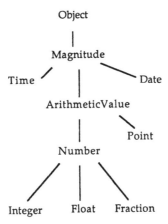

Figure 3. A class hierarchy for magnitudes. This example shows one possible inheritance hierarchy (class tree) for magnitude objects such as numbers. This is a subset of the actual Smalltalk Magnitude class hierarchy.

Polymorphism

In simple terms, polymorphism means being able to use the same function name with different types of arguments to evoke different behaviors. Most traditional programming languages allow for some polymorphism in the form of *over-loading* of their arithmetical operators, meaning that one can say (3 + 4) or (3.5 + 4.1) in order to add two integers or two floating-point numbers. The problem with limits on polymorphism (overloading) is that one is forced to have many names for the same function applied to different argument types (e.g., function names like playEvent(), playEventList(), playSound(), playMix(), etc.). In uniform O-O languages, all functions can be overloaded, so that one can create many types of objects that can be used interchangeably (e.g., many different classes of objects can handle the message play in their own particular ways).

Using polymorphism may mean that some additional run-time overhead is incurred, but it can be considered essential for a language on which to base an exploratory programming environment for music and multimedia applications. In message-passing O-O languages, the receiver of a message (i.e., the object to which the message is sent) determines what method to use to respond to a message. In this way, all the various types of (e.g.,) musical events and event collections can all receive the message play and will respond accordingly by performing themselves, although they may have very different methods for doing this.

Hybrid and uniform O-O programming languages

There are some systems that mix an "O-O flavor" into a programming language that is based on other principles, such as structured programming; Ada, Common Lisp, C++, and Objective C are examples of this kind of *hybrid* language. Several other languages provide only strictly O-O facilities (data types and operation paradigms), and can be said to be *uniformly* object oriented; examples of this are Smalltalk, Self, and Eiffel. There is some debate as to whether it is necessary to adopt a uniform O-O approach to achieve the full benefit of O-O software technology. Some commercial users of O-O technology (who are least likely to be interested in theoretical or "religious" arguments) cite a productivity increase of 600 percent when moving from a hybrid to a uniform O-O programming language (data from C++ relative to Smalltalk-80) and a 1400 percent difference in productivity between uniform O-O and structured languages (Hewlett–Packard 1993).

Other language, methodology, library, and tool issues

There are a number of other issues that influence how appropriate a software system will be for developing music representation tools. *Uniformity, simplicity, expressiveness*, and *terseness* are all important in a programming language; a large and well-documented *class library*, a set of integrated software development *tools*, and an appropriate analysis and design *methodology* are all necessary components of a programming system that will facilitate building sophisticated modern music software applications (Deutsch and Taft 1980; Barstow, Shrobe, and Sandewall 1985; Goldberg and Pope 1989; Pope 1994). As interesting as an in-depth discussion of these issues may be, it is outside of the scope of the present text.

Object-oriented music representation

Several O-O music description languages have been described in the literature, starting soon after the first O-O environments became practical (Krasner 1980; Rodet and Cointe 1984). Today, systems such as the Music Kit (Jaffe and Boynton 1989), Fugue/Nyquist (Dannenberg 1989), Common Music (Taube 1991), Kyma (Scaletti 1989), DMix (Oppenheim 1989), and the MODE (Pope 1993) are in wide-spread use.

In some of these systems (e.g., the NeXT Music Kit), the end-user is relatively unaware of the use of the object paradigm, while in others (e.g., Dmix, Kyma, and the MODE), it is presented directly to the user as the primary organizational technique for musical "objects." Most O-O music representation languages use a hierarchy of different classes to represent musical events and collections or sequences thereof. Some systems have many "event" or "note" classes (e.g., MIDI events vs. note-list events) and use polymorphism among their messages, while others have few of these classes and use "drivers" or "performers" to interpret events. As we will see below, the Smoke language (part of the MODE environment) falls into the latter category.

Language requirements

Several of the groups that have worked on developing music representations have started by drawing up lists of requirements on such a design (Dannenberg *et al.* 1989), and separating out which items are truly determined by the underlying representation, and which are interface or application issues. The group that designed the Smoke language developed the following list, using the results of several previous attempts as input.

A useful O-O music representation, description language, and interchange format should provide or support:

- abstract models of the basic musical magnitudes (units of measure such as pitch, loudness, and duration);
- sound objects represented as functions of time, grains, or other (non-note-oriented) abstractions;
- flexible grain-size of "events" in terms of "notes," "grains," "elements," or "textures";
- description and manipulation levels of data streams including event, control, and sampled function abstractions;
- flexible, hierarchical, event-trees (i.e., nested event lists) for "parts," "tracks," or other parallel or sequential structures;
- separation of "data" from "interpretation" (*what* vs. *how* in terms of having separate objects such as the note/instrument, event/voice, or part/performer abstractions);
- abstractions for the description of "middle-level" musical structures (e.g., chords, clusters, or trills);
- annotation of events supporting the creation of heterarchies (lattices with many roots) and hypermedia networks;
- graphical annotation including common-practice notation (this is an application issue);
- description of sound synthesis and processing models such as sound file mixing or DSP;
- convertors for many common formats, such as MIDI data, Adagio, note lists, HyTime/SMDL, DSP code, Music V-style instrument definitions, mixing scripts (this is an interface issue); and
- parsing live performance into some rendition of the representation, and of interpreting it in real-time (this is an application issue related to simplicity, terseness, etc.).

Programming environment requirements

The high-level components of a good O-O music language should be written in an rapid turnaround, incrementally compiled software development environment.

The use of a powerful and abstract central programming language integrated with the user interface "shell" is very important; the goal is to address the issues of learnability, scalability, abstraction, and flexibility, and provide a system that meets the requirements of *exploratory programming systems* as defined in (Deutsch and Taft 1980) or *interactive programming environments* as defined in (Barstow, Shrobe, and Sandewall 1985). The system should also be designed to support interchangeable ("pluggable") interactive front-ends (e.g., graphical editors, or musical structure description languages) and back-ends (e.g., MIDI output, sampled sound processing commands, sound compiler note-lists, or DSP coprocessor control). The components of such packages have been defined (see also Layer and Richardson 1991; Goldberg and Pope 1989), as: (1) a powerful, abstract programming language with automatic storage management, interpreted and/or incrementally-compiled execution, and a run-time available compiler; (2) software libraries including reusable low- and high-level modules; (3) a windowed interactive user interface "shell" text and/or menu system; (4) an integrated set of development, debugging, and code management tools; (5) an interface to "foreign-language" (often C and assembler) function calls; and (6) a software framework for constructing interactive graphical applications.

The primary languages for such systems have been Lisp and Smalltalk (and to a lesser extent Prolog and Forth), because of several basic concepts. Both languages provide an extremely simple, single-paradigm programming model and consistent syntax that scales well to complex expressions (a matter of debate). Both can be interpreted or compiled with ease and are often implemented within development environments based on one or more interactive "read-eval-print loop" objects. The history of the various Lisp machines demonstrates the scalability of Lisp both up and down, so that everything from high-level applications frameworks to device drivers can be developed in a single language system. The Smalltalk heritage shows the development of the programming language, the basic class libraries, the user interface framework, and the delivery platform across at least four full generations. The current VisualWorks system from ParcPlace-Digitalk, Inc. is a sophisticated development environment that is also portable, fast, commercially supported, and stable. Other commercial (e.g., from IBM) or public domain (e.g., Squeak or GNU) Smalltalk systems are largely source-code compatible with "standard" Smalltalk-80, and there is an ANSI standards effort under-way.

The remainder of this chapter will describe one O-O music description language—the Smalltalk music object kernel or *Smoke*—in detail. To a large degree, the same issues that arise in the design of music representation languages using non-O-O foundations (Dannenberg 1994; Wiggins *et al.* 1994) must also be addressed in O-O systems. Smoke shares many features with the other O-O

music languages mentioned above, and is radically different from most of them
in several ways as well.

The Smoke music representation

The Smalltalk music object kernel—*Smoke*—is a uniformly object-oriented representation, description language and interchange format for musical parameters,
events, and structures. This representation, and its linear ASCII text description,
are well-suited as a basis for: (1) concrete description interfaces in other languages, (2) binary storage and interchange formats, and (3) use within and
between interactive multimedia, hypermedia applications in several application
domains.

The textual versions of Smoke share the terseness of note-list-oriented music
input languages (e.g., Music V), the flexibility and extensibility of "real" music
programming languages (e.g., Common Music), and the non-sequential description and annotation features of hypermedia description formats (e.g., HTML).
The description given below presents the requirements and motivations for the
design of the representation language, defines its basic concepts and constructs,
and presents examples of the music magnitudes and event structures.

Summary of Smoke

The "executive summary" of Smoke from (Pope 1992) is as follows. Music (i.e.,
a musical surface or structure), can be represented as a series of *events* (which
generally last from tens of msec to tens of sec). Events are simply property
lists or dictionaries; they can have named properties whose values are arbitrary.
These properties may be music-specific objects (such as pitches or loudness
values), and models of many common musical magnitudes are provided. At the
minimum, all events have a duration property (which may be zero). Voice objects
and applications determine the interpretation of events' properties, and may use
standard property names such as *pitch, loudness, voice, duration,* or *position.*

Events are grouped into event collections or *event lists* by their relative start
times. Event lists are events themselves, and can therefore be nested into trees
(i.e., an event list can have another event list as one of its events); they can also
map their properties onto their component events. This means that an event can
be "shared" by being in more than one event list at different relative start times
and with different properties mapped onto it.

Events and event lists are performed by the action of a scheduler passing them
to an interpretation object or *voice*. Voices map event properties onto parameters

of input/output (I/O) devices; there can be a rich hierarchy of them. A scheduler expands and/or maps event lists and sends their events to their voices.

Sampled sounds are also describable, by means of synthesis "patches," or signal processing scripts involving a vocabulary of sound manipulation messages.

The Smoke language

The Smoke music representation can be linearized easily in the form of immediate object descriptions and message expressions. These descriptions can be thought of as being declarative (in the sense of static data definitions), or procedural (in the sense of messages sent to class "factory" objects). A text file can be freely edited as a data structure, but one can compile it with the Smalltalk compiler to "instantiate" the objects (rather than needing a special formatted reading function). The post-fix expression format taken from Smalltalk (`receiverObject keyword: argument`) is easily parseable in C++, Lisp, and other languages.

Language requirements

The Smoke representation itself is independent of its implementation language, but assumes that the following immediate types are representable as character strings in the host language:

- arbitrary-precision integers (or at least very large ones—64 or more bits);
- integer fractions (i.e., stored as numerator/denominator, rather than the resulting whole or real number);
- high-precision (64 or mote bits) floating-point numbers;
- arbitrary-length ASCII/ISO strings;
- unique symbols (i.e., strings that are managed with a hash table);
- 2- and 3-dimensional points (or n-dimensional complex numbers) (axial or polar representation); and
- functions of one or more variables described as breakpoints for linear, exponential or spline interpolation, Fourier summations, series, sample spaces, and various probability distributions.

The support of *block* objects (in Smalltalk), or *closures* (in Lisp), is defined as being optional, though it is considered important for complex scores, which will often need to be stored with interesting behavioral information. (It is beyond the scope of the present design to propose a meta-language for the interchange of algorithms). Associations (i.e., key/value tuples) and dictionaries (i.e., lists of associations that can be accessed by key) must also either be available in the host language or be implemented in a support library.

Naming and persistency

The names of abstract classes are widely known and are treated as special global objects. (As in Smalltalk, they are written with an initial capital letter, see Appendix 1). The names of abstract classes are used wherever possible, and instances of concrete subclasses are returned, as in the expressions (`Pitch value: 'c3'`) or (`'c3' pitch`) (strings are written between single-quotes in Smoke), which both return an instance of class SymbolicPitch. All central classes are assumed to support "persistency through naming" whereby any object that is explicitly named (e.g., (`Pitch named: #tonic value: 'c3'`)) gets stored in a global dictionary under that name until explicitly released. What the exact (temporal) scope of the persistency is, is not defined here. The (lexical) extent is assumed to be as Smoke "document" or "module."

Score format

A Smoke score consists of one or more parallel or sequential event lists whose events may have interesting properties and links among them. Magnitudes, events, and event lists are described using class messages that create instances, or using immediate objects and the terse post-fix operators demonstrated below. These objects can be named, used in one or more event lists, and their properties can change over time. There is no pre-defined "level" or "grain-size" of events; they can be used at the level of notes or envelope components, patterns, grains, etc. The same applies to event lists, which can be used in parallel or sequentially to manipulate the sub-sounds of a complex "note," or as "motives," "tracks," "measures," or "parts." Viewed as a document, a score consists of declarations of (or messages to) events, event lists and other Smoke structures. It can resemble a note list file or a DSP program. A score is structured as executable Smalltalk expressions, and can define one or more "root-level" event lists. There is no "section" or "wait" primitive; sections that are supposed to be sequential must be included in some higher-level event list to declare that sequence. A typical score will define and name a top-level event list, and then add sections and parts to it in different segments of the document (see the examples below).

Smoke music magnitudes

Descriptive models for the basic music-specific magnitudes—units of measure such as pitch, loudness and duration—are the foundation of Smoke. These are similar to Smalltalk magnitude objects in that they represent partially- or fully-ordered scalar or vector quantities with (e.g.,) numerical or symbolic values. Some of their behavior depends on what they stand for (the *representation* class), and some of it on how they are stored (the *implementation* class). These two aspects are the objects' *species* and their *class*. The two pitch-species objects described as (440.0 Hz) and ('c#3' pitch), for example, share some behavior, and can be mixed in arithmetic with no loss of precision. The expression ('f4' pitch + 261.26 Hz) should be handled differently than (1/4 beat + 80 msec). The class of a music magnitude object depends on the "type" of its value (e.g., a floating-point number or a string), while its species will denote what it represents. Only the species is visible to the user.

Music magnitudes can be described using prefix class names or post-fix type operators, e.g., (Pitch value: 440.0) or (440.0 Hz) or ('a3' pitch) all represent equivalent objects, as do (Amplitude value: 0.7071) and (-3 dB). The representation and interchange formats should support all manner of mixed-mode music magnitude expressions (e.g., ('c4' pitch + 78 cents + 12 Hz)), with "reasonable" assumptions as to the semantics of the operation (coerce to Hz in this case).

Applications for this representation should support interactive editors for music magnitude objects that support the manipulation of the basic hierarchy described below, as well as its extension via some form of "light-weight" programming.

Figure 4 shows the class hierarchy of the model classes—those used for the species (i.e., representation)—on the left side, and the partial hierarchy of the

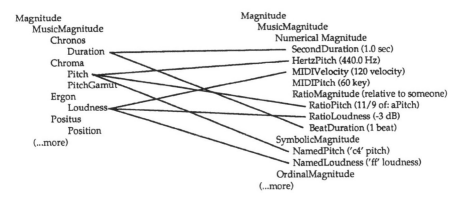

MusicMagnitude Representation Hierarchy   MusicMagnitude Implementation Hierarchy

Figure 4. Smoke music magnitude model abstractions and implementation classes. This figure shows the two hierarchies used for modeling music magnitudes: the representation or species hierarchy on the left, and the implementation or class hierarchy on the right.

```
"Verbose examples--Smalltalk class messages."
(Duration value: 1/16)          "Same as 1/16 beat--a 16th note duration"
(Pitch value: 60)               "Same as 60 pitch--middle C"
(Amplitude value: 'ff')         "Same as 'ff' dynamic--fortissimo"


"Music Magnitude coercion examples."
(Duration value: 1/16) asMS     "Answers 62 msec at tempo = mm 60"
(Pitch value: 36) asHertz       "Answers 261.623 Hz."
(Amplitude value: 'ff') asMIDI  "Answers MIDI velocity 106."


"Terse examples--value + post-operator."
"Pitches"       ('f#4' pitch)   (261 Hz)    (71 key)
"Dynamics"      ('pp' dynamic)  (-38 dB)    (56 velocity)
"Durations"      (1/4 beat)     (2381 msec) (2.3 sec)
"Spatial Positions"      (0@0 position)   (1@2@3 position)
```

Figure 5. Music magnitude usage examples.

concrete (implementation) classes on the right. The class inheritance hierarchy is denoted by the order and indentation of the list. The lines indicate the species relationships of several of the common music magnitudes.

The examples shown in Figure 5 demonstrate the verbose (class message) and terse (value + post-operator) forms of music magnitude description. Note that comments are delineated by double quotes (or nesting curly braces) in Smoke.

The minimal set of music magnitudes is illustrated in Figure 5. There are additional desirable formats (e.g., `Duration until: [some condition]`) that are more difficult to describe in a portable format, and so are not presented here.

Note that these music magnitudes ignore the "relative" quantities of pitch interval, meter, and relative loudness; each of these is handled by a special *ratio magnitude* class, for example (`Pitch value: 11/9 of: (Pitch named: #tonic)`).

The great perception debates of pitch vs. frequency and loudness vs. dynamic vs. amplitude are not addressed here; it is no problem to have a single event with contradictory or redundant magnitudes (e.g., `[anEvent pitch: ('a3' pitch); frequency: (446 Hz)]`). It is left up to voices or other interfaces to interpret these values as appropriate—a music-printing application might use the pitch rather than the frequency, but a note-list-oriented output voice might take the frequency value instead.

Smoke event objects

The simplest view of events is as Lisp-like property lists—dictionaries of prop-erty names and values, the relevance and interpretation of whom is left up to others (such as voices and applications). Events need not be thought of as mapping one-to-one to notes, though they can be used to represent note-level objects. There may be one-to-many or many-to-one relationships (or both) be-tween events and notes. Events may have arbitrary properties, some of whom will be common to most musical note-level events (such as duration, pitch or loudness), while others may be used more rarely or only for non-musical events.

An event's properties can be accessed as keyed dictionary items (i.e., events can be treated as record-like data structures), or as direct behaviors (i.e., events can be thought of as purely programmatic). One can set an event to "have the color blue" (for example), by saying

```
"dictionary-style accessing-use the at:put:  message"
(anEvent at:  #color put:  #blue)
```

or more simply

```
"behavioral accessing-use the prop.  name as a message"
(anEvent color:  #blue)
```

(whereby `#string` represents the unique symbol whose name is "string"—see Appendix 1). Events can be linked together by having properties that are asso-ciations to other events or event lists, as in (`anEvent soundsLike: anoth-erEvent`), enabling the creation of annotated hypermedia networks of events. Event properties can also be active blocks or procedures (in cases where the system supports compilation at run-time as in Smalltalk or Lisp), blurring the differentiation between events and "active agents." Events are created either by messages sent to the class *Event* (which may be a macro or binding to an-other class), or more tersely, simply by the concatenation of music magnitudes using the message "," (comma for concatenation), as shown in the examples in Figure 6. As shown there, the concatenation of several music magnitudes (properties) is read as the declaration of an event with the given properties. Applications should enable users to interactively edit the property lists of event objects, and to browse event networks via their times or their links using flexible link description and filtering editors. Common properties such as pitch, duration, position, amplitude, and voice are manipulated according to their "standard" se-mantics by many applications. Note that events have durations but no start times; this is provided by the context in which they are used (see below).

```
"Event creation examples--the verbose way (using class messages)."
"Create a named (and therefore persistent) event."
(Event newNamed: #flash)
        color: #white;
        place: #there.


"Create and play a musical event the long-hand way."
(Event duration: (Duration value: 1/2)
              pitch: (Pitch value: #c2)
              loudness: (Loudness value: #mf))
        playOn: (MIDIVoice onMIDIPort: 0 channel: 1)


"Create three events with mixed properties--the terse way."


        "Abstract properties, use the default voice"
event1 := (440 Hz), (1/4 beat), (-3 dB), Voice default.


        "MIDI-style properties, use a numbered voice"
event2 := 38 key, 280 ticks, 26 vel, (#voice -> 4).


        "Note-list-style properties, use a named voice"
#c4 pitch, 0.21 sec, 0.37 ampl, (Voice named: #oboe).


        "Create a named link between two events."
event1 isLouderThan: event2.
```

Figure 6. Event description examples.

Event lists

Events are grouped into collections—event lists—where a list is composed of associations between start times and events or sub-lists (nested to any depth). Schematically, this looks like:

```
(EventList:=  (dur1  =>  event1),
              (dur2  =>  event2),
```

where $(x => y)$ denotes an association or tuple with key x and value y. The durations that are the keys of these associations can be thought of as relative delays between the start of the enclosing event list, and the start of the events with which the delays are associated. A duration key with value zero means that the related event starts when the enclosing event list starts. In the case that `dur1` and `dur2` in the example above are equal, the two events will be simultaneous. If (`dur1` + `event1 duration`) = `dur2`, the two events will be sequential. Other cases—such as overlap or pause between the events—are also possible, depending on the values of the `dur1` and `dur2` variables and the durations of the events with which they are associated. There should be processing methods in the environment that supports Smoke to remove "gaps" between events, or to apply "duty cycle" factors to event durations, for example to make a *staccato* performance style.

Figure 7 shows a simple example of the use of the duration keys in event list declarations; in it, a G-major chord of three notes is followed by the first three steps of the G-major scale in sequence. Event lists can also have their own properties, and can map these onto their events eagerly (at definition time) or lazily (at "performance" time); they have all the property and link behavior of events, and special behaviors for mapping that are used by voices and event modifiers (see below). Event lists can be named, and when they are, they become persistent (until explicitly erased within a document or session).

The messages (`anEventList add: anAssociation`) and (`anEventList add: anEventOrEventList at: aDuration`) along with the corresponding event removal messages, can be used for manipulating event lists in the static representation or in applications. If the key of the argument to the add: message is a number (rather than a duration), it is assumed to be the value of a duration in seconds or milliseconds, "as appropriate." Event lists also respond to Smalltalk collection-style control structure messages such as (`anEventList collect: aSelectionBlock`) or (`anEventList select: aSelection-Block`), though this requires the representation of contexts/closures. The be-

```
EventList new
        "Add 3 simultaneous notes--a chord"
    add: (#g3 pitch, 1 beat) at: 0;
    add: (#b4 pitch, 1 beat) at: 0;
    add: (#d4 pitch, 1 beat) at: 0;
        "Then 3 notes in sequence after the chord"
    add: (#g3 pitch, 1 beat) at: 1 beat;
    add: (#a4 pitch, 1 beat) at: 2 beat;
    add: (#b4 pitch, 1 beat) at: 3 beat.
```

Figure 7. A mix of parallel and sequential events in an event list.

haviors for applying functions (see below) to the components of event lists can look applicative (e.g., anEventList apply: aFunction to: aPropertyName, eager evaluation), or one can use event modifier objects to have a concrete (reified) representation of the mapping (lazy evaluation). Applications will use event list hierarchies for browsing and annotation as well as for score following and performance control. The use of standard link types for such applications as version control (with such link types as #usedToBe or #via_script_14), is defined by applications and voices.

A named event list is created (and stored) in the first example in Figure 8, and two event associations are added to it, one starting at 0 second, and the second one starting at 1 second. Note that the two events can have different types of properties, and the handy instance creation messages such as (dur: d pitch: p amp: a). The second example is the terse format for event list declaration using

```
"Event List creation the verbose way."

(EventList newNamed: #test1)
                "Add an event with musical note-like properties"
        add: 0 sec => (Event dur: 1/4 pitch: 'c3' ampl: 'mf');
                "Add an event with a sampled sound's name"
        add: 1 sec => (Event new dur: 6.0; ampl: 0.3772; sound: #s73bw)


"Terse Lists--concatenation of events or (dur => event) associations."
                "First event--simple"
(440 Hz, 1 beat, -9.7 dB),
                "Second event--with a phoneme name"
((1.396 sec, 0.714 ampl) phoneme: #xu),
                "Third event--a MIDI-style note after a pause"
(4 sec, 250 msec, 64 key, 86 vel).


"Bach WTC C-minor fugue theme."
"start time        duration   pitch          voice"
(1/2 beat =>        (1/4 beat,  'c3' pitch, (#voice -> 'harpsichord'))),
                    (1/4 beat,  'b2' pitch),
                    (1/2 beat,  'c3' pitch),
                    (1/2 beat,  'g2' pitch),
                    (1/2 beat,  'a-flat2' pitch).
```

Figure 8. Simple event list examples.

the concatenation message (,)—concatenation of events, or of (duration =>
event) associations, is read as the declaration of an event list. One can use this
style of shorthand as a terse way of creating the anonymous (non-persistent) list
with three events shown in the second example in Figure 8. The third example
shows the first few notes from the C-minor fugue from J.S. Bach's *The Well-
Tempered Clavichord* in which the first note begins after a rest (that could also
be represented explicitly as an event with a duration and no other properties).

Note from the above examples that there is no model of time in Smoke; only
relative durations are used. Absolute time is not represented explicitly because
everything is thought to be "relative." An event is always contained within some
event list, so its start time is described as the relative delay (duration) from the
start of the enclosing event list to its own. Thus, a time model is not needed,
and events have no notion of their own start times, meaning that the same event
can be shared in several places by being "pointed to" by several event lists at
different relative delays.

Event generators and modifiers

The event generator and event modifier packages provide for music description
and performance using generic or composition-specific "middle-level" objects
(Pope 1989). Event generators are used to represent the common structures of
the musical vocabulary such as chords, ostinati, or compositional algorithms.
Each event generator class knows how it is described (e.g., a chord has type,
root, and inversion, or an ostinato has an event list and a repeat rate) and can
perform itself once or repeatedly—acting like a function, a control structure, or
a process, as appropriate.

Some event generators describe relationships among events in composite event
lists (e.g., chords described in terms of a root and an inversion), while others
describe melismatic embellishments of—or processes on—a note or collection
of notes (e.g., mordents). Still others are descriptions of event lists in terms
of their parameters (e.g., ostinati). Most standard examples (chords, ostinati,
rolls, etc.) above can be implemented in a simple set of event generator classes;
the challenge is to make an easily-extensible framework for composers whose
compositional process will often extend the event generator hierarchy.

All event generators can either return an event list, or they can behave like processes, and be told to play or to stop playing. We view this dichotomy—between
views of event generators as functions versus event generators as processes—as
a part of the domain, and differentiate on the basis of the musical abstractions.
It might, for example, be appropriate to view an ostinato as a process (and send
it messages such as start and stop), or to ask it to play thrice.

"Create a pentatonic cluster."
(Cluster dur: 2.0 sec
      pitches: #(c3 d3 e3 g3 a4)
      ampl: #mp
      voice: #piano)

"Create and manipulate a chord."
| aChord | "Declaration (optional)"
      "Create a C-Major tetrad in the root position lasting 1/2 beat"
aChord := Chord majorTetradOn: 'c3' inversion: 0 duration: 1/2.
aChord ampl: #mf.   "Make it mezzoforte"
aChord eventList.   "Answers an event list with the chord's 4 notes"

"A Simple Progression--C Major full cadence (with terrible voice-leading)."
(EventList newNamed: #progression1)
      add: (Chord majorTetradOn: 'c3' inversion: 0 duration: 1/2);
      add: (Chord majorTetradOn: 'f2' inversion: 2 duration: 1/2);
      add: (Chord majorTetradOn: 'g2' inversion: 1 duration: 1/2);
      add: (Chord majorTetradOn: 'c3' inversion: 0 duration: 1/2).

"Arpeggiate the Chord"
Arpeggio on: aChord
      delay: 100   "give a delay for arpeggiation (msec)"
      ampl: 'f'   "set the amplitude"

"Simple rolls and trills"
Roll length: 2 sec   "duration of roll"
      delay: 50   "delay between notes"
      note: #f2   "pitch = f2"
      ampl: #ff.   "amplitude"

"The unit messages here can be left out as they are assumed."
Trill length: 1   "1.0 sec duration"
      delay: 80   "80 msec per note"
      notes: #(c d)   "give the array of pitches"
      ampl: 100.   "loudness = MIDI velocity 100"

Figure 9a. Event generator description examples. Clusters.

"Create stochastic cloud with values taken from the given ranges. See figure 10a."

(Cloud dur: 4   "duration in seconds"

    pitch: (60 to: 69)   "pitch range--an interval (C to A)"

    ampl: (80 to: 120)   "amplitude range--an interval"

    voice: (1 to: 4)   "voice range--an interval"

    density: 10)   "density in notes-per-sec"

"Create a selection cloud with values from the given data sets."

(SelectionCloud dur: 2   "duration in seconds"

    pitch: #(c d f)   "select from this pitch array"

    ampl: #(mf mp pp)   "and this array of amplitudes"

    voice: #(viola)   "and this voice"

    density: 16)   "play 16 notes-per-sec"

"Make a low rising crescendo cloud."

(DynamicCloud dur: 6 sec

                 "starting and ending pitch ranges"

                 "i.e., focus onto one note"

    pitch: #((30 to: 44) (60 to: 60))

    ampl: #((40 to: 60) (80 to: 120)) "amplitude ranges--crescendo"

    voice: 1   "static voice"

    density: 20)   "20 notes-per-sec"

"Make a textured crescendo roll."

(DynamicCloud dur: 12

    pitch: (20 to: 20)   "fixed pitch"

                 "crescendo with a small random jitter"

    ampl: #((26 to: 30) (114 to: 120))

    voice: (1 to: 1)   "fixed voice"

    density: 20)   "20 notes-per-sec"

"Make a transition between two chords. The result is shown in figure 10b."

(DynamicSelectionCloud dur: 5

                 "starting and ending pitch sets"

    pitch: #(#(57 59 60) #(67 69 72 74))

    ampl: #(30 40 60)   "static amplitude set"

    voice: #(1 3)   "and voice set"

    density: 16)   "20 notes-per-sec"

Figure 9b. Event generator description examples. Clouds.

"Set up an Ostinato on the named scale."

(Ostinato named: #scale2 onList: (EventList named: #scale1)).

"Turn it on."

(Ostinato named: #scale2) play.

"Stop it."

(Ostinato named: #scale2) stop.

"Play it 5 times."

(Ostinato named: #scale2) play: 5.

Figure 9c. Event generator description examples. Ostinati.

Shared behavior of event generators

Every event generator class has behaviors for the creation of instances, including, normally, some terse description formats (see the examples below). All event generator instances must provide a way of returning their events—the eventList method. Process-like event generators such as ostinati also provide start/stop methods for their repeated performance. The examples in Figures 9a–c illustrate other event generator behaviors.

Abstract classes: cluster, cloud, and ostinato

There are three abstract classes of event generators: *cluster*, *cloud*, and *ostinato*. An instance of a cluster class is a description of the pitch set or a group of simultaneous or repeated events. Examples of concrete cluster classes are *chords* and *rolls*. A cloud is a pitch-time surface described in terms of its data sets or stochastic selection criteria. Ostinato objects describe the various ways of controlling the repetition of an event list.

The examples given in Figures 9a–c demonstrate the use of event generators and event modifiers. Figure 10 shows the output of two of the cloud examples from Figure 9b as represented in Hauer-Steffens notation. This is similar to piano-roll notation—lines in the staff correspond to accidentals, and the note heads map onto the "voice" used. The lines extending out from the note head are used to signify notes' durations (horizontal lines) and amplitudes (vertical lines). The basic set of event generators are illustrated in Figures 9a–c; there are several extensions in the standard MODE release, and a number of others in current usage. This begs the question of "how far to go." Are complex artificial-intelligence-based compositional expert systems themselves simply event generators with very complex selection criteria?

Event modifiers and operators

Event modifier objects hold onto a function of one variable and a property name; they can be told to apply their functions to any property of an event list eagerly

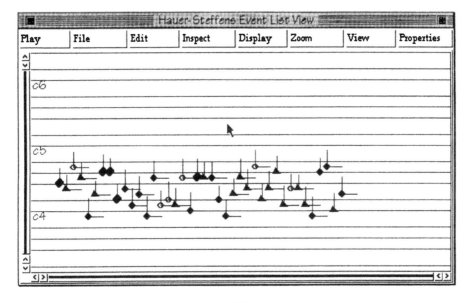

(a)

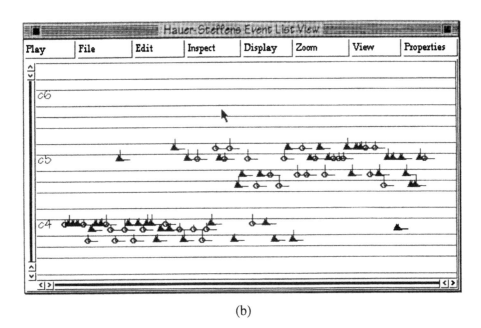

(b)

Figure 10. Output of example clouds in Hauer-Steffens notation.

"Apply a crescendo to an event list using a linear ramp function."

      "Declaration of temporary variables"

| roll fcn |

      "Create a roll 4 sec long with 20 notes-per-sec."

roll := (Roll length: 4.0 sec delay: 50 msec

          note: #d pitch ampl: #mf ampl) eventList.

      "Play it"

roll play.

      "Create a linear function that ramps from 0 to 1 over its extent."

      "An x/y plot of this function is shown in Figure 12a."

fcn := LinearFunction from: #((0@0) (1@1)).

      "Apply it immediately to the loudness of the roll."

roll apply: fcn to: #loudness.

      "Play the roll again."

roll play.

"Playing 'molto rubato'."

| roll fcn |

      "Create a roll using the assumed types of sec, msec, key, velocity"

roll := (Roll length: 4.0 delay: 80 note: 36 ampl: 100) eventList.

      "Apply a spline function to the start times."

roll apply:

      "An x/y plot of this function is shown in Figure 12b."

          (SplineFunction from: #((0@1) (0.35@1.2) (0.8@0.4) (1@1)))

          to: #start.

      "Play the roll."

roll play.

Figure 11. Event modifier examples.

(at creation time) or lazily (at performance time). Functions of one or more variables (see below) can be described in a number of ways, including linear, exponential, or cubic spline interpolation between breakpoints. The examples in Figure 11 illustrate the simple use of event modifiers. Figure 12 shows two simple functions: a linear ramp function from 0 to 1, and a spline curve that moves around the value 1.

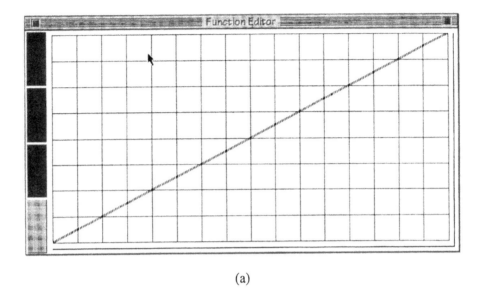

(a)

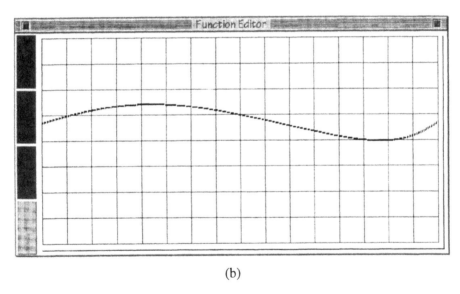

(b)

Figure 12. Linear (a) and (b) spline functions.

Functions, probability distributions and sounds

Smoke also defines several types of discrete or continuous probability distributions, and granular and sampled sounds. The description of these facilities is, however, outside the scope of this paper, and the reader is referred to (Pope 1992, 1993, 1995).

Voices and structure accessors

The "performance" of events takes place via *voice* objects. Event properties are assumed to be independent of the parameters of any synthesis instrument or algorithm. A voice object is a "property-to-parameter mapper" that knows about one or more output or input formats for Smoke data (e.g., MIDI, note list files, or DSP commands). A *structure accessor* is an object that acts as a translator or *protocol convertor*. An example might be an accessor that responds to the typical messages of a tree node or member of a hierarchy (e.g., *What's your name? Do you have any children/sub-nodes? Who are they? Add this child to them.*) and that knows how to apply that language to navigate through a hierarchical event list (e.g., by querying the event list's hierarchy). Smoke supports the description of voices and structure accessors in scores so that performance information or alternative interfaces can be embedded. The goal is to be able to annotate a score with possibly complex real-time control objects that manipulate its structure or interpretation. Voices and event interpretation are described in (Pope 1992, 1993).

The required voices include MIDI I/O (both real-time and file-based), Music V-style note-lists (for the Cmix, cmusic, and Csound formats), and real-time sound output. Others are optional. Figure 13 shows the desired usage of voices in shielding the user from the details of any particular output format. In this case, an event list is created and then played on both MIDI and Cmix output voices in turn.

```
"Create some notes in an event list"
| list cmVoice |
list := Trill length: 1 delay: 80 notes: #(c d  g) ampl: #mp.


        "Play it on a MIDI synthesizer."
list voice: (MIDIVoice on: (MIDIDevice new) channel: 1).
list play.


        "Create a Cmix format note-list voice for the given file."
cmVoice := CmixVoice on: ('test.out' asFilename writeStream).
        "Tell it how to map event properties to note command fields."
cmVoice map: #ampl toField: 4.
        "Play the event list onto the file."
list playOn: cmVoice on: aFileStream.
```

Figure 13. Voice usage example.

"Declare variable names and top-level event list."
| piece section1 section2 |
        "name declarations--optional but advised."
piece := EventList newNamed: #Opus1.

        "section 1--verbose, add events using add:at: message."
section1 := EventList newNamed: #section1.
section1 add: (first event--may have many properties ...) at: 0.
section1 add: (second event ...) at: 0.   "i.e., it starts with a chord."

"...section 1 events, in parallel or sequentially..."

"section 2--terse, add event associations using ',' for concatenation."
section2 := ((0 beat) => (...event1...)), ((1/4 beat) => (event2)),
        "...section 2 events...",
        ((2109/4 beats) => (event3308)).

"Event list composition (may be placed anywhere)"
piece add: section1; add: section2.   "add the sections in sequence."
piece add: (Event duration: (4/1 beat)).   "add one measure of rest after section 2."

"Add a section with event data taken from the given arrays."
piece add: (EventList
        durations: #(250 270 230 120 260 ...)   "duration data array"
        loudnesses: #(mp)   "loudness is all mp"
        pitches: #(c3 d e g ...)).   "pitch value array"

"Add an event with the given samples (the very-low-level!)"
piece add: (Event rate: 44100 channels: 1
                samples: #(0 121 184 327 441 ...)) at: 34 sec.

"Declare global (named) event modifiers, functions, etc."
(Rubato newNamed: #tempo)
                function: (...tempo spline function...)
                property: #startTime.
piece tempo: (Rubato named: #tempo).

"Optionally declare voices, accessors, other modifiers, etc."

Figure 14. Extended score example.

Smoke score example

In Smoke scores, sections with declarations of variables, naming of event lists, event definition, functions and event modifiers, and annotational links and data, can be freely interspersed. Note that one tries to avoid actually ever typing Smoke at all, leaving that to interactive graphical editors, algorithmic generation or manipulation programs, or read/write interfaces to other media, such as MIDI. The example given in Figure 14 shows the components of a Smoke score for a composition with several sections declared in different styles.

Conclusions

The Smalltalk music Object Kernel (Smoke) is a representation, description language, and interchange format for musical data that eases the creation of concrete description interfaces, the definition of storage formats, and is suitable for use in multimedia, hypermedia applications. The Smoke description format has several versions, ranging from very readable to very terse, and covering a wide range of signal, event, and structure types from sampled sounds to compositional algorithms. Smoke can be viewed as a procedural or a declarative description; it has been designed and implemented using an object-oriented methodology and is being tested in several applications. More explicit documents describing Smoke, and the Smalltalk-80 implementation of Smoke in the MODE system, are freely available via Internet file transfer (see Pope 1993, 1995 for details).

Acknowledgments

Smoke, and the MODE of which it is a part, is the work of many people. Craig Latta and Daniel Oppenheim came up with the names Smallmusic and Smoke. These two, and Guy Garnett and Jeff Gomsi, were part of the team that discussed the design of Smoke, and commented on its design documents. Many others have contributed to the MODE environment.

References

Barstow, D., H. Shrobe, and E. Sandewall. 1984. *Interactive Programming Environments.* New York: McGraw-Hill.
Dannenberg, R.B. 1989. "The Canon score language." *Computer Music Journal* 13(1): 47–56.

Dannenberg, R.B. 1993. "Music representation issues, techniques, and systems." *Computer Music Journal* 17(3): 20–30.

Dannenberg, R.B., L. Dyer, G.E. Garnett, S.T. Pope, and C. Roads. 1989. "Position papers for a panel on music representation." In *Proceedings of the 1989 International Computer Music Conference.* San Francisco: International Computer Music Association.

Deutsch, L.P. and E.A. Taft. 1980. "Requirements for an experimental programming environment." Research Report CSL-80-10. Palo Alto, California: Xerox PARC.

Goldberg, A. and D. Robson. 1989. *Smalltalk-80: The Language.* Revised edition. Menlo Park: Addison-Wesley.

Goldberg, A. and S.T. Pope. 1989. "Object-oriented is not enough!" *American Programmer: Ed Yourdon's Software Journal* 2(7): 46–59.

Hewlett–Packard. 1994. *Hewlett–Packard Distributed Smalltalk Release 2.0 Data Sheet.* Palo Alto, California: Hewlett–Packard Company.

Jaffe, D. and L. Boynton. 1989. "An overview of the Sound and Music Kits for the NeXT computer." *Computer Music Journal* 13(2): 48–55. Reprinted in S.T. Pope, ed. 1991. *The Well-Tempered Object: Musical Applications of Object-Oriented Software Technology.* Cambridge, Massachusetts: The MIT Press, pp. 107–118.

Krasner, G. 1980. Machine Tongues VIII: the design of a Smalltalk music system. *Computer Music Journal* 4(4): 4–22. Reprinted in S.T. Pope, ed. 1991. *The Well-Tempered Object: Musical Applications of Object-Oriented Software Technology.* Cambridge, Massachusetts: The MIT Press, pp. 7–17.

Layer, D.K. and C. Richardson. 1991. "Lisp systems in the 1990s." *Communications of the ACM* 34(9): 48–57.

Oppenheim, D. 1989. "DMix: an environment for composition." In *Proceedings of the 1989 International Computer Music Conference.* San Francisco: International Computer Music Association, pp. 226–233.

Pope, S.T. 1989. "Modeling musical structures as EventGenerators." In *Proceedings of the 1989 International Computer Music Conference.* San Francisco: International Computer Music Association.

Pope, S.T. 1992. "The Smoke music representation, description language, and interchange format." In *Proceedings of the 1992 International Computer Music Conference.* San Francisco: International Computer Music Association.

Pope, S.T. 1993. "The Interim DynaPiano: an integrated computer tool and instrument for composers." *Computer Music Journal* 16(3): 73–91.

Pope, S.T. 1994. "Letter to the editors." *International Computer Music Association Array* 14(1): 2–3.

Pope, S.T. 1995. *The Musical Object Development Environment Version 2 Software Release.* Source code and documentation files available from the Internet server ftp.create.ucsb.edu in the directory pub/stp/MODE.

Rodet, X. and P. Cointe. 1984. "FORMES: composition and scheduling of processes." *Computer Music Journal* 8(3): 32–50. Reprinted in S.T. Pope, ed. 1991. *The Well-Tempered Object: Musical Applications of Object-Oriented Software Technology.* Cambridge, Massachusetts: The MIT Press.

Scaletti, C. 1989. "The Kyma/Platypus computer music workstation." *Computer Music Journal* 13(2): 23–38. Reprinted in S.T. Pope, ed. 1991. *The Well-Tempered Object: Musical Applications of Object-Oriented Software Technology.* Cambridge, Massachusetts: The MIT Press, pp. 119–140.

Taube, H. 1991. "Common Music: a music composition language in Common Lisp and CLOS." *Computer Music Journal* 15(2): 21–32.

Wegner, P. 1987. "Dimensions of object-based language design." In *Proceedings of the 1987 ACM Conference on Object-Oriented Programming Systems, Languages, and Applications (OOPSLA).* New York: ACM Press, pp. 168–182.

Wiggins, G., E. Miranda, A. Smaill, and M. Harris. 1993. "A framework for the evaluation of music representation systems." *Computer Music Journal* 17(3): 31–42.

Appendix 1: Reading Smalltalk

Smalltalk is an object-oriented message-passing programming language where expressions are built to be read as English sentences. Names and identifiers in Smalltalk are separated by white space and are often composed of a con-catenated noun phrase written with embedded upper-case letters, e.g., anEvent or MusicMagnitude. By convention, shared or global objects (such as class names) are written with the first letter capitalized (e.g., MusicMagnitude, Ab-stractEvent, or HertzPitch), while private or temporary objects are written lower-case (e.g., anEventInstance or thePosition).

In a Smalltalk expression, the noun (i.e., the receiver object), comes first, followed by the message; e.g., to ask the size of an array, one sends it the message size, as in the expression (anArray size), which answers an integer object. This kind of message (without any arguments) is called *unary*.

If the message has any arguments, they are separated from the message key-words in that the keywords all end in ":" so for example to index the first element of the array, one writes (anArray at: 1); to set the first element to zero, use (anArray at: 1 put: 0). Note the use of multiple keywords (at: and put:), and the fact that the order is always to alternate keywords and argu-ments. This means that—if you choose your keyword names well—even rather complex messages with many arguments are quite readable.

There is a special case of keyword messages that is used for arithmetic and logical operations—binary messages. In this case, one can leave the colon off of the message keyword, allowing one, for example, to write $(3 + 4)$ or $(x > 0)$ as legal Smalltalk. There are several other binary messages that are widely used, among them "@ " for creating points—the expression 3@4 answers a point whose $x = 3$ and whose $y = 4$—and "->" for creating associations—the expression key -> value "associates" the given key with the given value.

Expressions can be nested using parentheses (i.e., evaluate what's inside the inner-most parentheses first), and fancy expression constructs and control struc-tures are possible. Normally, message expressions are separated by periods (.), but multiple messages sent to the same receiver object may be separated by semi-colons (;), in which case the receiver need not be repeated.

Double-quotes delineate comments in Smalltalk (e.g., "This is a com-ment."); single-quotes are used for immediate string objects (e.g., 'This is a string.'). Names for temporary variables are declared between vertical bars (e.g., | varName1 varName2 |). Symbols are special strings that are stored in a table so as to be unique; they are written with the hash-mark "#" as in #blue, meaning "the symbol blue."

Smalltalk supports deferred execution in the form of closures or anonymous functions called *blocks*; they are written in square brackets "[...]" and can have arguments and/or local temporary variables. The up-arrow or caret ($^\wedge$) is used to return values (objects) from within blocks. For example, a block that takes two arguments and answers their sum would look like

```
["arguments" :x :y | "body" ^x + y].
```

There are many more features of the language that are of interest to anyone concerned with programming in Smalltalk (e.g., how control structures work), but they are beyong the scope of the current discussion.

Smalltalk programs are organized as the behaviors (methods) of classes of objects. To program a graphical application, for example, one might start by adding new methods to the point and 3D point classes for graphical transformations, and build a family (a class hierarchy) of display objects that know how to present themselves in interesting ways. Classes are described as being abstract or concrete depending on whether they are meant as models for refinement within a framework (and not be instantiated), or for reuse "off the shelf" as in the elements in a tool kit. Inheritance and polymorphism mean that one reads Smalltalk programs by learning the basic protocol (messages/methods) of the abstract classes first; this gives one the feel for the basic behaviors of the system's objects and applications.

Appendix 2: MODE and Smoke availability

The definitive implementation of the Smoke music representation language is written in the ParcPlace-Digitalk dialect of Smalltalk-80, but it is portable to other dialects of Smalltalk such as Squeak, IBM or GNU Smalltalk. It is included in the Musical Object Development Environment (MODE), and serves as the basis of the MODE's applications. The MODE, version 2, is available via the World-wide Web from the URL http://www.create.ucsb.edu/~stp/MODE/.

10

AI-based music signal applications—a hybrid approach

Antonio Camurri and Marc Leman

In this chapter, we discuss the basic requirements of interactive music systems based on artificial intelligence (AI). The focus is on the integration of multiple representational levels and reasoning mechanisms, the grounding of such systems in the music signals environment, the importance of metaphors and analogies, and requirements related to real-time processing. An experimental AI-system—HARP—is then presented. Its integration with musical signals is discussed and examples of concrete applications are given.

Introduction

One of the most typical characteristics of AI-based systems is that they involve *knowledge* about a particular application domain. This knowledge is contained in some kind of database that is used to guide the solution of a task in an "intelligent" way. In practice, a musical task can be related to any kind of application

in composition, performance, listening, analysis, editing, etc. Tasks may deal
with the synthesis of sounds, the analysis or variation of structure, planning,
perception, control of action, and so on. Furthermore, tasks are not necessarily
limited to purely musical activities. They may involve multimodal perceptions
and actions, such as the perception of movement and translation of movement
into musical pitch, phrase, or form. They may involve the perception of speech
and translation of speech into computer animation of a face (Schomaker *et al.*
1995).

Multimodal interactive systems are the core of the next generation systems
that deal with environments for music, art, and entertainment. The focus of
this chapter, however, is not on one particular task but rather on the hybrid
architecture that is behind such tasks. We start with general observations and
give more concrete examples toward the end of the chapter.

The problem of representational closure

The knowledge domain of multimodal interactive environments is most often
vaguely constrained. In an environment with dancers, the movement of an arm
may be detected by sensors specialized to particular segments of the movement. The combination of the perceived movements may trigger a concept (or
"Gestalt") of a circle which may then be associated with further actions (e.g.
"stop the music," or "change speed," . . .). Typically, the kind of "objects" dealt
with here have a layered nature and their description may call for a multitude
of representational levels and of processing strategies embedded in a distributed
network of "expert agents". The completion of a particular task may furthermore
depend on unexpected input from the (multimodal) environment. A particular
sound perceived by the system may stop an ongoing process or change its parameters.

Obviously, the development of a knowledge-based design for multimodal interactive systems is a delicate task in which questions such as "Which domain
levels should be represented? How they should be represented, and how different levels of representation should be connected with each other?" are related to
a more general problem—the problem of *representational closure.* This implies
that in a rich environment—such as in a natural musical environment—people
are used to think in many levels at the same time, and they seem to shift their
focus of attention quite fluently to different aspects of the same musical material.
People have the capacity to deal somehow with micro-variations of pitch and
its contribution within the global structure of the piece at the same time. They
seem to jump fluently from one level to another, yet, when some aspects of this

natural environment have to be represented in a computerized environment, for-malized representations must be used and these imply that particular restrictions are imposed on the representation and manipulation of the objects represented.

Since the computer is used as an extension of the human mind, these restric-tions force users to think about musical objects in a way that is constrained by the formal representation of the knowledge used. In rich domains such as music and multimodal interaction, the closed nature of formal representations poses a real problem because according to the user's reasoning perspective and goals, a representation of the same musical object can vary from a single symbol in a high-level formalism to a waveform in the deepest view of the same material (Godoy 1993).

In a computer music environment, different views on a single musical entity are necessary and this involves bridges from abstract symbolic representations (e.g. the form of a fugue) to concrete subsymbolic representations (e.g. the pitch of a musical signal as perceived by the human auditory system). All this should moreover be integrated within an easy-to-use graphical and textual interface.

A main research goal of AI is therefore to develop formalisms that are able to manage different representational levels. Although most of the current systems provide but partial solutions (or proposals of solutions) towards the achieve-ment of that goal at long term, some of them are quite interesting and generate promising applications in the field of multi-modal interactive computing. Some examples are given in the second part of this paper.

Symbolic and subsymbolic knowledge-based systems

Translating a natural musical environment into a computer is a complicated enterprise that requires an interdisciplinary approach based on cognitive sciences. The challenge is to find a representation system that allows the user to extend the natural way of thinking and behaving in the digital environment.

From this perspective, it is easy to understand that the development of neural networks and connectionism in the 1980s has largely influenced the classical notion of "knowledge-based system".

The classical AI-approach relied almost exclusively on *symbolic* and non-analogical representations (e.g. rule-based systems). Knowledge was thought of in terms of static *explicit* structures which describe the world in terms of predicates and manipulations of predicates.

The connectionist and *subsymbolic* accounts, on the other hand, introduced many new representational ideas including images, responsive and reactive sys-tems, self-organization, and topological memory organizations (Kohonen 1984;

McClelland and Rumelhart 1986). Many of the interesting features of the sub-symbolic approach rely on the distinction between macro-level and micro-level. The interaction of elements at the micro-level typically produce effects which are most relevant at the macro-level.

It is now widely accepted that important parts of domain knowledge can be built up by learning and adaptation to statistical constraints of the environment. As a result, the study of emergent behavior (how global properties result from the interaction of elements at a micro-level), perceptual learning, and ecological modeling are now considered to be genuine topics of AI.

Once it is accepted that knowledge can be non-symbolic, one is forced to admit (a) that knowledge is not confined to a database of descriptions and heuristics, but may as well emerge from low-level (data-driven) information processing, and (b) that the application of knowledge as a guide to solutions can be embedded within the framework of dynamic systems theory.

Non-symbolic knowledge need not be expressed in an explicit way; it can be cast in terms of schema-driven processing of an attractor dynamics or force field. The resulting notion of a knowledge-based system has therefore been extended with *implicit* and dynamic structures—often called *schemata* (Arbib 1995; Leman 1995a). The completion of a particular task may then be seen as the trajectory of the state-space of a dynamic system in interaction with the environment (the user, audio sounds, dance movements, the audience, . . .).

Optimal interaction will be achieved when the knowledge-base itself has been built up during the interaction with such an environment.

A number of authors have recently examined the role of non-symbolic knowledge systems for music. Examples are found in the area of rhythmical grouping (Todd 1994), as well as in self-organizing knowledge structures for tone center and timbre perception (Leman 1994a; Cosi *et al.* 1994; Toiviainen 1996). The applications are based on so-called analogical representations, which often allude to metaphors of musical expression, physical motion (including concepts of dynamics, energy and mass), attractor dynamics, etc.

A taxonomy of representational systems

The use of symbolic as well as subsymbolic knowledge raises questions about the nature of representational formalisms. Recently, some attempts have been undertaken to classify the different approaches to musical representation. Much attention, thus far, has been focused on representational systems for music generation (synthesis and symbolic manipulation).

Geraint Wiggins et al. (Wiggins *et al.* 1993) consider the merits of representational systems along two orthogonal dimensions: *expressive completeness* and *structural generality*. Expressive completeness refers to the range of raw musical data that can be expressed; structural generality refers to the range of high-level structures that can be represented and manipulated. A sound waveform, for example, is one extreme, since it has the maximum amount of expressiveness, but does not allow one to easily capture abstract features of the music signal.

At the opposite extreme, traditional music notation has a good support of abstraction and generality, but is restricted in expressive completeness. On the basis of these two dimensions, a taxonomy is proposed for some of the existent systems in the literature.

Another overall taxonomy has been proposed by Stephen Travis Pope (Pope 1993). In his view, composition systems are compared along different criteria such as the level of representation (event-control such as MIDI, time model, pitch or voice-based), the possibility of expressing representational hierarchies, multiple levels of control, multiple tasks, the special-purpose hardware or software required, and so on.

Although most representation systems have a control structure by which it is possible to plan actions of the system, only few of them contain some sort of "intelligence"—knowledge by which actions are guided and adapt themselves to the environment in a way that resembles human information processing. In (Leman 1993) music representation is considered within a context of music cognition. A distinction is made between the acoustical or signal representation, the symbolic or conceptual representation and the subsymbolic or auditory representation. Analogical representations are characterized by the property that the representation has some structural features in common with the relations between the objects in the environment. According to (Camurri *et al.* 1994) the analogical type of representation provides a means to connect the subsymbolic representational level with the symbolic representational level. We will go deeper into these distinctions in the next section.

Basic properties of hybrid systems

Non-symbolic AI has shown that AI applications in music cannot be restricted to a static explicit and abstract knowledge-database. A representation in terms of discrete symbols onto which formal operations are then doing knowledge-driven symbol manipulation should be extended with non-symbolic descriptions of the world in terms of images, gestures, and dynamic implicit knowledge structures (schemata). The hybrid approach may therefore offer a way to deal with both symbolic and subsymbolic formalisms for the representation of musical and

multimodal information. In fact, hybrid systems aim to combine the useful properties of both approaches into a single computer environment. What properties,
then, define the architecture for multimodal interactive music systems?

The following list of requirements is a first step towards the characterization
of these hybrid systems.

The system should integrate multiple representational levels

It is useful to rely on the distinction between acoustical, symbolic, subsymbolic
and analogical representations.

- The acoustical representation is closest to the physical properties of a
  sound. The waveform is a representation of the variance of amplitude.
  For our purposes, it is important to notice that the acoustical representation is characterized by the unity of form and content. The form of
  the wave defines the characteristics of the tone that is represented; hence
  the representation is iconic. Fourier or wavelet transformations may be
  considered descriptions derived from the waveform.

- The term "symbolic" is adopted for those representational systems whose
  "atomic" constituents are in fact pointers to objects in the real world.
  Think here of a propositional logic in which "p" is an atomic proposition.
  "p" is a pointer to something in the world. As a matter of fact, "p" is itself
  a representation. Such systems have a syntax (which defines well-formed
  expressions), and a semantics (which defines what the symbol represents
  and how the logical relationships between them should be interpreted). An
  interpreted logical theory is a typical example of a symbolic system. For
  musical applications of logical theories, see, e.g. (Blevis 1989; Bel 1990;
  Courtot 1992). Musical scores, MIDI-files and most musical languages
  (Wiggins *et al.* 1993; Pope 1993) including Nyquist (see the chapter in
  this book by Dannenberg *et al.*) rely on symbolic representations.

- A representation is called "subsymbolic" if it is made of constituent entities that have *reflective* properties. Filtered signals, auditory images and
  schemata belong to this category. It may be useful to make a distinction
  between icons and images. Iconic representations have the property that
  the form is identical to the content; the representation is self-contained
  as in sound waveforms. Fourier transforms (see the chapters by Serra)
  and wavelet transforms (see the chapter by Evangelista) can be considered
  as icons, since they allow an inverse process by which the sound waveform can be obtained. It is useful to think of an icon as something that

can be put into a real sound (e.g. by means of a simple digital-to-analog conversion). Images on the other hand reflect certain properties of wave-forms and are used as such. Auditory images show aspects of the sound waveforms as filtered through the human auditory system. Non-symbolic knowledge structures (schemata) may respond to images. The response itself may be called an images (see below). Sometimes, a filtered signal is not used as an image (reflecting something) but rather as a proper icon.

- The term "analogical" refers to a representation in which the constituents and their relations are one-to-one with the represented reality. It is important to notice that an analogical representation can be either symbolic or subsymbolic. In the AI literature, the "vivid" knowledge base of H. Levesque (Levesque 1986) is analogical and symbolic, while Funt's diagrams (Funt 1980) are analogical and subsymbolic. In music perception, the schema theory introduced by M. Leman is based on a type of representation which is both subsymbolic and analogical. On the other hand, the HARP system developed by A. Camurri and collaborators allows the specification of one-to-one connections between symbolic entities and subsymbolic entities (auditory images) or even acoustical signals (icons). These connections are possible because the analogical structure both symbolic and subsymbolic types of representation allow a straight-forward mapping.

The multiple representational system should be flexible

Flexibility is a concept that indicates the ease with which connections between representations can be made. The human mind is considered to be very flexible. On the other hand, hybrid systems aim to gain more flexibility by integrating the symbolic and subsymbolic representational levels. Given the fact that both levels can deal with analogical representations, connections are possible between structures of knowledge units.

An example is an interactive computer music system that performs functional harmonic analysis starting from musical sounds. Such a system should first be able to track musical entities in terms of auditory images about which the system may start reasoning in terms of musical objects such as chords and tone centers. The connection between the subsymbolic part and the symbolic part may be realized by hooking a subsymbolic topological dynamic schema to an analogical symbolic database. The recognition of chords and tone centers may rely on an auditory model and artificial neural networks, while reasoning about harmonic functions proceeds with the help of a symbolic knowledge-base. (See the TCAD-HARP example below).

The system should be embedded in the natural environment

Hybrid systems interact with a natural environment by means of actions and perceptions. Hybrid systems act partly as autonomous agents and part of their actions may be "situated" actions, i.e. learned responses to structures in the environment. Therefore, rather than working only with abstract concepts or symbolic representations of music (such as in most MIDI-based interactive systems), we require that some representational entities should be grounded in the perception of the physical environment. Auditory models provide justified tools for building connections between audio signals and higher-level representations (Leman 1994a, b). In multimodal systems, however, one may try to incorporate the perception of movement, and incorporate haptic (tactile), visual and olfactory features (Schomaker *et al.* 1995). At the highest level, the environment-embedded images can be connected to symbolic entities which then form a vivid knowledge representation. In a multimodal interactive system, dance movements may be captured and used for the control of musical sounds. (See the DANCE-MUSIC example below.) In a similar way, physical models for sound generation (see the chapter by Smith) may be controlled by gestures which are captured and ultimately represented by single symbolic entities.

The system should integrate multiple modes of reasoning and dynamics, and should exhibit learning capabilities

Computer systems, able to support multiple representational levels should provide mechanisms for reasoning on actions and plans, for analyzing alternative solutions, strategies and goals. They should also provide both formal and informal analysis capabilities for inspecting the objects represented. F. Courtot, for example, mentions that a computer-assisted-composition environment should allow a composer to add new musical composition programs, without any skill in the particular programming language chosen for the system (Courtot 1992, p. 191). This requirement points to the fundamental issue of learning and the related question of how to automatically update the system knowledge (new analysis data, new composition strategies)—for example by means of generalizations processes starting from examples presented by the user. Some solutions proposed in the literature are based on purely symbolic approaches (e.g. Cope 1989; Widmer 1992; Westhead and Smaill 1994) others rely on learning systems and neural networks (Todd and Loy 1991). The latter are dealing with the adaptation of memory structures to properties of the musical environment. Learning is involved because these properties is often context dependent. Straightforward examples are available in learning computers how to perform a score in a musical relevant way (Bresin 1993).

The system should be able to handle metaphors and analogies as a conceptual tool for increasing its representation and reasoning capabilities

Music languages and theories are traditionally rich in metaphors derived from the real world dynamics. In musicology, the tonal system is often described in terms of "energies," "forces," "tension," and "relaxation". Also in computer music systems, metaphors may be at the basis of languages for the integration

Figure 1. Navigation of a robot in a space. Force fields (in white) are used as metaphor for navigation.

of different representational levels and they provide a basic conceptual tool for transfering knowledge about music dimensions to other modality dimensions (e.g. gestural, visual), and vice-versa.

The issue of reasoning based on metaphors has been widely studied from different points of view in AI, psychology and philosophy, and it plays a fundamental role in the design of music and multimedia systems. In (Camurri 1986b) the analogies between languages for movement, dance and music are discussed. Terms and descriptions in one modality can be used to express intuitively "similar" concepts in other modalities. Combined with subsymbolic representations, however, metaphors may offer a powerful tool similar to the effects of *synesthesia*—a process in which a real information of one sense also elicits perception in another sense. The hypotheses about synesthesia is that the sensory inputs, regardless their nature, ultimately may have access to the same neurons in the brain, hence causing effects in other perceptual modalities (Stein and Meredith 1993). This idea can be exploited in a straightforward way at the level of subsymbolic processing. One idea is to cast metaphors in terms of similarities of topological structures between dimensions in a conceptual space (Gärdenfors 1988, 1992). In a similar way, relations between metaphors and diagrammatic or pictorial representations are possible (Narayanan 1993; Glasgow and Papadias 1992). Mental models and analogical representations based on metaphors are more common in cognitive musicology nowadays. The subsymbolic approaches are mostly related to issues in music imagery. For example, (Todd 1992) argues that musical phrasing has its origin in the kinematics and the self-stimulation of (virtual) self-movement. This is grounded on the psychophysical structure of the human auditory system. Another example comes from robot navigation in a three-dimensional space. In this task domain, a bipolar force field is a useful metaphor; the moving robot corresponds to an electric charge, and a target to be reached corresponds to a charge of opposite sign (Figure 1). Obstacles correspond to charges of the same sign. Metaphorical reasoning implies the use of multiple representational levels and environment-based representations. The metaphor of a snail-like elastic object moving in a space has been used to implement the attractor dynamics of schema-driven tone center recognition (Leman 1995c).

The system should work with multiple time levels

In his survey on musical signal representations, G. Garnett (1991, p. 343) proposes a four-level time model:

- implicit time, or stream time, is at the lowest level, which denotes the ongoing flow of time in event streams;
- calendar time refers to a calendar or a clock;
- music time "consists of either of the above two kinds of time as well as temporal concepts particular to music ... includes times that are ... unspecified or imprecise";
- logical time is the level which supports the explicit (i.e. symbolic) reasoning mechanisms involving time.

This distinction seems to correspond with the above distinction between the acoustical, subsymbolic and symbolic levels of representation. Obviously, it is important to vary, in a fluent way, the "grain" of reasoning about time (Allen 1984) and the musical objects that are related to the different time levels. Temporal knowledge models should therefore exhibit flexibility as well as fluent connections between different levels.

The relationship between input and output is multivariable

The relationship between input and output is an intricate one. Interactive instruments, like physical musical instruments, allow performers to map gestures and continuous movement into sounds (Machover and Chung 1989; Sawada *et al.* 1995; Vertegaal and Ungvary 1995; Winkler 1995). Hybrid systems add more flexibility in that some input (e.g. recognized movement) may have some direct causal effect on sound, while other inputs may release certain actions or just change the course of a process. In short, the cognitive architecture allows a planning of multivariable actions. Furthermore, their firing may be context-dependent and may be learned beforehand.

System tasks should happen in-time rather than out-of-time

Systems that perform actions and perceptions in the environment work with schedules—much like humans use schedules to plan their actions. What is meant by the requirement that the system should perform *in-time* rather than *out-of-time* is that the system should schedule concepts and actions only when needed, so that, in principle, the system should be able act in a real musical environment. The "in-time" time needed to perform a specific music task may vary according to the type of task and it is a prerequisite to fast (real-time) responses to the musical environment. In jazz improvisation, for example, the system has to follow the performance time, but it will use the available time to reason "forward" in time, that is, to anticipate the behavior of the system in a time window of a few seconds. Of course, representations of the past events should also be considered by the system to decide the new actions. This means that the system can build up some hypotheses of the actions it will perform in the near future, which can be possibly retracted, corrected, or substituted within the "latest moment" (in the performance time axis) on the basis of new upcoming information and/or reasoning results.

HARP: the basic architecture of a hybrid system

HARP is a hybrid system for the representation and *in-time* processing of multimodal information. HARP is structured as a development environment and a run-time environment. The former, at a first glance, may be conceived of as a sort of hybrid expert-system shell which—like any shell—allows the application programmer to do several things. It is useful to make a distinction between the programmer mode, the users mode and the analysis mode. In order to use HARP, domain knowledge should be put into the system by means of the development environment. The user enters the programming mode and typically starts with defining a set or structured set of labels (sometimes called "symbols" or "concepts"), which usually stand for agents and situations, and their relations (or "roles"). Agents are program modules that perform certain tasks like for example logical reasoning about symbols, or perception of audio input.

In the run-time system, the user typically uses the system as a prolongation of human activity within a digital environment. In this mode, the system typically creates, deletes, influences agents according to the needs of that moment. For example, if an agent comes up with the recognition of a particular chord, then the system creates a corresponding new situation, describing that chord in symbolic terms. This may also cause the creation of an agent which reasons about the chord in relation to the context in which it appeared. In addition to programming and use, HARP allows the user to switch to an analysis mode in which the user can exploit the system to infer properties of its own actions. All this makes of HARP a quite complex but highly flexible system. Its architecture is shown in Figure 2.

The overall system architecture is based on a distributed network of agents. In some respect, the system is similar to Cypher (Rowe 1993), TouringMachines (Ferguson 1992), M (Riecken 1994) and NetNeg (Goldman, Gang, and Rosenschein 1995). We will go deeper into some basic features of the system below.

Input/output and processing building blocks

Following the scheme depicted in Figure 2, we can make a distinction between the following building blocks in user mode:

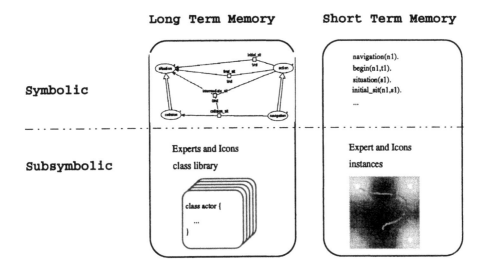

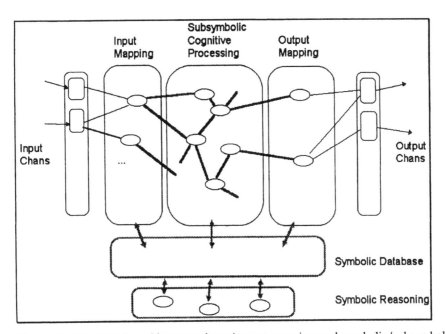

Figure 2. The HARP architecture: input/output mapping and symbolic/subsymbolic division.

- Input mapping. The input mapping consists of a group of agents that are able to receive signals from sensors and map them onto schemata. A schema can be a self-organizing neural network, for example, one that has been trained to organize some specific statistical properties of context-dependent patterns into some global structure. The recorded signals may be mapped onto the schema in terms of movement trajectories.

- Output mapping. The output mapping consists of a set of agents that manage the orders given by the cognitive processing agents. The orders may pertain to high level parameters. As stated, the output may be of any kind and need not be restricted to direct causal transformation of the input.

- Cognitive processing. Cognitive processing is about reasoning and planning. This layer deals with two kinds of activities: subsymbolic and symbolic agents performing subsymbolic reasoning and planning. For example, the map may contain tone centers which are structured according to the circle of fifths and the musical information flow may be mapped onto this structure by the input mapping processes. The (subsymbolic) schema may then be active in that the trajectory on the map is subject to attraction forces. Attractors are representations in the schema that may force the trajectory of an input to move in a different way or towards a particular attractor. This is useful in case of ambiguous or incomplete input. In a similar way, the movement of a dancer may be projected onto a map and its trajectory may be influenced by attraction. Symbolic reasoning can only perform symbolic inference and planning in the symbolic database.

- Symbolic database. The symbolic database is a high-level, symbolic representation of the domain space(s) (e.g. music composition and performance spaces, movement and gesture spaces). It consists of a symbolic knowledge base written in a standard representation language (a subset of first order predicates), structured in a *long-term memory* (LTM) and in a *short-term memory* (STM). LTM stores taxonomies (or "ontologies") related to general definitions of events, situations, facts, objects, and relations. Instances of relevant facts about events, situations, objects, and related features are stored during a work session in the STM. The agents are responsible to update the STM, and some agents can start their activity according to particular events that occur in the STM.

- Agents communication. The agent communication component implements a declarative communication protocol that is used for inter-agent communication. We adopt for this module a subset of KQML—Knowledge Query and Manipulation Language—standard (Genesereth and Ketchpel 1994). Agents can also communicate indirectly by means of modifications of the common domain worlds.

Long-term and short-term memory

The dynamics of HARP is based on a distinction between LTM and STM.

The LTM is the permanent and "encyclopedic" storage of general knowledge. It contains two knowledge-bases: a symbolic—analogical as well as non-analogical—component. The information processing dealt with at this level is done in terms of symbol manipulation based on three types of formalisms: (i) a representation language derived from semantic networks of the family of KL-ONE (Woods and Schmolze 1992); (ii) a simple temporal logic language for high-level, logical time management; and (iii) production rules to represent factual long term knowledge about the domain, including inferences.

In the programming mode of the development environment, the user will give "labels" to the different agents and situations. At this level, it is possible to describe relationships between the labels (symbols) in terms of an inheritance semantic network formalism. Subsymbolic component is based on a library of schemata ("skills", "behaviors", and "memory structures") that can (if required) be learned by the system by means of self-organization (e.g. procedures, maps). The above mentioned attraction dynamics is situated at this level.

The STM is the working memory in which the actual context regarding the state of affairs of the world is dealt with. The STM represents data about what is happening when the system is at work in user-mode. It is the place where the system stores temporary information, such as information about the birth of agents that are suddenly triggered by some input, or about their death when the task is completed. The distinction between symbolic and subsymbolic levels of representation is here dealt with in the following way:

- Symbolic components point to individual entities (icons, images, objects in the real world, or abstract concepts) by means of a formalism that is based on a subset of first-order logic. The processing in the symbolic part of the STM is based on reasoning by procedures and defined in the symbolic LTM.

- Subsymbolic components are iconic representations (e.g. signals, FFTs), images (auditory images) or actions. The processing in the subsymbolic part of the STM is based on reasoning by means of dynamic systems, utilizing the schema dynamics ("behaviors", "skills", and "metaphors") that is present in the subsymbolic LTM.

Connections between representational levels

The symbolic STM works as a sort of interface between the LTM symbolic component and the subsymbolic STM; it is the core of the "fluent" connection between the representational levels. The symbolic part of the STM is "vivid" in the sense of (Levesque 1986); this means that its constituent individual constants are linked one-to-one to entities (images, signals, agents) in the subsymbolic STM.

The architecture is also inspired by Johnson-Laird's mental model (Johnson-Laird 1983). The subsymbolic STM minimal structure consists therefore of two components: a knowledge base of instanced icons or images, and some generative process for managing icons, for acting on them and manage their interactions with the symbolic memory. A subset of these entities are linked to symbols in the STM and emerge in the symbolic STM. This is implemented by extending the symbolic language to support this grounding mechanism (Camurri 1994).

Modes of reasoning

HARP makes a distinction between three types of reasoning: classification, subsymbolic reasoning, and hybrid planning.

- The symbolic components are characterized by the well-known classification and recognition algorithms typical of term-subsumption languages (Woods and Schmolze 1992). They are here integrated with rule-based inference mechanisms. Given a taxonomy of symbolic entities and relationships between them (an example is shown in Figure 3), symbolic classification algorithms allow to find the correct position of any newly introduced concept, starting from its properties. Recognition algorithms allow furthermore the classification of individual constants. For example, a subsymbolic perception module might be able to generate at the symbolic level a new chord instance with a set of properties, at a given instant of the performance. The symbolic recognition algorithm then takes the new object, and tries to discover which kind of object it is, then it is added to the symbolic knowledge-base. In the taxonomy of Figure 3, the symbolic recognizer might generate a instance of Cmajor, where Cmajor is a specialization (sub-concept) of chord. The rate at which this type of reasoning takes place is slow. It is typically in the order of 0.5 to 3 seconds (it is invoked periodically or evoked on demand by agents effects on the STM).

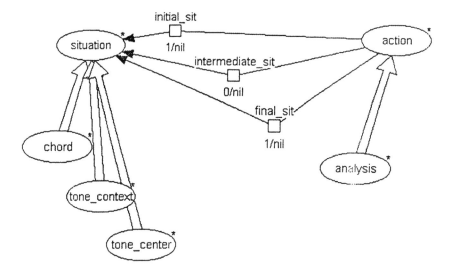

Figure 3. A taxonomy of symbolic entities and relationships.

- Subsymbolic reasoning can involve special-purpose dynamic systems which depend on the particular domain or metaphor used. For example, in an abstract potential metaphor, a reasoning mechanism corresponds to an algorithm for finding out a global minimum in the given landscape of potential. This corresponds to a choice of a music parameter during a composition process. Subsymbolic reasoning can be fast, the rate is typically in the order of few milliseconds.

- A further example of a reasoning mechanism in HARP is the "hybrid" planner, which allows the coordination of the activities of both symbolic and subsymbolic reasoners (both in LTM and STM), for reaching some goals. In the previous example of symbolic classification, the input to the symbolic recognition module is furnished by a subsymbolic module; as a whole, this is an example of a hybrid reasoning mechanism.

Time levels

The symbolic time level, characterized by a coarse granularity, corresponds to the logical time of Garnett; only the "relevant" situations that emerge from the subsymbolic level to the symbolic levels (both in LTM and STM) have an explicit symbolic time representation. For example, only the instants in which a new chord is recognized emerge in the symbolic STM. The subsymbolic time levels (characterized by a medium- and fine-grain time) are necessary to allow the coordination of the simulations, the measurements, and the executions performed in the subsymbolic STM. However, only "relevant" time instants emerge from the subsymbolic to the symbolic levels (e.g. only the time when the abstract potential reaches a minimum or the time at which a new chord has been detected).

HARP applications

HARP offers a conceptual framework to deal with multiple representational levels. In this section, we present two examples of how to integrate subsymbolic and symbolic processing in HARP. The first example describes how a subsymbolic model for chord and tone center recognition is integrated with HARP. The second example briefly mentions an interactive multimodal application for dance and music.

The integration of TCAD in HARP

The subsymbolic model for chord and tone center recognition is called TCAD (Leman 1995a, b). The motivation for integrating TCAD into HARP was to perform harmonic analysis starting from a musical signal. But rather than trying to recognize the individual pitches and use this information for making inferences about the harmonic structure of the piece, we adopted a more global approach based on the recognition of chord-types and tone centers.

Tone centers can be conceived as contexts in which chord-types appear. Once chord-type and tone center are known it is possible to make inferences and guesses about the harmonic structure.

The subsymbolic part (TCAD) thus provides chords and tone centers. The symbolic part (of HARP) uses the information provided by TCAD to reason about the harmonic structure. The latter can improve the outcome of TCAD and it can be used to recognize more general objects such as cadences.

Below we describe how we pass from signals to the AI-based application. The presentation of the different steps involved is done using of an excerpt from the *Prelude* No. 20 in C minor by F. Chopin (Figure 4).

The TCAD framework is based on three subsymbolic representational entities: musical signals, auditory images, and schemata. Signals are transformed into auditory images. Images organize into schemata by a *long-term* and *data-driven* process of self-organization. For a detailed discussion of the latter aspect, see (Leman 1995a). In the present context, schemata are merely considered from the

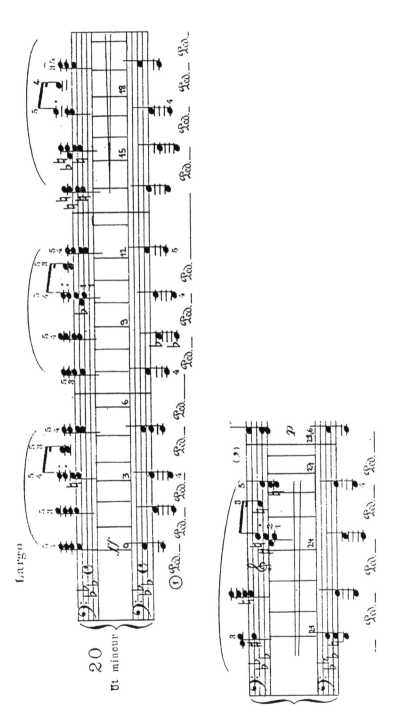

Figure 4. The first four measures from the Prelude No. 20 in C minor by F. Chopin.

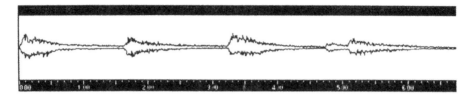

Figure 5. Waveform corresponding to the first measure of *Prelude* No. 20.

point of view of recognition, not from the point of view of learning. Recognition is *short-term* and *schema-driven*.

Musical signal. A *signal* refers to the acoustical or waveform representation of the music. Signals are digitally represented by an array of numbers. In this example, we rely on a sampling rate of 20000 Hz and 16-bit sample resolution. A waveform of the first measure of the *Prelude* No. 20 is shown in Figure 5.

Auditory images. An auditory image is conceived of as a state or snapshot of the neural activity in a region of the auditory system during a defined time interval. It is modeled as an ordered array of numbers (a vector). From an auditory modeling point of view, the most complete auditory image is assumed to occur at the level of the *auditory nerve*.

Figure 6 shows the auditory nerve images of the first 2 second of *Prelude* No. 20. The images (one vector of 20 components every 0.4 msecond) have been obtained by filtering the musical signal using a bank of 20 overlapping asymmetric bandpass filters (range: 220 Hz to 7075 Hz, separated: 1 Bark) and a subsequent translation of the filtered signals to neural firing patterns according to a design by L. Van Immerseel and J.-P. Martens (Van Immerseel and Martens 1992). The bandpass filters reflect the kind of signal decomposition that is done by the human ear. The signals shown in Figure 6 represent the probability of neuronal firing during an interval of 0.4 msecond. The vertical lines show marks at 0.1 second.

Subsequent processing of these images is based on their spatial and temporal properties.

- Spatial Encoding. When a sound reaches the ear, the eardrum takes over the variations of sound pressure. The middle ear bones transmit the vibration to the cochlea and a sophisticated hydromechanical system in the cochlea then converts the vibration into electrochemical pulses. Depending on the temporal pattern of the signal, a traveling wave pattern is generated in the cochlear partition which produces a characteristic spatial configuration. Some images like spectral images (see (Cosi *et al.* 1994)) are therefore based on the spatial configuration of Figure 6.

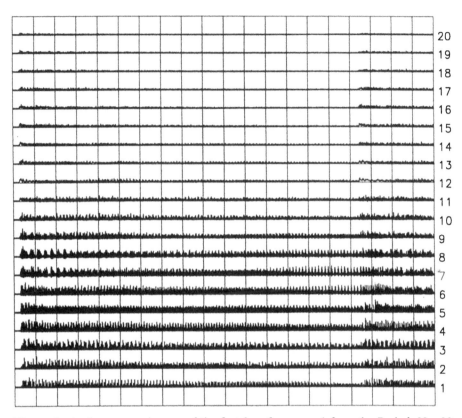

Figure 6. Auditory nerve images of the first 2 s of measure 1 from the *Prelude* No. 20 by F. Chopin. The horizontal axis is time, while the vertical axis shows the neural firing patterns in 20 auditory nerve fibers (central frequency range: 220–7055 Hz).

   – Temporal Encoding. Due to the membrane properties of the spiral ganglion cell, the graded activity of the inner hair cells generate all-or-non activity (action potentials or *spikes* in the auditory nerve fibers that innervate the cells. Taking into account the limits of neural firing (neurons are incapable of generating more than 500–1000 action potentials or spikes per second), the response envelope will reflect the time structure of the stimulating waveform. This is the basis of neuronal *synchronization*. Temporal encoding is very important for low pitch perception and tone center perception. Some images are therefore based on an analysis of the amplitude modulation of the signals in Figure 6.

    TCAD does not rely on spatial encoding and derived spectral images. Instead it is based on an analysis of periodicities in the neural firing patterns of the 20 auditory nerve fibers (channels). Every 10 msecond, a frame of 30 msecond in

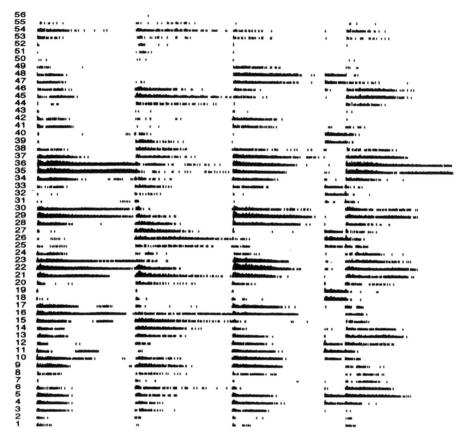

Figure 7. Completition images of the Chopin *Prelude*.

length is analyzed (using autocorrelation) for all 20 channels. The results are then summed over all channels, which gives the *completion image* (also called *summary autocorrelation image* or *virtual pitch image*). The term completion image refers to the fact that the image completes incomplete spectra. For example, if the signal would contain frequencies at 600, 800 and 1000 Hz, then the resulting image would contain the frequency of 200 Hz. Figure 7 shows the completion images of the first measure of *Prelude* No. 20. The horizontal axis is the time and the vertical axis represents the time-lags of the autocorrelation analysis. Frequencies can be deduced from it but as mentioned above, we are not interested in the exact frequencies, only in the global form of the pattern.

The next step involves a time integration of the completion image. This is necessary in order to take into account the formation of context and global patterns. A sequence of chords, for example, based on the degrees I-IV-V has indeed a different tonal feeling than the same sequence in reversed order (V-IV-I).

Figure 8. Context images of the Chopin *Prelude*.

Hence, aspects of integration at a rather large time scale is necessary in order to account for context. In the present example, we use two types of integration: one with a time-constant of 3 second, which accounts for tone centers, and another with a time-constant of 0.5 second for the chords. The time-constant of 3 second leads to the picture shown in Figure 8.

This is perhaps the place to note that the exploration and combination of different types of auditory images is a fascinating research domain. Since the information encoding by the auditory system is multiple it makes sense to distinguish between different types of images. G. Brown (Brown 1992) makes a distinction between auditory nerve images, onset images, offset images, residue images, frequency transition images, and others. In rhythm research, relevant images are provided by the rhythmogram (Todd 1994). In timbre research, envelope spectrum images or synchrony spectrum images can be used (Cosi *et al.* 1994). As we saw, in chord and tone center recognition, the relevant images are called: auditory nerve images, autocorrelation images, completion images, and context images.

A final category of images useful for our purposes are the semantic images. The semantic images provide information about the recognition. They involve already the schema.

Schemata. In the model, the images of the periphery are updated faster than those of the center levels. The auditory nerve images Figure 6 are updated every 0.4 msecond, the completion and context images only every 10 msesond Figure 7.

The semantic images provide information about chord and tone center analysis every 0.1 second. It is this information, finally, which is going to be processed by the symbolic engine of HARP—which will group several images into symbolic blocks with a beginning and ending.

Figure 9 shows an example of a semantic analysis of the first four measures of *Prelude* No. 20. Each vector at time t has 24 components and each value stands for the distance between the context image at time t and the schema

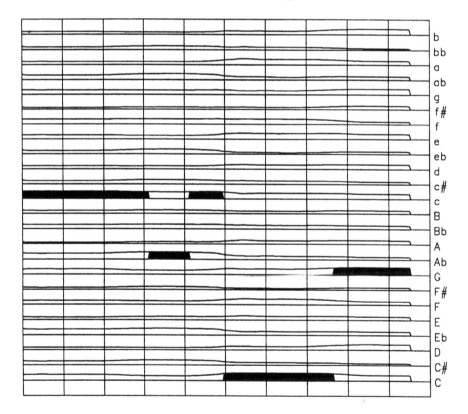

Figure 9. Semantic images of the first four measures of *Prelude* No. 20.

containing stable information about tone centers. In fact, the schema is hereby reduced to those 24 vectors which contain the most relevant information about the tone centers. Schemata may indeed be quite large and contain up to 10,000 neurons (Leman and Carreras 1996b). In a similar way, the context images for chords are compared with a schema containing information about chords. The schema is furthermore thought of as an active structure that controls the recognition of an object in terms of an attractor dynamics. It would lead us too far to go into the details of this dynamics but a useful metaphor is in terms of an elastic snail-like object that moves in a space. The head of the snail is the time index of the music, the tail is a buffer of about 3 second. Every new instance (0.1 sesond), a context image enters the "head" and an adapted image leaves the "tail". As such, the object moves in a space of tone centers. The latter should be conceived of as attractors. The position of the moving snail with respect to the attractors (hence: its semantic content) is depending on the nature of the information contained in the head (data-driven) in addition to the forces exerted by the attraction (schema-driven). The application of this dynamics to tone center recognition has improved the performance by about 10% (Leman 1995a).

To implement TCAD in HARP, a first step consists of defining a suitable ontology, that is, the dictionary of terms and relations. As described in the previous section, ontologies are stored in the symbolic LTM. An excerpt of the TCAD ontology is depicted in Figure 10. The ontology is structured in two main parts. The part at the left of Figure 10 gives the definition of the schema in terms of tone properties, i.e. "music fragments," "tone centers," "tone contexts," "chords," and their features and relations. The part at the (upper) right side of Figure 10 gives the definition of the agents that are involved in the application. The concepts "chord" and "tone center" are roots of sub-taxonomies. They are associated with the subconcepts of all possible chords and tone centers, respectively. These subtaxonomies are only partially shown in the Figure 10: they start from the gray concepts (graphic aliases). The definition of the TCAD agents is then completed by specification of their interface with the symbolic LTM, their bodies and forms of communication. During a specific music recognition process, agents can be activated to produce new facts and situations, asserted in the STM. This process is taking place at run-time.

In the present example, two types of assertions may be added to the symbolic knowledge base (KB): assertions about tone context, and assertions about chords. For example, let us consider the TCAD agent that, at a certain point, recognizes a chord; a corresponding new assertion of that chord is then added in the symbolic KB, together with a merit value (computed by TCAD), and its beginning and ending. The latter defines the time interval during which the chord has been

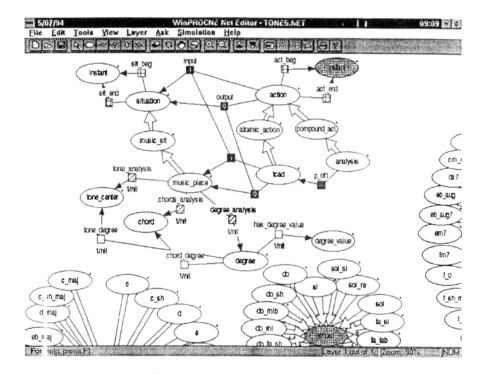

Figure 10. An excerpt of the HARP symbolic KB for the TCAD experiment.

recognized. Note that, in this way, only relevant time instants emerge from the subsymbolic (TCAD) to the symbolic level. Otherwise stated, only those instants in which a significant change of interpretation of chord or tone center is found are added to the symbolic KB. Figure 11 shows the assertions produced by the TCAD agent during the processing of the first measure of the music example.

Symbolic descriptions have been introduced for tone center, chord, and music fragment. A number of agents, such as cadence_analyser, are hooked to TCAD and to roles of music_fragment. The prolog window shows the new assertions of chords and the tone centers that are found by the TCAD agent while processing the first measure of *Prelude* No. 20. This window is activated by using HARP in the analysis mode (e.g. activation is done by selecting the Query option in the Ask menu).

The main role of HARP in this example is thus to integrate subsymbolic with symbolic reasoning in order to improve the harmonic analysis of the input piece by adding aspects of symbolic reasoning. HARP infers the harmonic function of chords on the basis of information about the tone centers (the context in which chords appear), the recognition of cadences, and other properties inferred by the underlying subsymbolic TCAD engine embedded in the TCAD agent. Suitable

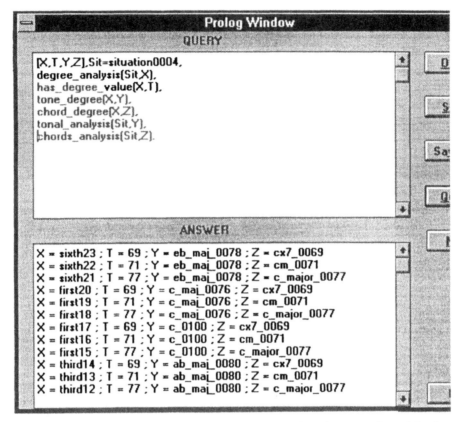

Figure 11. Assertion produced by the TCAD agent during the processing of the first measure of the musical example.

rules in the LTM inspect that given a tone center, say, A-flat, the recognized chord of C-sharp should be considered as a IV degree (therefore D-flat), and a possible cadence involving that chord as a IV degree of A-flat is searched to confirm the hypothesis. In general, symbolic knowledge can be useful for the solution of problems which are difficult to realize by subsymbolic processes, such as the recognition of cadences.

Integration of dance and music: multimodal environments

Hybrid systems are particularly useful in the design of *multimodal environments* (MEs). These environments include agents capable of establishing creative multimodal user interaction and exhibiting dynamic, intelligent, real-time, and adaptive behaviors.

In a typical scenario, one or more users are immersed in an environment that allows them to communicate by means of body movement (dance and gestures), by audio signals (singing, talking), and by controlling equipment (playing on an instrument or keyboard). Users get feedback from the environment in real time, in terms of sound, music, visual media, and actuators in general (e.g. movements of semi-autonomous mobile systems). We can think of a future, real-time version of the TCAD-HARP agent application described in the previous sections as an acquisition module of a ME, delegated to the sound acquisition task. Multimodal environments thus are digital environments used as a prolongation of the human mind/behavior. Several experimental MEs for different applications, based on the HARP architecture, have been developed.

They cover music and interactive arts, museal applications, and entertainment applications (in collaboration with SoundCage Srl):

- the HARP/Vscope was built for the tracking of human movement by means of on-body, wireless sensors, gesture recognition, and real-time control of computer-generated music and animation;

- the SoundCage Interactive Music Machine (IMM) is a system based on a set of spatial sensors displaced in a sort of "cage", whose design has been focused to track overall human movement features;

- the HARP/DanceWeb is a different human movement acquisition system, which can be used both in stand-alone installations and integrated with the SoundCage IMM for an improved movement and gesture tracking;

- the Theatrical and Museal Machine, consists of a supervision system based on HARP, and small, cheap mobile robots on wheels capable to perform tasks like Cicerone in a museum, or actor on stage in theater/dance/music events. HARP/Vscope, SoundCage IMM, and HARP DanceWeb are shown in Figure 12, during the EITC '95 Exhibition.

Let us discuss the features of our systems that distinguish them from the state of the art. Up to now, systems like virtual environments (VEs) and hyper-instruments have typically been static environments which can only be explored or navigated by users, or simply played as virtual musical instruments. They do not change their structure and behavior over time; for example, they do not adapt themselves to users, neither do they try to guess what the user is doing or wants. An exception is the MIT Media Lab's ALIVE system (Maesetal 1995).

Most of the existing state-of-the-art systems fall into two main categories. In the former, they consist of real-time systems that basically involve simple, low-level cause-effects mechanisms between modalities: the metaphor usually

Figure 12. Multimodal environment for dance and music I.

adopted is that of a musical (hyper)instrument where a fixed, simple mapping between human movement and sound output is defined. In the other category— i.e. animation production for films and computer games—the goal is to track as precisely as possible the human movement and to use this information as-is in an off-line design process to animate believable artificial characters. In contrast, our main goal is to observe a user and to derive sufficient information in real time in order to perform an overall evaluation of the actions (such as the style of the movement) to communicate with the user and to change the behavior of the ME to adapt to the actions of the user. A main focus is to observe general body movement features, in a sort of Gestalt approach. In that approach, it is not necessary to go into all the deep local movements. The main goal is not a very precise reconstruction of the body movements, but rather to extract global features as they are integrated by real-time motion detection capabilities of atomic, local movement features.

The paradigm adopted is that of a human observer of a dance, where the focus of attention changes dynamically according to the evolution of the dance itself and of the music produced. MEs should therefore be able to change its reactions and its social interaction and rules over time. Towards this aim, MEs embed multilevel representations of different media and modalities, as well as representations of communication metaphors and of analogies to integrate modalities. In such a way, MEs should be able to decide and apply plans in response to users actions and behavior.

We classify MEs as a sort of extension of Augmented Reality environments. They integrate intelligent features, as for example in software agents. We therefore envisage an audio-visual environment which can be communicated to other humans and machines, either other actors participating in the same event (including autonomous robots) or external spectators of the action. A typical sample scenario regards an integrated system which is driven, tuned, molded by the movements and by the sounds produced by the user(s), (actors, dancers, players), using specific metaphors for reaching, grasping, turning, pushing, navigating, playing, or communicating states or emotions. The system presented in this chapter constitutes a step toward this generation of MEs. A number of multi-modal environments have been developed thanks to the partial support of the Esprit Project 8579 MIAMI (Multimodal Interaction for Advanced Multimedia Interfaces). These applications have been used in several music and multimedia events, including concerts (e.g. Reina Sofia Conservatory, Madrid, 1995), mu-

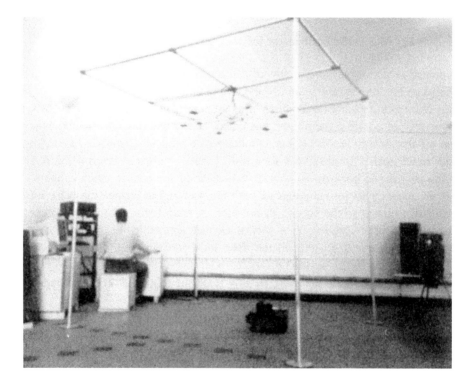

Figure 13. Multimodal environment for dance and music II.

seum exhibitions and atelier-laboratories, and have been selected by the CEC for live demonstrations at the European Information Technology Conference in the Brussels Congress Center. Figure 13 shows the Theatrical and Museal Machine presented in our Laboratory-Atelier during the national exhibition "Mostra della Cultura Scientifica e Tecnologica ImparaGiocando" at the Palazzo Ducale, Genoa, 1996. See (Camurri 1996; Camurri *et al.* 1996) for a deeper discussion on these families of MEs.

Conclusion

The state of the art of the research in AI-based systems is continuously growing; a new generation of systems fulfilling the requirements discussed in this chapter is expected in the near future. The TCAD/HARP experiment and the multimodal environments described in the second half of the paper constitute first steps in this direction. The motivation for the TCAD/HARP experiment is two-fold: on the one hand, it contributes to studies in music theory and music understanding; on the other hand, it is a preliminary attempt toward a new architecture for interactive music systems. In the latter, a listener module is able to acquire sound signals, based on models of the human ear rather than on MIDI signals. The system is furthermore integrated with the processing and performing modules in an overall AI-based hybrid architecture. With the availability of new powerful low-cost hardware, the goal is therefore to develop interactive music systems able to modify their behavior on the basis of an input analysis of complex signals.

Acknowledgments

Thanks to H. Sabbe and the Belgian Foundation for Scientific Research (NFWO/FKFO) for support. We thank also G. Allasia and C. Innocenti for their fundamental contributions to the design and implementation of the TCAD/HARP system.

References

Allen, J. 1984. "Towards a general theory of action and time." *Artificial Intelligence* 15: 123–154.
Arbib, M. 1995. *Schema Theory*. The Handbook of Brain Theory and Neural Networks. Cambridge, MA: The MIT Press.
Bel, B. 1990. "Time and musical structures." *Interface—Journal of New Music Research* 19(2–3): 107–136.
Blevis, E., M. Jenkins, and E. Robinson. 1989. "On Seeger's music logic." *Interface—Journal of New Music Research* 18(1–2): 9–31.

Bresin, R. 1993. "Melodia: e program for performance rules testing, teaching, and piano score performance." In G. Haus and I. Pighi, eds. *Atti di X Colloquio Informatica. Musicale* Universita degli Studi di Milano: AIMI.

Brown, G. 1992. "Computational auditory scene analysis." Technical report. Sheffield: Department of Computing Science, University of Sheffield.

Camurri, A. 1996. "Multimodal environments for music, art, and entertainment." Technical report. Genoa: DIST, University of Genoa.

Camurri, A., M. Frixione, and C. Innocenti. 1994. "A cognitive model and a knowledge representation architecture for music and multimedia." Technical Report. Genoa: DIST (submitted to *Journal of New Music Research*).

Camurri, A., M. Leman, and G. Palmieri. 1996. "Gestalt-based composition and performance in multimodal environments." In *Proceedings of the Joint International Conference on Systemtic and Cognitive Musicology – JIC96*. IPEM, University of Ghent.

Camurri, A., P. Morasso, V. Tagliasco, and R. Zaccaria. 1986. "Dance and movement notation." In P. Morasso and V. Tagliasco, eds. *Human Movement Understanding*. Amsterdam: Elsevier Science.

Cope, D. 1989. "Experiments in musical intelligence (EMI): non-linear linguistic-based composition." *Interface—Journal of New Music Research* 18(1–2): 117–139.

Cosi, P., G. DePoli, and G. Lauzzana. 1994. "Auditory modelling and self-organizing neural networks for timbre classification." *Journal of New Music Research* 23(1): 71–98.

Courtot, F. 1992. "Carla: knowledge acquisition and induction for computer assisted composition." *Interface—Journal of New Music Research* 21(3–4): 191–217.

Ferguson, I. (1992). "Touringmachines: autonomous agents with attitudes." *IEEE Computer* 25(5).

Funt, B. 1980. "Problem solving with diagrammatic representations." *Artificial Intelligence* 13.

Gärdenfors, P. 1988. "Semantics, conceptual spaces and the dimensions of music." *Acta Philosophica Fennica, Essays on the Philosophy of Music* 43: 9–27.

Gärdenfors, P. 1992. "How logic emerges from the dynamics of information." *Lund University Cognitive Studies* 15.

Garnett, G. 1991. "Music, signals, and representations: A survey." In G. De Poli, A. Piccialli, and C. Roads, eds. *Representations of Musical Signals*. Cambridge, MA: The MIT Press, pp. 325–370.

Genesereth, M. and S. Ketchpel. 1994. "Software agents." Special issue of *Communication of the ACM* 37(7).

Glasgow, J. and D. Papadias. 1992. "Computational imagery." *Cognitive Science* 16: 355–394.

Godoy, R. 1993. Formalization and epistemology. PhD thesis. Oslo: University of Oslo Department of Musicology, Oslo.

Goldman, C., D. Gang, and J. Rosenschein. 1995. "Netneg: A hybrid system architecture for composing polyphonic music." In *Proceedings of the IJCAI-95 Workshop on Artificial Intelligence and Music*. IJCAI, pp. 11–15.

Johnson-Laird, P. 1983. *Mental Models*. Cambridge: Cambridge University Press.

Kohonen, T. 1984. *Self-Organization and Associative Memory*. Berlin: Springer-Verlag.

Leman, M. 1993. "Symbolic and subsymbolic description of music." In G. Haus, ed. *Music Processing*. Madison: A-R Editions, pp. 119–164.

Leman, M. 1994a. "Auditory models in music research. Part I." Special issue of the *Journal of New Music Research*. Lisse: Published by Swets and Zeitlinger.

Leman, M. 1994b. "Auditory models in music research. Part II." Special issue of the *Journal of New Music Research*. Lisse: Published by Swets and Zeitlinger.

Leman, M. 1994c. "Schema-based tone center recognition of musical signals." *Journal of New Music Research* 23(2): 169–204.

Leman, M. 1995a. "A model of retroactive tone center perception." *Music Perception* 12(4): 439–471.

Leman, M. 1995b. *Music and Schema Theory—Cognitive Foundations of Systematic Musicology*. Berlin, Heidelberg: Springer-Verlag.

Leman, M. and F. Carreras. 1996. "The self-organization of stable perceptual maps in a realistic musical environment." In G. Assayah, M. Chemillier, and C. Eloy, eds. *Troisiéme Journées d'Informatique Musicale*. Caen, France: Les Cahiers du GREYC Université de Caen, pp. 156–169.

Levesque, H. 1986. "Making believers out of computers." *Artificial Intelligence* 30(1): 81–108.

Machover, T. and J. Chung. 1989. "Hyperinstruments: musically intelligent and interactive performance and creativity systems." In *Proc. Int. Computer Music Conference – ICMC 89*. Columbus, Ohio, USA: ICMA.

Maes, P., B. Blumberg, T. Darrel, A. Pentland, and A. Wexelblat. 1995. "Modeling interactive agents in ALIVE". In *Proc. Int. Joint Conf. on Artificial Intelligence IJCAI-95*. Montreal: IJCAI-95.

McClelland, J. and D. Rumelhart, eds. 1986. *Parallel Distributed Processing: Explorations in the Microstructure of Cognition*. Cambridge, MA: The MIT Press.

Narayanan, N.H., ed. 1993. Special issue on computational imagery. *Computational Intelligence* 9.

Pope, S.T. 1993. "Music composition and editing by computer." In G. Haus, ed. *Music Processing*. Madison: A-R Editions, pp. 25–72.

Riecken, D. 1994. *Intelligent Agents*. Special issue of *Communication of the ACM*, July.

Rowe, R. 1993. *Interactive Music Systems*. Cambridge, MA: The MIT Press.

Sawada, H., S. Ohkura, and S. Hashimoto. 1995. "Gesture analysis using 3D acceleration sensor for music control." In *Proc. Int. Computer Music Conference – ICMC 95*. Banff, Canada: ICMA.

Schomaker, L., J. Nijtmans, A. Camurri, F. Lavagetto, P. Morasso, C. Benoît, T. Guiard-Marigny, B.L. Goff, J. Robert-Ribes, A. Adjoudani, I. Defée, S. Münch, K. Hartung, and J. Blauert. 1995. A taxonomy of multimodal interaction in the human information processing system. Technical Report WP1, ESPRIT Project 8579 MIAMI.

Stein, B.E. and M. Meredith. 1993. *The Merging of the Senses*. Cambridge, MA: The MIT Press.

Todd, N. 1992. "The dynamics of dynamics: a model of musical expression." *Journal of the Acoustical Society of America* 91(6): 3540–3550.

Todd, N. 1994. "The auditory "primal sketch": A multiscale model of rhythmic grouping." *Journal of New Music Research* 23(1): 25–70.

Todd, P. and D.G. Loy, eds. 1991. *Music and Connectionism*. Cambridge, MA: The MIT Press.

Toiviainen, P. 1996. "Timbre maps, auditory images, and distance metrics." *Journal of New Music Research* 25(1): 1–30.

Van Immerseel, L. and J. Martens. 1992. "Pitch and voiced/unvoiced determination with an auditory model." *Journal of the Acoustical Society of America* 91(6): 3511–3526.

Vertegaal, R. and T. Ungvary. 1995. "The sentograph: Input devices and the communication of bodily expression." In *Proc. Int. Computer Music Conference – ICMC 95*. Banff, Canada: ICMA.

Westhead, M.D. and A. Smaill. 1994. "Automatic characterization of musical style." In M. Smith, A. Smaill, and G.A. Wiggins, eds. *Music Education: An Artificial Intelligence Approach*. Berlin: Springer-Verlag, pp. 157–170.

Widmer, G. 1992. "Qualitative perception modeling and intelligent muscial learning." *Computer Music Journal* 16(2): 51–68.

Wiggins, G., E. Miranda, A. Smaill, and M. Harris. 1993. "A framework for the evaluation of music representation systems." *Computer Music Journal* 17(3): 31–42.

Winkler, T. 1995. "Making motion musical: Gesture mapping strategies for interactive computer music." In *Proc. Int. Computer Music Conference – ICMC 95*. Banff, Canada: ICMA.

Woods, W. and J. Schmolze. 1992. "The KL-ONE family." *Computers Mathematical Applications* 23(2–5): 133–177.

Part IV

**Composition
and musical signal
processing**

Part IV

Overview

Curtis Roads

Before 1988, the idea of the affordable audio media computer was still a dream. Microprocessors were slow, quality audio converters were expensive, and audio software was nonexistent. Computer sound processing meant working in laboratory environments and programming in arcane music languages. Interactive editors were available only to a handful. Operations such as convolution, spectrum editing, sound granulation, and spatialization were exotic procedures practiced by specialists in research institutions. Today all this has changed. In a short period of time, digital sound transformation has moved from a fledgling technology to a sophisticated artform. Techniques that were considered experimental a few years ago have been built into inexpensive synthesizers or effects processors, or codified into documented personal computer applications that can be learned quickly.

At the same time, musical imagination has expanded to the point that our composing universe has become what Varèse called the domain of *organized sound*. This sweeping vision, coupled with the sheer number of technical possibilities available, poses problems for musicians trained within the confines of a traditional model of composition. They may fail to comprehend the change that has taken place, importing restrictions of a bygone era into a world where they no longer apply. Just as composers of the past participated in the development of new instruments, and took into account the properties of the instruments for which they composed, so composers of today must take an active interest in the growing possibilities in the electronic medium. This demands an ongoing education; even informed composers struggle to keep pace with rapidly-evolving technical developments.

If much of this book is a celebration of how far the field has progressed since the early years of computer music, Chapter 11, written by a veteran and prolific composer of both instrumental and electronic works, shows us how far we have to go in bringing the musician's interface up to the level of the composer. Synthesis and signal processing techniques have made obvious advances, but it is more difficult to see a direct line of progress in notations and interfaces. Giancarlo Sica's chapter points out the problems remaining, but also traces some possible paths towards their resolution. These take the form of hierarchical languages for algorithmic composition and innovative physical controllers—the instruments stroked, plucked, and blown by musicians in performance.

Sound waves convolve all around us. Yet digital convolution remains a rare specialty to many, perhaps due to lack of information. The goal of Chapter 12 is to introduce the universe of sound transformations made possible by convolution in order to further encourage the creative use of this powerful technique.

The interpreter has been around as long as electronic instruments have existed, from Clara Rockmore and her Theremin, to Oskar Sala and his Mixtur-Trautonium, to Wendy Carlos and her Moog and Synergy synthesizers. But the interpreter that Alvise Vidolin discusses in Chapter 13 is not simply an instrumentalist in the traditional sense. The interpreter he speaks of does not play a single instrument but rather configures, programs, and performs on an array of equipment in order to transform a composer's abstract concepts into a practical realization. The keyword that defines this new role is collaboration.

Vidolin observes that the concept of the *note*—the pillar of music for many centuries—is more and more replaced by the more general notion of *sound event,* allowing for complicated sonic morphologies and noise materials. Moreover, the concept of the event is placed on an equal footing with that of *process,* in that a score is no longer defined as merely a succession of events, but also by transformations effectuated by signal processing techniques.

11

Notations and interfaces for musical signal processing

Giancarlo Sica

The computer has been applied to musical tasks for over four decades, but with different degrees of success depending on the problem to which it is assigned. Highly sophisticated sound synthesis architectures and software environments are the undeniable achievements of computer science. Progress in applied digital signal processing has also been varied and considerable. By contrast, an efficient multilevel representation of musical signals still remains an unresolved issue. Many aspects of music representation continue to be debated or remain obscure. High-level representations of music have tended to be rather neglected.

Many researchers and composers still operate with virtual machine languages such as Music V and its many descendents (Mathews 1969). These languages were created as tools for developing sound synthesis techniques, and not for composition of high-level musical structure. Their awkwardness in handling the structural abstractions used in musical composition (hierarchical phrases, for example) is no secret. Thus there is a need to examine questions of form, notation, and interfaces from the composer's point of view, which is the goal of this chapter. In particular, this chapter examines the central problems in the representation of musical signals on computers, with a special focus on questions of music notation and the musician's interface. Without presuming to have exhausted these themes, we explore each topic and highlight cases that seem most significant. Our goal is to make more clear the difficulties that a composer confronts when realizing a computer-based composition and to suggest approaches that could make music interfaces more efficient.

Form, process, algorithm

One of the basic problems that has motivated musical researchers of our century, from Heinrich Schenker onwards, has been the definition of the concept of *form*. This has been attempted via the mechanisms of musical analysis and the erection of countless paradigms developed to corroborate the validity of the proposed theories. In the 1940s, Arnold Schoenberg wrote: "The term form means that the piece is 'organized', that it is constituted by elements operating like a living organism... The essential and necessary requirements to the creation of an understandable form are logic and coherence: the presentation, the development and the reciprocal links of ideas have to base themselves on internal connections, and the ideas have to be differentiated on the ground of their weight and function" (Schoenberg 1969).

Through a variety of formalisms, such as set theories, computational models, stochastic processes, Chomsky's (1956) *grammars*, and Berry's (1976) *structures,* many music researchers have emphasized the structured aspects of musical language in all its modalities and compositional expressions. Thus if we wish to create a parallel between the concepts of form and process we can quote that "A process can be compared to the time evolution of a system, that is, the evolution of the entities in an ordered set (physical or logical) related among them" (Haus 1984). Here we find the basic principles of form expressed by Schoenberg and other composers. On the basis of merely these criteria, a compositional form and a computational process would seem to differ only in terms of their implementations; in reality the problem of musical composition has to be defined less simplistically.

Let us assume that a composition can be compared to a process—a structure realized by a set of rules. But it is also the product of a *knowledge base.* A knowledge base is an unordered collection of descriptions of objects, relationships among them, facts, and situations of various kinds. The way these descriptions and relations are applied is quite free, and in any case is more flexible than the frozen logic that we commonly call an algorithm. Musical form is not an "unchangeable mold," but rather a "basic layout" that every composer adapts according to their aesthetic vision. An algorithm that implements such a basic layout will necessarily have to allow for *user-defined rules,* allowing composers to define their own forms, or to make changes in existing ones.

In the next section we explore some programs (in a MIDI environment) in order to evaluate how they let composers design and manipulate musical structures. Our goal is to see whether these systems could serve as general compositional tools.

List-driven and event-driven languages

Various programs support the possibility of creating and handling musical structures by means of *modules* with alphanumerical or graphical input. To clearly analyze these programs, we have to define two kinds of languages, which we call *list-driven* and *event-driven*. List-driven programs work by means of a predefined *event list,* in which opcodes and their arguments generate or process musical events. The values in these event lists have been first stipulated by the composer in a more-or-less precise way. According to this operational philosophy, composers can design their event list to exactly obtain what they desire. On the other hand, such a methodology does not permit real-time interaction, but this is a choice of the composer.

Event-driven (or performance-driven) programs do not require a prestored musical representation. Rather, they are based around processing algorithms that manipulate the data streaming in to their inputs. That is, the system's behavior (and its output) is determined by the response of the preprogrammed processing elements, triggered by its data inputs.

In this way, by means of an adequate interface, a composer (or performer) can develop a real-time performance, giving more priority to gestural control with less structural rigidity in the performance. Later in this chapter we study the interface directly, keeping in mind that an "interface" can be either a piece of hardware or a software module.

In order to clarify the presentation, we demonstrate two MIDI environment programs: Opcode Max, an *event-driven* program, and Tonality Systems' Symbolic Composer, a *list-driven* program. This distinction between list and event-driven programs is only an initial step in order to group programs that follow a certain philosophy. In fact, as we can show later, Max can also use preprogrammed lists in conjunction with real-time data, while Symbolic Composer can process any signal (self-generated or imported from other programs).

Now we begin to navigate between the two programs by means of some examples. The first of these has been devised by the author using the Opcode

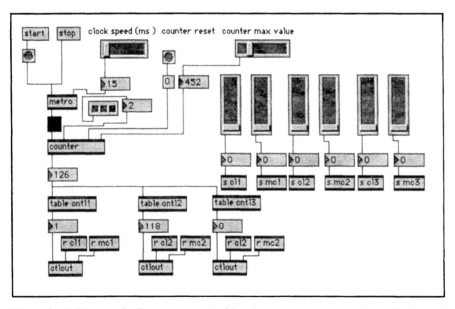

Figure 1. A Max patch. Boxes represent either data or operations on data. The flow of control runs, in general, from top to bottom.

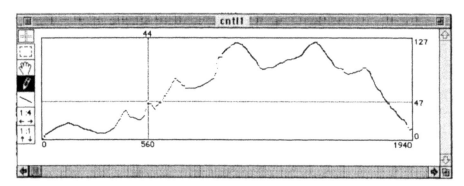

Figure 2. Max table object, graphical representation.

Max program. Figure 1 shows a typical Max *patch,* containing modules defining a virtual instrument. The purpose of this patch is to scan MIDI controllers values by means of a programmable counter of three tables. A Max *table* is a two-dimensional data representation: on the x axis there are the addresses of the real-time stored values, and y axis indicates their programmable range, as we can see in Figure 2.

The size of the *cntl* table has been established by means of the dialog box shown in Figure 3.

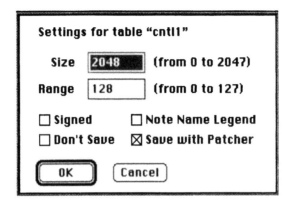

Figure 3. Table settings dialog box.

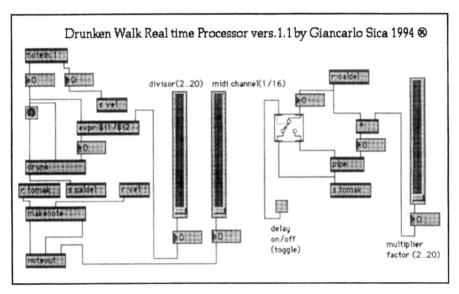

Figure 4. Drunken Walk Real Time Processor, a Max patch for control from an external MIDI input device.

Max lets musicians manage composition data either using graphical virtual controllers such as sliders, knobs, push buttons and so on (as displayed in Figure 1), or using an external MIDI command controller, (such a keyboard) as shown in Figure 4.

Here, data coming in from a keyboard are received by the Max module **notein**, and then further processed by means of the modules **pipe**, that generates a programmable delay, and **drunk**, that applies a random walk process to the pitch and duration information, and whose control parameter ranges can be managed with virtual slider objects. Obviously, other MIDI controllers can be easily used, such as physical potentiometers or a data glove interface.

The Max object **table** can handle a large amount of data. Visually, one sees a global view. When used to represent pitch data it it is not easy for a human being to read the data in a **table** object precisely. A better use of it could be as a *tendency path* for manipulation of large or small variations of control data (as, for instance, pitch shifting and so on).

On the other hand, Symbolic Composer's approach is much different. Not by chance, the developer's choice for this software environment has fallen on Common Lisp, a list-based language. (For further information on Symbolic Composer, see the review in *Computer Music Journal*, Summer 1994, pp. 107–111.) Here real-time processing has to be forgotten, one must work in in deferred time, as the venerable Csound language has taught us. Users edit and compile a program to obtain a MIDI file that can be played later with a sequencer program. The most important strength of Symbolic Composer (S-Com) is that we can both generate and/or process any kind of signal: to obtain this result, we have to well keep in mind the two basic concepts that are S-Com's framework: *mapping* and *conversion*.

Before we enter into these topics, however, we have to introduce the Lisp programming language itself. We begin with the lowest-level unit, the *atom*. Atoms are string of characters beginning with a letter, digit, or a special character other than a left "(" or right ")" parenthesis. Here are some atoms:

```
a f edo hero 2048 composer heaven
```

Lists look like this:

```
(m n)
(rhytm3 rhytm4 rhytm5)
(60 62 64 66 68 70)
(c d e f# g# a#)
```

that is, lists are collections of atoms surrounded by parenthesis.

To complete our brief introduction to Lisp, we have to mention the basic function setq. The function of setq is to create a *variable*. The *mapping* concept consists of a one-to-one processing connection between two lists. The first, called *input list,* is *mapped* onto the *second list*. The first is basically a *data list,* while the latter is the *processing list*. After the *mapping* operation, we obtain a *third list* that is the result of the process. The exciting thing is that if we change the *processing list* without altering the *input list,* we obtain a new sequence whose sounds are quite different. In any case, the internal structure organization of the *input list* will be preserved. We will see this *mapping* action at work later in the chapter.

The *conversion* concept is related to the transforming one representation into another without loss of meaning in the data (for instance, converting a symbol pattern into a numerical pattern and vice versa). The large number of built-in S-Com functions allow us of generating, processing, analyzing and reprocessing any kind of data, following the basic concepts above defined.

Now we demonstrate the high-abstraction level handling capabilities of S-Com by working with complex structures such as formal grammars, rewriting rules, and Lindenmayer systems, or L-Systems for short. (For an introduction to the topic of musical grammars see Roads (1985a).) In the simplest L-systems class, that is, *deterministic* and *context-free,* the rewriting rule:

$$a \to acb$$

means that the letter *a* has to be replaced by the string *acb*: also, the rule:

$$b \to a$$

means that the letter *b* has to be replaced by letter *a*, and:

$$c \to acba$$

means that the letter *c* has to be replaced by the string *acba*. The rewriting process starts from a initial, special string called the *axiom*. In our example, we assume that this axiom is the single letter *b*. In the first step of rewriting, the axiom *b* is replaced by *a*, following the rule $b \to a$.

In the second step *a* is replaced by *ab* by means of the rule $a \to ab$. The word *ab* consists of two letters: they are simultaneously replaced in the third step from the string *aba*, because *a* is replaced by *ab* and *b* by *a*, and so on, as shown in Figure 5.

A more complex and formally correct example stipulates that the the Greek letter ω represents the axiom, and the letters from p1 to p3 represent the production rules:

$$\omega : b$$
$$\text{p1} : b \to a$$
$$\text{p2} : a \to acb$$
$$\text{p3} : c \to acba$$

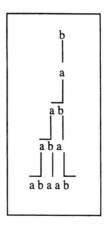

Figure 5. Derivation of terminal string by rewriting rules.

In short, starting from the axiom, the following sequence of words is generated:

$$b$$
$$a$$
$$acb$$
$$acbacbaa$$

and so forth.

Finally, we can see how we can obtain this process using only the following few S-Com instructions:

```
(initdef)

(defsym b 'a)
(defsym a '(a c b))
(defsym c '(a c b a))

(setq alpha)
(gen-lsystem b 3)
)

(listdef b 3)

;**** comments *****

; in alpha:
```

```
;result --> b
;result --> a
;result --> acb
;result --> acbacbaa
```

Here is a short explanation of the code. Function (initdef) initializes the symbol rewriting system. Function (defsym) defines a recursive rewriting rule. Function (gen-lsystem), whose syntax is [axiom depth valid-symbols] rewrites axiom at the depth depth, transforms it into a symbol, preserves only valid-symbols (in this example, all), and returns the new list. Comments aside, we need few S-Com code lines to obtain all that we want. And this is only the beginning.

A more complex way to manipulate L-systems has given by generating axial trees by means of strings with brackets, that allow us to delimit a branch. (For a fascinating introduction to L-systems and other growing simulation systems, we recommend *The Algorithmic Beauty of Plants* by Prusinkiewicz and Lindenmayer, published by Springer-Verlag.) The syntax is the following:

The symbol < pushes the current state onto a pushdown stack.

The symbol > pops a state from the stack and make it the current state.

The symbol + adds transposed value by 1.

The symbol − subtracts transposed value by 1.

We can generate a whole complex structure using only a root symbol. In the following graphic example, we have chosen the letter f, as shown in Figure 6. The data flow of the structure gives a taste of the power of this generative algorithm.

Figure 7 presents its implementation in S-Com. This L-system generates the following output, stored in the beta variable:

```
(f g e d e f g e g h f e f g h f e f d c d e f d d e c b c
d e c e f d c d e f d f g e d e f g e g h f e f g h f e f d
c d e f d)
```

The root symbol f has been modified only by means of stack operators (< > + −) in conjunction with the previously-mentioned rewriting rules.

Figure 7 is a complete example in S-Com. It yields as final output a standard MIDI file that we can play with any MIDI-controlled synthesizer. What we can

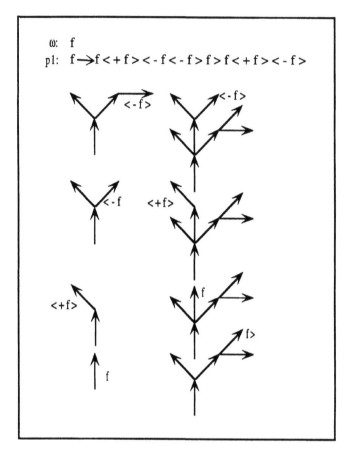

Figure 6. L-systems tree structure.

deduce from this quick exploration of just one of S-Com's capabilities? A list-driven environment lets musicians explore compositional structures normally forbidden to composers. It offers a way to hierarchically organize and elaborate raw materials into complete compositional architectures.

Our first question "Do these programs begin to offer to the composer some real compositional tools?" yields a positive response. Specifically, they provide interesting ways to explore the musical capabilities of event-driven and list-driven programs. They introduce musicians to different ways to represent and notate their compositions. At the same time, keep in mind that these possibilities remain within the well-known limits of the MIDI protocol. A more advanced use of these programs is possible, however. Depending on the configuration, each offers interesting possibilities of interfacing with the world of programmable digital music synthesis.

```
(initdef)

(defsym f '(f < + f > < - f < - f > f > f < + f > < - f >))
(defsym - '-)
(defsym + '+)
(defsym < '<)
(defsym > '>)

(setq alpha
(gen-rewrite f 2))

; alpha:
;(f < + f > < - f < - f > f > f < + f > < - f >
;< + f < + f > < - f < - f > f > f < + f > < - f > >
;< - f < + f > < - f < - f > f > f < + f > < - f >
;< - f < + f > < - f < - f > f > f < + f > < - f > >
;f < + f > < - f < - f > f > f < + f > < - f > >
;f < + f > < - f < - f > f > f < + f > < - f >
;< + f < + f > < - f < - f > f > f < + f > < - f > >
;< - f < + f > < - f < - f > f > f < + f > < - f > >)

(setq beta
(gen-lsystem f 2' (f < > + -)))

(def-instrument-symbol
    instr1 beta)

(def-instrument-length
    instr1
      (setq dur
          (symbol-to-vector  20 100  beta)))

(def-instrument-velocity
    instr1
      (setq vel
          (symbol-to-velocity 40 110 3 beta)))

(def-instrument-channel
  instr1 1)

(setq tons (activate-tonality (overtone c 4)))

(compile-song "ccl;Output:" 4\/4 "L-system A"

; BARS                   |---|---|---|---|

changes tons         ". "
instr1    changes "----------------------------------------")
```

Figure 7. L-systems implemented in S-Com Lisp.

The notation problem

The question of an appropriate computer-based music notation remains a difficult one. In the most general sense, to represent means "describing by means of signs and symbols." In our case, a symbol is a graphical sign whose interpretation is bound to a convention. Obviously, common musical notation (CMN) is also included in these definitions, but its inadequacy in handling many aspects of contemporary music (not to mention electronic and computer music) is well known. Especially in the twentieth century there have been many attempts by composers to devise personal representations of their work, but these modifications have not had a continuing impact, because the basis of traditional musical pedagogy and performance depends on CMN.

What has really changed, from the seventeenth century century until today, is the attitude assumed by the composer in relation to the score and the performer. During the Middle Ages and the Renaissance, musical notation was only a kind of schematic layout that the performer's active interpretation had to transform in performance. From the seventeenth century onwards the increasing definitions of new symbols indicated a growing rigidity of the composer towards the performer. Notation became more and more precise, and performance instructions became more detailed and specific. By the mid-twentieth century, it was not uncommon to see some sort of comment applied to every note in a score in an attempt to control the sonic continuum in all aspects. But even extreme examples of notational complexity (witness the current fashion of hypercomplex scores) do not result in more precise or repeatable performances. This is because CMN itself is ambiguous and inherently subjective. What is the difference in decibels between *mezzoforte* and *pianoforte*, for example? CMN cannot be realized precisely because of natural human inaccuracies.

By the late 1950s experiments with computer-generated sound proved that one could specify individual sonic events with ultrafine resolution, stipulating—to a numerical precision of several decimal places—sound parameters such as pitch, duration, spectral content, amplitude envelope, and spatial position. Paradoxically, these extended possibilities of definition, control, and processing of the single event caused difficulties in representing globally the compositional process in a clear manner. Indeed, global representations were entirely neglected in favor of hierarchically flat lists of numbers representing individual note events, as in languages such as Music V and its imitations. These languages allow great precision in the local definition of a sonic event, but on the contrary are practically unreadable in a global level. By contrast, CMN allows us to scan the overall shape of a composition at a glance.

There have been various attempts at using computer-graphics representations that have an aesthetically interesting form. But there is always the problem of global versus local representation: that is, if we want to examine the single event, we lose the global view. One exception is Xenakis's UPIC synthesis system (Xenakis 1992). Although this instrument does represent music on multiple time scales, it does not attempt to provide a complete solution to the problem of synthesis and signal processing.

Common music notation provides a split-level view of a composition, at least for some styles of occidental music. That is, it offers a good global representation and an fair local representation that musicians consider an acceptable compromise. After all, the scores developed with such a system are addressed to subjective human beings, and not to precise electronic machines.

Keeping in mind these observations, we will try to trace a map of seven problems related to notation of electronic music.

1. Notational ambiguity (hidden or intrinsic elements).

2. Representation of micro- and macro-structures.

3. Representation of spatial distribution.

4. Representation of musical time.

5. Representation of timbre.

6. The creation and definition of new symbols. Iconic or symbolic?

7. Readibility.

Notational ambiguity

Ambiguity is endemic to many symbolic representations since the interpretation of these symbols is often highly subjective. As we have already pointed out, a trivial example is that of the interpretation of a range of dynamical levels related to CMN, such as those defined by the symbols p, mf, f, and so on. What specific amplitude can be ascribed to mf? In the temporal domain, what quantified variation will take place when in an *andante* passage we encounter the term *accelerando*?

These ambiguities in CMN were acceptable in the past since they constituted a situation that de facto was transformed to de jure in performance. In the twentieth century the standard has not adapted well to the new electronic instruments. For many people these ambiguities in notation represent a degree of musical freedom that should be retained. On the other hand, it is one of the major obstacles to the trend toward musical determinism by many composers.

The musical determinism of the 1950s and 1960s was dictated by the philoso-phies of structuralism and serialism. Certain graphical representations of elec-tronic and acoustic musical scores, in spite of their geometrical precision, suf-fered, perhaps even more than CMN, from this "interpretative randomness". This is justified in some cases by a sort of "poetry of the indeterminate" (as in Cage's and Nono's music), while in other situations it happens because the amount of control parameters cannot be really represented on a single diagram without reaching an enormous complexity. (See, for example, *Pithoprakta* for string orchestra by Iannis Xenakis, which exists in both graphic and CMN score forms.) We would point out that we have not assumed a critical position towards these philosophies of representation, but we feel the necessity of highlighting the difficulties regarding the readability and the intepretation of the score, in both macro- and microstructural environments. We dissect some of these points in the next section.

Macro- and microstructure

A flexible representation must handle both micro- and macrostructures. What do we mean by "structure"? In a broad sense, this term is a synonym of "process" and "form". By extension, microstructure is a synonym of a basic element in a logical relationship with other elements on the same time scale, while macrostructure is synonym of a superset that includes many of these elements. Let us to define these lemmas more accurately. We will try to do this by means of a simple Csound example based on the technique of *asynchronous granular synthesis* (Roads 1985b, 1991). The synthesis orchestra is listed below. Semicolons denote comments.

```
sr = 44100          ;sampling rate
kr = 22050          ;control rate
ksmps = 2
nchnls = 1          ;monaural

instr 10                      ;begin instrument definition
iamp = ampdb(p4)              ;read amplitude in decibels
iper1 = p5                    ;sine frequency expressed in
                               terms of a period in ms
icps1 = (1/iper1)*1000        ;period-to-frequency conver-
                               sion of 'iper1'
```

```
      iper2 = p6                    ;'gaussian-like' envelope
                                     duration expressed in ms
      icps2 = (1/iper2)*1000        ;period-to-frequency conver-
                                     sion of 'iper2'

      ilen1 = p7
      ilen2 = p8
      ifuntab1 = p9
      ifuntab2 = p10
      andx phasor icps1
      kndx phasor icps2
      a1 table andx*ilen1,ifuntab1
      k1 table kndx*ilen2,ifuntab2
      k2 = iamp*k1
      a1 = a1*k2
      display andx,p3               ;display the signals
      display kndx,p3
      display a1,p3
      out a1                        ;write the samples to the
                                     output file

      endin
```

In the Csound environment, this list represents a *virtual instrument description* in which are specified all the operations needed to implement a particular sound synthesis algorithm. Here one specifies the signal generators and processors that emit a particular type of sonic microstructure. In the following score file we specify the temporal event structure and also the list of parameter values to be assigned to the generators defined in the orchestra file.

```
;AGS.sco
f1 0 4096 10 1                                    ;sine waveform
f3 0 4096 10 1 0 .2 .5 .7 .8 .7 .5 .2             ;a kind of
                                                   formant
f2 0 4096 8 0.000000 2080 1.000000 2016  0.000000 ;gaussian-
                                                   like envelope
```

;p1	p2	p3	p4	p5	p6	p7	p8	p9	p10
;instr	start	dur	amp	iper1	iper2	ilen1	ilen2	iftab1	iftab2
i10	0	0.1	85	1	100	4096	4096	1	2
i10	0.2	0.1	85	3	100	4096	4096	3	2
i10	0.3	0.1	85	2	100	4096	4096	1	2
i10	0.4	0.1	85	4	100	4096	4096	3	2
i10	0.6	0.1	85	6	100	4096	4096	1	2
i10	0.8	0.1	85	1	100	4096	4096	3	2
i10	1.0	0.2	85	10	100	4096	4096	1	2
i10	1.4	0.2	85	5	100	4096	4096	3	2
e									

Figure 8 shows a time-domain view of the sound file produced by this score. Here we observe a microstructure made up of fundamental sonic particles called *grains*. In this technique the pitch, amplitude, spectrum, duration, and spatial distribution have to be specified for each event, which mandates a high-level control mechanism in order to drive such a great amount of data. An advantage of the granular technique is that it constitutes an elegant system to create a well-defined hierarchy between microstructure and macrostructure.

Now we turn to problems involved in representing the musical parameters of space, timbre, and time.

Representation of spatial position

Spatial projection changes dramatically the musical "weight" of sounds. Yet the spatial projection of sound is an often neglected representation problem, perhaps because the efficient control of space has always been quite complicated. The hardware required for real-time spatial projection is still expensive and complex. Only a few synthesis languages offer primitives for spatial distribution with their modules. Csound, for example, has instructions such as **out, outs, outq**, and

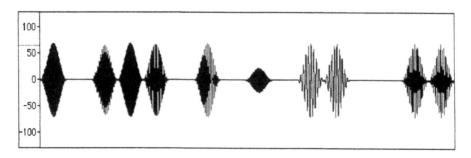

Figure 8. Time-domain view of granular synthesis microstructure.

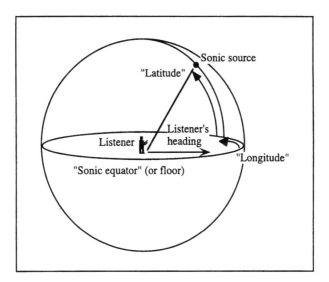

Figure 9. A picture of a virtual ambience for sound sources in three-dimensional space.

pan, that let one control a simple spatial trajectory of up to four channels of panning. But spatial projection is more complex than these primitives would imply. Indeed, some composers spatialize their compositions by associating a specific location to each sound source, by means of a *virtual ambience* as shown in Figure 9.

The sonic source location(s) of a single loudspeaker or of a loudspeaker array has been determined by means of geographical coordinates of latitude and longitude (expressed by degrees), where our "Greenwich meridian" is represented by the listener's head. The composer should be able to define these acoustical paths by means of graphical trajectories.

If we imagine a spherical loudspeaker array, it would not be difficult to imagine how fascinating an experience it could be to locate single streams or clouds of grains in a precise acoustical space! Here, effects like *cloud evaporation* could be implemented also as spatial effects. The problem of building an appropriate spatial projection system for concert use remains expensive and technically complex. We can only hope that affordable devices are developed in the future, and that these will offer programmability and versatility, thus allowing composers to create their own spatial distributions.

Representation of musical time

The question of representing both global and local time remains an unresolved issue. For example, in certain graphical scores one notices such a high density of points that it is impossible to distinguish them individually. These dense sonic masses are comprised of events having a very short duration. Their definition in detail would require another scale of representation. A similar situation can occur in common music notation, where the solution is to not try to represent the entire process on a single sheet but to subdivide it over several pages and parts. They key is the subdivision inherent in music notation. The global score is subdivided into individual pages and parts, pages are subdivided in measures, and measures are divided into beats. This objective of a hierarchy of time scales, capturing both global and local time, must also be reached in representations for computer music. This observation should underline the necessity of defining a different symbology than the note lists and sequences currently in use today. A first step in this direction is seen in the UPIC system, which offers the possibility of defining graphical pages whose synthesized playback duration can vary from 6 ms to two hours.

Representation of timbre

The representation of timbre—spectrum, envelope, and articulation—is certainly one of the most complex problems in computer music. If we examine the evolution of music notation we see that from the seventeenth century onwards composers have added special markings and Italian terms in order to specify aspects of timbre and performance articulation. On a violin, for example, one notes the string to play, the bow stroke (up or down), the bow *alla punta* (on the tip), on the keyboard, *staccato, martellato, vibrato,* and so on. These additional notation elements have been universally accepted in the tradition of performing practice. The situation for virtual instruments, defined in software, is completely different. Here the control parameters must be rigorously specified on an event-by-event basis. In this environment a universal notation does not exist for controlling the timbre of a given instrument.

Graphic functions are often employed, but there is no common standard for these functions. And the problem still remains that graphical representations may give only an approximate idea of the synthesis process, while a deeper analysis of the synthesis instrument is often necessary in order to understand the actual timbral evolution it generates.

A concrete example of what we are saying can be shown in the Csound language. Figure 10 presents an instrument in which an **oscili** unit is amplitude modulating another **oscili** unit. We use a function that controls the *modulation index* (the overall amplitude of the modulating oscillator) by means of a **linseg** unit, whose parameters are specified in the score file. We can visualize the

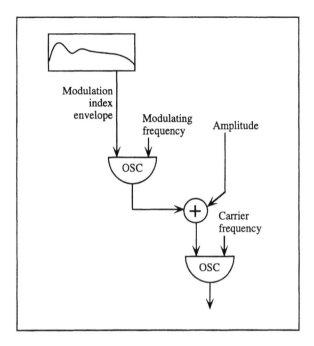

Figure 10. Example of an instrument patch diagram.

function curve by means of the **display** unit (during the compilation) to examine its overall course but we lose the local meaning of the data, which we can see only by studying the score file itself.

In other cases, notably synthesis by physical models, it is the *combined* effect of a multitude of control parameters that determines what sound is produced. Looking at any one of these curves separately tells us little about what we may hear.

These represent just two cases among an endless catalog of examples of this problem. A general solution seems difficult at the present time because there are too many different philosophical and practical approaches to this representational issue, in many different programs.

Iconic or symbolic notation?

The question of iconic versus symbolic notation is a perennial one. Abstract symbolic representations are familiar from texts and mathematics. Iconic representations, on the other hand, have a strong point in that the symbol has a topological similarity between the signifier (the sign) and what it represents (Sebeok 1975). Various software packages typically have only an iconic representation,

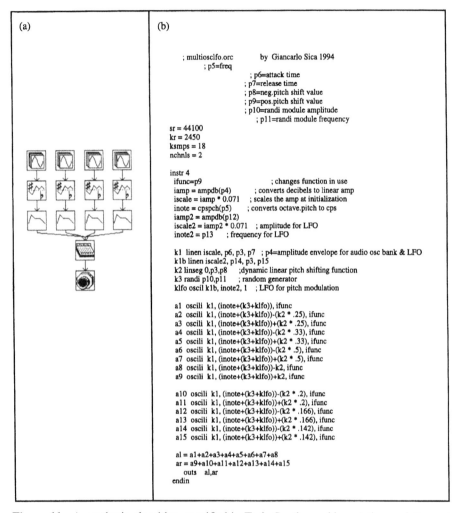

```
(a)                   (b)

                      ; multiosclfo.orc          by Giancarlo Sica 1994
                          ; p5=freq
                                           ; p6=attack time
                                        ; p7=release time
                                        ; p8=neg.pitch shift value
                                        ; p9=pos.pitch shift value
                                        ; p10=randi module amplitude
                                            ; p11=randi module frequency
                      sr = 44100
                      kr = 2450
                      ksmps = 18
                      nchnls = 2

                      instr 4
                        ifunc=p9                      ; changes function in use
                        iamp = ampdb(p4)       ; converts decibels to linear amp
                        iscale = iamp * 0.071  ; scales the amp at initialization
                        inote = cpspch(p5)     ; converts octave.pitch to cps
                        iamp2 = ampdb(p12)
                        iscale2 = iamp2 * 0.071   ; amplitude for LFO
                        inote2 = p13      ; frequency for LFO

                        k1  linen iscale, p6, p3, p7  ; p4=amplitude envelope for audio osc bank & LFO
                        k1b linen iscale2, p14, p3, p15
                        k2 linseg 0,p3,p8      ;dynamic linear pitch shifting function
                        k3 randi p10,p11      ; random generator
                        k1fo oscil k1b, inote2, 1  ; LFO for pitch modulation

                        a1  oscili k1, (inote+(k3+klfo)), ifunc
                        a2  oscili k1, (inote+(k3+klfo))-(k2 * .25), ifunc
                        a3  oscili k1, (inote+(k3+klfo))+(k2 * .25), ifunc
                        a4  oscili k1, (inote+(k3+klfo))-(k2 * .33), ifunc
                        a5  oscili k1, (inote+(k3+klfo))+(k2 * .33), ifunc
                        a6  oscili k1, (inote+(k3+klfo))-(k2 * .5), ifunc
                        a7  oscili k1, (inote+(k3+klfo))+(k2 * .5), ifunc
                        a8  oscili k1, (inote+(k3+klfo))-k2, ifunc
                        a9  oscili k1, (inote+(k3+klfo))+k2, ifunc

                        a10 oscili k1, (inote+(k3+klfo))-(k2 * .2), ifunc
                        a11 oscili k1, (inote+(k3+klfo))+(k2 * .2), ifunc
                        a12 oscili k1, (inote+(k3+klfo))-(k2 * .166), ifunc
                        a13 oscili k1, (inote+(k3+klfo))+(k2 * .166), ifunc
                        a14 oscili k1, (inote+(k3+klfo))-(k2 * .142), ifunc
                        a15 oscili k1, (inote+(k3+klfo))+(k2 * .142), ifunc

                        al = a1+a2+a3+a4+a5+a6+a7+a8
                        ar = a9+a10+a11+a12+a13+a14+a15
                          outs  al,ar
                      endin
```

Figure 11. A synthesis algorithm specified in TurboSynth graphic notation and Csound alphanumeric notation.

or mixed iconic-simbolic representation, but there is room for a great deal of improvement in making the music notation generated by music sequencers, for example, more readable.

An example that highlights the problem can be easily furnished using the language Csound and the program TurboSynth by Digidesign. TurboSynth is an iconic DSP environment designed for building virtual synthesis instruments. As shown in Figure 11, a direct comparison between them is impossible. Csound lets one specify an instrument in fine numerical precision. The instrument is driven by a alphanumeric score. TurboSynth, on the other hand, is more intuitive and easier to use, but does not allow us to play the instrument directly on the computer. The sounds generated by TurboSynth are meant to be transferred to a sampler where they are triggered by a performer or by MIDI note-on messages sent by a sequencer. What is needed, of course, is a program that is both easy to use, with graphical and MIDI controls, but that also allows the possibility of control via a score. The recent program SuperCollider by James McCartney goes in this direction.

Notation readability

With regards to new musical notation, we must underline the fact that notation must be easily legible, both in local and global ranges. This legibility must be independent of the type of representation used, and must preserve precision of information in both ranges. The problem of redundant alphanumeric data—well known to those whose have used Music V and its variants—should diminish through the use of graphic interfaces and algorithmic techniques. Ideally, representations must also be connected to performance gestures. This immediately raises the issue of the musician-machine interface, discussed next.

The interface problem

A limiting factor in the use of present computer systems is that of controlling the parameters of real-time synthesis, that is: pitch, duration, amplitude, spectrum, and spatial distribution, in a live performance. A musical performer must be able to control all aspects at the same time. This degree of control, while also preserving expressivity to the fullest extent, allows continuous mutations in the interpretation of a score. This is something that has been impossible to realize with computers until recently. These possibilities have been enabled by new "alternative" controllers coupled with sophisticated performance software.

Alternative controllers

Expressive control is not difficult for a virtuoso performer playing an acoustic instrument, or even an analog instrument. Speaking of the analog world, let us recall the touch-sensitive controllers of the Buchla Electric Music Boxes, not to mention of the expressivity of a magnificent instrument like the Theremin in the hands of a virtuoso like Clara Rockmore. (See *The Art of the Theremin,* Delos

D/CD 1014, available from Big Briar, Inc.) Robert Moog's factory still makes advanced controllers like the Theremin.

After many years with the keyboard-oriented MIDI protocol, we can only agree with the late Vladimir Ussachevsky, who wisely observed that the continuing use of keyboard controllers leads only to more sophisticated transistor organs. Fortunately a number of research centers and instrument manufacturers are making alternative controllers. One such instrument is the Radio Baton three-dimensional controller and its Conductor software, developed by Max Mathews and his colleagues at Stanford University. Mathews has pointed out that in western music a composition can be separated into two parts: the aspects fixed by composer (usually pitch) and the ones left to the expressive capabilities of the performer. He suggests that computers can perform the fixed parts established by the composer, while the performer should only be concerned with expressive parameters. With the Radio Baton, the computer plays the notes while the performer controls the onset time of each note, its timbre, loudness, and so on.

Robert Moog and John Eaton have also developed a *multiply touch-sensitive keyboard.* On every key are three different sensors that are able to recognize the following data:

1. The position of the finger compared to key length.
2. The position of the finger compared to key width.
3. The area of the finger contacting with the key surface.
4. How much the key is depressed.
5. The pressure amount after the key has totally depressed.

Such a keyboard presents a serious challenge to the control capabilities of a virtuoso.

Another interesting controller has been developed by the German company Doepfer. The MOGLI (Midi Output GLove Interface) generates MIDI events (such as note, pitch bending, velocity, modulation), as the hand moves in a three-dimensional space surrounded by sensors. The MOGLI is, however, difficult to use and requires practice and talent. But it seems to be an intelligent way to develop a controller. This instrument probably works best controlling just one MIDI parameter at time during performance.

Students researchers at the Massachusetts Institute of Technology have devised a set of "virtual gestural real-time controllers". The gestural data produced with these controllers are sent to a network of MacOS computers, each running a program that analyzes the input data and produces a musical result according to its own processing algorithm. Yet another alternative controller is Buchla's

Thunder device that has been adapted to gather data related to the position and pressure of the fingers in order control musical phrasing.

Our list of alternative controllers could go on, but there is a problematical aspect that we would like to point out: how can the composer notate these often subtle gestures in order to exactly reproduce them? Looking at a device like Buchla's Thunder, how can we find reference points that allow a performer to repeat a composition correctly every time? The answer could come from neural networks or from *learning instruments*. The network could follow the performer's gestures and, after a training time, it could learn the pitches played by the performer. But will such a gadget be precise and yet allow variations as would a nonlearning instrument?

Requirements of future musical interfaces

Based on current experiments, the next generation of musical interfaces must possess the following features:

- Flexibility to adapt to various situations furnished them from several different kind of sensors.
- Programmability of the feedback between the musician and the interface itself.
- The ability to generate graphical representations of the input process. For instance, if a performer generates a sequence of pitch data in a non-well-tempered tuning, the interface should be able to display the range and the steps among the pitches, in order to reproduce the performance with a high degree of precision.

Conclusions

Despite many heroic efforts, representations of musical form and process are inherently difficult to adapt to computer technology. During the forty years since the beginning of computer music history, researchers have been lost in a sea of representation criteria, modalities, and philosophies without finding definitive solutions of these problems. Because of the proliferation of idiosyncratic "personal representations" (some of which are marketed as more general solutions or packaged in the form of toolkits), the problem has grown larger in a negative sense. Perhaps the moment has finally arrived to develop a real high-level language that allows a musician to control—from a high level of abstraction—all aspects of musical signals, from both musical and technical perspectives.

References

Berry, W. 1976. *Structural Functions in Music.* Englewood Cliffs: Prentice Hall.

Chomsky, N. 1956. "Three models for the description of language." *IRE Transactions on Information Theory* 2(3): 113–124.

Haus, G. 1984. *Elementi di Informatica Musicale.* Milan: Ed. Jackson.

Lohner, H. 1986a. "The UPIC system: a user's report." *Computer Music Journal* 10(4): 42–49.

Lohner, H. 1986b. "Interview with Iannis Xenakis." *Computer Music Journal* 10(4): 50–55.

Mathews, M. 1969. *The Technology of Computer Music.* Cambridge, Massachusetts: The MIT Press.

Marino, G., J.-M. Raczinski, and M.-H. Serra. 1990. "The new UPIC system." In S. Arnold and G. Hair, eds. *Proceedings of the 1990 International Computer Music Conference.* San Francisco: International Computer Music Association, pp. 249–252.

Roads, C. 1985a. "Grammars as representations for music." In C. Roads and J. Strawn, eds. *Foundations of Computer Music.* Cambridge, Massachusetts: The MIT Press, pp. 403–442.

Roads, C. 1985b. "Granular synthesis of sound." In C. Roads and J. Strawn, eds. *Foundations of Computer Music.* Cambridge, Massachusetts: The MIT Press, pp. 145–159.

Roads, C. 1991. "Asynchronous granular synthesis." In G. De Poli, A. Piccialli, and C. Roads, eds. *Representations of Musical Signals.* Cambridge, Massachusetts: The MIT Press, pp. 143–185.

Schoenberg, A. 1969. *Elementi di Composizione Musicale.* Milan: Ed. Suvini-Zerboni.

Sebeok, T.A. 1975. "Six species of signs: some propositions and structures." *Semiotica* 13(3): 233–260.

Winston, P. and B. Horn. 1989. *LISP.* Third edition. Reading, Massachusetts: Addison-Wesley.

Xenakis, I. 1992. *Formalized Music.* Revised edition. New York: Pendragon Press.

12

Sound transformation by convolution

Curtis Roads

Since the invention of the vacuum tube, musicians have sought to transform sounds by electronic means (Bode 1984). In the 1950s, the invention of devices that could convert between the continuous-time (analog) and discrete-time (digital) domains opened up the vast potential of programmable signal processing (David, Mathews, and McDonald 1958). Today, ever-increasing processor speeds make it possible to realize previously exotic and computationally-intensive techniques on inexpensive personal computers. *Convolution* is one such technique (Rabiner and Gold 1975). A fundamental operation in signal processing, convolution "marries" two signals. It is also implicit in signal processing operations such as filtering, modulation, excitation/resonance modeling, cross-filtering, spatialization, and reverberation. By implementing these operations as convolutions, we can take them in new and interesting directions.

Convolution can destroy the temporal morphology of its input sounds. Thus in order to apply convolution effectively, musicians should have a full understanding of its sensitivities as well as its manifold possibilities. This chapter reviews the theory and presents the results of systematic experimentation with this technique. Throughout we offer practical guidelines for effective musical use of convolution.

We also present the results of new applications such as sound mapping from performed rhythms and convolutions with sonic grains and pulsars.

Status of convolution

The theory of convolution remains unknown to most musicians, yet to signal processing engineers it is a basic topic, a foundation stone of linear system theory. But modern signal processing textbooks present it tersely, reducing it to a handful of generalized mathematical clichés. The profound acoustical significance of convolution is rarely discussed (an exceptional text is Dolson and Boulanger 1985).

Listeners are familiar with the effects of convolution, even if they are not aware of its theory. Convolution is disguised under more familiar terms such as filtering, modulation, and reverberation. Recent software tools running on personal computers unbundle convolution, offering it as an explicit operation, and allowing any two sampled files to be convolved (MathWorks 1995; Bias 1996; Erbe 1995). Such tools provide a stable basis for musical exploration of the technique, and prompt a need for more universal understanding of its powers. We begin this teaching task here. Those already familiar with the theory of convolution may want to skip to the section "Musical significance of convolution." (See also Roads 1996.)

Impulse response and cross-synthesis

A filter is a very general concept (Rabiner *et al.* 1972). Virtually any system that accepts an input signal and emits an output is a filter. And convolution certainly is a filter. A good way to examine the effect of a filter is to see how it reacts to test signals. One of the most important test signals in signal processing is the *unit impulse*—an instantaneous burst of energy at maximum amplitude. In a digital system, the briefest possible signal lasts one sample period. This signal contains energy at all frequencies that can be represented at the given sampling frequency. The output signal generated by a filter that is fed a unit impulse is the *impulse response* (IR) of the filter. The IR corresponds to the system's *amplitude-versus-frequency response* (often abbreviated to "frequency response"). The IR and the frequency response contain the same information—the filter's response to the unit impulse—but plotted in different domains. That is, the IR is a time-domain representation, and the frequency response is a frequency-domain representation. The bridge between these domains is convolution. A filter convolves its impulse response with the input signal to produce the output signal.

The implications of convolution in music and audio engineering are immense. One can start from the measured IR of any audio-frequency system (microphone, instrument, loudspeaker, room, distortion, delay effect, filter, modulator, etc.); through convolution, one can impose the characteristics of this system on any audio signal.

This much is well understood in the engineering community. By generalizing the notion of impulse response, however, one arrives at quite another set of possibilities. Let us consider any sequence of samples as the impulse response of a hypothetical system. Now we arrive at a new and musically potent application of convolution: *cross-synthesis* by convolution of two arbitrary sound signals. In musical signal processing, the term cross-synthesis describes a number of different techniques that in some way combine the properties of two sounds into a single sound. This can involve shaping the spectrum, time, or spatial pattern of one sound by the other. We return to the subject of cross-synthesis later.

What precisely is convolution? The next section presents an intuitive review of the theory. Then we assess the musical significance of convolution and offer guidelines for effective musical use.

Review of convolution theory

To understand convolution, let us look at the simplest case: convolution of a signal a with a unit impulse, which we call $unit[n]$. A unit impulse is a digital sequence defined for any value of n. At time $n = 0$, $unit[n] = 1$, but for all other values of n, $unit[n] = 0$. The convolution of $a[n]$ with $unit[n]$ can be denoted as follows:

$$output[n] = a[n] * unit[n] = a[n].$$

Here the sign "$*$" signifies convolution. As Figure 1(a) shows, this results in a set of values for *output* that are the same as the original signal $a[n]$. Thus, convolution with the unit impulse is said to be an *identity operation* with respect to convolution, because any function convolved with $unit[n]$ leaves that function unchanged.

Convolution by scaled and delayed unit impulses

Two other simple cases of convolution tell us enough to predict what will happen at the sample level with any convolution. If we scale the amplitude of $unit[n]$

by a constant c, the operation can be written as follows:

$$output[n] = a[n] * (c \times unit[n]).$$

The result is simply:

$$output[n] = c \times a[n].$$

In other words, we obtain the identity of a, scaled by the constant c, as shown in Figure 1(b).

In the third case, we convolve signal a by a unit impulse that has been time-shifted by t samples. Now the impulse appears at sample $n - t$ instead of at $n = 0$. This can be expressed as follows:

$$output[n] = a[n] * unit[n - t].$$

The result of which is:

$$output[n] = a[n - t].$$

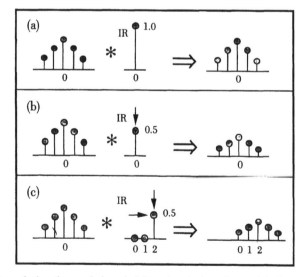

Figure 1. Convolution by scaled and delayed unit impulses. (a) Convolution with a unit impulse is an identity operation. (b) Convolution with a delayed impulse delays the output. (c) Convolution with a scaled and delayed impulse.

That is, *output* is identical to *a* except that it is time-shifted by the difference between *n* and *t*. Figure 1(c) shows a combination of scaling and time-shifting.

Putting together these three cases, we can view any sampled function as a sequence of scaled and delayed unit impulse functions. For example, the convolution of any signal *a* with another signal *b* that contains two impulses spaced widely apart results in a repetition or echo of *a* starting at the second impulse in *b* (Figure 2). When the impulses in *b* move closer together, the scaled repetitions start to overlap each other. Thus, to convolve an input sequence $a[n]$ with an arbitrary function $b[n]$, we place a copy of $b[n]$ at each point of $a[n]$, scaled by the value of $a[n]$ at that point. As Figure 3 shows, the convolution of *a* and *b* is the sum of these scaled and delayed functions. Clearly convolution is not the same as simple multiplication of two signals. The multiplication of a one signal *a* by another signal *b* means that each sample of *a* is multiplied by the corresponding sample in *b*. Thus:

$$output[1] = a[1] \times b[1]$$
$$output[2] = a[2] \times b[2]$$

etc.

By contrast, in convolution *each* sample of *a* is multiplied by *every* sample of *b*, creating an array of samples of length *b* for every sample of *a*. The convolution is the sum of these arrays. Compare convolution by the unit impulse (discussed previously) with multiplication by the unit impulse. In sharp contrast to convolution, the multiplication of *a* by the unit impulse $unit[n]$ results in all values of $output[n]$ being set to zero except for $output[0]$, where $unit[n]$ equals 1.

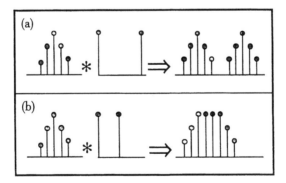

Figure 2. Echo and time-smearing induced by convolution. (a) A perceivable echo occurs when the impulses are greater than about 50 ms apart. (b) Time-smearing occurs when the pulses in the IR are so close as to cause copies of the input signal to overlap.

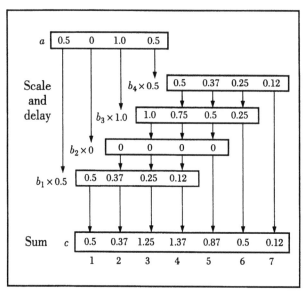

Figure 3. Direct convolution viewed as a sum of many delayed and scaled copies of signal b. The impulse response $a = \{0.5, 0, 1.0, 0.5\}$ scales and delays copies of $b = \{1.0, 0.75, 0.5, 0.25\}$. There are as many copies of b as there are values in a.

Mathematical definition of convolution

A mathematical definition of the convolution of two finite sequences of samples $a[n]$ and $b[n]$ of length N and M, respectively, is as follows:

$$a[n] * b[n] = output[n] = \sum_{m=0}^{N} a[m] \times b[n - m].$$

In effect, each sample of a serves as a weighting function for a delayed copy of b; these weighted "echoes" all add together. The conventional way to calculate this equation is to evaluate the sum for each value of m. This is *direct convolution*. The result of this method of convolution is usually rescaled (i.e., *normalized*) afterward.

Convolution lengthens its inputs. The length of the output sequence generated by direct convolution is:

$$\textbf{length}(output) = \textbf{length}(a) + \textbf{length}(b) - 1.$$

In the typical case of an audio filter (lowpass, highpass, bandpass, bandreject), a is an IR that is very short compared to the length of the b signal. (For a smooth rolloff lowpass or highpass filter, for example, the IR lasts less than a millisecond.) It does not, however, matter whether a or b is considered to be the impulse response, because convolution is commutative. That is, $a[n] * b[n] = b[n] * a[n]$.

The law of convolution

A fundamental law of signal processing is that the convolution of two waveforms is equivalent to the multiplication of their spectra. The dual also holds. That is, the multiplication of two waveforms is equal to the convolution of their spectra. Another way of stating this is as follows:

> *Convolution in the time domain is equal to multiplication in the frequency domain and vice versa.*

The law of convolution has profound implications. In particular, convolution of two audio signals is equivalent to filtering the spectrum of one sound by the spectrum of another sound. Inversely, multiplying two audio signals (i.e., performing *ring modulation*), is equal to convolving their spectra. Convolution of spectra means that each point in the discrete frequency spectrum of input a is convolved with every point in the spectrum of b. Convolution does not distinguish whether its input sequences represent samples or spectra. To the convolution algorithm they are both just discrete sequences.

Another implication of the law of convolution is that every time we reshape the envelope of a sound, we also convolve the spectrum of the envelope with the spectrum of the reshaped sound. In other words, every time-domain transformation results in a corresponding frequency-domain transformation, and vice versa.

Relationship of convolution to filtering

Convolution is directly related to filtering. An equation for a general *finite-impulse-response* (FIR) filter is as follows:

$$y[n] = (a_0 x[n]) \pm (a_1 x[n-1]) \pm \cdots \pm (a_m x[n-m]). \qquad (1)$$

We can think of the coefficients $a_0, a_1, \ldots, a_m$ as elements in an array $h(m)$, where each element in $h(m)$ is multiplied by the corresponding element in array

$x[n]$. With this in mind, equation (1) can be restated as a convolution:

$$y[n] = \sum_{m=0}^{N} h[m] \times x[n - m],$$

where m ranges over the length of x. Notice that the coefficients h play the role of the impulse response in the convolution equation. And indeed, the impulse response of an FIR filter can be derived directly from the value of its coefficients. Thus any FIR filter can be expressed as a convolution, and vice versa.

Fast and single-pulse convolution

Direct convolution is notoriously intensive computationally, requiring on the order of N^2 operations, where N is the length of the longest input sequence. Thus direct convolution is rarely used to implement narrow band filters or reverberators (both of which have long impulse responses) when more efficient methods suffice. Many practical applications of convolution employ a method called *fast convolution* (Stockham 1969). Fast convolution for long sequences takes advantage of the fact that the product of two N-point *fast Fourier transforms* (FFTs) is equal to the FFT of the convolution of two N-point sequences.

Fast convolution means that one can replace direct convolution by FFTs, which are dramatically quicker for large values of N. In particular, fast convolution takes on the order of $N \times \log_2(N)$ operations. Speedups begin to occur as soon as N exceeds 64 samples. Consider, for example, the direct convolution of a pair of two-second sounds sampled at 48 kHz. This requires on the order of $96,000^2$ or 9.2 billion operations. Fast convolution with the same two sounds requires less than 3.5 million operations, a speedup by a factor of about 2660. Put another way, a microprocessor that can perform a fast convolution of a pair of two-second sounds in real time would take 1 h and 18 min to calculate their direct convolution.

Aldo Piccialli applied the concept of *single-pulse* convolution to maximize the efficiency of a pitch-synchronous granular analysis/resynthesis system (De Poli and Piccialli 1991; see also Chapter 5). Single-pulse convolution is a slight-of-hand that takes advantage of the fact that the convolution of a signal x with a unit impulse is an identity operation. That is, the convolution of any finite-duration signal x with a series of impulses reduces to a series of additions of x. In Piccialli's system x was a grain template that imposed a timbre onto the pitch determined by the impulse train.

Real-time implementation of convolution

In the *block-transform implementation* of fast convolution, the spectrum multiplication occurs only after a block of input samples have been collected in memory and analyzed. Depending on the length of the input signals, this may involve a significant delay. Direct convolution has no such delay, but can require an enormous amount of computation. Fortunately for real-time applications where immediate output is needed, it is also possible to implement fast convolution in *sections,* that is, a few samples at a time. Sectioned and nonsectioned convolution generate equivalent results. Rabiner and Gold (1975), Kunt (1981), and Sorensen and Burrus (1993) present techniques for sectioned convolution with hints for real-time implementations. Gardner (1995) describes a novel technique that combines direct and sectioned convolution to eliminate processing delays.

Musical significance of convolution

A veritable catalog of sonic transformations emerge out of convolution: filtration, modulation, models of excitation/resonance, spatialization, and time-domain effects. Some of the most dramatic effects induced by convolution involve temporal and spatial transformations: attack smoothing, multiple echoes, room simulation, time smearing, spatial positioning, and reverberation. The type of effect achieved depends entirely on the nature of the input signals. Pure convolution has no control parameters.

The following sections spotlight each type of transformation. A dot in front of an indented section indicates a practical guideline.

Cross-filtering

One can implement any filter by convolving an input signal with the impulse response of the desired filter. In the usual type of FIR audio filter the IR is typically less than a few dozen samples in length. By generalizing the notion of impulse response to include signals of any length, we enter into the domain of *cross-filtering*: mapping the time-varying spectrum envelope of one sound onto another.

- If both signals are long in duration, the main effect of convolution is a spectrum alteration.

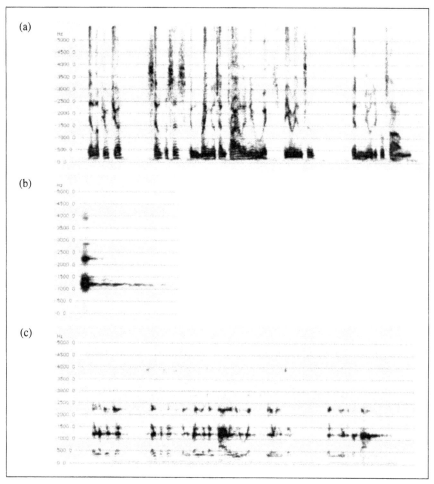

Figure 4. Spectrum filtering by convolution. (a) Male voice saying "In the future [pause] synthesis can bring us entirely new experiences [pause] in musical sound". (b) Tap of drumstick on woodblock. (c) Convolution of (a) with (b) results in the voice speaking through the sharply filtered spectrum of the woodblock with its three narrow formants.

Let us call two sources a and b and their corresponding analyzed spectra A and B. If we multiply each point in A with each corresponding point in B and then resynthesize the resulting spectrum, we obtain a time-domain waveform that is the convolution of a with b. Figures 4 and 5 demonstrate the spectrum-alteration effects of convolution of percussive sounds on speaking voices.

- If both sources are long duration and each has a strong pitch and one or both of the sources has a smooth attack, the result will contain both pitches and the intersection of their spectra.

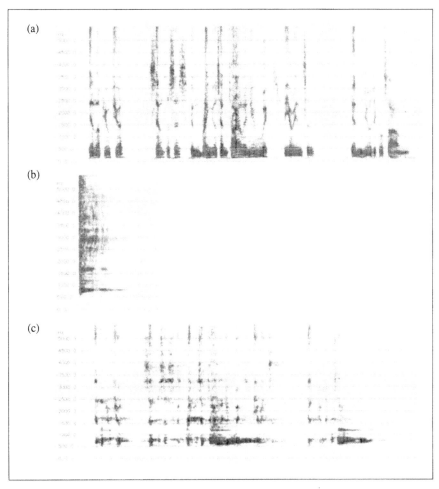

Figure 5. Using the same spoken phrase as in Figure 4, this time filtered by the twang of a plucked metal spring. (a) Male voice saying "In the future [pause] synthesis can bring us entirely new experiences [pause] in musical sound." (b) Twang of metal spring. (c) Convolution of (a) with (b) results in the voice speaking through the ascending pitched spectrum of the spring.

As another example, the convolution of two saxophone tones, each with a smooth attack, mixes their pitches, creating a sound like the two tones are being played simultaneously. Unlike simple mixing, however, the filtering effect in convolution accentuates metallic resonances that are common in both tones.

Convolution is particularly sensitive to the attack of its inputs.

- If either source has a smooth attack, the output will have a smooth attack.

Listening to the results of cross-filtering, one sometimes wishes to increase the presence of one signal at the expense of the other. Unfortunately, there is no straightforward way to adjust the "balance" of the two sources or to lessen the convolution effect. After the convolution is accomplished, however, one can mix some of the original sound with the convolved sound to deemphasize the effect.

Spatio-temporal transformations

Space-time transformations are among the most important effects induced by convolution. These include echo, time smearing, and reverberation.

Echoes
Any unit impulse in one of the inputs to the convolution results in a copy of the other signal. Thus if we convolve any sound with an IR consisting of two unit impulses spaced one second apart, the result is an echo of the first sound (Figure 2(a)).

- To create a multiple echo effect, convolve any sound with a series of impulses spaced at the desired delay times. For a decaying echo, lower the amplitude of each successive impulse.

Time-smearing
Figure 2(b) showed an example of "time-smearing," when the pulses in the IR are spaced close together, causing the convolved copies of the input sound to overlap. If, for example, the IR consists of a series of twenty impulses spaced 10 ms apart, and the input sound is 500 ms in duration, then multiple copies of the input sound overlap, blurring the attack and every other temporal landmark. Whenever the IR is anything other than a collection of widely-spaced impulses, then time-smearing alters the temporal morphology of the output signal.

Room simulation and reverberation
The IR of a room contains many impulses, corresponding to reflections off various surfaces of the room—its echo pattern. When such an IR is convolved with an arbitrary sound, the result is as if that sound had been played in that room, because it has been mapped into the room's echo pattern.

- If we convolve sound *a* with the IR of an acoustic space, and then mix this convolution with *a*, the result sounds like *a* has been placed in the acoustic space.

We hear reverberation in large churches, concert halls, and other spaces with high ceilings and reflective surfaces. Sounds emitted in these spaces are reinforced by thousands of closely-spaced echoes bouncing off the ceiling, walls, and floors. Many of these echoes arrive at our ears after reflecting off several surfaces, so we hear them after the original sound has reached our ears. The myriad echoes fuse in our ear into a lingering acoustical "halo" following the original sound.

From the point of view of convolution, a reverberator is nothing more than a particular type of filter with a long IR. Thus we can sample the IR of a reverberant space and then convolve that IR with an input signal. When the convolved sound is mixed with the original sound, the result sounds like the input signal has been played in the reverberant space.

Importance of mixing
For realistic spatial effects, it is essential to blend the output of the convolution with the original signal. In the parlance of reverberation, the convolved output is the *wet* (i.e., processed) signal, and the original signal is the *dry* (i.e., unprocessed) signal.

- It is typical to mix the wet signal down -15 dB or more with respect to the level of the dry signal.

Noise reverberation
When the peaks in the IR are longer than one sample, the repetitions are time-smeared. The combination of time-smearing and echo explains why an exponentially-decaying noise signal, which contains thousands of sharp peaks in its attack, results in reverberation effects when convolved with acoustically "dry" signals.

- If the amplitude envelope of a noise signal has a sharp attack and a fast exponential decay (Figure 6), the result of convolution resembles a natural reverberation envelope.
- To color this reverberation, one can filter the noise before or after convolving it.

Another type of effect, combining reverberation and time distortion, occurs when the noise is shaped by a slow logarithmic decay.

- If the noise has a slow logarithmic decay, the second sound appears to be suspended in time before the decay.

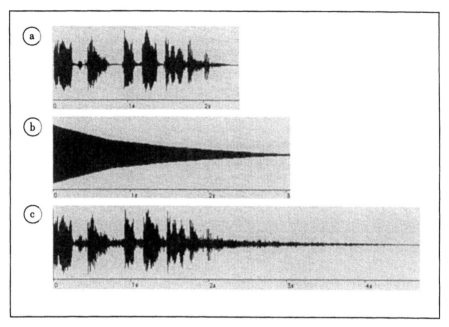

Figure 6. Synthetic reverberation. (a) Original signal. (b) Exponentially-decaying white noise. (c) Convolution of (a) and (b) results in a reverberation effect.

Modulation as convolution

Amplitude and *ring modulation* (AM and RM) both call for multiplication of time-domain waveforms. The law of convolution states that multiplication of two waveforms convolves their spectra. Hence, convolution accounts for the sidebands that result. Consider the examples in Figure 1, and imagine that instead of impulses in the time domain, convolution is working on line spectra in the frequency domain. The same rules apply—with the important difference that the arithmetic of complex numbers applies. The FFT, for example, generates a complex number for each spectrum component. Here the main point is that this representation is symmetric about 0 Hz, with a complex conjugate in the negative frequency domain. This negative spectrum is rarely plotted, since it only has significance inside the FFT. But it helps explain the double sidebands generated by AM and RM.

Excitation/resonance modeling

Many vocal and instrumental sounds can be simulated by a two-part model: an *excitation* signal that is filtered by a *resonance*. The excitation is a nonlinear switching action, like the pluck of a string, the buzz of a reed, or a jet of air into a tube. The resonance is the filtering response of the body of an instrument. Convolution lets us explore a virtual world in which one sound excites the resonances of another.

By a careful choice of input signals, convolution can simulate improbable or impossible performance situations—as if one instrument is somehow playing another. In some cases (e.g., a chain of bells striking a gong), the interaction could be realized in the physical world. Other cases (e.g., a harpsichord playing a gong), can only be realized in the virtual reality of convolution.

- To achieve a plausible simulation, the excitation must be a brief, impulse-like signal, (typically percussive), with a sharp attack (or multiple sharp attacks). The resonance can be any sound.

New applications of convolution in sound transformation

This section surveys three new uses of convolution in sound transformation: rhythm mapping, convolution with clouds of grains, and pulsar synthesis.

Rhythm mapping

We have seen that a series of impulses convolved with a brief sound maps that sound into the time pattern of the impulses. Thus a new application of convolution is precise input of performed rhythms. To map a performed rhythm to an arbitrary sound, one need only tap with drumsticks on a hard surface, and then convolve those taps with the desired sound (Figure 7).

- The convolution of a tapped rhythmic pattern with any sound having a sharp attack causes each tap to be replaced by a copy of the input sound.

This is a direct method of mapping performed rhythms to arbitrary sounds. Since convolution aligns the sounds to the rhythm with a time resolution of the sampling rate, this approach is much more precise than a MIDI percussion controller with its temporal resolution of several milliseconds. One can also layer convolutions using different patterns and input sounds. After pre-positioning each tap in stereo space, convolution automatically distributes them spatially.

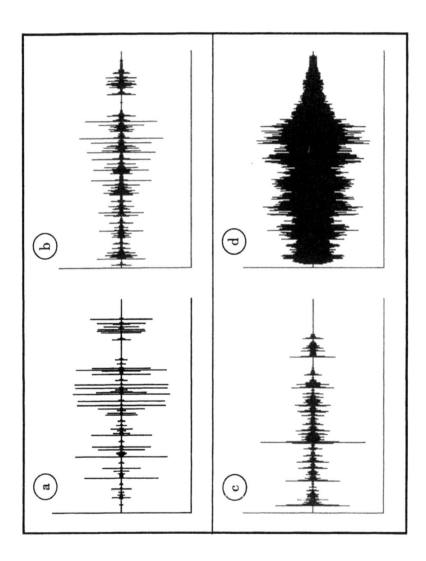

Figure 7. Rhythmic mapping. (a) Original taps of drum sticks. (b) Taps convolved with bongo drum. (c) Taps convolved with conga drum. (d) Taps convolved with cymbal crash.

Convolutions with clouds of sonic grains

An interesting family of sound transformations involves convolutions with *clouds* of sonic grains (Gabor 1946, 1947, 1952; Xenakis 1960; Roads 1978, 1991). A *grain* is a brief acoustical event, typically lasting between 1 and 100 ms. This event contains a waveform that is shaped by a Gaussian or quasi-Gaussian envelope.

We can divide granular techniques into two broad classes, depending on how the grains are scattered in time: *synchronous* and *asynchronous clouds* (Figure 8). In a *synchronous* cloud the grains follow one another in a strictly metrical order, although the meter can change to allow accelerating and decelerating sequences. In an asynchronous cloud the grains are scattered at random time points. In either case, the *density* of grains in a cloud has a determining effect on its time structure.

As a further distinction, when the grains are emitted by a table-lookup oscillator we say the grains are *synthetic*. The frequency of the synthetic grains are assigned within the bandlimits of a cloud region inscribed on the time-versus-frequency plane. This stands in opposition to *sampled grains* that play without pitch transposition.

The results of convolution with grains vary greatly, depending on the properties of the granular cloud and the input signal (Figure 9). If each grain was only a single-sample pulse, then the echoes would be faithful copies of the original input. Since each grain may contain hundreds of samples, however, each echo is locally time-smeared. In the case of a *synthetic asynchronous* cloud, the grains can be thought of as the *virtual impulse response* of an unusual filter or synthetic space (Roads 1992). For a brief sharp-attacked input signal, convolution with a sparse cloud containing a few dozen short grains contributes a statistical distribution of echoes of the input sound. The denser the cloud, the more the echoes fuse into an irregular reverberation effect, often undulating with odd peaks and valleys of intensity.

Short grains realize time-domain effects, while longer grains accentuate time-smearing and filtering. For example, a stream of 1-ms grains at 440 Hz acts mainly as an echo generator, while a stream of 10-ms grains imposes a sharp bandpass filter. When the input sound has a smooth attack—as in a legato saxophone tone—the result is a time-varying filtering effect superimposed on the tone.

Convolutions with *synthetic synchronous* clouds resemble tape echo at low densities (< 10 grains/s). Short grains produce clear echoes, while long grains accentuate the bandpass filtering effect. At high densities the echoes fuse into buzzing and ringing sonorities and the source identity of the input signal is obliterated.

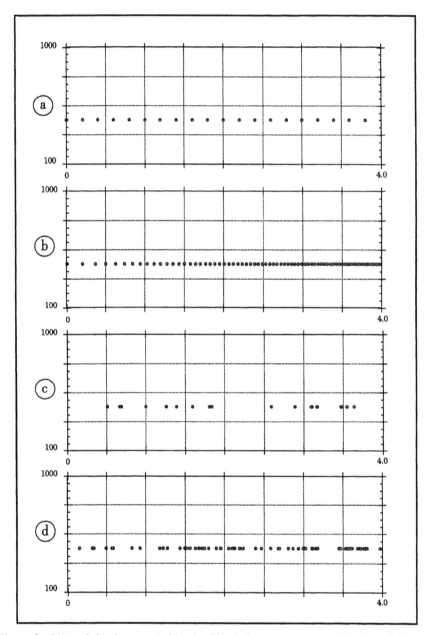

Figure 8. Plots of clouds generated by the Cloud Generator program (Roads and Alexander 1996). The horizontal axis is time and the vertical axis is frequency. (a) Synchronous cloud in which each grain follows the next in a strictly metrical order. The density is constant at 4 grains/s. (b) Increasing density creates an accelerando effect. (c) Asynchronous cloud at constant density of 4 grains/s. Notice the irregular clustering on the time axis. (d) Asynchronous cloud with increasing density.

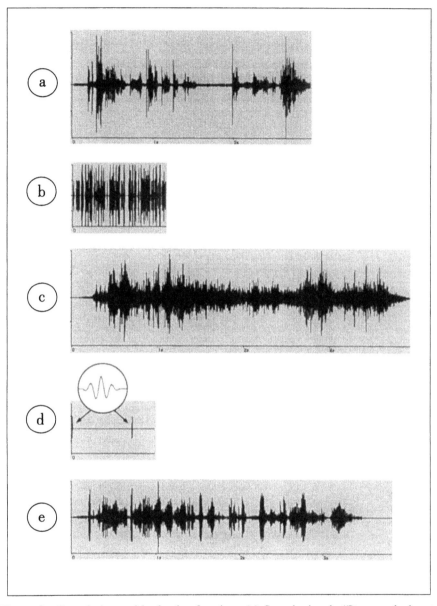

Figure 9. Convolutions with clouds of grains. (a) Speech signal: "It can only be attributed to human error." (b) Asynchronous cloud of 200 10-ms grains spread across the frequency bandwidth from 60 Hz to 12 000 Hz. (c) The convolution of (a) and (b) resulting in the speech being heard amidst an irregular "liquid" echo/reverberation effect. (d) Synchronous cloud of two 10-ms grains at 440 Hz. The circled inset shows the form of the grain in detail. (e) Convolution of (a) and (d) results in a strongly filtered but intelligible echo of (a).

Pulsar synthesis

Pulsar synthesis is an efficient method of sound synthesis developed by the author in the course of composing *Clang-tint*. This technique generates a stream of microsonic events at a continuously variable rate, from the audio range down to the infrasonic frequency domain. At audio rates the distance between successive events is so brief (less than 1/50th of a second) that we perceive the pulsar stream as a pitched continuum. When the rate of emission crosses the infrasonic threshold (less than about 20 Hz), the perception of pitch fades as we perceive each event separately. Thus pulsar synthesis merges synthesis on the microsonic level with gestures at the phrase level of composition.

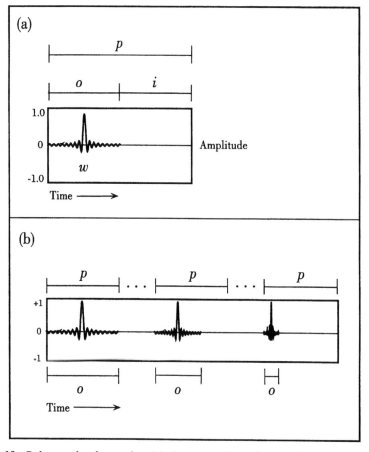

Figure 10. Pulsar and pulsar train. (a) Anatomy of a pulsar consisting of one period of an arbitrary waveform w (the *pulsaret*) with a duty cycle o followed by an arbitrary time interval i. (b) Three periods of a pulsar train with constant p and shrinking o. Intermediate steps are deleted.

We define a single *pulsar* as consisting of one period of an arbitrary waveform w (the *pulsaret*) with a period o followed by an arbitrary time interval i (Figure 10(a)). Thus the total duration $p = o+i$, where p is called the *pulsar period* and o is called the *duty cycle*. Galileo and Mersenne observed in 1636 that when the distance between successive impulses is brief, one perceives a continuous

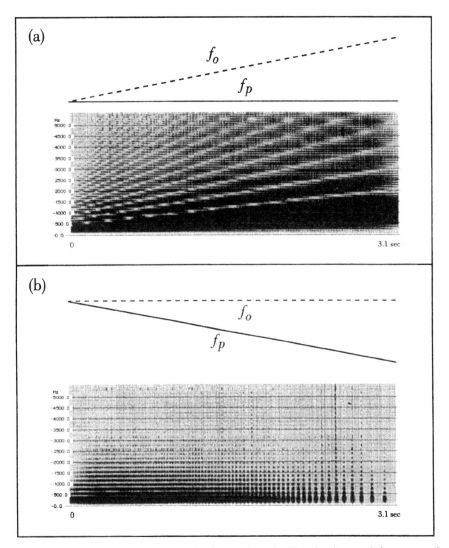

Figure 11. Envelopes and spectra of pulsar trains. (a) The fundamental frequency f_p remains constant at 100 Hz while the formant frequency f_o sweeps from 100 to 1000 Hz. (b) The formant frequency f_o remains constant while the fundamental frequency f_p sweeps downward from 50 Hz to 4 Hz. Notice the individual pulsars at the end.

tone. For p between approximately 5 ms (20 Hz) and 200 μs (5000 Hz) one ascribes the perceptual characteristic of pitch to the tone.

We can divide pulsar synthesis into two variants: 'a "basic" technique and an "advanced" technique that employs convolution. In basic pulsar synthesis, the composer can simultaneously control both fundamental frequency (rate of pulsar emission) and a *formant* frequency (corresponding to the period of the duty cycle)—each according to separate envelopes. For example, Figure 10(b) shows a pulsar train in which the period p remains constant while the duty cycle o shrinks.

We can define the frequency corresponding to the period p as f_p and the frequency corresponding to the duty cycle o as f_o. Keeping f_p constant and varying f_o on a continuous basis creates the effect of a resonant filter swept across a tone (Figure 11). There is, of course, no filter in this circuit. Rather, the frequency corresponding to the period o appears in the spectrum as a narrow *formant peak*.

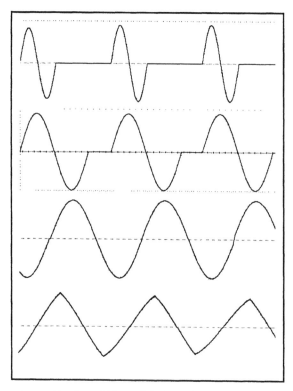

Figure 12. Four stages of pulse-width modulation with a sinusoidal pulsaret waveform. In the top two images $f_o \leqslant f_p$. In the third image $f_o = f_p$, and in the bottom image $f_o \geqslant f_p$.

As a special case, pulsar synthesis realizes *pulse-width modulation* (PWM) effects when $f_o \leqslant f_p$. Of course, w is not limited to rectangular pulse, and can be any waveform (Figure 12).

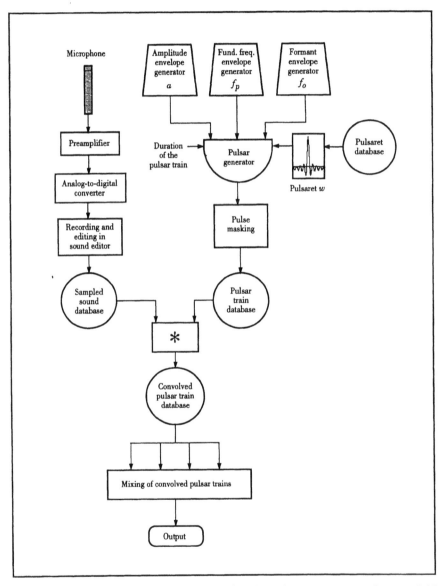

Figure 13. Overall schema of pulsar synthesis. The pulsar generator produces variable impulses in the continuum between the infrasonic and audio frequencies. Pulse masking breaks up the train. The pulsar trains are convolved (denoted by "$*$") with sampled sounds, and possibly mixed with other convolved pulsar trains into a single texture.

In advanced pulsar synthesis, each pulsar acts an impulse response in a convolution operation, imposing its fundamental, formant spectrum, and spatial properties onto a sampled sound. Figure 13 depicts the overall schema of advanced pulsar synthesis. Let us assume that the pulsar generator emits a regular sequence of pulsars according to f_p. We can break up this emission by selective *pulsar masking*. Pulsar masking means "clearing" individual pulsars in a sequence, leaving momentary silences in their place. For example, consider two patterns a and b, each of which has been convolved with a separate sampled sound. When both sequences are played simultaneously neither is heard distinctly. But when one masks certain pulsars in a this creates a gap that allows those in b to stand out. By selectively masking pulsars in a and b one creates a dialog within a phrase, articulating each stream in turn, as shown below, where a is the top pattern and b is the bottom pattern.

In the infrasonic range (below about 20 Hz) these contrapuntal sequences create rhythmic patterns. In the audio frequency range (above about 20 Hz) they create timbral effects. The tempo of these sequences need not be constant, and can vary according to the curve of the fundamental frequency envelope f_p of the pulsar train.

A second application of masking is spatialization. Imagine the pulsar sequences in row a above assigned to the left channel and the pulsar sequences in row b assigned to the right channel, both played at low speed. One obtains the effect of a sequence that alternates between two channels.

Each pulsar, when convolved with a sampled sound, maps to a particular region in timbre space. If the same sampled sound is mapped to every pulsar, timbral variations derive from two factors: (1) the filtering effect imposed by the spectrum of each pulsar, and (2) the time-smearing effects caused by convolution with pulsar trains whose period is shorter than the duration of the sampled sound.

A database of sampled sound objects serves as stockpile to be crossed with trains selected from the pulsar database. A collection of percussion samples is a good initial set for a sound database. The percussion samples should be of short duration and have a sharp attack (e.g., a rise time less than 100 ms). These constraints can be relaxed if the composer seeks a smoother and more continuous texture; long durations and slow attacks cause multiple copies of the sampled object to overlap, creating a rippling yet continuous sound stream.

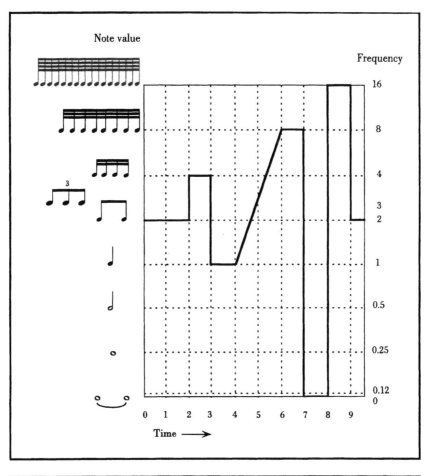

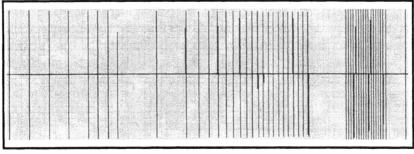

Figure 14. Pulsar rhythms. Top: Pulse graph of rhythm showing rate of pulsar emission (vertical scale) plotted against time (horizontal scale). The left-hand scale measures traditional note values, while the right-hand scale measures frequencies. Bottom: Time-domain image of generated pulsar train corresponding to the plot above.

Pulse graphs

In advanced pulsar synthesis, the final stage of synthesis involves the merger of several pulsar trains to form a composite. Each layer may have its own rhythmic pattern, formant frequency envelope, and choice of convolved objects, creating an intricate counterpoint on the microsound level.

Figure 7 showed that any series of impulses convolved with a brief sound maps that sound into the time pattern of the impulses. The impulses in Figure 7 were played by a percussionist, but they can also be emitted at a precisely controlled rate by a pulsar generator. If the pulsar train frequency falls within the infrasonic range, then each instance of a pulsar is replaced by a copy of the sampled sound object, creating a rhythmic pattern.

Figure 14 shows a *pulse graph,* which plots the rate of pulsar emission versus time. Pulse graphs can serve as an alternative form of notation for one dimension of rhythmic structure, namely the onset or attack time of events. In order to determine the rhythm generated by a function inscribed on a pulse graph, one has to calculate the duration of the pulsar emission curve at a given fixed frequency rate. For example, a pulsar emission at 4 Hz that lasts for 0.75 s emits 3 pulsars.

Conclusions

The "liberation of sound" predicted by Edgard Varèse is now in full bloom, and has deeply affected the art of composition. Among known transformations, convolution is most versatile, simultaneously transforming the time-space structure and spectral morphology of its inputs. Its effects range from subtle enhancements to destructive distortions. But only a knowledgeable and experienced user can predict what the outcome of certain convolutions will be. Many convolutions that appear to be interesting musical ideas ("How about convolving a clarinet with a speaking voice?") result in amorphous sound blobs. Thus a thorough exploration of the terrain is necessary before this technique can be applied systematically in composition. This chapter has only begun the task of charting this frontier.

Acknowledgements

My interest in this subject was sparked by conversations in Naples and Paris with my friend and colleague the late Professor Aldo Piccialli. During the period of my first experiments with convolution, I benefited from discussions of signal processing with Dr Marie-Hélène Serra. Mr Tom Erbe was helpful in answering questions about the internal operation of his algorithms in the excellent Sound Hack program. I would like to also thank Gerard Pape, Brigitte Robindoré, and Les Ateliers UPIC for their support, as well as Horacio Vaggione and the Music Department at the Université Paris VIII. My thanks also to Gianpaolo Evangelista for reviewing the draft of this chapter and offering thoughtful suggestions.

References

Bias. 1996. *Peak User's Guide*. Sausalito: Bias.

Bode, H. 1984. "History of electronic sound modification." *Journal of the Audio Engineering Society* 32(10): 730–739.

David, E., M. Mathews, and H. McDonald. 1958. "Description and results of experiments with speech using digital computer simulation." In *Proceedings of the National Electronics Conference*. Vol. IV. Chicago: National Electronics Conference, pp. 766–775.

De Poli, G. and A. Piccialli. 1991. "Pitch-synchronous granular synthesis." In G. De Poli, A. Piccialli, and C. Roads, eds. *Representations of Musical Signals*. Cambridge, Massachusetts: The MIT Press, pp. 187–219.

Dolson, M. and R. Boulanger. 1985. "New directions in the musical use of resonators." Unpublished manuscript.

Erbe, T. 1995. *SoundHack User's Manual*. Oakland: Mills College.

Gabor, D. 1946. "Theory of communication." *Journal of the Institute of Electrical Engineers*. Part 3, 93: 429–457.

Gabor, D. 1947. "Acoustical quanta and the theory of hearing." *Nature* 159(1044): 591–594.

Gabor, D. 1952. "Lectures on communication theory." Technical Report 238. Cambridge, Massachusetts: MIT Research Laboratory of Electronics.

Gardner, W. 1995. "Efficient convolution without input-output delay." *Journal of the Audio Engineering Society* 43(3): 127–136.

Kunt, M. 1981. *Traitement Numérique des Signaux*. Paris: Dunod.

MathWorks, The. 1995. *Matlab Reference Guide*. Natick: The MathWorks.

Moore, F.R. 1985. "The mathematics of digital signal processing." In J. Strawn, ed. *Digital Audio Signal Procesing: An Anthology*. Madison: A-R Editions, pp. 1–67.

Rabiner, L., J. Cooley, H. Helms, L. Jackson, J. Kaiser, C. Rader, R. Schafer, K. Steiglitz, and C. Weinstein. 1972. "Terminology in digital signal processing." *IEEE Transactions on Audio and Electroacoustics* AU-20: 322–327.

Rabiner, L. and B. Gold. 1975. *Theory and Application of Digital Signal Processing*. Englewood Cliffs: Prentice Hall.

Roads, C. 1978. "Automated granular synthesis of sound." *Computer Music Journal* 2(2): 61–62. Revised and updated version printed as "Granular synthesis of sound" in C. Roads and J. Strawn, eds. 1985. *Foundations of Computer Music*. Cambridge, Massachusetts: The MIT Press, pp. 145–159.

Roads, C. 1991. "Asynchronous granular synthesis." In G. De Poli, A. Piccialli, and C. Roads, eds. *Representations of Musical Signals*. Cambridge, Massachusetts: The MIT Press, pp. 143–185.

Roads, C. 1992. "Musical applications of advanced signal transformations." In A. Piccialli, ed. *Proceedings of the Capri Workshop on Models and Representations of Musical Signals*. Naples: University of Naples "Federico II", Department of Physics.

Roads, C. 1996. *The Computer Music Tutorial*. Cambridge, Massachusetts: The MIT Press.

Roads, C. and J. Alexander. 1996. *Cloud Generator Manual*. Distributed with the program Cloud Generator.

Sorensen, H. and C.S. Burrus. 1993. "Fast DFT and convolution algorithms." In S. Mitra and J. Kaiser, eds. *Handbook of Digital Signal Processing*. New York: Wiley, pp. 491–610.

Stockham, T. 1969. "High-speed convolution and convolution with applications to digital filtering." In B. Gold and C. Rader, eds. *Digital Processing of Signals.* New York: McGraw-Hill, pp. 203–232.

Xenakis, I. 1960. "Elements of stochastic music." *Gravesaner Blätter* 18: 84–105.

13

Musical interpretation and signal processing

Alvise Vidolin

Changes in the musical language of the twentieth century and the advent of electronic technology have favored the birth of a new musical figure: the interpreter of electronic musical instruments. This interpreter must not only be musically competent in the traditional sense, but must also be a signal processing expert. The interpreter not only "plays" during a concert but also designs the *performance environment* for the piece and acts as an interface between the composer's musical idea and its transformation into sound.

The performance environment consists of the hardware and software components that transform a technological system into a musical "instrument" for executing a specific musical text during a concert. The main elements in the design include sound processing techniques, the human interface, the ergonomics of controlling gestures, the synchronization traditional instrument players with electronic processes, as well as the rapid transition from one performance environment to another.

This chapter discusses the techniques of musical interpretation with electronic instruments, placing greater emphasis on the sound rather than on the text (score). We start from the primary musical parameters of duration, pitch, intensity, timbre and space. Many of the techniques discussed here have been developed in the laboratory and numerous articles have been published about them. This chapter, therefore, concerns, above all, their application during a live performance and contemporary musical works will be used as examples.

The role of the interpreter

In traditional music, interpreters translate into sound what the composer has written on paper in a graphic-symbolic language. In part, they serve an operative role, in the sense that they must realize exactly what has been written, and in part they have a creative role, in that they must complete in a stylistically correct manner, and sometimes even invent, the elements and gestures that the notation language cannot express in detailed terms, or that the composer has deliberately left open to interpretation.

In the twentieth century, musical language has been enriched by new sound materials and techniques that are difficult to express on paper with traditional language. The concept of the *note,* which has been the pillar of music for many centuries, is more and more often replaced by the more general notion of *sound event,* which includes the world of indeterminate sound pitches and sound-noises. Nowadays, experimental composition frequently involves a long period of experimentation in collaboration with the interpreters before the score finally is written. Thus, with the advent of electronic music, the concept of the sound event was placed alongside that of a *process,* in that a musical part of the score was no longer defined as a simple succession of events, but also by the transformations these have been subjected to.

It is inevitable that such considerable changes in the language and techniques used in the realization of music means that the interpreter's role has also changed radically, as well as altering his competence and function. During this century, the interpreter of traditional instruments has specialized, learning new techniques for the execution of music (for example, multiphonic sound techniques with wind instruments). Thus, the role and competence of interpreters of electronic musical instruments has not yet been well defined (Davies 1984), in that these range from the players of synthesizers to signal processing researchers, with many intermediate levels of specialization. In many cases, in fact, the interpreter does not play a single instrument but rather, programs and controls the equipment. The interpreter does not simply translate a score into a sound, but transforms the composer's abstract musical project into an operative fact, making use of digital technology and new developments in the synthesis and signal processing (Vidolin 1993).

That the interpreter has a wide range of functions, is also seen when the various phases that music produced with electrophonic instruments are examined. This is due, very probably, to the rapid developments in technology and musical language, so that the same person can be either all or in part, researcher, inventor of instruments, composer and performer. During the first half of this century, the inventor of electronic musical instruments and the performer were often one and the same person, which is the case of Lev Termen and his Theremin, and the Ondes Martenot created by Maurice Martenot, who were among the first and most famous inventors and interpreters of electronic instruments, in the 1930s. Starting from the 1950s when electroacoustic music was produced in a studio, the composer began to dominate the scene so that the creative and realisation phases of the piece are almost always interwoven. This method of working, which is typical of experimental music, has also been used successively by those composers of computer music who have chosen the computer as an aid to composing.

The studio interpreter

The fact that one person could be the creator of the entire musical product, a popular utopia that was fashionable in the 1950s, not only led to important musical results but also underlined its limits. If the figure of the composer prevails, his only interest lies in turning a musical idea into a concrete sound, without being excessively bothered about the quality of the details. Moreover, once the work has been realized, he is no longer interested in the work's successive performances, in that his attention moves immediately to the next work. On the other hand, if the interpreter prevails, the formal construction is overwhelmed by the pleasurable effect he is able to create by demonstrating his own technical brilliance. However, the advantage of being in charge of the entire composition and realisation very often means that the composer-interpreter is distracted by frequent and banal technical problems linked to his own computer system. On the other hand, this means that he only seems to be consulting some manual, or indulging in his hobby of updating his computer software, so that his original imagination has been reduced to implementing a new algorithm.

The necessity of separating the role of composer from that of the interpreter was noted as far back as the 1950s in the WDR Studio for electronic music, in Cologne. The young Gottfried Micheal Koenig worked in this studio and his role was to transform the graphic scores produced by the various invited composers into electronic sound. Similarly, Marino Zuccheri, who worked at the RAI (Italian Radio and Television) Fonologia Musicale (Musical Phonology) studio in Milan, was an incomparable assistant to the various composers, in that he was deeply sensitive and had great musical talent (Doati and Vidolin 1986).

More recently, composers who have been invited to the Ircam center in Paris to produce a musical compositions using computer technology are provided with a highly skilled musical assistant whose role is similar to that of the traditional interpreter. This way of working is practiced in many centers producing music with a high technology component.

The live-electronics interpreter

Digital techniques generating and processing signals can turn many of the timbres that the composers of the 1900s could only dream about into real sounds. Knowledge of sound, the mechanisms of perceiving it, together with the development of technology that can manipulate the acoustic universe, have changed the way of creating and realizing a musical work.

The traditional orchestra, in terms of signals, realizes a continuous sound by summing numerous complex sources. Furthermore, in addition, electronics means that such individual or groups of sources can be changed, by multiplying or subtracting the spectral contents or other forms of treatment to increase or decrease the density of the event. In musical terms this means an amplification of the traditional concept of *variation*.

Similarly, the roles of the composer, the orchestra conductor and musicians, all of whom reflect the *modus operandi* of the last century's mechanistic society, have been modified, reflecting the changes in the way work is organized when producing goods on an industrial scale. Nowadays, large orchestras have been substituted by large sound-generating systems or they have been reduced to just a few soloists, whose music is then processed by live electronics. A new figure has arisen, the interpreter of electrophonic instruments, who must realize the processing system and plan the performance environment. A large part of the interpreter's work is carried out while the work is being prepared, while during the live performance he makes sure that the machines function correctly, manages the interaction between the machines and any soloists, calibrates the overall dynamic levels and realizes the spatial projection of the sounds. This interpreter, who is often called the sound director, has a role that is conceptually much closer to that of the orchestra conductor than the player.

In the production of a musical work, the experimentation that precedes and accompanies the real composition phase is very important. Thus, the composer must often rely on virtuosi of traditional musical instruments and must also, and just as frequently, rely on experts in modern technology who help in the various planning phases of the work. The interpreter of electronic musical instruments becomes, therefore, a kind of interface between the idea that forms the basis of the composition and the sound. A sound no longer grows from the mechanical vocalization alone or from the gestures used when playing an acoustical instrument, but it develops, rather, from the planning of an algorithmic synthesis, a processing "played" in the performance environment.

The performance environment

Traditional musicians play codified instruments that have been stable for centuries and learn by imitating the "Maestro" and develop gesture skills that make the most of an instrument, using it as if it were an extension of their own bodies. In the world of signal processing, however, new equipment evolves as a result of technological improvements and, therefore, the life-cycle of a technological generation is often less than ten years. Moreover, very little equipment is autonomous, as the acoustical musical instruments are, in that each piece of equipment is part of a group which, when conveniently connected to each other and programmed, make up a single unit that can be compared to the old concept of an instrument and which, in the world of technology, is called a *system*.

In this case, the system input consists of the audio signals to be processed. It is fitted with controls so that the parameters of a sound can be varied to produce the output signals. In order to transform this system into a musical instrument, the controls must be suitable for the performance. Therefore, they must vary according to a measuring unit of psychoacoustics or better yet, a musical one (intensity, for example: dB, phon, sone or the dynamic scale from *ppp* to *fff*), and they must have a predefined range of variability and be able to obey an opportune law of variation (for example, linear, exponential or arbitrary), in order to make easier to execute a specific musical part.

The interpreters, who are often also the designers of the performance environment, must choose the equipment for the processing system. Furthermore, they must construct the interface between the *performer's controls*, or rather, the musical parameters that must be varied during the performance but that have been fixed by the composition, and the *system controls*, which depend on the equipment chosen. Very often it is more convenient to have a consistent multifunctional control device, so that by means of a single gesture, a number of parameters in the system can be varied both coherently and simultaneously. Continuing along the lines of the previous example, it is best to connect a single performer control to several varieties of system controls such as, amplitude, low-pass filter for *piano* and an *exciter* for *forte* in order to obtain dynamic variations ranging from *ppp* to *fff*. Furthermore, during the performance, it would be more efficient to use responsive input devices that can extract a variety of information from a single gesture and that would, in fact, subject the interpreter to greater physical stress when he aims for the extreme execution zones (Cadoz, Luciani, and Florens 1984). The need to have gesture controls that favor the natural actions of the performer and that also allow, with a single gesture, for the coherent variation of several musical parameters, has led to the development of new control devices that are used with, or even substitute for the traditional potentiometers, keyboards and pushbuttons. Many examples can be found in literature on the subject (Mathews and Abbott 1980; Davies 1984; Waiwisz 1985; Chabot 1990; Rubine and McAvinney 1990; Bertini and Carosi 1991; Genovese, Cocco, De Micheli, and Buttazzo 1991).

The performer controls must be limited in number in order to understand the performance environment quickly and favor immediate access to the main executive functions. For example, the traditional mixer, which is one of the most widely used instruments in live electronics concerts, is not ergonometrically suitable for the execution of live performances in that all the controls are monodimensional and the calibration and execution controls are both found on the same level. However, of the hundreds of potentiometers and switches on it, only slightly more than ten are varied when playing one single score in a concert, and these can not be easily grouped in one single accessible area so the position of the keys must be well known. It is, therefore, more convenient to have a remote control device for those elements that are likely to be varied.

When a piece is being played and even more during a succession of pieces that make up a concert, there is a rotation of several performance environments. This must be taken into account both when choosing the equipment and when planning the environments. For example, the transition from one environment to another must be instantaneous and should not cause any disturbance, and the performer controls must be organized in such a way that the change is reduced to a minimum. Moreover, interpreters must be free to choose their own position in the hall, depending on the architectural characteristics, or wherever else the score is to be played. Sometimes the best position is in the center of the theater whilst in other case the interpreter must be on stage together with the other musicians. Therefore, it is necessary to have a relatively small remote control device and which can, therefore, be easily transported, even by a single person, as well as being fitted with a visual feedback system attached to the main technological one. In some cases, to facilitate freedom of movement, a radio connection can be used rather than the traditional cables.

For relatively simple performance environments, a MIDI remote control, connected to equipment and software that can easily be found on the market, could provide a simple and economic answer. Unfortunately, the amount of information that a MIDI line can carry is very limited (31250 bits/s) and the data are organized in such a way that only excursion ranges from 0 to 127 can be handled with ease. These limits considerably reduce the advantages deriving from the extensive distribution of the MIDI code in the musical and signal processing worlds. Therefore, if many parameters must be continuously varied in the performance environment, it is necessary to use several independent MIDI lines or for particularly complex cases, alternative control systems must be utilized.

In conclusion, a performance environment is the musical interface (hardware and software) that allows for transforming a complex technological system into a kind of general musical instrument, which the interpreter can use when playing a specific musical composition. The planning of any such environment is left to the interpreter in order to reconcile the personal performing style with the characteristics of a single work.

The performance style of an environment can not be compared to the traditional one for an acoustical musical instrument, in that the environment is intrinsically linked to the music that must be produced and the interpreter who has projected it. Therefore, learning cannot be by intuition or imitation, as is the usual practice. The interpreter must, instead, develop a learning capacity based on the analytical nature of the technologies and signal processing techniques, and must be able to pass rapidly from a variety of situations and configurations to others that are very different, which may also occur even in a single piece.

Performance environments, unlike musical scores, are subject to periodic changes in that many devices become obsolete and must be replaced by new equipment that is conceptually similar to the previous system but which is operated differently. Over longer periods, the structure of the system also changes, as has occurred in the transition from analog performance environments to mixed ones (digital-controlled-analog) and then to completely digital ones. Technological developments constantly lead to changes in the performance environments and can, thus, improve the execution of a musical work in that when redesigning the performance environment, the technical solutions or some parts of the score can make the new "orchestration" of the electronic part more efficient.

Signal models for the interpreter

The traditional, classical music repertory uses various techniques for developing the musical discourse (repetition, variation, development, counterpoint, harmony, foreground, background, etc.), and these are applied while writing the piece or rather, while composing the score. With signal processing instruments, however, it is possible to organize the musical discourse by acting directly on the sound rather than on a text.

For example, with traditional techniques, before a phrase can be varied it must be rewritten, modifying the desired elements. With signal processing any variation is obtained by directly processing the sound, starting from the acoustic realization of the original phrase and proceeding to the successive transformations both of the original and the various elaborations.

Tables 1–5 lists the main sound processing techniques organized according to the musical parameters of timing, pitch, dynamics, timbre and space. As an introduction to such techniques, it is advisable to consult the texts listed in the bibliography (Mathews 1969; Roads and Strawn 1985; Strawn 1985; Wasserman 1985; Mathews and Pierce 1989; Roads 1989, 1996; Moore 1990; De Poli, Piccialli, and Roads 1991). In theory, many of the processes are

Table 1.

Time processing

Processing	Technique	Results
Time translation	Delay, $t > 50$ ms	Simple echo, repetition
Accumulation	Feedback delay, $t > 50$ ms, gain < 1. Other transformation elements such as filters, transpositions, etc. can be put into the feedback line	Repetition and accumulation. Canon structure with some variations when there is transformation in the feed-back
Slowing down and quickening the pace	Sampling	The pitch goes down when the times slows down and vice versa
Backwards	Backward sampling	Temporal sound inversion; transient inversion
Augmentation or diminution of the duration	Sampling with looping or skipping segment	Augmentation or diminution of sound duration, attack and decay characteristics remaining the same. True of steady state sounds
Freezing	Asynchronous granular feedback delay, grain duration > 1 s; loop time $<$ grain time; gain < 1	Prolongation of sound time window. Use a gaussian type time window to avoid clicks
Foot tapping	Adaptive and/or cognitive system	Beat extraction from rhythmic music
Stretching and shrinking	Phase vocoder; wavelet; linear prediction	Duration of a musical section is stretched or shrunk without varying the pitch. Transient modification

Table 2.

Pitch processing

Processing	Technique	Results
Transposition	Harmonizer; phase vocoder; wavelet; LPC	Varies pitch of the sound but not the duration. Formant transpositions varies pitch of the sound but not the duration. Constant formants
Vibrato	Low frequency (4–8 Hz) frequency modulation	Periodic pitch fluctuation
Detection (pitch follower)	Zero crossing; tunable IIR filter; FFT	Extracting a sound pitch. Works only with periodic sounds

Table 3.

Dynamic processing

Processing	Technique	Results
Increment or reduction	Amplitude scaling	More than a dynamic variation, can sometimes give the effect of increasing or reducing the source distance
Increment	Distortion; excitement	Enriches supplementary harmonic sound in acute register
Reinforcement	Doubling by FIR comb filter, delay < 30 ms	Reinforces sound. Adds a spatial prospective
Reduction	Low-pass filtering, cut-off frequency = 1–10 kHz	Reduced upper harmonic energy
Tremolo	Low frequency (4–8 Hz) amplitude modulation	Slow periodic amplitude variation
Expansion or compression	Amplitude scaling dependent on signal power	Strong signals are amplified more than weak ones; vice versa in the event of compression
Gate	Threshold switch	Only signals above a certain amplitude threshold pass through follows the amplitude variations
Detection (envelope follower)	Low-pass filtering the RMS value	Extracting the envelope
Hybridization	Amplitude scaling by the envelope detected from another signal	Fragmentation of a signal by another one

similar but there are operational differences between working in a studio and a live performance. Therefore, in live electronics some processes can not be realized or they give results that can not be so well controlled. A symbolic case

Table 4.

Timbre processing

Processing	Technique	Results
Spectral transformation	Linear filtering: low-pass, band-pass high-pass, band-rejection etc.	Spectral deformation by amplitude scaling of a signal band
Flanger effect; chorus effect	Low frequency (0.05–10 Hz) time-varying recursive comb filter, delay (1–30 ms), and amplitude modification	Richer sound variable in terms of timbre
Specular spectrum translation	Ring modulation by audio sinusoidal carrier	Inharmonic sound with energy centred on carrier and band width is double the modulation signal band
Spectrum translation	Single side ring modulation	Spectrum translated by a constant value frequency making a harmonic sound inharmonic
Transformation (harmonic translation)	Pitch synchronous ring or frequency modulation of a harmonic sound. Multiple pitch carrier	Sound is still harmonic and is translated with combination of harmonics
Periodic part amplification or attenuation	Pitch synchronous FIR comb filter of a harmonic sound, delay $= 1/f$	Separation of harmonic and inharmonic part of a sound
Hybridization	Pitch synchronous resonant filtering. Control: harmonic sound, controlled: any sound	Controlled sound filtered on the basis of the pitch of the sound control
Hybridization	Vocoder; convolution; LPC	Controlled sound filtered on the basis of the spectrum sound control

is the shrinking of the sound's duration that, if realized in real time, should be projected into the future. On the other hand, the interaction between acoustic instruments and electronic ones played live can be improved during a concert thanks to the positive tension that is created because of the presence of the public and because of the expectancy linked to the event.

Tables 1–5 list the main sound elaboration techniques from the point of view of the interpreter or rather, on the basis of their effect on the primary musical parameters of duration, pitch, intensity, timbre and space. It is important to note that the separation between the parameters shown appears to be much more distinct than they are in reality, in that normally, even when one single parameter

Table 5.

Space processing

Processing	Technique	Results
Room reverberation	Multitap delays, recursive comb and all-pass filters	First echoes simulated and reverberation diffused in the hall
Stereo placing	Stereo balance; stereo delay; stereo low-pass filtering	Interaural time, intensity, and timbre difference
Stereo phasing effect	Low frequency time varying stereo comb filter	Timbre and spatial effect
Near-far placing	Balancing direct to reverberated signal	Reverberated sound fixes the maximum distance, progressively adding the direct signal brings the sound closer
Movement speed	Frequency transposition	Doppler effect simulation
Resonant room; resonant cavity	Feedback delay network	Multiple reflections simulation of a resonant cavity
Auralization	Binaural filtering and convolution by the room impulse response	Fixing a sound at any point in a real theatre; heard in stereo
Sound placing	Multiloudspeaker projection	The sound depends on the location of the loudspeakers. Stereo techniques can be added dynamically to each pair of loudspeakers in order to simulate sound movement

is varied, it will influence the some or all of the others, to a greater or lesser degree.

Examples of performance environments

In the world of art music, interest is not so much turned towards technological or scientific novelty as an end in itself but rather what this new technology can offer to reach precise expressive or aesthetic results. This section presents three performance environments chosen as significant examples of the integration between signal processing technology and contemporary music. The examples are based on musical works produced during the last ten years that have already established a place for themselves in theater and modern musical festival repertories. In these examples, even though the technology used was not always the most sophisticated, it has played an important role in the evolution of musical language and thought.

All three works involve interaction between traditional and electronic instruments, and the scores have been written using traditional methods. This is not always suitable for the needs of live electronics, in that the parameters to be controlled cannot always be represented on the staves. This lack of a standardized notation system for live electronics has led to the mistaken idea that the role of the electronic instruments interpreter is less important and that he has a greater degree of liberty. This is not true in that the work to be carried out is just as precise and deterministic, unless the composer has specifically requested improvisation. The difficulty in annotating parts for live electronics lies in the fact that there is not, as yet, any convention that allows the technical-operative data to be translated into graphic symbols that indicate what type of acoustic result is desired. Therefore, most scores for live electronics consist of an initial technical section where the operative schemes of algorithmic synthesis or the treatment of the sound are described, while the real score written on traditional staves is combined with the indications set out for the electronic parts. These latter generally are similar to the old tablatures in that they are nearer the action for varying some of the parameters in the performance environment, rather than being based on the music desired.

Ofanim by Luciano Berio
for voices, children's chorus, orchestra and live electronics

Ofanim by Luciano Berio is a work in progress that was first performed in Prato, Italy (Berio 1988) and has been repeated on numerous occasions, each of which has resulted in a different version of the composition. In some cases the differences between versions have been slight while in others, they have been quite considerable. This analysis will focus on the performance that took place in December 1993, played by the Berlin Philharmonic Orchestra.

The live electronics, which were realized by the Centro Tempo Reale, Florence (Bernardini and Otto 1989a), have three main functions: the movement of sound in space, the transformation of the chorus and orchestra, the processing of the sounds played by the soloists. The performance environment was rather complex in that it was necessary to capture all the sounds emitted by the performers via microphone (making sure that undesired sounds were reduced to a minimum) and mix the different groups separately (orchestra I, orchestra II, chorus I, chorus II, percussion I, percussion II, etc.), both for the movement of sound in space and for its transformation. In the Berlin performance, a main mixer with 40 inputs and 8 outputs was used, together with an auxiliary mixer with 12 in and

4 out and a 8 in and 2 out mixer that could be controlled via MIDI. These last two were used for sound procesing. The movement of the sounds in space was realized by the Minitrails system (Bernardini and Otto 1989b), which used an 8-by-8 voltage-controlled amplifier (VCA) computer-controlled matrix. This meant that eight independent lines could be used on eight amplification channels for the dynamic balancing between the channels. The sequence of movements was stored on a *playlist*, the various starting points being activated manually, following the conductor's signals. Luciano Berio, who was sitting in the middle of the theatre, used a small control desk with eight potentiometers for the remote control of the fine calibration of the amplification level of the eight lines.

Ofanim is subdivided into twelve sections that follow each other without any interruption. The most critical phases for the live electronics are the transitions from one section to next. To ease these commutations and eventual variations in the level, the MAX program was chosen (Puckette 1988; Opcode 1990) to handle the manually-controlled sequence of MIDI messages. The first section is dominated by a duet between a child's voice and a clarinet. Both are subject to various electronic transformations: feedback delay lines, transpositions, filtering and *hybridization*. Attempts at hybridization, or crossing of the characteristics of two sounds, required many experiments; it would be interesting to summarize the main results.

Berio's composition aims at transforming a child's voice into a clarinet and vice versa. Then both should be transformed into a trombone. The musical interest, therefore, does not lie in the terminal mimesis but rather in the various intermediate sounds between the beginning and the end. Moreover, it should be underlined that the two soloists sing and play at the same time, so that the hybrid sound has to be much more pronounced, because it must be well distinguished from the original ones. The transformation system used for both was based on the extraction of pitch by means of a pitch detector and on the successive synthetic generation or manipulation of the original sound. The first versions were based on sound generation by means of a sampler that exploited the crossed fading away of the voice and the clarinet. Later, when the Centro Tempo Reale acquired the Iris MARS workstation (Andrenacci, Favreau, Larosa, Prestigia-como, Rosati and Sapir 1992) various algorithms were tried out. For example, consider the transformation of the voice. The first completely synthetic solution used frequency modulation to generate sound. The frequency was extracted from the pitch detector that controlled the carrier and the modulation frequency (with a $3:2$ ratio) while the amplitude values were extracted from an envelope follower and then used to control both the amplitude and the modulation index. By assigning a multiplication index factor to an external controller, it was possible to pass from a sinusoidal sound to one that was richer in odd harmonics.

Another solution was based on ring modulation where the carrier was still a sinusoidal generator controlled by the pitch detector while the modulator was the signal itself. Using a 1 : 2 ratio, odd harmonics prevail which in the low register is similar to the sound of a clarinet. A third solution made use of the waveshaping technique where the voice is filtered in such a way as to obtain a sinusoidal sound which is then distorted with a suitable distortion function.

These three solutions however, consider the transformation only from the point of view of sound. However, it was also necessary to take into account the performance aspects, such as, for example, eliminating all the typical vocal *portamento* and making a more rapid transition from one note to another, in order to better represent the characteristic articulation of the clarinet. This was brought about by inserting a sample-and-hold unit that held the current note until the successive one had been established. On the other hand, in the passage from the clarinet to the voice it was necessary to do the opposite, so a low-pass filter with a cutoff frequency of only a few hertz at the exit of the pitch detector was used to smooth out the rapid transitions, in order to introduce the vocal *portamento*.

These experiments have shown that a voice or an instrument is not only a sound spectrum and the microtemporal factors that define its evolution, but a sound is recognized, above all, by gestures and agogic execution. Moreover, even the writing of music is closely connected to the technical aspects of the instrument. Therefore, the phrases written for the clarinet are morphologically different from those written for a voice. In the transformation from a voice to a clarinet, within the ambitus of this example, a sound can be transformed in real time but, as yet, the tools to process the agogic-executive aspects are still weak.

Prometeo by Luigi Nono
for soloists, chorus, orchestra and live electronics

Prometeo was first performed was at the Biennial International Festival of Contemporary Music, Venice, the 25 September 1984 (Nono 1984; Cacciari 1984). The chosen theater was worthy of note because of the implications for the composition of the work. In the first place, the opera was not performed in a traditional concert hall but in a completely empty, deconsecrated church in Venice, the Church of San Lorenzo. This was transformed by the architect Renzo Piano into a congenial musical space by constructing a suspended wooden structure inside it (which will be simply called the "structure"). In terms of size, this structure resembled the empty hulk of a ship but in terms of its function, it would be more correct to compare it to the harmonic body of a musical instrument. It was designed to hold both the public, sitting on the bottom of the structure, and the performers, arranged on three balconies at different heights (Simonelli 1985).

The theme of music within space, was very dear to Luigi Nono and had its roots in the ancient Venitian culture (similar to the Gabrieli *battenti* choruses of the 1500s). San Lorenzo and the structure proved to be a fortunate experiment. In *Prometeo*, in fact, there is an interaction between the spatial composition of the acoustic sounds of the orchestra (subdivided into four groups arranged asymmetrically at the four corners of the structure and on different levels) and the multi-channel projection of electroacoustic sounds produced by the soloists. The latter were manipulated and increased during the live performance, by means of various electronic techniques (Haller 1985). Thanks to the structure and the electroacoustic spatialization system, Nono was able to organize the sounds within this space using the contrast between various dimensions: acoustic/electroacoustic, internal/external, horizontal/vertical, static/dynamic, distant/near. Moreover, the voices and the soloists, thanks to the live electronics, took on a phonic richness that countered the sound of the orchestra.

The live electronics system came from the Heinrich Strobel Stiftung Experimental Studio SWF, Freiburg, Germany and was completely managed by remote control and automatic commutation of the connections by a 48-by-48 active matrix piloted by a computer. The main sound processes used by Nono were: feedback delay; pitch transposition; filtering with banks of very narrow filters (second and fifth); a 48-filter vocoder; automatic variation of amplitude depending on the envelope extracted by a voice or instrument; the movement of sound within the space with automatic or manual variation of the amplitude over 12 independent channels.

One of the most fascinating parts of *Prometeo* is the section dedicated to Hölderlin for two sopranos, bass flute, doublebass clarinet, reciting voices and live electronics. This section is dominated by the two sopranos, which are gradually transformed into what becomes, virtually, an obsessive and hypnotic virtual chorus by means of two independent delay accumulation lines, respectively, 4 and 8 s. The dense, vibrant texture of the voices counter the rich wind sounds and the inharmonic sounds of the two wind instruments which were subject to hybridization by means of a vocoder. The sound of the doublebass clarinet was analyzed by the bank of analysis filters to give a spectral envelope over which the sound-noise of the flute was molded by means of the synthesis filters. In Hölderlin, the linear relationship that normally connects the vocoder analysis filters to the synthesis ones, were overturned by Nono, associating the bass filters to the treble ones and vice versa. In this way, the low resonance of the doublebass clarinet opened the filters corresponding to the high register of the flute. Finally, the reciting voices were amplified.

Another interesting part, from the point of view of this analysis, was the *Island I* (*Isola I*) where the acoustic sounds of the orchestra and the electroacoustic sounds of the soloists were added to the synthetic ones generated in real-time by the 4i system (Di Giugno 1984; Sapir 1984; Azzolini and Sapir 1984) developed by the Centro di Sonologia Computazionale (CSC) at Padua University (Debiasi, De Poli, Tisato, and Vidolin 1984). The performance environment for the synthetic section had to guarantee maximum liberty, in that the interpreter had to improvise vocal and choral sonorities by interacting with the string soloists (Sapir and Vidolin 1985). To this end, a granular synthesis environment composed of 24 voices in frequency modulation was developed. The grains were very long with a 200 ms trapezoidal envelope and had a sustained duration varying randomly between 0.5 and 1 s. The grain parameters were adjusted at the beginning of each new envelope, and were controlled in real-time by six potentiometers. To make the performance more secure, the variation field of some of the potentiometers was limited to a precise interval with the addition of preset controls that could be chosen by using the control computer keyboard (Digital Equipment Corporation PDP-11/34).

The following is an example of the configuration of the potentiometer excursion field: polyphonic density (0–24 voices), overall amplitude (0–90 dB), base frequency for calculating the carriers (116.5–232 Hz), carrier multiplication factor for calculating the modulator (0.5–2), modulator amplitude (0–500 Hz), and random deviation of the various grains with respect to the base frequency to obtain the microinterval (0–0.08). With the function keys instead, it was possible to carry out transposition and assign harmonic structures to groups of voices. The following group of structures was used: keynote; keynote and second minor; keynote and tritone; keynote and fifth; keynote and descending minor second; keynote and descending fourth; keynote and octave; keynote, fifth and eighth; seven octaves on a single note.

By means of this environment, therefore, it was possible to pass from a soft unison chorality of sinusoidal sounds with small frequency deviations, to a sound that more closely evoked the human voice transposing the carrier by an octave and with only slight variations in the modulation index. The unison chorus sound could evolve according to the preset harmonic structures that could be chosen by using the function keys, and could become completely inharmonic by moving the modulator to an irrational ratio with respect to the carrier.

In the 1984 Venice version of *Prometeo*, Nono began by conjuring up the chord that opens the *First Symphony* of Mahler and the 4i system was chosen to intone the 116.5 Hz B-flat, projected by the loudspeakers set under the base of the structure, then expanding it gradually over seven octaves and transforming it, finally, into the dimmed sound of a distant chorus.

Perseo and Andromeda by Salvatore Sciarrino
for soprano, mezzo-soprano, two baritones and synthesis sounds

Perseo and Andromeda by Salvatore Sciarrino would be a completely traditional opera if the orchestra were also a traditional one instead of being completely synthetic and played live by only two people. The synthetic sounds, however, are not an imitation of the traditional acoustic ones. They are, indeed, anything but orchestral. The aim was to create an abstract musical game, where the sounds are designed to suggest the soundscape of the island of Andromeda: wind, the sea, the seagulls, the horizon, the pebbles, drops of water, etc.

All the sounds arise from a single synthesis algorithm that, in its most elementary form, consists of a white noise filtered through a second order low-pass resonant filter. Therefore, amplitude, cutoff frequency and the filter resonance factor are the parameters of this algorithm, which can be conveniently varied according to a specific function of time.

Sciarrino used traditional graphic notation to write the entire score and added, for the synthetic parts, a quantitative description of the filter resonance and stylized graphics for the dynamic trend of the three parameters (Sciarrino 1990). This opera was first performed the 29 January 1990 at the Staattheater, Stuttgart in Germany and was successively repeated, with different scenery, at the Gibellina Festival (July 1991) and at the La Scala Theater, Milan (April 1992).

With regards to the performance, if it had been possible to record the synthetic parts on tape with the voices singing live, the performance environment of this opera would have been extremely simple. But this type of solution would have resulted in an unacceptably rigid performance because of the negative conditioning of the singers, also on a psychological plane, who would, probably, have felt restrained by the time constriction of the tape and the singing would, thus, have lost its naturalness, which the score called for. Furthermore, there would have been similar difficulties for the scenic part, in that there are various free musical parts in the opera where the duration is not established, a priori.

The synthesized sounds, on the other hand, could not be completely played live by various performers on commercial keyboards for a variety of reasons. For instance, there was no commercial synthesizer capable of generating the sounds developed in the laboratory. The number of simultaneous independent voices and the difficulty in executing some of the musical parts, as well as increased costs due to more players and rehearsals. Moreover, from a musical point of view, it would not have necessarily produced the best results.

From among the various solutions studied, the chosen performance environment allowed for a certain temporal freedom but also the performance precision required by the score that was best resolved by using the computerized batch system. The system used consisted of a general-purpose signal processor in real time: the 4i system (later replaced by the Iris MARS workstation), played by gesture control and by two personal computers fitted with good quality sound cards. The sound was triggered by means of independent *playlist* sequences of precalculated sound files, activated by keys on a normal computer keyboard (Vidolin 1991). The system was developed by the CSC at Padua University. The resulting performance technique was, thus, not so very different from a traditional one.

In classical orchestral performance, the conductor establishes the beat and brings in the single instruments or groups of instruments, which then play their part of the score "independently" until the next time they are to play. Therefore, a traditional score is rather like a series of segments that are brought in at the opportune moment (by the conductor) and then continue freely, but executing their part according to the general timing set out in the score.

In this case too, there is a conductor who indicates when the singers should come in and when the computer operators should intervene at particular key points. Therefore, Sciarrino's score was divided into various parts, relying on the real-time processor to handle those parts that could not be fixed and the remaining parts to the other two computers. The duration of each piece depends on the music itself, or rather the possibility and necessity of dividing the piece into ever smaller segments with respect to the singers' parts. If necessary, it is possible to subdivide the segments even to the level of a single sonorous event.

The performance environment must also allow for the movement of the synthetic sound in space. The greater part of the sounds, according to Sciarrino, should be sonorous objects that pass over the heads of the listeners, starting from a distant horizon in front of them and which then disappear behind their backs. In other cases, the sounds must completely envelope the listener, to give the impression that the sounds arrive from all around them.

All the sound movements are indicated in the score and their complexity does not allow for manual execution. Therefore, a fourth computer was used to make the spatial movements automatic or rather, to generate the control signals for the bank of potentiometers that can be controlled by a MIDI. The performance philosophy chosen for the spatial dimension was similar to the sound synthesis one. The movements were written into the score, dividing it into segments that were then translated and memorized in a computer. During the performance, the spatial segments that corresponded to the sound segments were activated.

Conclusions

From these three examples, it can be seen that a musical composition is a complex work that involves various types of musical and theatrical traditions. The musical style of *live electronics* is as yet still young and requires a certain flexibility on the part of everyone concerned in order to obtain the best results from an artistic point of view. Generally, orchestra conductors are careful about what their instrumentalists play, but do not pay too much attention to the electronic parts that are included in the opera. Therefore, the sound director must find the correct balance between the acoustic and electroacoustic sounds and this equilibrium can only be found if there is sufficient time to rehearse. More time should be left for these rehearsals than is normally the case when playing repertory music.

These examples also bring to light the role of the interpreter of electronic musical instruments. His main activity concerns the planning of the performance environments for performing a live electronics musical concert. This requires not only traditional musical competence but also, a good knowledge of signal processing techniques. It also means that he must know about the most modern hardware and software packages that are available on the market and he must be able to assemble the various pieces of equipment to optimize the performance environment, creating an immediate and powerful musical interface.

During this century, many mixed works involing electronic music have been composed. Yet the greater part of these are no longer played because of the difficulty in recreating the performance environment either because the equipment is obsolete or the composer's score is inadequate. The interpreter should make every effort to save this musical heritage, by performing it and thus making it known to the public. Today, there are digital systems that can simulate any instrument of the past, so that it is possible to bring back to life many of the electronic works that have disappeared with the disappearance of an instrument or on the death of the composer. Therefore, it is to be hoped that the new interpreters also learn to transcribe the performance environment both in order to conserve the music of the past, and also in order to guarantee the survival of today's music, given that it, too, may become "obsolete" within a few years.

References

Andrenacci, P., E. Favreau, N. Larosa, A. Prestigiacomo, C. Rosati, and S. Sapir. 1992. "MARS: RT20M/EDIT20—development tools and graphical user interface for a sound generation board." In *Proceedings of the 1992 International Computer Music Conference*. San Francisco: International Computer Music Association, pp. 344–347.

Azzolini, F. and S. Sapir. 1984. "Score and/or gesture–the system RTI4i for real time control of the digital processor 4i." In *Proceedings of the 1984 International Computer Music Conference*. San Francisco: International Computer Music Association, pp. 25–34.

Berio, L. 1988. *Ofanim*. Score. Vienna: Universal Edition.

Bernardini, N. and P. Otto. 1989a. "Il Centro Tempo Reale: uno studio report." In F. Casti and A. Doro, eds. *Atti dell' VIII Colloquio di Informatica Musicale*. Cagliari: Spaziomusica, pp. 111–116.

Bernardini, N. and P. Otto. 1989b. "TRAILS: an interactive system for sound location." In *Proceedings of the 1989 International Computer Music Conference*. San Francisco: International Computer Music Association.

Bertini, G. and P. Carosi. 1991. "The Light Baton: a system for conducting computer music performance." In *Proceedings of the International Workshop on Man-Machine Interaction in Live Performance*. Pisa: CNUCE/CNR, pp. 9–18.

Cacciari, M., ed. 1984. *Verso Prometeo. Luigi Nono*. Venezia: La Biennale.

Cadoz, C., A. Luciani, and J.L. Florens. 1984. "Responsive input devices and sound synthesis by simulation of instrumental mechanisms: the cordis system." *Computer Music Journal* 8(3): 60–73. Reprinted in C. Roads, ed. 1989. *The Music Machine*. Cambridge, Massachusetts: The MIT Press, pp. 495–508.

Cadoz, C., L. Lisowski, and J.L. Florens. 1990. "A modular feedback keyboard design." *Computer Music Journal* 14(2): 47–51.

Chabot, X. 1990. "Gesture interfaces and software toolkit for performance with electronics." *Computer Music Journal* 14(2): 15–27.

Davies, H. 1984. "Electronic instruments." In *The New Grove Dictionary of Musical Intruments*. London: MacMillan.

Debiasi, G.B., G. De Poli, G. Tisato, and A. Vidolin. 1984. "Center of Computational Sonology (CSC) Padova University." In *Proceedings of the 1984 International Computer Music Conference*. San Francisco: International Computer Music Association, pp. 287–297.

De Poli, G., A. Piccialli, and C. Roads, eds. 1991. *Representations of Musical Signals*. Cambridge, Massachusetts: The MIT Press.

Di Giugno, G. 1984. "Il processore 4i." *Bollettino LIMB* 4. Venezia: La Biennale, pp. 25–27.

Doati, R. and A. Vidolin, eds. 1986. "Lavorando con Marino Zuccheri." In *Nuova Atlantide. Il Continente della Musica Elettronica*. Venezia: La Biennale.

Genovese, V., M. Cocco, D.M. De Micheli, and G.C. Buttazzo. 1991. "Infrared-based MIDI event generator." In *Proceedings of the International Workshop on Man-Machine Interaction in Live Performance*. Pisa: CNUCE/CNR, pp. 1–8.

Haller, H.P. 1985. "Prometeo e il trattamento elettronico del suono." In *Bollettino LIMB* 5. Venezia: La Biennale, pp. 21–24.

Mathews, M.V. 1969. *The Technology of Computer Music*. Cambridge, Massachusetts: The MIT Press.

Mathews, M.V. and C. Abbott. 1980. "The sequential drum." *Computer Music Journal* 4(4): 45–59.

Mathews, M.V. and J.R. Pierce, eds. 1989. *Current Direction in Computer Music Research*. Cambridge, Massachusetts: The MIT Press.

Moore, F.R. 1990. *Elements of Computer Music*. Englewood Cliffs: Prentice Hall.

Nono, L. 1984. *Prometeo. Tragedia dell'ascolto*. Score. Milano: Ricordi.

Opcode, Inc. 1990. *Max Documentation*. Palo Alto: Opcode.

Puckette, M. 1988. "The Patcher." In C. Lischka and J. Fritsch, eds. *Proceedings of the 1988 International Computer Music Conference*. San Francisco: International Computer Music Association, pp. 420–425.

Rubine, D. and P. McAvinney. 1990. "Programmable finger-tracking Instrument Controllers." *Computer Music Journal* 14(1): 26–41.

Roads, C. and J. Strawn, eds. 1985. *Foundations of Computer Music*. Cambridge, Massachusetts: The MIT Press.

Roads, C., ed. 1989. *The Music Machine*. Cambridge, Massachusetts: The MIT Press.

Roads, C. 1996. *The Computer Music Tutorial*. Cambridge, Massachusetts: The MIT Press.

Sapir, S. 1984. "Il Sistema 4i." In *Bollettino LIMB* 4. Venezia: La Biennale, pp. 15–24.

Sapir, S. and A. Vidolin 1985. "Interazioni fra tempo e gesto. Note tecniche alla realizzazione informatica di Prometeo." In *Bollettino LIMB* 5. Venezia: La Biennale, pp. 25–33.

Sciarrino, S. 1990. *Perseo e Andromeda*. Score. Milano: Ricordi.

Simonelli, G. 1985. "La grande nave lignea." In *Bollettino LIMB* 5. Venezia: La Biennale, pp. 15–19.

Strawn, J., ed. 1985. *Digital Audio Signal Processing: An Anthology*. Madison: A-R Editions.

Vidolin, A. 1991. "I suoni di sintesi di *Perseo e Andromeda*." In R. Doati, ed. *Orestiadi di Gibellina*. Milano: Ricordi.

Vidolin, A. 1993. "Problematiche e prospettive dell'esecuzione musicale con il mezzo elettronico." In R. Favaro, ed. *Suono e Cultura. CERM-Materiali di ricerca 1990–92.* Quaderni M/R 31. Modena: Mucchi.

Waisvisz, M. 1985. "THE HANDS, a set of remote MIDI-controllers." In *Proceedings of the 1985 International Computer Music Conference.* San Francisco: International Computer Music Association, pp. 313–318.

Wasserman, A., ed. 1985. "Computer music." Special issue. *ACM Computing Surveys* 17(2).

NAME INDEX

A

Adrien, J.M. *20*
Allen, J.B. *93, 128*
Arfib, D. *121*

B

Backus, J. *215, 218*
Bartolozzi, B. *207, 208, 212–214*
Beauchamp, J. *103*
Benade, A.H. *216, 218*
Berio, L. *450–452*
Bernardi, A. *126, 187* ff.
Berry, W. *388*
Borin, G. *5* ff.
Bugna, G.-P. *126, 187* ff., *197, 218*

C

Cage, J. *400*
Camurri, A. *268, 349* ff., *353, 355*
Carlos, W. *336*
Cavaliere, S. *126, 155* ff.
Chomsky, N. *388*
Clarke, J. *188*

D

d'Alembert, J. *226*
Dannenberg, R. *267, 268, 271* ff., *325, 354*
De Poli, G. *5* ff., *12, 125, 126, 158, 159, 187* ff.
Desain, P. *267, 268, 271* ff.

E

Eaton, J. *408*
Erbe, T. *436*
Evangelista, G. *126, 127* ff., *141, 159, 437*

F

Florens, J. *14*
Friedlander, B. *93*

G

Gabor, D. *125, 128, 132, 155, 156, 158*
Gabrieli, A. *453*
Galileo, G. *431*
Garbarino, G. *207, 208*
Gardner, W. *419*
Garnett, G. *344, 358, 365*
Gibiat, V. *218*
Gomsi, J. *344*

H

Haar, J. *134*
Helmholtz, H.L.F. *188*
Hilbert, D. *141*
Hölderlin, F. *453*
Honing, H. *267* ff., *296*
Hooke, R. *223*
Hopf, H. *217*

J

Jones, D. *157*

K

Karplus, K. *250, 251, 252*
Koenig, G.M. *441*

L

Leman, M. *268, 349* ff., *355*
Lienard, J. *159*

M

Maher, R.C. *103*

SUBJECT INDEX

STUDIES ON NEW MUSIC RESEARCH

1. *Signal Processing, Speech and Music.* Stan Tempelaars.
  1996. ISBN 90 265 1481 6

2. *Musical Signal Processing.* Edited by C. Roads, S.T. Pope, A. Piccialli, G. de Poli.
  1997. ISBN 90 265 1482 4 (hardback)
      ISBN 90 265 1483 2 (paperback)

For Product Safety Concerns and Information please contact our EU
representative GPSR@taylorandfrancis.com
Taylor & Francis Verlag GmbH, Kaufingerstraße 24, 80331 München, Germany

 www.ingramcontent.com/pod-product-compliance
Ingram Content Group UK Ltd.
Pitfield, Milton Keynes, MK11 3LW, UK
UKHW051828180425
457613UK00007B/257